£13.95+

WITHDRAWN
FROM STOCK

Religious change in contemporary Poland

INTERNATIONAL LIBRARY OF SOCIOLOGY

Founded by Karl Mannheim

Editor: John Rex, University of Aston in Birmingham

Arbor Scientiae

Arbor Vitae

A catalogue of the books available in the INTERNATIONAL
LIBRARY OF SOCIOLOGY and other series of Social Science
books published by Routledge & Kegan Paul will be found
at the end of this volume.

RELIGIOUS CHANGE IN CONTEMPORARY POLAND
Secularization and politics

Maciej Pomian-Srzednicki

Routledge & Kegan Paul
London, Boston, Melbourne and Henley

To Hania and Wojtek

First published in 1982
by Routledge & Kegan Paul Ltd
39 Store Street, London WC1E 7DD,
9 Park Street, Boston, Mass, 02108, USA,
296 Beaconsfield Parade, Middle Park,
Melbourne, 3206, Australia and
Broadway House, Newtown Road,
Henley-on-Thames, Oxon RG9 1EN
Printed in Great Britain by
St Edmundsbury Press, Suffolk
© Maciej Pomian-Srzednicki 1982

Library of Congress Cataloging in Publication Data

Pomian-Srzednicki, Maciej.
Religious Change in Contemporary Poland.
  (International library of sociology)
  Bibliography' p.
  Includes index.
  1. Secularism-Poland. 2. Communism and culture-
Poland. 3. Poland-Intellectual life. I. Title
II. Series.
BL2747.8.P65   306'.6'09438   82-500
ISBN 0-7100-9245-8   AACR2

CONTENTS

FOREWORD

There could hardly be a more appropriate time for the appearance of this splendid book. The election of a Polish Pope and the recent repression of working-class institutions in Poland make it very topical. Unfortunately, what we know of Poland from newspapers and television is superficial, because we have no genuine access to the conditions under which 'mental fight' is carried out on the other side of the European border. We may read of a sermon by Archbishop Glemp or a statement by Poland's military leaders and so think we pick up some echoes of the battle. But there are deeper entrenchments staked out all over the intellectual field and these are invisible in the West, indeed almost unimaginable. We can imagine martyrdoms and we know what the sign of the cross means in the Polish films recently on our screens, but we have no first-hand acquaintance with the tools of ideological nihilation. These are screened out of our consciousness.

Nor, I think, do we imagine what it is like for these tools of nihilation, assiduously and dishonestly deployed, to be supplemented by secular rituals. The propagation of party doctrine and the rewriting of history as a form of secular heilsgeschichte are backed up by pervasive rituals. These are certain formulae which are repeated endlessly and used to box reality into categories useful to those in power. There are also various kinds of ceremonious induction - secular confirmations - designed to ensure that Poles inhabit a world limited to the horizons required by their masters. These are not remotely as pervasive as in the Soviet Union, but they are a part of Polish reality we do not really understand. In short, we do not enter into the deep structure within which the Poles have been incarcerated.

That deep structure is religious in the worst sense of the word, partly by transmuting the categories of Christianity into a mechanical and immanent philosophy of history, and partly by developing a system of Inquisition that claims to ensure that human beings are circumscribed by 'socialist reality'. 'Socialist reality' is, of course, precisely one of those ritual formulae just referred to.

What Dr Maciej Pomian-Srzednicki has done is to introduce us to that deep structure as it is played out, not in the salons of Western intellectuals, but in the propaganda apparatus of the state. That structure is fairly uniform throughout the eastern bloc, although specially virulent in Albania and relatively relaxed in Yugoslavia. Only if you have read much of this material

do you enter into a real tragedy of the mind, executed under
the aegis of a system which proclaims itself the real, practical
realisation of man's highest hopes, including his religious aspirations. Hitler's perverse millennium was at least largely theoretical and bizarre, in spite of the flashes of insight which
appear in 'Mein Kampf'. But here we have the theory of enlightenment enacted as the practice of misery. It is the world up-
side down, proclaimed to be the right way up by party intellectuals, and held in that position by guns. No wonder the symbol
of the cross holds the whole world of meaning for Poles as
Pontius Pilate rules the roost and has not even the grace to
wash his hands. Metternich was a graceful liberal compared to
what has now befallen the Polish pioneers of European democracy,
and the nineteenth-century oppressions against which Marx
railed so properly and vigorously look mild and almost bene-
ficent. There is now no inevitable trumpet to release the prisoners as in 'Fidelio', because they are held down by the theory
of their own liberation.

It must also be said that the theories of religion emanating
from the Polish positivist tradition look less impressive in retrospect than they presumably did at the time. I find it particularly
interesting that these early theorists were so inclined to relate
religiosity to the conditions of peasant existence. The overtones
of contempt and superiority, as well as the kinds of simple
theory espoused, tell us at least as much about the social position and assumptions of part of the intelligentsia as they do
about the phenomena of religiosity. At the same time, Dr Maciej
Pomian-Srzednicki performs a useful service in introducing us
to an early tradition of investigation in the sociology of religion
which is too little known outside Poland.

Just because secular ideology deploys the categories and
apparatus of religion at its worst, it does not follow that
traditional religion must be true. To be harassed and even
persecuted is not necessarily to be right. What one does
realise is that when a system declares itself a unique union of
political power and truth we are in for hell on earth. There
have been times in the European past when Catholicism did
precisely that, but at least the dissident could always appeal to
a transcendence that was not wholly pocketed by the authorities. Now, however, in many parts of the world, Catholicism
can stand for human rights, in El Salvador or South Korea as
well as in Poland, and having been evicted from the seats of
power - or never having occupied them - it can adopt positions
which promote both decent material conditions and the rights
of religion and conscience. Indeed, more than that, it is clear
that in the conditions of contemporary Poland, as many times
before, the Roman Church is the one institution able to hold
the soul of a nation in safe keeping.

David Martin

PREFACE

The initial idea for this study was conceived in 1973 - long before the election of Pope John Paul II and subsequent events hit the world headlines. In this sense, therefore, the importance of the subject has been vindicated. The material began to take shape as a doctoral thesis written with the aim of exploring the state of both Catholicism and its sociology in Poland. It has since been substantially restructured, rewritten and extended as well as corrected.

My deepest gratitude goes to Professor David Martin who was always ready to listen, read and advise - probably far more than was good for him - during my years at the London School of Economics. Without his concern and encouragement it is unlikely that the study would have acquired the present form. I am also indebted to the late Lucjan Blit who advised me during the early stages of writing. My other thanks must go to my wife Hania who read and re-read the manuscript in order to weed out inconsistencies and stylistic ponderosities as well as to my parents who helped me in a way that is best known to them alone. My general thanks would be incomplete without mentioning the Social Science Research Council which provided me with finance at the outset of my research.

Specific thanks must also go to Alexander Tomsky (Keston College) for his indefatigable and expert advice during the period of writing and for his reading of the original manuscript; Dr Maria Hirszowicz (Reading University) also read the manuscript and provided many useful comments. In addition, I would like to express my indebtedness to the following who helped me in many ways including the simple offering of both academic and physical hospitality during my wanderings: Leszek Kołakowski (All Souls College, formerly of UW), Fr Jerzy Mirewicz (Polish Jesuit Fathers, London), Adam Podgórecki (formerly of PAN), Olgierd Stepan (London), Fr Władysław Piwowarski (KUL), Andrzej Święcicki (ATK and KIK), Fr Józef Majka (Wrocław Catholic Seminary, formerly of KUL), Anna Pawełczyńska (PAN), Edward Ciupak (UW and WSNS), Andrzej Wójtowicz (PAN), Józef Keller (PAN), Józef Grudzień (IPP), Franciszek Adamski (KUL), Fr Władysław Prężyna (KUL), Jerzy Mikułowski Pomorski (WSE, Kraków), Ryszard Dyoniziak (WSE, Kraków), Barbara Leś (UJ), Fr Józef Tischner (Theological College, Kraków), Halina Moszczyńska (UJ), Hubert Domagała (UJ), Fr Jacek Salij (Dominican Fathers, Warsaw), Halina Bortnowska ('Znak'), Juliusz Eska ('Więź'), Janina Słomińska (KIK),

Fr Stefan Dobrzanowski (Kraków), Marek Skwarnicki ('Tygodnik powszechny'), Fr Jan Pałyga (Pallottine Fathers, Warsaw), Fr Stanisław Małkowski (Warsaw) and Fr Adam Boniecki (Vatican staff, formerly of the Kraków Diocese).

Finally, my thanks go to the staff of the following institutions: The British Library, The Polish Library (London), Keston College, The Polish National Library (Warsaw), the UW Library and the KUL Library.

M.P.S.
Selsey, Sussex

KEY TO ABBREVIATIONS
USED IN THE TEXT

ATK   Akademia Teologii Katolickiej, The Catholic Academy

GUKPPiW   Główyny Urząd Kontroli Prasy, Publikacji i Widowisk, The Central Office for the Control of the Press, Publications and Performances

IFIS   Instytut Filozofii i Socjologii, The Institute of Philosophy and Sociology (of the PAN)

IPP(ML)   Instytut Podstawowych Problemów Marksizmu-Leninizmu KC PZPR, The Institute for the Study of Marxism-Leninism

KC   Komitet Centralny, The Central Committee (of the PZPR)

KIK   Klub Inteligencji Katolickiej, Club of the Catholic Intelligentsia

KPP   Komunistyczna Partia Polska, The Polish Communist Party

KUL   Katolicki Uniwersytet Lubelski, The Catholic University of Lublin

NKVD   The People's Commissariat for Internal Affairs (a past name for the Soviet security apparatus)

OBOP   Ośrodek Badania Opinii Publicznej przy Polskim Radio i T.V., The Public Opinion Research Centre of the Polish Radio and Television

PAN   Polska Akademia Nauk, The Polish Academy of Sciences

PPR   Polska Partia Robotnicza, The Polish Workers' Party

PPS   Polska Partia Socjalistyczna, The Polish Socialist Party

PRL   Polska Rzeczpospolita Ludowa, The Polish People's Republic

PTR   Polskie Towarzystwo Religioznawcze, The Polish Religiological Society

PZPR   Polska Zjednoczona Partia Robotnicza, The Polish United Workers' Party

ROPCiO   Ruch Obrony Praw Człowieka i Obywatela, The Movement for the Defence of Human and Civil Rights

SDKPiL   Socjaldemocracja Królestwa Polskiego i Litwy, The Social Democratic Party of the Kingdom of Poland and Lithuania

TKKŚ   Towarzystwo Krzewienia Kultury Świeckiej, The Society for the Propagation of Secular Culture

UJ   Uniwersytet Jagielloński, The Jagellonian University (Kraków University)

UW   Uniwersytet Warszawski, Warsaw University
WSNS   Wyższa Szkoła Nauk Społecznych przy KC PZPR, The
            Central Committee School of the Social Sciences

INTRODUCTION

The aims of this book are modest. I propose to use the concept of secularization as a signpost indicating the direction of the path we can use in order to explore religion in Polish society. It is as well to point out immediately that although I use the term 'secularization' in the title, I am equally concerned with its opposite. It is through a quirk of usage that the concept of secularization can be just as appropriately applied to the understanding of the reverse process of desecularization.

The use of this signpost proved more difficult than may appear from a mere glance at the contents page: the field of inquiry was not at all clear at the outset of the research. In this sense the study marks a true exploration which - like all exploration - often has to stop at new and interesting ground in order not to over-expand and lose its purpose. The path will take the reader through some early Polish sociology - much of it quite new to Western readers - then on to Polish history, thought, culture, politics and empirical sociology as well as touching on Soviet empire-building. The object is to show where answers might be found to questions of religious vitality and weakness: in particular, the path will show where such answers are emphatically not to be found.

The book will be of interest both to specialists in a variety of areas - religion and Christianity, Eastern Europe and the Soviet bloc, the sociology and politics of religion - and to the curious non-specialists.

There are fundamental differences between the position of religion under communist regimes and its position in the western liberal democracies. These differences stem mainly from the totalitarian character of the regimes on the one hand, and from the atheist nature of communist totalitarianism on the other. Consequently, any attempt to deal with religion and secularization in Poland, while clearly remaining within the bounds of the sociology of religion, also becomes an exercise in political sociology with the result that the final product necessarily becomes a political sociology of religion and secularization.

But Poland is worthy of note for two other reasons. Firstly, it has a very strong Catholic tradition; secondly, since the turn of the century Polish society has been undergoing fairly intense if erratic urbanization and modernization - processes which have gone hand in hand with industrialization and the spread of various versions of empiricist Weltanschauungen. Since the end

1

of the Second World War the state authorities have sought to intensify the process of industrialization.

Although it is clear today that the contemporary political structure of Poland (and of all Soviet bloc societies) is unintelligible unless seen in terms of totalitarianism, this view has by no means always been held. Even the term itself was in disrepute during recent years and was obviously unpopular in the bulk of Western writing on the subject of Eastern Europe. One of the reasons was political climate: the 1960s saw an end to the 'cold war' and a development of a spirit of 'détente' in the West. These changes were paralleled by suggestions that the Soviet bloc was evolving either towards a Western form of democracy ('convergence' theory) or towards some sort of benign dictatorship. Such hopes were, quite naturally, inimical to the concept of totalitarianism. But they proved to be false hopes and a return to a more realistic appraisal is visible today.

Another reason for the reluctance to apply the term totalitarian in this context has been the unwillingness to attribute central importance to the function of Marxist-Leninist ideology within Soviet bloc societies. This in turn stemmed from the correct observation that very few of the citizens of those societies believed in either the truth or the value of Marxism-Leninism. It has become clear, however, that ideology occupies a central position in Soviet-dominated societies despite its almost total rejection by the populations. In addition to legitimizing the power of the rulers, Marxism-Leninism has the dual function of laying down the principles of totalitarianism while at the same time camouflaging the nature of the political structure; in the words of Raymond Aron: 'If the Party stopped thinking of itself as the vanguard of the proletariat, it would become the collective tyrant, the Prince who governs according to his whims and in his own interest.'(1) Without coming to terms with the function of ideology it is impossible to appreciate the significance of totalitarian features such as the one-party system, the monopoly of the mass media, the monopoly of the armed forces and of the police, the secret police and the use of terror. These are all classic features of totalitarianism and also characteristics of Polish society.(2) These features are all welded together and nourished through the medium of state ideology and give rise to secondary totalitarian features: the great emphasis placed on industrialization, the attempted monopoly of all social and political organizations, the programme of the secularization of society, the persecution and harassment of the Church.

I am also inclined to accept Maurice Cranston's view that an ideal totalitarian regime is one where 'the populace is not simply subdued but brainwashed:'(3) such a view takes Marxist-Leninist ideology to be central to communist totalitarianism. While regimes may differ in terms of degree of totalitarianism, Cranston concludes that 'the *most* totalitarian régime is the one where the penetration of the régime into the soul of the individual is complete.'(4) Thus we are dealing here with a regime whose aim, though not always and everywhere successful to the same extent, is to monopolize the personality of the individual.(5) It has also been argued that a fully successful totalitarianism is impossible. Stanislaw Malkowski suggests that 'totalitarian systems are bursting from internal contradictions: a perfect totalitarian system will end up by destroying itself.'(6) It is not open to any doubt that Poland since the war has had one of the least successful totalitarianisms of Eastern Europe if not the very least successful.

Instability has always been a feature of totalitarianism in Poland. The events of 1980 – particularly the establishment of the free trade unions – have dramatically demonstrated this instability. Indeed, totalitarianism in Poland is unlikely to be the same ever again: it will either continue to decay, taking much of the East European communist world with it, or reassert itself in a far stronger version.

Totalitarianism, however, is not the only feature of communist societies which is of relevance to the position of religion in those societies. Christel Lane, in her study of Christian religion in the Soviet Union,(7) draws attention to the effects of intense industrialization.

In my examination of material from Poland I have taken a broad view of the concept of secularization and have avoided any discussion of definitions. I simply took those definitions which were offered by the authors whose work I have taken into account.

I must mention here that in selecting relevant issues and material I took as a guide the generally accepted meaning of the Polish term 'laicyzacja.' Although 'laicyzacja' can be roughly translated as secularization, its use does, nevertheless, allow a distinction to be made between the usual sociological sense of the word and 'sekularyzacja', which is usually applied to the policy of secularizing ecclesiastical property, land and institutions.(8) This latter phenomenon, while of great significance to the position of religion in Polish society, is not a central concern of the present study.

Another frequently used and related term is 'dechrystianizacja' – meaning dechristianization. This term has a specific meaning in the context of secularization: firstly, and most obviously, it is only applicable to a process occurring within the confines of Christian society or tradition; secondly, its use is rather more restricted than that of 'laicyzacja' since it relates to the question of religiosity alone, that is to say, it is concerned with the question of whether an individual or a group is 'no longer Christian'. In other words, it is concerned with the disappearance of Christian belief and practice.

The term religion is, of course, a very broad category – too broad to be encompassed satisfactorily by the material selected. Therefore, my main concern will be with Christianity and, in a more precise way, with Roman Catholicism. This is in keeping with both the almost exclusively Catholic tradition of present-day Polish society and also with the orientations of the material. Also in keeping with the orientations of the material is an often loose use of the word religion where Christianity or Catholicism are being specifically referred to in this study. There should not be any ambiguity since the meaning will always be clear from the context.

Other terms which will be used interchangeably in the course of this book are: Marxist-Leninist, socialist and communist – especially where a political system or regime as opposed to a belief is being referred to. I do not wish to deny that differences exist in the meanings of the terms or suggest that the differences are of no consequence – I merely wish to point out that the differences need not be taken into account for the purposes of this study. However, it may be useful to point out that the rulers of Poland (in common with all rulers of Soviet bloc societies) claim to be a Marxist-Leninist inspired body which, under the conditions of a socialist political system, is leading the building of a communist society.

Some comment is required regarding the use of the terms science and scientific. Although I have based my use of these words on the Polish term 'nauka' this is not a satisfactory translation. 'Nauka' encompasses the whole of learning, including metaphysics, and is best seen as the equivalent of the Latin 'scientia'. What is referred to in the English language as science forms but a fragment of 'nauka'. It is therefore important to bear in mind that whenever the term science is used in this book it has to be understood as conveying the ideas of learning, truth and objectivity in the broadest possible sense.

Although I have used the term 'laicyzacja' as a guide I have nevertheless tried to avoid the constrictions on the use of the word that have been imposed by conventional Polish sociological definitions. These definitions tend to limit the sociology of secularization to questions of dechristianization – a most unwelcome restriction on the mobility of the sociology of religion. The approach used here, therefore, has been based on the acceptance of criteria and definitions similar to those used by David Martin.(9)

Martin has also provided some of the more important elements of the framework which I use in my approach to this subject. Consequently, there is a sense in which this study can be considered as a test of the validity of these elements in addition to being an elaboration of the problem of secularization in Polish society. There are five areas in which the observation of secularization can be attempted: the area of religiosity, the area of history and tradition, the questions concerned with power relations in society, the issues of planned secularization, the area of the disappearance of the sacred. The Polish sociology of religion, as has been noted, is principally concerned with the first area as the legitimate field of investigation. The categorization into the above areas does not involve any implicit theory of society, religion or secularization, but is intended simply to act as an arbitrary but useful signpost indicating where attention should be directed. As a result of the wide scope of this study only a relatively small amount of attention has been given to studies of dechristianization and religiosity in proportion to the amount of material available in this one area.

While it is the primary intention of this study to understand the concept of secularization as presented in Polish writings, the secondary though no less important intention is to arrive at a picture of religiosity, religious change and the associated social and political processes in Poland today.

There are several reasons why a study of secularization in Poland is of interest to the sociologist. Firstly, such a study is concerned with one of the most sensitive issues which can be identified in a communist totalitarian state. Much of the material available has been produced under the conditions of that totalitarian state itself. This is a subject which has been hitherto little explored and it is most fortunate, in more ways than one, that in Poland totalitarianism is not as successful or extreme as it is in the Soviet Union, for example: under the latter conditions such a study would have been impossible on account of the unavailability and inaccessibility of much of the material. Although I am principally concerned with material from Poland, I have, for the sake of completeness, made an exception in the case of the later contributions of Leszek Kolakowski who had to leave Poland after the purge of Marxist revisionists in the late 1960s.

Related to this point is the similarity between Poland and the rest of Eastern Europe; there are, of course, some vast and very significant differences.(10) Of the similarities I have in mind such features as the phenomenon of planned secularization (anti-religious policy and propaganda), the rewriting of history and the way in which the communist authorities attempt to determine the kind of information which is freely available for general consumption. In other words, some of the external constraints on religion are similar in other Soviet bloc states.

Secondly, Poland is of interest on account of some very serious doubts which can be raised regarding the process of secularization. This is especially significant in view of the fact that Poland today possesses many features which might, at first sight, suggest that there should be a relatively high rate of secularization within the society. Such features include intense industrialization and urbanization, increasing levels of education, the inconveniencing and harassment (rather than all-out persecution) of believers. While there are undoubtedly some signs of secularization in some spheres, there is also exceptionally strong contrary evidence which suggests that Catholicism in Poland is of exceptional vitality. It is becoming easier to argue that there is a process of desecularization going on in Poland.

Thirdly, Poland is one of the few countries which can take pride in a long tradition in the sociology of religion. Although this tradition was largely influenced by West European and, in particular, French sociology it did nevertheless produce original and generally valuable contributions. The field is relatively well-developed today and much empirical material is available.

The final reason is connected with the idea that Catholicism in Poland may turn out to be a deciding factor in determining the outcome of the tensions within the Soviet bloc. As a result the Christian tradition would again be seen as reasserting itself decisively as a key factor in the development of European history.

In the classification and arrangement of the contemporary material I have relied more on institutional than other criteria. I have done so for three reasons: firstly, such an arrangement is convenient; secondly, the arrangement is one which is commonly accepted in Poland; finally, because a presentation based on such an arrangement has stronger explanatory power.

1 'ARCHAIC MAN' AND RELIGION: THE BEGINNINGS OF THE SOCIOLOGY OF RELIGION IN POLAND

The question of secularization has been receiving more and more attention in sociological circles in Poland in recent years. It may even be true to say that more time and paper have been devoted to this aspect than to any other single issue in the sociology of religion. Thought on this subject, however, is not new. The beginnings of systematic sociological thought on the subject of religion in Poland can be traced back to the turn of the century. This indigenous Polish thought, drawing heavily on the socio-logical and philosophical thought of Western Europe, produced a characteristic picture of religion and religiosity which is still widely recognized as a starting-point for the contemporary Polish sociology of religion. Nevertheless, it is worth pointing out that the validity of this picture - while never accepted by Polish ecclesiastical circles - has become gradually more questionable over the years to the extent that a reappraisal may be necessary. Broadly speaking, this early view identified Catholicism with an archaic peasant society while at the same time suggesting a depen-dence of Catholicism on that type of society. This chapter will be concerned with an examination and brief appraisal of the work of the early Polish sociologists of religion.

At the turn of the century Poland had been divided between three occupying powers (Russia, Prussia, Austria) for over one hundred years. One of the consequences of these occupations was the lack of a full, independent and free academic life. Academic discussions, lectures and seminars took place privately - this was the tradition of the 'flying university' - and intellectuals were harassed. Articles in learned journals (and also in some of the more popular publications) complemented this clandestine academic life. But it is beyond doubt that intellectual life suffered as a consequence. For this one reason alone it would not be surpris-ing to find that, despite the availability of talent, Poland was unable to produce thinkers of any great standing. In the realm of sociology, Poland did not produce a Durkheim or a Weber. It is almost as though all the nation's intellectual resources were directed towards a struggle against the occupying powers and towards the finding of a way to national independence. Poland did, however, produce some thinkers whose contributions to the sociology of religion should not be ignored. The reinstatement of Poland's statehood after the First World War provided an atmosphere more conducive to academic work; this period gave rise to a fair number of sociological publications.

Another consequence of the occupations was the country's

relative economic backwardness with all its concomitants. Perhaps
the most significant aspect of this backwardness, for our present
purposes, were the primitive living conditions of the great mass
of the peasantry who greatly outnumbered the town-dwellers. In
fact, even many of the latter belonged to the first generation of
peasants who were rapidly swelling the ranks of the still comparatively small working class. It is hardly surprising, therefore, to find that at least some of the educated town-dwellers of
the time would be prone to regard the uneducated, illiterate and
primitive peasant with whom they could scarcely converse in the
same language as a member of some other nation, as belonging
to a different people. Generations of serfdom in much of the land
would have reinforced this attitude. Such an attitude, however,
is not unique to Poland. Even relatively recent descriptions of
the Scottish Highlands, for example, contain very similar ideas
regarding the native population. But in Poland this view contributed to the notion of the 'two nations' of which the peasant,
with his manifestly ludicrous methods of reasoning and superstitious mind, was 'the other'.

The notion of the 'two nations' was never expressed in quite
this way. Evidence for its existence can be traced back to the
beginning of the nineteenth century: Polish literature was soon
to become almost saturated with works on the subject of peasants.
There were those authors who romanticized the peasant - like
Adam Mickiewicz and later Władysław Reymont - and there were
others who looked at him clinically, though not unkindly. Still
others were to hold him in contempt. The ethnographer Jan
Stanisław Bystroń has observed that the interest in the quaint
ways of the Polish peasant had become so intense amongst the
educated that it can only be described as 'peasantomania'.(1)
Well-known figures from cultured circles would dress up as peasants and take part in peasant celebrations. Cultured evenings
in salons would include a peasant or two. Some of the more adven-
turous and fashionable would even go as far as to marry peasant
girls - at least this is what was said.(2) All this serves to illustrate that the peasant was sufficiently different to merit special
attention.

Franciszek Mirek explains how the partitions themselves could
have influenced the interest in the peasant. He suggests that the
quest for the 'roots of the nation' - the search for a rationale
of national identity - led observers to the peasant who, despite
the disruptive effects and the persecution of the partitions, survived as a characteristic and identifiable unit right across the
nation. In addition, the development of the notion of brotherhood
and the struggle for independence brought with it an interest
in the national culture of which the peasant was an important
carrier.(3)

Sociologists as such were relative latecomers to this already
well-established scene. They were at once anxious to offer their
own versions of the peasant's quaintness while at the same time
establishing their own position as modern men in the spirit of

positivism and empiricism. They found that the 'other nation' provided them with fertile ground for the application of the ideas of Spencer, Durkheim and Marx and also, to no lesser an extent, the ideas of the early anthropologists like Frazer and Tylor. Observations of the 'other nation' were also to provide the early Polish sociologists with an opportunity to offer explanations of the then still weak but already prominent processes of social change and modernization which were beginning to grip Polish society.

An interesting, though unarticulated, assumption of the early Polish sociology of religion begins to emerge here. This is the way in which religion was implicitly treated as characteristic of the primitive mind to the exclusion of any possibility of religious manifestation amongst the educated or 'modernized'. Below we will examine the way in which this assumption anchored itself firmly within the early sociological tradition. Even today we commonly find peasant religiosity used as a reference point in models of secularization as indeed we also find attempts to correlate decreasing levels of religiosity with increasing levels of education. In passing, it is perhaps necessary to point out that we will not be concerned with a history of trends in the Polish sociology of religion but merely concentrate in some detail on one trend which has been generally passed by – the approach to secularization. An excellent general résumé of all the early work has been made by Piwowarski.(4)

The first account of religion in Poland as seen through the spectacles of sociology came from Ludwik Krzywicki. As well as being a sociologist, Krzywicki was an active Marxist who in his youth was closely associated with the revolutionary movements of the turn of the century. In his well-known account of pilgrims on their way to the Abbey of Our Lady of Częstochowa(5) Krzywicki combined Marx's very low opinion of the peasant with the notion of the 'two nations'.

Perhaps the most striking characteristic of this, Krzywicki's most important sociological account of religion is the uncompromising contempt which he exhibits for the peasant and for peasant religiosity in particular. Indeed, his contempt may even be greater than Marx's when he describes the peasants' behaviour during the pilgrimage. Krzywicki is deeply convinced of the Marxist 'opium theory' of religion and his account marks an attempt to develop it further. Like Marx, he too had a highly emotive turn of phrase and the appeal of his writings on religion and capitalist society was, in the final analysis, emotional. Further, Krzywicki is explicit in his claim that his analysis can be the only valid one since, as a non-participant, he is in the privileged position of standing apart. Any interpretation by participants is not and cannot be valid.(6) On this basis Krzywicki describes what he sees as the real Hell of the peasants' conditions of existence, the Hell which forces them to seek out the illusory Heaven of religious experience also on earth.

Krzywicki sought the causes of religious manifestations, as

observed amongst the peasantry, in the conditions of existence -
physical and social. He described what he saw as a 'collective
ecstasy' which allowed the peasant to cope with the brutal reality
of his everyday life. The pilgrimage to Częstochowa which he
describes is an event in which the vast mass of the peasantry
participates. While Częstochowa is the most important national
shrine with the famous image of the Black Madonna, there are
other, less important, local centres. Pilgrimages to Częstochowa
are traditionally made on foot and the journey takes several days
with excitement mounting as the holy place draws near. Krzywicki
observed that often, already within sight of the towers of the
abbey, mass weeping breaks out amongst the pilgrims. This
weeping, wrote Krzywicki:(7)

> rose up in such a way that it became a groan - almost a roar
> - flooding minds and hearts, crushing all into one solid con-
> vulsing and sobbing mass. This weeping broke loose in one
> all-embracing outburst and so wrenched from all hearts the
> sorrow, the pain and the whole bitterness of existence.

In what way do the peasant's living conditions explain this
curious phenomenon? Krzywicki states: 'These spasms and
groans, this whole pulsation which is so characteristic of the
peasants' religiosity arise only at a certain stage of history and
will continue for as long as certain circumstances remain unal-
tered in their entirety'.(8) Krzywicki thus begins to lay the
basis for a theory of secularization. He distinguishes two main
causes of this collective ecstasy. The first of these is concerned
with the peasants' general feeling of impotence and powerlessness experienced in their confrontation with the harsh physical
environment, in a word - fear. 'All the conditions of his existence contribute to such a spasm of impotence', writes Krzywicki.(9) At this point Krzywicki begins to diverge somewhat
from Marx in so far as he begins to lay stress on the physical
environment and conditions as key factors in his analysis instead
of relying principally on a concept of social relations. The latter
are not, however, excluded in principle, since mastery of the
physical world can be quite easily seen as requiring certain social
preconditions. He continues:(10)

> The peasant lives in a state of constant terror, directly face
> to face with the unharnessed power of nature's vagaries. His
> way of life nay his very surroundings lack the elements which
> could inspire his courage and give him that unshakeable con-
> fidence which is so characteristic of the town dweller... This
> feeling of impotence never leaves him, fear always lurks in his
> heart.

The only fear ever experienced by the town-dweller, Krzywicki
explains, is the fear of death; but, he continues, such fear is
neither constant nor intense enough to produce the pulsations

observed amongst the peasants. Moreover, he adds, any mis-
demeanour, any sin is enough to tear the peasant's conscience
apart with guilt and send his world crashing down even further
into the depths of his manifest Hell: 'There are times when they
writhe like vermin thinking about their sins and about the
responsibility which they bear for any hurricanes, droughts,
famines or pestilence.'(11)
   The other source of ecstasy lies in the day-to-day work of
the peasant. Day in and day out he works 'in the sweat of his
brow' with(12)

> his neck drooping from sunrise to sunset, his muscles strain-
> ing from the constant effort in the scorching heat... Come
> Sunday, crowds gather in the church. The singing of the
> choir, the music of the organ, the smell of incense seeping
> away from the alter, the relaxation of his muscles, these are
> all stimulants of spiritual ecstasy.

Krzywicki's analysis so far does not stand up very well to
close inspection: the conclusions are dubious and the categories
used are not subject to any form of discussion. Since it was
Krzywicki's intention to be polemical, some of his excesses can
be forgiven. Nevertheless, there still remain some unacceptable
problems, perhaps the most damning of which arises from the
popularity of the pilgrimage to Czestochowa today and what is
more, its popularity amongst people from all walks of life including those with higher education. It has become generally acceptable that even gross blunders - theoretical, logical or otherwise
- do not necessarily mean that a view is doomed to oblivion.(13)
Sometimes the exact opposite is the case, provided that the writing is forceful in some other way. Krzywicki's account is best
understood as typical of a scientistic attitude common in certain
Polish learned circles at the time.
   Having carefully identified the conditions which give rise to
religious ecstasy, Krzywicki is in a position to suggest reasons
for the eventual decline of religion. He argues that on the one
hand:(14)

> The present period is one of profound changes in the living
> conditions of the peasant: the impotence in the face of the
> vagaries of nature is being destroyed. The forces of nature
> are being harnessed and are being used for the benefit of
> mankind.... I certainly doubt whether the peasant today,
> faced with that iron monster on rails, would be capable of
> emitting the mournful notes of hymns like 'Dies irae, Dies
> illa', bequeathed to us by the Middle Ages.

Krzywicki continues that on the other hand 'technology, the
exchange of a scythe for a motor-mower, a sickle for a reaping
machine - all begin to erode the elements of physiological ecstasy
and tend to change its form.'(15) Where previously sheer brute

strength saw the peasant through his day's work, now sight and
hearing become the key qualities. The peasant now trains his
eyes to see whether the furrows run true and his ears to detect
the state of health of his newly acquired mechanical horse. It is
therefore hardly surprising, concludes Krzywicki, that the
peasant uses his now available spare time in unloading a huge
surplus of physical energy: the ecstasy changes from physiological to physical. The peasant thus seeks out motion, exertion,
sport.

Stated briefly, Krzywicki's theory of secularization suggests
that religious manifestations (at least in the case of the Polish
peasant) are some sort of crude psycho-biological reaction to a
stimulus which is a combination of terror and fatigue. He also
assumes that the peasant is endowed biologically with a vast
reservoir of energy which must be used up. When the application of more advanced technology lessens both the peasant's terror and his work-load he will no longer need the recompensation
and safety-valve of religious ecstasy: he will turn to sport. It
would be interesting to know why Krzywicki does not attribute
significance to ecstasy produced by the fatigue resulting from
sport.

Krzywicki's argument that fear of death – as in the case of the
town-dweller – should be discounted as fear is yet another hallmark
of the inadequacy of the account. The whole piece conveys the
impression that Krzywicki had no intention of producing a sound
contribution to the sociology of the peasant. Rather, it would
appear to be evidence that he had a hard ideological axe to grind.

In limiting his definition of religiosity to 'collective ecstasy',
Krzywicki precludes the existence of any doctrinal elements in
the religious life of the peasant. The peasant's clear and concise
notion of what does and does not constitute sin, for example,
appears not to be enough to qualify as doctrinal or philosophical
content. Nor is any attention paid to the Church as an institution – to Krzywicki the Church appears to be nothing more than
a building, a meeting place, a centre for religious ecstasy. He
explains that 'In this unloading of emotion, in this ecstasy of
sobbing, Church dogma does not play the least part.'(16) He
continues his description as follows:(17)

> The Mass ceases to be contemplation of the articles of the
> faith and I even doubt whether it is contemplation of any
> sort at all. Instead, it is a state of lulled sleep and oblivion,
> not unlike that of an infant rocked to sleep in his cradle to
> the sound of his mother's lullaby.

The suggestion that the peasant's religiosity is devoid of intellectual content implies, nevertheless, that religion does have
such a content although Krzywicki does not believe the peasant
to be capable of ever grasping it. But the intellectual elements
of religion are not the key to the apparently extreme piety and
devotion of the peasant. In other words, piety and devotion

can exist and be observed widely to be such without the presence of any formalized doctrine or philosophy. Amongst the
complexities which this question raises on close inspection, one
is particularly worthy of note since it marks the first sign of a
skeleton in the cupboard of the Polish sociology of religion and
is especially relevant to the question of secularization in general.
Two related issues are involved: firstly, the definition of what
does and does not constitute a 'Christian' people; secondly,
the extent to which the Polish peasant, and indeed any group of
nominally Christian people, was in fact 'Christianized' in the
first place.(18) These issues will be cropping up in various
forms throughout this book.

The next important observer of the Polish peasant and of his
religious ways is Florian Znaniecki. His most important contributions on the subject are to be found in the monumental work,
'The Polish Peasant', which he co-authored with William Isaac
Thomas.(19) The work of these two sociologists was concerned
with the problems resulting from the large-scale migrations of
Polish peasants to the United States - a process which started in
earnest towards the end of the last century. Thomas and
Znaniecki, in contrast with the then current practice among
sociologists, emphasized the importance of individual and general
attitudes, case histories and other subjective data in the gaining
of insights into social cohesion and social disorganization. The
information which they provide on the subject of religion and
related beliefs is based to a large extent on secondary source
material. Nevertheless, there is a clear attempt to 'enter the
mind' of the peasant despite the authors' own positivistic points
of reference. It is as well to note that in 'The Polish Peasant'
religion is not treated extensively - the authors clearly found it
of only secondary relevance to their central interest. Znaniecki
also introduced to the Polish sociology of religion the notion of
the structure and function of the religious group and of the
local territorial organization of the Church.(20) It is under the
influence of these ideas that Franciszek Mirek produced a major
contribution to the sociology of the parish; this work is now
considered to be one of the classics of Polish sociology.(21)
Mirek's work is also commonly identified with the beginnings of
the sociology of religion at KUL. But the work of Znaniecki is
also receiving increasing attention from Marxist sociologists of
religion in Poland: Edward Ciupak has been engaged in an
appraisal of Znaniecki's relevance to the contemporary sociology
of religion. Let us now turn to the picture of the Polish peasant's
religiosity as illustrated by Thomas and Znaniecki.

If Krzywicki's peasant is a miserable and pathetic creature,
worthy only of pity or contempt, then the peasant of Thomas
and Znaniecki is a strange and mysterious type of animal. He
lives in the backwaters of the modernizing world and has difficulty in coming to terms with it whenever he finds himself up
against it. He also inhabits an unfamiliar fairy-tale universe,
part this-worldly and part other-worldly, populated by monstrous

and miraculous beings of whom the Holy Family, angels, saints
and devils are but part. It is through the totality of these
beliefs and the practices associated with them that the peasant
becomes united into the social organization of the Church;
according to the authors, the peasant's religion is 'a matter of
social organization on the basis of given mythical beliefs and
magical practices rather than of personal mystical connection
with the divinity'.(22) In addition, the peasant reasons in ways
which modern man, with his respect for positivism and empiricism, would find alien and unproductive. In other words, the
peasant is absurd. One could almost say that he lives and reasons in terms of different conceptual categories - those of his
strange world.

It is worth quoting at length from Thomas and Znaniecki's
description of the peasant's intellectual process:(23)

> The peasant seldom uses dialectic in criticizing any view and
> can hardly be persuaded by dialectic. He simply opposes his
> opinion to another; and the more effort the elaboration of this
> opinion has cost him, the less willing is he to exchange it for
> another. He may even acknowledge that the contrary opinion
> is right, but he holds that his own is also right, and he feels
> no necessity of solving the apparent contradiction unless the
> problem is important enough to compel him to do some more
> thinking and to elaborate a third, intermediary opinion. He
> is so accustomed to live among partial and one-sided general-
> izations that he likes to collect all the opinions on some impor-
> tant issue, listens with seeming approval to every one, and
> finally does what he intended to do at first or sets about
> reflecting and elaborates his own view. If he selects the
> opinion of anybody else, he is led, not by the intrinsic merit
> of the opinion, but by his appreciation of the man. If only he
> has confidence in the man's sincerity and intelligence, he
> supposes that the man's advice was the result of a sufficient
> process of thinking and considers it useless to repeat this
> thinking himself in order to appreciate the advice on its own
> merits.

To take issue with this statement as an accurate description of
how the peasant 'thinks' would be pointless. It is far more useful
to question the statement's validity as a criterion for distinguishing the thought processes of the peasant from those of
modern man. As such it would fail disastrously. If we are to
trust our own personal observations of the way in which the most
educated members of the most modern societies think today, we
cannot fail to conclude that the 'peasant mentality' as outlined
above is common everywhere, even amongst the most modern of
men. In fact, even a not-too-satirical account of sociological
writings would not sound very much different.(24) It is doubtful
whether Thomas and Znaniecki themselves were entirely unaffected by this oddity of reasoning.

This characterization of the peasant's thought process is
significant in other respects. Firstly, it stresses 'mistakes' in
the peasant's thought process. If mistakes indeed they are, they
belong to the very same category of mistake which modern man,
and especially modern men like Thomas and Znaniecki, should at
all costs avoid. They are not compatible with the canons of
positivism and empiricism. Secondly, Thomas and Znaniecki
imply that this archaic mode of thought is bound to disappear
as the peasant becomes more and more educated. This idea
requires the assumption that man is in principle above all else
a reasoning, rational and cognitive being and that his ultimate
goal is the realization of this potential to its fullest. This assumption is clearly part of a theory of human nature. Thirdly, the
statement illustrates an attitude typical of the time: the belief in
the inadequacy of the peasant's conceptual apparatus. The relevance of this idea to religion is clear. The acceptance of religious
belief can be seen to be associated with faulty reasoning.

To Thomas and Znaniecki the 'peasant mentality' is significant
in terms of its consequences for the peasant's life in his rural
environment. Firstly, it removes any problems which he otherwise might have in accepting the multitude of fairy-tale and
spiritual beings which inhabit his universe and where the existence of some contradicts or precludes the existence of others.
Secondly, it provides the peasant with the respect for his surroundings so necessary for one who is so dependent on the
physical environment; so much so that one might almost be able
to speak of the functional adaptation of thought processes.

Thomas and Znaniecki describe the Polish peasant's perception
of the cosmos in a section which deals with both religious and
magical attitudes.(25) This is because they do not believe that
the distinction between magic and religion exists in the mind of
the peasant - to him both magic and religion are seen to form part
of the same reality in which he finds himself.(26) A large and
significant part of the peasant's perceptions of his world consists of elements which are of pagan, pre-Christian or non-
Christian origin. Even many of the seemingly Christian beliefs
can be quite easily traced back to their non-Christian origins.
Thus Thomas and Znaniecki find the peasant's world consisting
of animated objects, days and seasons; in this world animals,
plants, heavenly bodies, earth, fire, water are all living and
sentient entities: they possess knowledge, they are capable of
thought and they have an understanding of the moral value of
deeds and, what is more, can perceive a man's actions, judge
them and so reward or punish the doer. In this scheme of things
the peasant's notion of the solidarity of nature plays an important part: plants can, if entreated correctly, cure animals; the
death of a cow, for example, will always cause the death of a
weasel somewhere, and vice versa. The greatest solidarity, as
might be expected, occurs between animals of the same species;
we therefore find that some animals have their animal kings whom
they obey: there is the king serpent, wolf, owl, deer and boar.

This idea of the solidarity of nature has an important consequence for the life of the peasant: it makes him suspicious of
technological innovation and hostile to large-scale industrial
projects on the grounds that they disturb the age-old harmony
of nature. Such a view of the peasant's ideas as being fundamentally opposed to modernization could be used as a justification
of a complementary view suggesting that pressure can justifiably
be used in order to modernize him and his rural environment.

The detailed knowledge of the peasant's animated world, being
so extensive, is normally in the hands of a specialist to whom
the peasant goes for advice. Since these specialists are also
Christian believers, it becomes clear that the peasant is quite
capable of ignoring any contradictions between the existence
of this world and the one postulated by Christian teaching.

In addition to the belief in the animation of the physical world,
the peasant believes in the existence of beings, referred to here
as spirits, which are very much part and parcel of the world
of nature as opposed to a supernatural structure standing to the
outside of it. Thomas and Znaniecki refer to these spirits as
forming an imaginary extension of the natural world. These
spirits are the leprechauns and kelpies of the Slavs and they
must, if they are of the evil type, be treated with the respect
that they deserve. They are quite numerous in their varieties,
ranging from the obviously non-Christian ones like the 'boginki'
(spirits of lakes and rivers), the 'płanetniki' (cloud spirits
capable of bringing rain and hail), the 'skrzaty' (forest and
home spirits or gnomes), 'jędze' (hags who eat children), 'zmory'
(nightmare spirits), through the less obviously non-Christian
ones like vampires,(27) souls doing penance on earth, devils
of various sorts, to spirits based on Christian belief: God the
Father, Jesus, the Holy Spirit, the Virgin Mary, saints and
angels.(28) Although Thomas and Znaniecki do not mention it,
it would appear that the Christian figures have simply become
incorporated into a mythical landscape which existed prior to the
arrival of the first missionary.

Another important part of the peasant's belief system is his
belief in magic. Thomas and Znaniecki, in a way similar to that of
the early anthropologists, consider magic in terms of a system
of causal relations and therefore as an inferior and failed version
of physical science. They state:(29)

> Magical action differs essentially from physical action in that
> the process by which one object influences another is given
> and can be analysed in physical action, while in magical action
> it is not given and avoids analysis. There is a continuity
> between physical cause and effect; there is an immediate pas-
> sage, without intermediary stages, between magical cause and
> magical effect.

This sort of definition of magical action has been generally referred to as the 'intellectualist critique' and has, in various forms,

been applied by sociologists and anthropologists to both magic
and religion. The definition has its problems; also, the definition of physical science which it necessarily involves is questionable and the circular reasoning centring on what can or cannot
be analysed and how is unacceptable. Nevertheless, Thomas and
Znaniecki conclude here that since magic is a bankrupt science
its practice by the peasant must lead to a profound feeling of
not being in control and of helplessness vis à vis the environment. However, the explanation of helplessness, if indeed such
a feeling exists at all, is bound to be much more complicated.
It is quite possible, for example, that magical attitudes are the
result rather than the cause of feelings of helplessness - a point
which Thomas and Znaniecki do not consider; nor do they consider any of the peasant's own explanations of the obvious fail-
ures of magical technique. It is likely, however, that magic and
the sort of helplessness described are two quite independent
variables.

The authors' account so far stresses once again albeit indirectly the issue regarding the incomplete christianization of the
Polish peasant: we can observe non-Christian beliefs existing
side by side with the comparatively more recent Christian ones
despite the theoretical incompatibility of the two - at least from
the Christian point of view.

In their description of the peasant's religious system, Thomas
and Znaniecki lay stress on the role of religion in the maintenance of the social bond.(30) We thus see that the historical
development of the sociological concept of social bond is closely
linked with an appraisal of religion in society. Central to this
role of religion is the parish of which the territorial structure
unites the parishioners into a 'family'. The authors write:(31)

> The divine service, at which all the parishioners meet, is the
> main factor in the moral unity of the group. Now in the reli-
> gious meeting, during the divine service, the group is uni-
> fied, not only by the mere fact of its presence in one place,
> but also by the community of interests and attitudes, and this
> community itself has particular features which distinguish it
> from any other form in which solidarity and self-consciousness
> of the group are elaborated.

The Mass, however, is not the only factor producing the social
cohesion of the parish. There is also the general ceremonial of
religious life in the parish, the songs and prayers of the period
of Lent, the 'kolęda' (visits made by the parish priest to all the
parishioners in the period after Christmas: during the 'kolęda'
personal contact is renewed, the home is blessed, money is
collected), the 'Gorzkie żale' (or 'Bitter Regrets' - services in
remembrance of Our Lord's Passion). The rites of passage -
baptisms, weddings, funerals - in particular 'arouse in all the
assistants the consciousness of an identity of interests and
attitudes'.(32) Also important are the activities in which the

parishioner actively participates, the most notable being confession and communion. Participation in these is traditionally high amongst the Polish peasantry.

The final type of religious attitude or belief which is described in 'The Polish Peasant' is mysticism. Normally this is a rare phenomenon in Poland and tends to become general only in periods of stress like wartime, for example. Otherwise it is to be found amongst isolated individuals possessing an exceptionally low level of cultivation. Thomas and Znaniecki describe the Polish peasant's mysticism in the following way:(33)

> He [the Polish peasant] is in this respect radically different from the Russian peasant. Still, there are cases in which a mystical attitude develops during extraordinary religious meetings – revivals, pilgrimages – when the usual environment and the usual interests are for a while forgotten, and the individual is aroused from his normal state by the example and devotion of others and by the influence of the mob of which he is part.

Modern men as we have defined them are likely to be more perplexed by mysticism than by religion and Thomas and Znaniecki are no exception. Mysticism lacks even the dogma to give it shape and form: it tends to appear fluid, amorphous and elusive. It is only to be expected, therefore, that the positivist frame of reference will attribute even greater conceptual inadequacy to mystics.

Thomas and Znaniecki's view of the process of secularization requires the gradual recognition by the peasant of the deficiencies of religious and magical explanations of the physical world. The authors suggest that this process has already been occurring for some time and the observable aesthetic interests of the peasant in fact represent long-forgotten religious or other beliefs whose seriousness and significance has been lost.(34) With the advent of education for everybody the physical sciences will begin to compete forcefully with religion as an explanation of the physical world and the old beliefs will eventually shift into the realm of aesthetic interests. Thomas and Znaniecki conclude: 'Lately the explanatory sciences – physics, chemistry, biology, geology – have begun to take the place of religion.'(35)

Less famous in Western Europe than Znaniecki, but no less important as a founding father of Polish sociology, is Stefan Czarnowski. Czarnowski made his name mainly through his writings on culture, Celtology,(36) and, like Krzywicki, on the then current political and social questions. Ten years of his early life were spent in Paris where he became an active member of the Durkheimian school of thought, the influence of which is so evident in his work.

Czarnowski's best-known contribution to the sociology of religion is a series of observations concerning the religiosity of the peasant.(37) In this piece we find none of Krzywicki's scorn and disdain and little of Thomas and Znaniecki's mystery. Instead, we find all the novelty which normally accompanies the discovery of some exotic tribe, about to fall off the edge of the world, the meaning of whose customs is gradually and methodically unravelled. The descriptions and explanations, while imbued with respect for the peasant's ways, nevertheless suggest the existence of an ocean between his archaic way of life and that of the man of modern society.

In 1912 Czarnowski published a theoretical contribution to the sociology of religion in the form of two articles in 'The Polish Weekly'.(38) In the two articles Czarnowski introduced the Durkheimian criterion for distinguishing religious social facts from other social facts. In doing so he discarded the approaches of Spencer, Tylor, MacLennan and Frazer who, according to him, suggest that 'religion is an attempt to grasp that which the intellect in its desire to explain phenomena, cannot grasp':(39) in other words, the comprehending of the incomprehensible. Czarnowski, however, is satisfied that these phenomena are really very clear to the mind of the primitive man: 'everything is clear to him, the very thing which appears miraculous to us is quite commonplace to him'.(40) Czarnowski also rejects Spencer's notion of animism on the grounds that the only point in its favour is that it sounds 'likely' as an explanation of the origin or, what to Czarnowski amounts to the same thing, the essence of religion; the problem with animism is that it cannot satisfactorily account for the immense variety of religions in the world. At this point Czarnowski turns to the French school. The French sociologists, writes Czarnowski, have observed that both religious belief and religious practice are obligatory and not, as might be supposed, only the latter:(41)

Each member of a religion not only believes in the articles of faith and is obliged to act as though he believes in them but is also bound by the obligatory nature of the belief itself. In this way they [the French sociologists] have arrived at a criterion whereby they can distinguish between religious facts and facts concerned with morals, legality, etc., which are characterized only by behavioural norms and scientific beliefs or opinions which have no social obligation.

The obligatory nature of beliefs has its origin in an authority higher than man. The only authority higher than man is society. The authority of society is so mighty that it can even successfully challenge the sense experiences of individual men. Czarnowski writes: 'Believers will always doubt the reality of their own sense experiences if the latter happen to contradict a particular religious belief but they will never subject the belief itself to doubt.'(42) In any case, he continues, believers always invoke the authority of tradition and 'whoever says tradition means society.'(43)

In a way similar to Durkheim, Czarnowski identifies that sacred

core within society on which all religion is based. This is the
principle of the quintessence or mana which is in turn responsible for the origin of the notion of 'sacred'.(44) The petitio
principii involved here is well known:(45) the definition of religion in terms of society and the definition of society in terms of
religion. Despite this problem,(46) the Durkheimian framework
proved to be a very tempting proposition in that it appeared,
firstly, to be ideally suited to the observation of primitive peoples
and their religion and, secondly, to have strong explanatory
potential;(47) finally and no less significantly, it held that the
only authority above man was society. For Czarnowski, the
immediate practical consequences of this methodological stance
are two: firstly, he immediately chooses the peasant as the subject of his investigations and, secondly, he looks at the peasant's
social organization and social conditions in order to see religion
and, of course, vice versa. This Czarnowski could do in a way
which was totally novel at the time.

Before turning to Czarnowski's account of the Polish peasant's
religious culture it is worth making a few remarks about his
study of the religiosity of the Polish gentry of the sixteenth and
seventeenth centuries.(48) By contrast, this account is distinctly
Marxist in the way in which it attempts to explain gentry religiosity as depending on class position, interests and circumstances and not on any intellectual commitment to religious truth
or dogma. The identification of the Catholic hierarchy with the
upper social strata - a result of the recruitment of the former
from the latter - meant that there was a strong overlap in the
religiosity of the two groups. As a result, continues Czarnowski,
Polish Catholicism became identified with the Polish national senti-
ment and lacked any intellectual tradition:(49)

Polish Catholicism is entirely superficial. As a whole it is
limited to the observance of the external rules of Christianity:
fasts, participation in services, prayer, processions, pilgrimages. From this point of view the Polish gentry were willing to
do even more than the Church required. Self-mortification,
flagellation, falling prostrate and going barefoot on long pilgrimages were all practiced. They gave alms to beggars, paid
for Masses, donated to churches and demanded that in return
they should be prayed for after death. They thus judged that
they had paid the required tribute to God and to their con-
sciences. At the same time they drink, they refuse to deny
themselves any sensual pleasures and they torment their serfs
without mercy. In business matters they are far from scrupu-
lous. They are so little concerned with matters of doctrine
that they willingly marry a Protestant so long as they do not
suffer materially as a result. Papal nuncios bitterly complain
and as a consequence accuse the Poles of coldness and even
indifference in matters of religion.

A characteristic of Poland, however, is that in contrast to other states like Spain or Italy religiosity started and finished at the level of superficiality. Such a form of worship, concludes Czarnowski, is significant in so far as it unites the otherwise disunited gentry: it provides them with a means of self-admiration and expresses their class sovereignty.(50)

The two important points which emerge from these comments are similar to those which emerge from Krzywicki's account: firstly, there is the suggestion that the level to which the nation (or, at least, one social group within the nation) was Christianized was not particularly high; secondly, there is the idea of the marginality of Polish religiosity with respect to intellectual life and the marginality of the doctrinal content within it - in practical terms at least. In addition there is the implication that there exists somewhere a context within which true respect for the intellectual and doctrinal elements of religion can be found.

The times which Czarnowski describes were special. They marked the end of the Reformation period and the beginning of the Counter-Reformation. It should be stressed, therefore, that the religiosity of that period should be understood against the background of a massive rejection of the established Church (amongst the gentry in particular) followed by an intense policy of Christianization.

Let us now turn to Czarnowski's account of the religious culture of the peasantry. Czarnowski's central idea is that the identity of the Polish peasant and the social cohesion of the peasant community both maintain themselves through religion; to be more precise, through the totality of religious practice in its broadest sense. Czarnowski states that the phenomenon at hand is not so much religion as what he calls religious culture. Religious culture is that which enables us to distinguish, for example, the Catholicism of the village folk of Poland from that of the village folk of Italy. Whilst both sets of beliefs may be nominally Catholic, they nevertheless possess very characteristic elements in their respective structures of belief, practice and ritual; these characteristic elements exist in conjunction with the overarching Catholic beliefs and practices. So much emphasis is placed on these additional local elements that the significance of the overarching Catholicism is decidedly low; nevertheless, no serious conflict occurs between the two. The reasons for the dissimilarities in the different religious cultures are to be sought in the conditions, both physical and social, under which the individual religious group finds itself. For example:(51)

> The Polish peasant subconsciously adapts his Catholicism to the images and emotions characteristic of him as a peasant, of one who is in direct contact with the land. This land, in turn, is of a particular fertility and likewise is subject to specific influences. He also adapts his Catholicism to the images and emotions of a people who were, until very recently, under the yoke of serfdom and who, even after its abolition, remained

dependent economically, socially and spiritually on the historically established superiority of other rural strata. Thus
the Catholic rituals and beliefs, despite the fact they they
are basically the same in other classes of the same nation and
also in other Catholic nations, are nevertheless coloured in a
specific way by the village folk of Poland. They are closely
enmeshed with the peasant's anxieties, needs and particular
aspirations; they are also bound up with his beliefs and
superstitions regarding farming and society.

Czarnowski thus sees one level of religious expression which
corresponds exactly to another level of manifest and tangible
social relations and needs.

This final point is best understood by considering the conversion of a people from paganism to Christianity. Czarnowski
argues that:(52)

> The accepted religion endeavours to shape the new social
> environment according to its own pattern. However, this new
> social environment is not itself a passive object but a living
> and active collectivity which irresistibly strives to express
> itself in the fullest possible way in all fields. It exerts its
> own force on the religion. It introduces alien elements of
> belief and ritual into it. It fuses its practice with social
> values which have nothing to do with it. It transforms the
> religion for its own purposes and fashions it according to
> its own image and likeness.

Religion thus inevitably develops a religious culture where the
collectivity concerned 'looks at its beliefs and practices as though
it were looking into a mirror'.(53)

Czarnowski's belief that religion becomes, in the form of religious culture, a reflection of the essential characteristics of the
social group had important consequences for the future development of the sociology of religion in Poland. Particularly important
is its capacity to form a synthesis with a Marxist-type approach.
Czarnowski's ideas are to be found in the work of the contemporary Edward Ciupak, who is often accused of sociologism by
Catholic sociologists of religion.

One of the most characteristic qualities of the Polish peasant,
Czarnowski observes, is his 'confessional nationalism'. This
simply means that the peasant's strong nationalistic feelings
become expressed through the medium of religious culture. This
being the case, it is inevitable that Catholicism should become
the criterion of Polish nationality and that Polish nationality
should become the criterion of Catholicism.

Another important element of the Polish peasant's religious
culture is the way in which social bonds, from the local to the
national level, are religious in their form and are expressed and
maintained by local practices and by national participation in
the pilgrimage to Częstochowa.

This is not all, however. The very patterns of differentiation within peasant society (age and sex, for example) are reflected in differential participation in religious practices. Different levels of piety reflect different positions within the social structure: the older one is, the more pious one is expected to be; also, women are expected to be more pious than men.(54) Even the agricultural calendar can be read with accuracy while in fact looking at the liturgical one.

Side by side with these and other expressions of the collective through religious culture Czarnowski finds that the doctrinal elements by which Roman Catholicism is commonly recognized are sadly lacking amongst the Polish peasantry. The religious practice, he notes, 'possesses no content other than that which originates from the everyday existence of the peasant'.(55) Czarnowski calls this type of religious behaviour 'ritualistic'. Yet ritualism is not the only type of religious behaviour which can be observed amongst the peasants of Poland. The other type is what Czarnowski terms 'private religiosity' (religijność prywatna). Private religiosity has a deeper spiritual and doctrinal content than ritualism and it becomes stronger as the traditional forms of collective life disintegrate. Czarnowski's theory of secularization is thus more of a theory of religious change where private religiosity corresponds to the new and developing (i.e. future) society of technological and industrial innovation - the society of modern man - in the same way as ritualism corresponds to the traditional peasant community. Czarnowski, however, is not willing to commit himself as to the exact nature of the private religion's relationship to the new society. He simply states that:(56)

> The Polish village...is in a state of spiritual ferment. This spiritual ferment is becoming more and more violent as well as becoming deeper. It is closely related to changes occurring on a nationwide scale and seems to herald far-reaching changes in religious life: not only the emancipation of religion from the hitherto existing totality of collective life but also the deepening of its ethical and doctrinal content.

The next writer who contributed to the sociology of religion in Poland is the sociologist and ethnographer Jan Stanisław Bystroń. Bystroń was primarily interested in Polish folk culture and made some important contributions regarding its origins and history. He considers religion to be an integral part of folk culture and also essential to the understanding of the history and development of folk culture.(57)

In his book on Polish folk culture(58) Bystroń examines the influence of the Church on its formation in Poland and suggests that there has been a gradual decline, over the centuries, of the authority of the Church at village level. Bystroń argues as follows:(59)

The Church very powerfully influenced the development of
folk culture: for many centuries it remained the mightiest,
and practically the only, force. Later it stood equal with the
dwór [manor] and cooperated with it. Finally, already during
the nineteenth century it recedes somewhat into the background but, nevertheless, right up to this day it remains
very much alive and active. One thousand years ago, when
the Church first began its activity on Polish soil, the numer-
ically weak clergy were the most significant force which consciously organized new forms of cultural life. This cultural
supremacy of the Church lasted for the whole period of the
Middle Ages.

But Bystroń does not see the role of the Church as something
positive in Polish history. The Church was against all forms of
progress, he often stresses,(60) 'turning more and more to
medieval tradition, becoming more and more of a mass movement
and employing demagogic arguments'.(61)

Like the other authors whom we have considered, Bystroń
could not refrain from a characterization of the peasant. Bystroń's
peasant possesses a very determined and often absurd conservative nature and lives by tradition - by 'what always was and by
what our fathers did'. So strong is his resistance to change that
the whole history of the Polish peasantry is deeply marked by
the struggle of the old ways with the new. Thus from the dawn
of Christianity in Poland the pagan medicine men fought strongly
against the new beliefs and, in consequence, the Catholicism of
the peasant is to this day saturated with pagan relics. This
struggle is no less obvious today where the peasant, confronted
with an iron ploughshare, cannot believe that this is an improvement or that the earth itself will not eventually rust and so lose
all its fertility. In addition to this conservatism, Bystroń notes
the peasant's passivity, his heritage of serfdom and his poverty
- all of which reduce his desire for any sort of cultural or
political activity.(62)

Bystroń also describes the animated physical world and the
spirits and other beings that the peasant sees around him.(63)
This account is very similar to that of Thomas and Znaniecki
except that it stresses the more terrifying aspects: cats are in
league with evil, dogs can sense and communicate knowledge of
imminent disaster like war or death, the owl is half-devil half-
bird and maintains close contact with the diabolical powers. Such
a world leads Bystroń to conclude that:(64)

Man was unsure of himself and surrounded by mysterious
powers: from all quarters he was threatened by the influence
of evil behind which stands the enemy of mankind - Satan.
Heavenly and earthly portents and visions in dreams foretold
his future and directed his actions. Alone he was powerless,
helpless and incapable of understanding the real world and
unable to act according to his own thoughts. The need to

depend on some unshakeable and supernatural principle
became his prime concern: such aid and defence was to be
found in religion.

Quite clearly, then, Bystroń agrees with Krzywicki's thesis
concerning the causal connection between fear and religion
although, in this case, it is fear of the demoniacal.

Not all of Bystroń's remarks about religion are compatible with
one another, with the result that it is difficult to express his
ideas in an ordered way. For example, it is not entirely clear
whether the wondrous world of the peasant, the fear which turns
him to religious belief, is not itself rooted in a religious tradition: surely Satan is an important part of Christian belief? From
Bystroń's account it would appear that the peasant believes in
God because he is scared of the devil.

Bystroń agrees that the religiosity of the Polish peasant is
rather superficial. He writes:(65)

> The religiosity of Old Poland is effusive, affective and exter-
> nal; its often theatrical and demonstrative observance is its
> key feature: loud forms of worship, donations to convents
> and monasteries, pilgrimages to the Holy Image form the main
> substance of religious life. This is why less attention is paid
> to Church teaching in matters of either dogma or morals. The
> content of the religious beliefs of an averagely educated man
> of these times was significantly different from that required
> by the Church and visibly depended on legend and supersti-
> tion.

Although these remarks are addressed to much earlier times - the
sixteenth, seventeenth and eighteenth centuries - it is clear from
Bystroń's other remarks that it is only during his time that any
substantial changes are beginning to take place. It is perhaps
worth noting the similarity of the above description with Czarnowski's account of the religiosity of the Polish gentry.

According to Bystroń, the religious life of the peasant is subject to the same influences as the totality of folk culture. Folk
culture, he notes, is handed down from generation to generation
in a very direct way: by word of mouth. This direct way of
handing it down makes it relatively stable. However, with the
advent of the written word and of increasing education in the
village certain consequences are bound to follow: 'as soon as a
society begins to use indirect means of handing down tradition...
the old folk culture begins to disappear'.(66) But this is not the
only aspect of the breakdown of the old religious folk culture.
The other is that the Church is now competing with sources of
authority which it had not known previously. What Bystroń has
in mind particularly is not so much the authority as the influences
of the urban-industrial environment which are becoming stronger
with the coming of large-scale industrialization and the trade and
exchange which it stimulates. Although this is the nearest that

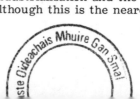

Bystroń gets to a theory of secularization, he is nevertheless
quite convinced that the totality of folk culture, including the
religious elements will not survive the onslaught of progress and
retain its original form.
The final sociologist whose work we shall consider is Józef
Chałasiński. Together with Czarnowski, Bystroń and Znaniecki
he was a member of the editorial board of the Polish sociological
journal - the 'Przegląd socjologiczny' (the 'Sociological Review')
- which first appeared in 1934. Chałasiński thus neatly rounds
off the group of early and pre-war Polish sociologists. The mass
migrations of peasants from Poland to the United States gave him
(as they had previously given to Thomas and Znaniecki) the
opportunity to study their behaviour and institutions in the new
environment. Chałasiński's interest in peasants was much broader,
however. He is especially noted for his part in editing the
'Młode pokolenie chłopów' (the 'New Peasant Generation')(67)
which, in a way similar to the 'Polish Peasant', was based on
biographical material.
In his work on the Polish peasant immigrant community in the
United States Chałasiński observes how loath the peasant is to
part with the past. In this case the Poland which he has left
behind represents the past and so the peasant tries to re-create
this past society, the society of his values and of his dignity.
Some of these constructions may appear rather banal: the newly
established colony resembles a Polish village more than it does
an American industrial settlement.(68) Other features began to
show evidence of functional value, like the mutual aid societies,
until finally, out of one of these societies, the Polish parish
organization was born. The functions of the Polish parish in the
United States had been noticed already by Thomas and Znaniecki
who wrote: 'The parish is, indeed, simply the old primary community, reorganized and concentrated.'(69) The sociological
study of the parish had almost become a topic in itself and today
constitutes a major part of the sociology of religion in Poland.(70)
Chałasiński treats the parish in terms of what we recognize
today as structural-functionalism. He describes the parish in
the following way:(71)

> The parish is a social entity which is of deep significance to
> the life of the Polish colony in America. It permeates all
> spheres of collective life as the fundamental and leading
> group. It is the basic model with the help of which the mig-
> rant thinks about the community and about questions of soci-
> ety in general as well as about himself. His values and his
> feeling of dignity are both intimately associated with the model
> of the parish.

Chałasiński divides the functions of the parish into two distinct
categories: firstly, it is an organization which caters for collective worship and a symbol of all that was left behind in Poland.
As such it gives stability and continuity in the presence of

changes and upheavals involved in the process of emigrating and in the new life itself. This stability and continuity imparted by the parish organization may become so strong that the migrant may not, as a result, be able to come to terms fully with his new social environment: the parish then becomes 'harmful and causes him problems with his adaptation to the new conditions of life and to the struggle for a better place in American society'.(72)

The other function of the parish is the way in which it acts as a 'group of one's own people' (grupa swoich)(73) which is, of course, another way of looking at the notion of community. In this respect the parish, in addition to its religious elements, embodies all the common social values of its members and is therefore a unifying factor. Chałasiński refers to this as its 'gathering' or 'concentrating' function.

The approach in this study of the parish contrasts with the previous ones in one basic way: it does not concern itself with trying to explain the form, content or origin of religion. It would thus appear to stay clear of the question of secularization. However, the question must inevitably arise whenever the functionality or dysfunctionality of religious belief or organization is touched upon. As we have already shown in other examples, dysfunctionality would appear to favour a process of secularization and vice versa. Chałasiński's approach has been clearly one where both functionality and dysfunctionality of the parish were singled out.

We have so far looked at, in broad outline, the main substance of Polish sociological writing concerning religion and secularization up to the eve of the Second World War. In terms of sheer volume, far more has been written than could possibly have been adequately summarized in this chapter, but the fundamental arguments have all been presented. It is perhaps worth mentioning Oskar Kolberg's 'Lud' and also the 'Pamiętniki chłopów', both of which, while not concerned directly with religion, contain much valuable information on the subject.(74) Let us now turn to some concluding remarks.

The strong elements of crude positivism, empiricism and Marxism which can be observed in the works of the founding fathers of the Polish sociology of religion contributed towards a most unflattering picture of religion. This was the sole sociological picture available until the publication of Mirek's book in 1928;(75) in the preface to this book Znaniecki notes that neither the clergy nor the sociologists in the Church have been interested in sociology. This is partly because 'previously, philosophical sociology had a definite materialistic orientation and many sociologists were personally hostile to either Christianity in general or to Catholicism in particular'.(76) It was Znaniecki's school which only later attempted to break with this tradition.(77)

In the early development of the Polish sociological tradition the near-obsession with the need to modernize man and society can be seen to have existed hand in hand with at best a suspicion and at worst a deep contempt for religion. This tradition

presented a composite theory of modernization and secularization
where an attempt was made to equate the concept of archaic man
with a concept of religious man. Further, the calling of modern
man led the early sociologists to accept the ideal of a secular
society.
Religious explanations were dismissed as inferior and mistaken
forms of scientific explanation. These explanations are therefore found to be associated with primitivism, ignorance and
magic; evidence for this was found by pointing to the strength
of religion in the uneducated peasant class. It was also argued
that religious explanations are only one part of the huge folk
culture and lore of the peasant or even just one absurdity
amongst many: they cannot be expected to possess any philosophical or dogmatic content. It is doubtful, in any case, whether
the early sociologists would have rejoiced at finding such content. The general argument concludes that religion - as part of
folklore, as a mistaken explanation and as a refuge from misery
and terror - is on the way out together with all the other ancient
cultural elements: there will be no more folklore, false explanations or misery and terror. The inevitability of progress will
see to that.
Progress, in the very sense in which it was used, has left
some of the most absurd superstitions intact like, for example,
the very widespread belief that individuals' fate can be traced
in the stars or others concerning cats running across one's
path. Indeed, certain beliefs in progress are no less irrational
than some of the beliefs criticized by the observers of the
peasant.
Perhaps most characteristic of all is that the early tradition
held that religion could be explained totally in terms of non-
religious factors - physical, social or ideological - without the
need to either consider the belief system itself or to differentiate
between belief systems. 'All religion is the same' might have been
a suitable catchword. This reductionism turned out to be an ideal
receptacle for anti-religious sentiments both then and in later
times.
The general approach of the early Polish sociologists was
firmly rooted in the European sociological tradition. In other
words, the authors used, either directly or by implication, the
concepts generally employed by the sociologists of the time in
order to explain social change. The concepts were often used in
unfamiliar forms. Table 1.1 contains a list of most of the concepts as used by the authors together with the more common
sociological equivalents where necessary. The list is not exhaus-
tive and it may contain some versions which were not specifically
referred to in the text. The table is not analytical in purpose -
its aim is to illustrate.
The concepts listed are presented in terms of polar opposites.
Each pair of these polar opposites itself embodies a theory of
social change and is also seen to be associated with the opposites
'religious:secular' which, in turn, suggests a theory of religious

change. The polar opposites also summarize the main differences between the 'archaic' and the 'modern'.

TABLE 1.1 Concepts related to secularization[a]

Concepts employed	Common sociological equivalents
Helplessness:mastery of nature	Alienation:self-realization
Terror:domination	Irrational:rational
Religious:empirical	Irrational:rational
Analogical:dialectical	Irrational:rational
Ecstasy:recreation	?
Emotion:sport	?
Home village:American society	Community:society
Old society:modern society	Community:society
Parish:society	Community:society
Peasant:industrial worker	Rural:urban or agricultural: industrial
Religious culture: private religiosity	Religious:secular?
Folklore:modernism	?
Conservatism:radicalism	?
Tradition or continuity:change	?
	Primitive:technological
	Mythological:factual
	Magical:causal
	Religious:scientific

[a] Some of the concepts were employed in a direct, familiar form.

Czarnowski provides us with what might be an interesting exception to this general scheme. This exception illustrates the ambiguity of the traditional sociological concepts and especially of the categories 'religious' and 'secular'.(78) The issue here is whether ritualism, on the one hand, or private religiosity, on the other, constitutes the less secularized version. This point becomes clearer when we consider that ritualistic religion is more easily observable than private religiosity and that a decline in the previous ceremonies and rituals would suggest a process of secularization. At the same time, the deepening of the intellectual content cannot be unambiguously interpreted in terms of secularization (nor can it even be put on the same scale of measurement). A practical consequence of this problem may be that either secularization or desecularization will be inferred depending on whether the decline of ceremony and ritual or the intellectual deepening is observed or recognized as the key criterion.

One of the consequences of the materialistic orientation of the early sociologists was that a quite obvious point was missed. In their treatment of religion and religiosity as a product of society they were unable to also treat it sociologically as a form of worship. In this way it would be quite appropriate to look at different

religious manifestations in terms of different forms of worship.
For example, the peasant's form of worship will centre on his
ritualism whereas an intellectual's form of worship may stress an
understanding of the Church's teaching. Here it is important
not to confuse changes in form of worship with a decline in the
worship. If, on the other hand, ritualism and 'intellectualism'
are treated as phenomena in their own right and not as forms of
worship it is difficult not to favour the higher intellectual level
represented by the latter as opposed to the primitivism of the
former: this is exactly what was done by the early Polish sociologists.

Another advantage of using this sort of approach is that the
process of religious change as opposed to decline can be more
clearly seen. It provides a way out of some of the problems which
emerge from Czarnowski's account of religious change.

One final aspect deserves a mention. This is the problem caused by a vacillation between the idea of the peasant as representing a high point of Catholicism and a notion of him as being
incompletely Christianized and primitive in his Catholicism. This
vacillation can be understood as arising out of the weaknesses of
a view of secularization which is based on ideas of social, technological and educational change. It is argued, as we have seen,
that as the peasant moves out of archaism and into the modern
world he becomes less religious. However, if his original religiosity is now also put in question then it must be conceded that
his move from high to low religiosity must be similarly put in
question. In other words, the secularization thesis is considerably weakened by suggestions of religious primitivism amongst
the peasantry. It is clear that despite the immensely informative
nature of some of the early studies the overall framework of
understanding lacked some fundamental elements of consistency
and cohesion.

2 FROM PAGANISM TO HEATHENISM VIA CHRISTIANITY: RELIGION IN POLAND PAST AND PRESENT

Any attempt to understand both religion and its sociology in a society cannot afford to ignore the history of that society. This is particularly true of Poland where an even superficial understanding of the society is not possible without an understanding of the role of Christianity in its history. Such an approach is not rooted in mere ideological bias, dogma or apologetics - it is essential to the very intelligibility of an account of Polish history. What we require, therefore, is a characterization of the relationship between religion and the rest of society, both in the past and during present times. There is, of course, some room for bias but such bias resides only in an evaluation of the role of religion: for example, a view may consider the relationship between religion and society as significant or as not significant; alternatively, it may regard the influence of religion as either positive or negative.

The solution which we shall choose is one in which alternative biases can be juxtaposed. Such a juxtaposition of biases enables the observation of different points of reference in terms of which religion, society and history can be understood. There is, of course, no empirical guide to choosing between biases or points of reference: such a choice, however, can be made by asking the question whether a particular option can or cannot be accepted into our system of meaning and understanding. In other words, the question 'Does an interpretation make sense?'. All the different points of reference are themselves quite real in the sense that they are all part of the broad axis around which revolves the process of change which encompasses religion and the Church. In this chapter, therefore, we will elaborate on the relationship between religion and the history, society and politics of Poland. Later, in chapter 4, we will examine an alternative interpretative bias.

POLAND UNTIL THE SECOND WORLD WAR

Polonia semper fidelis!
(Traditional motto of the Polish gentry)

Poland is a fine example of the Christian tradition. The date normally given for the acceptance of Christianity is 966. This is certainly the date which saw the baptism of Mieszko I, the powerful ruler of the area which was later to become Poland. From

this point Christianity was to assert itself as the greatest unifying and nation-creating force in the whole of Polish history.
Mieszko, however, was not the first of his people to become
converted: the disciples of Cyril and Methodius had already been
active in the region for some time and there is reason to think
that they may even have established a number of Romano-Slav
dioceses as early as a century before. Some archaeological evidence would appear to date the first signs of Christianity on
Polish soil at around the third century.

Side by side with the Romano-Slav rite there was the Latin
rite and it was the latter which was finally accepted by Mieszko.
He felt, perhaps, that the Latin rite, whose prestige was greater
both in Rome and in Christendom in general on account of its
universality, would be more likely to secure him entry into the
family of Christian nations and, by the same token, enable him
to oppose more effectively the Germanic pressure from the west.
Mieszko was thus no longer exposed to Christianization through
conquest.

After Mieszko's baptism and the conversion of the court circles
there followed a rapid mass Christianization where the rest of
society was indeed Christianized and baptized en masse with little
or no doctrinal preparation. It appears that this process went
relatively smoothly. But in many cases the lives of the inhabitants
continued very much as before and it was centuries before the
ancient pagan beliefs ceased to give the Church concern. Even
today, as we have seen, relics of paganism continue to survive.
The Romano-Slav rite continued to coexist precariously with the
Latin: its decline began after the middle of the eleventh century
and its disappearance on Polish soil was complete in the twelfth.
Its later reappearance in Poland was due not to its rebirth in the
kingdom but to the incorporation into Poland of lands to the
east. By this time, however, the allegiance of the Romano-Slav
Church had changed from Rome to Byzantium and it had become
known as the Graeco-Ruthenian Church.

A very important figure in early Polish history is Stanisław
Szczepanowski who was Bishop of Kraków from 1072 to 1079.
Stanisław entered into a dispute with King Boleslaus the Bold
about the way that monarchs should treat their subjects. He had
long witnessed that the king had been treating his subjects
arbitrarily, according to his whims, and not in accordance with
Christian law. Nobody, not even the king, is above the law,
maintained Stanisław. This angered Boleslaus who ordered that
Stanisław be axed to death. After all, Boleslaus had been brought
up on the tradition of his predecessors who had always expected
absolute obedience from their subjects. The martyrdom of
Stanisław, his canonization 200 years later and his subsequent
veneration have produced a deep conviction in the Polish spiritual
and national consciousness that 'might need not be right'. The
whole event soon acquired the significance of a Magna Carta as
successive kings were brought to swear oaths of respect on the
tomb of St Stanisław. The echoes of St Stanisław were respon-

sible for the early experiments in Polish democracy during the
Renaissance as they are today responsible for the particular
concern that the Polish Church has for human rights. There is a
more than just symbolic sense in which St Stanisław is regarded
as the patron of Poland.

Almost from the very moment of Poland's conversion, its rulers
engaged in what the historian Walerian Meysztowicz has characterized as a 'croisade permanente'. The core trait of the 'croisade
permanente' was the high degree to which Polish foreign policy
was motivated by religious and moral considerations rather than
by material and political ones alone. This motivation was not without significance as far as its historical consequences are concerned: King Sigismund III's tenacious adherence to Rome during Russia's Time of Troubles and his refusal to embrace Orthodoxy contributed to his losing control of Russia; on the other
hand, the successful conversion of the Princedom of Lithuania
enabled an extremely powerful Polish-Lithuanian state to emerge
during the Middle Ages. The 'croisade permanente' was first
a struggle between Christian Poland and her pagan neighbours
and later became the struggle of a Catholic Poland against non-
Catholic neighbours (Protestantism, Russian Orthodoxy, communism).

In the early days Poland's enemies were the pagan nations
and tribes: the Western Slavs of Pomerania, the Prussian and
the Lithuanian peoples to the north and north-east, the Tartar
hordes to the east and, later, the Turks in the south of Europe.
None of them caused Poland any grave problems: Pomerania was
conquered and converted, Lithuania was simply converted to
become united with Poland under the former Prince of Lithuania
as monarch. The Polish-Lithuanian state which now emerged was
successful in defending its eastern borders against the Tartars
and in defeating the Teutonic Knights who had settled in Prussia
and then threatened both Poland and Lithuania. There was,
therefore, also a definite sense in which Poland was regarded
in Europe as a 'bulwark and rampart' of Christendom.

From the time of their first attack on Poland in 1241, the Tartar hordes proved to be more of a cruel and brutal nuisance
than a serious threat of invasion. Their occasional blitzkrieg-
like sorties against Polish and Lithuanian towns did, however,
wreak havoc and instil terror into the populations. The Tartars
were brought up on iron discipline and were absolutely ruthless.
One of the consequences of the Tartar attacks and of their
consolidation to the east during the thirteenth century was the
establishment by Rome of close links with the European monarchs
with the aim of containing the Tartars and of defending the
Christian nations against the expansion of the hordes' territories.
But although the Tartars were never defeated in battle, they did
not manage to expand any further: their fortunes gradually
declined and their power and traditions became gradually trans-
ferred to the Dukes of Muscovy. This marked the beginnings of
Russia.

The situation in the south of Europe was quite different: the Moslem Turks were a far more pressing threat to Europe than the Tartars had ever been. This was crusading Islam at its peak, ready to strike at the very heart of Christendom. The Tsars had been unwilling to take part in any action against them despite requests from both Rome and the Christian monarchs. Beaten by Poland in 1621 and in 1673 they returned to be finally and decisively defeated by King John Sobieski in 1683 at the Battle of Vienna. In his letter to Pope Innocent XI after the victory, King John Sobieski made it clear that it was God who had won the day.

The well-known Polish characteristic, the identification of religious sentiments with national ones, owes much of its rationale to the 'croisade permanente'. This characteristic in turn gave the Poles the reputation of basing their patriotism on their Catholicism and, of course, vice versa. One of the consequences of this combination of sentiments was that all enemy efforts to destroy Polish national feeling (during the partitions, during the occupations of the Second World War and during the present post-war period) have been clearly harmonized with attacks on the Roman Catholic Church.

The veneration of the Virgin Mary is inseparably linked with the above sentiments. One of the first concrete signs of this veneration is to be observed during the Deluge - a period of general disorder and repeated invasion - when, in 1656, the Kingdom of Poland was dedicated to the Blessed Virgin by King John Casimir whilst he was facing defeat in battle. This act was the result of what was considered to be the miraculous defence of the Shrine of Jasna Góra the previous year. The Virgin Mary has since been regarded by the Poles as the Queen of Poland. This image of Queen is strongly bound up with an image of a protective spiritual mother to the nation.

During the partitions religion and the Church survived under conditions of intolerance and persecution in the Prussian and Russian zones.(1) These two powers were particularly insistent in their respective policies of Germanization and Russification of their shares of Poland. They both hoped somehow to use the Polish Church to further their aims. Although life in neither of the zones was in any sense free, constant fear of deportation to Siberia plagued the minds of those living under Russian occupation. In the Austrian-occupied zone the situation was different. Because of the strong Catholic traditions within the Austrian empire itself with its numerous nationalities and also because of the empire's weakness, the Church in this zone together with the theology departments at the Universities of Kraków and Lwów remained untouched as an institution. The theology departments were the only two open in all three occupied zones, indeed, this was also the case with the two universities. The Austrian state did manage to succeed where the Prussians and the Russians had failed, namely, in the penetration of the Polish Church and in the subordination of even its

most trivial secular functions. This process has come to be
known as 'Josephism', after Emperor Joseph II who was especially vehement in his pursuit of the policy.
  As a result of the different conditions prevailing under the
different occupations - including the short-lived Grand Duchy
of Warsaw and the Congress Kingdom of Poland - and also of the
rapid changes in policy by the occupying powers, the Polish
Church had to develop a political and pastoral flexibility while
at the same time maintaining its unity across the whole nation.
This flexibility was to prove invaluable in times to come.
  Direct action against Roman (Latin rite) Catholics in the
Prussian and Russian zones ranged from the closing of convents
and theology departments, the continual surveillance of priests
and bishops with frequent imprisonments to the occasional massacre here and there. In the Russian zone the Graeco-Ruthenians
came off worse. They had, since the time of Casimir the Great
in the fourteenth century, returned to their original allegiance
to Rome and had become known as the Uniates.(2) Their re-
incorporation into the Orthodox Church had become a matter of
honour for the Russians during the partitions; because of their
relatively small numbers, their poor organization and their
Romano-Slav rite the Uniates were easy prey for conversion to
Orthodoxy and subsequent Russification. Deportation and the
imprisonment of both clergy and faithful were used to encourage
potential converts. The particularly strong drive against the
Uniates suggests that the Russians perhaps also feared that they
might act as a bridge between Rome and Orthodoxy. Attempts
to convert Roman Catholics were less intense and produced no
successes worth mentioning.
  The period of the partitions is most noteworthy on account of
the intense opposition to the occupying powers which was gen-
erated: this opposition was most strongly directed against Prussia and Russia. The relatively mild Austrian regime provided
favourable conditions for this zone to become the centre for
revolutionary organization for the three zones. Between 1830 and
1905 there were five armed uprisings. The role of the Catholic
Church as a rallying point for feelings of national identity during this period has been noted by many writers. The clergy, in
particular, became famous for their patriotism and many took an
active part in the insurrections. Most important of all was that
the Church was the only Polish institution whose unifying influence transcended the imposed boundaries: it became a surrogate
state. This could not have occurred without the tacit approval
of the Vatican.
  Even before the partitions the authority of the Church had
been unquestionable. This was due to the part which it had
played in crucial historical events and also by its more general
role within society: it had played a decisive part in the restora-
tion of the Polish monarchy in the thirteenth century, it had
been actively involved in the legal reforms of Casimir the Great
in the fourteenth century, already by the thirteenth century

it had fully organized a network of parishes throughout the kingdom, in the sixteenth century the position of Primate acquired the additional function of regency during interregna;(3) from then on the Polish Primate has always been regarded as 'interrex'. Finally, the Catholic Church had emerged triumphant after its fight with the currents of the Reformation in Poland.

It is worth noting that, as a result of Christianization, the cultural heritage of Poland owes much to the ancient Greek - in particular Aristotelian - traditions in science and philosophy and to the Roman legal tradition as well as incorporating the more characteristic features of the Judaeo-Christian tradition. Scholasticism was especially strong in Polish thought. These traditions first found their anchorage in the Jagellonian University in Kraków which was founded in 1364 by Casimir the Great. At first, the University comprised the Faculties of Philosophy and of Law; later, in the fifteenth century, the Faculty of Theology was established. This faculty was to become the centre of learning for the Polish bishops. However, the teaching of philosophy, law, theology and Latin was not limited to the University alone even during the early period: schools were established in monasteries and even some of the local churches became centres of learning. Soon other important academies were founded: Poznań, Zamość and Wilno were among the first.

The period of the Renaissance in Poland is often referred to as the Golden Age. Renaissance ideas reached Poland quite easily albeit late: all learned men in Poland spoke Latin and in Kraków there was no shortage of men of learning from Italy and other places. Many Poles underwent education in Italy. Communication and communications, therefore, were no problem. But the Renaissance did not spread any further: it halted at Poland's eastern border. It was during the Renaissance that the Jagellonian University produced many figures of repute of whom Nicolas Copernicus is perhaps the best known. Thought at the University also undoubtedly influenced the Polish legal system as regards the acceptance of the principle of 'Neminem captivabimus nisi iure victum',(4) the equivalent of the 'Habeas corpus', in the 1430s; also passed was the Law of Religious Tolerance in 1573. This law conferred equal rights on members of all religious creeds. The 'democratization' of decision-making amongst the gentry and the establishment of an elective monarchy both owe their inspiration to a fusion of a Renaissance ideas with earlier traditions favouring democracy.

These legal and political developments were therefore well in advance of analogous ones in the neighbouring states, some of which possessed similar traditions. The attitude towards Muscovy (and later towards Russia), whose traditions concerning social order and moral virtue had been inherited from the Tartars, was a combination of fear and contempt: in such traditions the 'will of the monarch' replaced all notions of justice and law. The will of the Tsar, as manifest in his decrees, had the force of law and the righteousness of justice: the Tsar was thus above all law.

In Poland, Stanisław Szczepanowski had been canonized for having put an end to such ideas centuries before. The Polish attitude, strengthened by a view of Russian Orthodoxy as a refusal of the traditions of Rome and Christendom, led to the Poles considering Russia as a rather abhorrent kind of enemy.

The Golden Age was also the period of the Reformation in Poland. The complexity of the religious movements of the time and of their interrelationships defies simple description but four directions can be roughly distinguished: Hussitism, Arianism, Lutheranism and Calvinism, of which the latter was unquestionably the strongest. In the course of only a few decades Poland had become, in the words of a Vatican official, a 'paradisus hereticorum'. A Protestant majority in the Sejm (parliament) seemed to mark the final victory of Calvinism on Polish soil, but in fact marked only its highest point. During this period the idea of forming a National Church became an issue. Despite appearances, however, Reformation currents were weak in Poland: Calvin, despite repeated attempts, had not managed either to reform the Polish monarchy or to make any impression on the peasantry. As a result the Church hierarchy was able to rely on royal support for the Polish Counter-Reformation. The Union of Brest was one of the incidental results of the Counter-Reformation and succeeded in bringing back into the Catholic Church the almost forgotten Graeco-Ruthenians.(5)

The exhaustion of the creative drive of the Renaissance towards the end of the sixteenth century coincided with the Counter-Reformation. This was the end of the Golden Age. Although the subsequent period is often dismissed as one of cultural, intellectual and political stagnation as well as one of uncertainty it was, nevertheless, one of frenzied activity for the Church. The Jesuit Order formed the spearhead of this activity: the Jesuits were charged with the implementation of the Tridentine reforms. In practical terms their object was a pastoral one - the deepening of Catholic belief at all levels within Polish society. This object was to be accomplished by means of developing education, mission work and by involvement in extensive charity work. During this period we observe the expansion of seminaries, the growth of religious orders and the general raising of the intellectual level of the clergy. Amongst the mass of the population there was the spread of popular Church hymns, the spread of the veneration of the Virgin Mary and a popularization of pilgrimages; it was then that the first pilgrimage to the Black Madonna of Częstochowa took place. The Jesuits were also responsible for introducing Spanish mysticism to religious elites; the Polish Pope John Paul II, while still a priest studying in Rome, was to echo this interest 300 years later.

With the eighteenth century came the Enlightenment which brought with it an interest in reform, education and deism. In Poland, the Enlightenment was a strictly elite phenomenon which left the vast majority of the population untouched. It also lacked the strong anti-religious flavours of its French cousin: two of

its principle figures - Stanisław Staszic and Hugo Kołłątaj - were
both Catholic priests although, admittedly, not particularly
devout ones. But the Polish Enlightenment was specific in other
ways. Its distinctness can only be understood against the background of internal disharmony and strife of the Deluge and the
tragic débâcle of the partitions. It erupted as a deep-seated
desire for more than mere reform: it demanded a total reconstruction of Polish society. The Church, affected by the euphoria, joined in. However, the currents of utilitarianism, prag-
matism, liberalism and political expediency were dangerous
ground for the Church: 'useless' religious orders disappeared,
'superstitious' forms of religious expression were attacked,
'religious tolerance' dampened evangelizing fervour. Ironically,
all these measures originated from within a very confused
Catholic establishment which thereby unwittingly implemented
some of the occupying powers' anti-religious and depolonizing
policies.

The Enlightenment is also significant in that it marks the point
at which Polish intellectual and cultural life becomes pluralist in
character: Catholicism and the Church are no longer seen as the
sole and unquestioned sources of ideas and inspiration. The
origins of the concept of 'modern man', described in the previous
chapter, can already be seen here. The period of the Enlightenment was relatively short-lived and faded into the background
where it patiently waited for happier days as the nation was
swept off its feet by an even greater euphoria.

Romanticism took Poland by storm. The Polish Primate of the
time, John Paul Woronicz, declared that tragedy had befallen
the nation because it had turned away from God: a return to
Him was the only answer. The Polish Romantics were quick to
snatch up this theme. Although they were originally inspired by
western Romanticism and especially by the works and image of
Lord Byron, the Polish Romantics' unique character was immediately apparent when they dedicated themselves to fierce patriotism and to the ideal of national liberation and fashioned what
has since been called 'the Polish national philosophy' (polska
filozofia narodowa). Various aspects and variants of this national
philosophy can be found in the works of Adam Mickiewicz,
Juliusz Słowacki, Zygmunt Krasiński (the three Polish 'bards')
and also in the works of August Cieszkowski, Bronisław Tren-
towski, Kornel Ujejski and perhaps also of Henryk Sienkiewicz
and others. The Polish national philosophy has often been referred to as Polish messianism.

Messianism appears as a specifically national characteristic
bearing little or no relation to any mainstream European thought.
Polish messianism has never been a homogenous and well-ordered
body of ideas, but more of a mystical vision. Briefly stated,
the messianic view suggests that the Polish nation is the 'chosen
people' of the New Covenant and is destined, through its suffering and constant martyrdom, to lead the nations of the world to
salvation and to the Kingdom of God. While the Kingdom of God

referred to here is most certainly one belonging to the other
world, the road to this salvation is itself to mark the opening of
an era of justice and happiness in this world. Furthermore,
the misfortunes of Poland must be brought before the judgment
of all nations in order for this destiny to be fulfilled. At the
same time there is a strong feeling of guilt for the past sins of
Poland, a guilt which can be expiated only through an unconditional struggle for freedom and a dedication to God: the cult
of the hero-leader together with a glorification of dying for one's
native land are therefore central features of messianism. Messianic ideas were undoubtedly the principal source of inspiration
for the insurrections especially during the period 1831-63.
Although officially disapproved of by the Catholic Church, messianism did not lack sympathizers amongst the clergy and even
higher: it did, after all, contribute greatly to a revival and
renewal of Catholicism in Poland. Also the clergy were themselves
patriotic and longed for independence. Messianism, therefore,
can be thus considered as a sort of 'unofficial extension' of
Catholicism or even as a local national variant. It might even be
possible to see it in terms of a national religious culture.
    It is these messianic elements which, in fusing with the offi-
cially defined Roman Catholicism, produced the patriotic Catholicism of Poland. This version of patriotic Catholicism is characteristic of Poland alone. Despite its strong ethnocentric character
there has been no observable tendency in Poland towards any
form of national sectarianism or towards the formation of a schis-
matic 'National Church':(6) Polish messianism appears to be well
contained within the bounds of Catholicism proper by its even
stronger inherent universalist tendencies which envisage the
salvation of all mankind - Poles and non-Poles alike - and by what
amounts to a rejection of a this-worldly paradise. The contain-
ment of messianism, however, has as its unavoidable consequence
a degree of tension which has long been a characteristic of the
relationship between national attitudes and official Church teaching. There has, occasionally, even been some mistrust of the
universal successor of St Peter. The election of a Polish Pope
will no doubt be of far-reaching significance for the future of
messianism: on the one hand, there will be a strengthening of
the messianic idea, especially since the Romantic bard Słowacki,
during the first half of the nineteenth century, prophesied the
coming of a Slav Pope. In 1848 Słowacki wrote this about the
Pope: 'He will cast out all corruption from the world's wounds,
All vermin and foulness; Instead, he will bring health and kindle
the fire of love - And the world he will save.'(7) On the other
hand, a resolution, perhaps only temporary, of the traditional
tension might be expected and be accompanied by an influx of
strong Polish Catholic traditions into the 'universal' Catholicism.
There is evidence of these two processes and the latter in particular can be observed in the appearance of Marianism in the
foreground of Catholicism since the advent of Pope John Paul
II.(8)

The history of messianism can be traced back to the beginnings of Poland's crusading tradition. The first concrete reference to Poland as a chosen nation can be found in the middle of the sixteenth century. This suggests that messianic ideas are more than just a product of Poland's Romantic climate and of the partitions. Further, these ideas did not disappear with the end of the Romantic era: messianism is still a force today, despite accusations that it is no more than a skeleton in the closet of Polish dreams appearing only when the second bottle of vodka is being opened.

Closely allied to Polish messianism is the philosophic messianism or 'absolute philosophy' of Józef Hoene Wroński. Curiously, Wroński's claim to a Polish heritage is dubious and most of his writing was done in France. Wroński believed that it is possible to arrive at the salvation of the whole of mankind through the discovery of absolute truth. Absolute truth is, according to Wroński, accessible to man and consists of the unconditional union of goodness and truth or, in other words, of science and religion. It is this fusion of values with knowledge that can reveal humanity's destiny and so put it on the road to salvation. Wroński's quest has not been abandoned, however, and today Władysław Bruliński in Warsaw claims to be in the final stages of producing a scheme of the absolute as was originally envisaged by Wroński.

After the abortive uprising of 1863 the dormant Enlightenment surfaced in the new form of positivism. Its proponents accused Romanticism and messianism of fruitlessness. Lwów and Kraków, both in the Austrian zone, became centres of positivist thought. Later, after the First World War, the Polish positivists were to become closely associated with the Vienna Circle and published their work in the journal 'Erkenntnis'. The works of Darwin and Spencer were most enthusiastically received by positivists at the time.

The strong influence of positivism can be observed in the sphere of early Polish sociology and many of the sociologists' pronouncements regarding religion can be seen as critiques from the positivist frame of reference. Any form of critique or criticism of Catholicism, however, was a very delicate issue since it always implied the additional questioning of traditional Polish national feeling. This strong national feeling would tend to reassert itself in the condemnations by members of the Catholic elite of the sociologists as enemies of Poland and of Catholicism. The feeling against the sociologists also partly accounts for the small volume of sociological studies of religion in Poland especially in the very early days.

The early days of positivism in Europe coincided with the days of Marx, Engels and dreams of the proletarian revolution. In Poland, however, native communist thought and tradition amounted to no more than a very muddy dribble. The KPP, which emerged from the fusion of the left wing of Józef Piłsudski's PPS with the SDKPiL towards the end of the nineteenth century, hardly met with any success. Having dumped his left wing and pronounced himself in favour of a nationalist solution, Piłsudski was to become the undisputed leader of Poland after the end of the First World War. In addition to the PPS there were two other important clandestine political movements in Poland during this period. One was Roman Dmowski's National Democratic Party - strongly Catholic (even messianic) and anti-socialist. Although it was never to come to power, it remained as an opposition party between the wars and its influence is still very strongly felt. The other was the Peasant Party, generally associated with Wincenty Witos. This grouping, while not directly anti-Catholic, did have some strong anticlerical tendencies despite the fact that Witos was himself a practising Catholic. Meanwhile the KPP was to remain a pathetic movement fighting against overwhelming odds and with little support other than itself. This view of early Polish communism is not shared by the official communist historians of today simply because communist leaders base much of their prestige and legitimacy on historical justifications and on traditions of struggle.

The original Marxist revolutionary movement was strongly associated with Russia - a traditional enemy and the occupying power; the slogan of the 'international revolution' adopted by Rosa Luxemburg, the leader of the revolutionaries, meant very little to most Poles whose prime concern was the independence and unity of Poland ('Poland is already international enough under the three occupations', they might have said). Luxemburg's slogan resulted in her incurring the nationalists' wrath and being branded as 'anti-Polish'. Ironically, she also incurred the wrath of Lenin himself who feared that too great an emphasis on non-Russian problems and on internationalism within his party would jeopardize his chances of coming to power in Russia: Lenin was, after all, a politician. Rosa Luxemburg's Jewish origins were not a point in her favour; the Jews had always been a marginal group in Polish society: they tended to live in separate communities, they had their own language, customs, style of dress and general appearance. A small trickle from these communities fed the tiny though economically and professionally significant Jewish middle class and the extreme radicals who, although ethnically mixed, possessed a very strong Jewish contingent. Thus Poles and Jews, with the exception of this small radical group, were foreigners in each other's eyes.

Another handicap of the Marxist revolutionaries was their dogmatic rejection of religion. In a country whose very rationale for independence was firmly anchored in the Catholic tradition they could not have been expected to have gained much support.

The stand taken by the Polish communists on some key national issues during the inter-war period of independence only contributed to a weakening of their position: they refused to accept the legality of Pilsudski's new government with the result that they became outlawed as a party; they supported Russia and its invasion of Poland during the Polish-Soviet War; they supported the territorial claims made against Poland by Russia, Germany and Lithuania. The taking of such positions is evidence of the communists' political immaturity: each of these positions taken alone would have been sufficiently damning - together and in combination with the abovementioned handicaps they simply deprived the communists of all traces of credibility. The communists failed even as a funnel for discontent: Piłsudski's PPS had long siphoned off all the significant discontent resulting from the occupations leaving only those individuals with incurable internationalist or pro-Russian yearnings.

The KPP was finally physically liquidated on the instigation of Stalin in 1938 because it was still too 'internationally' minded and Stalin was not only still preoccupied with the task of building 'socialism in one country', but also feared the presence of a fifth column in a rapidly deteriorating Europe.

After the end of the First World War Poland was not finally at peace until the Treaty of Riga was concluded with Soviet Russia in 1920. This treaty marked the end of the Polish-Soviet War in which the decisive victory was obtained by Piłsudski's troops when they routed the Red Army at the Battle of Warsaw in August 1920. This victory has been attributed by many to divine intervention and has become famous as the Miracle of the Vistula (Cud nad Wisłą); it was certainly an unexpected victory since the odds were very much against the Polish army, especially during the final stages of the war.

The wars left the Roman Catholic Church with some 21 million faithful. In addition, there were about 3 million Uniates which put the total number of Catholics at around 75 per cent of the population.(9) With the constraints of the partitions gone, the Catholic Church was able to resume normal activity in the open. The problem of national unification was a priority. Although the Church favoured the National Democrats (the ND or Endecja) and had always been suspicious of the PPS, its tacit alliance with the elite in power was probably a significant factor contributing to the thriving of Catholic life between the wars. It adopted a broad pastoral strategy. The year 1918 saw the opening of KUL which, apart from its functions as a university, became an important centre of intellectual life in Poland;(10) in 1919 the papal nuncio arrived from Rome and the groundwork was done for the Concordat of 1925; during the whole inter-war period the numbers of bishops, priests, nuns and monks more or less doubled - for example, in 1918 there were 23 bishops and in 1939 there were 51; religious instruction in schools was made obligatory for each denomination;(11) the term 'Catholic press' loosely describes an assortment of newspapers and periodicals which gave prominence to Catholic news and features (a Catholic press agency was also established). In addition, catechetal activity intensified, parish life showed signs of a considerable revival, religious orders expanded and missionary activity abroad increased. The development of Catholic lay organizations is an important feature of this period. Most of these organizations were centred on Catholic Action (Akcja Katolicka); of particular note is Odrodzenie (Rebirth) - a national student organization with strong links with KUL. Outside Catholic Action there was Iuventus christiana - also principally a student organization. While it could be said that the Catholic Church and the associated intellectual elites tended towards the right, an important and influential section of Polish intellectuals had strong left-wing and anticlerical leanings.(12) But militant atheism as such, however, was unknown. These left-wing tendencies are particularly significant as they were to impinge strongly on intellectual and political developments in Poland after the Second World War. During the inter-war years the traditions of the Enlightenment, of Positivism and of early socialism all mingled together in the typical left-wing humanist intellectual. Some of the more able minds of the time, Tadeusz Kotarbiński and Stanisław Ossowski for example, were attracted and fed by these traditions. Church obscurantism was attacked and the Church was identified as an obstacle to social progress. It is worth recalling that Krzywicki was firmly anchored in this tradition.

The most important movement associated with the anticlerical currents was the Association for Free Thought (Stowarzyszenie Wolnej Myśli, later to become the Związek Myśli Wolnej) and its student equivalent the Legion of Youth (Legion Młodych). The movement was also represented at secondary school level by Vanguard (Straż Przednia). A prominent aim of the movement was the abolition of religious instruction in schools: the principal supporter of this aim was the Union of Polish Teachers. Two other youth organizations incorporating a degree of anticlericalism were the rural Wici and the young worker organization OMTUR.

The Second World War hit Poland like a thunderbolt. It brought with it massive persecution of the clergy: out of a total of 10,017 priests in 1939 no less than 2,647 (20 per cent) had, by 1944, suffered a violent death in concentration camps or prisons or were killed at home or at work. Constant attempts at weakening the spiritual leadership of Poland had the very opposite effect - the reinforcement of the authority of those who remained. The suffering and self-sacrifice of the war years stands out in the figure of Fr Maksymilian Kolbe who, while imprisoned in Auschwitz, volunteered to take the place of another prisoner in the death cell and was subsequently starved to death.

At the beginning of the war Poland was invaded by both Germany and the Soviet Union. The country was duly partitioned according to the terms of the secret protocol of the Nazi-Soviet pact. Two years later Poland was to fall entirely under German occupation. In the meantime the Soviet authorities decided to cleanse their zone of all potential intellectual and military leadership - those who might be able to offer any resistance - by sending some one and a half million Polish citizens to 'corrective labour camps' for what was euphemistically called 'citizens' re-education' inside the Soviet Union proper. The Soviet Union is

also known to have liquidated about 15,000 Polish officers whom
they had first deported and imprisoned.(13) The Polish government, having fled to Paris and later to London, was both too far
from Poland and too weak to be able to influence the flow of
political and military events either directly or through the intervention of the Western Allies. Its links with Allied decision-
making circles, with the Polish population and with its guerrilla
force in Poland were poor. Under such circumstances the Soviet
Union did not encounter any serious obstacles when it organized
its workers' party, the PPR together with a militia (the People's
Guard - Gwardia Ludowa) which began to engage in some very
minor anti-German guerrilla activity on Polish soil after 1941.(14)
All along, the Soviet intention had been to set up a puppet
government in Poland without itself appearing to be involved. It
was important, therefore, for the PPR to appear to be in full
control of its own destiny. Meanwhile, the 'regular' guerrilla
force, the Home Army (Armia Krajowa), tended to disregard the
People's Guard which it considered as some sort of temporary
aberration. However, the PPR soon founded a National Council
- the KRN. After this all went smoothly for the Soviet Union with
the result that on 31 December 1944 the KRN declared itself to
be the provisional government of Poland. The formation of this
provisional government was met with disbelief: the view that it
was doomed to failure was taken by both the Church and by the
remnants of the pre-war government who had remained in Poland.
But although the provisional government appeared both pre-
carious and preposterous, the closeness of its Soviet protector
enabled an extremely rapid consolidation of power with the result
that by 1947 all governmental anti-communist opposition ceased.
(15)
    The fundamental pattern of the whole structure of the new
power apparatus in Poland, of which the new government was
part, was now the same as that of the Soviet Union. Indeed, the
Soviet model of state power was eventually imposed on all the
countries which were absorbed into the Soviet orbit during the
war. Because of the very low support for the provisional government (by July 1944 the PPR had only 20,000 members - a strange
combination of idealists, fatalists and pragmatists) and because
of a lack of a true grasp of the new realities by the vast majority
of the war-weary population the new authorities, after a short
period of cautious treading during which they wanted to give the
impression of a strong desire to befriend the Church, began to
rely extensively on a high degree of overt coercion which was
always loudly justified in terms of pro-Soviet, Marxist-Leninist
and anti-fascist slogans.(16) Later, as power became consolidated,
this coercion was replaced by threats - both implicit and explicit.
    It was perhaps not entirely a surprise to find that one promin-
ent section of the population was quick to declare its support for
the new regime. This group was composed of the freethinking
left-wing intellectuals who in most cases genuinely believed that
Soviet Marxism-Leninism in Poland would in the long run and

despite some of its grotesque facets lead towards the realization of all the noble values. The fusion of their anticlericalism with the regime's militant atheism was a feature which not only brought the freethinkers and the communists together, but also one which presented the Church and the Catholic community with a new kind of threat.

In general the intellectuals tended to close their eyes even to the cruder measures of the regime: they often argued that such measures were necessary for the future realization of justice in society. Their absolute loyalty, however, was to prove relatively short-lived as we will see below.

During the early years Marxist-Leninist slogans were used to justify the policy of nationalizing the economy: state control of production, exchange and services meant that the state, as virtually the sole employer, was provided with a vast reserve of an additional type of power - remunerative power. 'He who does not support us will not work and will thus starve' became the authorities' never publically admitted motto. The exercise of remunerative power by the state in communist countries remains to this day similar in character and is a particularly important instrument of rule. However, the military might of the Soviet Union has remained as the principal reminder of the need for absolute conformity. During the early days the Soviet Union, not wishing to take any chances, made the Soviet Marshall Constanty Rokossovsky head of the Polish Armed Forces.

The double invasion of Poland in 1939 confirmed the so-called 'theory of two enemies' (teoria dwóch wrogów). The 'theory of two enemies' is a reference to the age-old Polish political debate regarding Poland's geographical position between Germany and Russia. It is maintained, on the one hand, that Poland should ally herself with Germany - an advanced nation and a part of Western Europe and Roman tradition - in order to oppose the westward expansion of the savage and primitive Russia; on the other hand, it is maintained that Poland should ally herself with Russia, like Poland a Slav nation and thus similar racially and spiritually, against the brutal and inexorable Drang nach Osten of the Germans. This debate is unresolvable and in the final analysis both are regarded as enemies for the reasons given - it is a choice between two extreme evils. The new authorities, wishing to exploit the debate in favour of the Soviet Union, began to build on the horrors of the Nazi occupation and stress the continual danger of 'German revisionism'. A prominent feature of the maintenance of the Nazi concentration camps as monuments to human bestiality is the heavy stress laid on the constant German danger; this stress is at least equal to that concerned with the condemnation of the horrendous crime of the camps. Multitudes of books and articles have been written on the 'German problem'. The anti-German line, however, suffers major problems of consistency when it stresses the difference between the 'friendly' German Democratic State and the potential or even actual fascism of Federal Germany.(17) The authorities' avowed hatred of Germany is the only patch of ground on which they can hope to receive anything resembling support from the population.

POLAND SINCE THE SECOND WORLD WAR

> O God, who hast for centuries long
> Surrounded Poland with power and glory,
> With protective shield guarded
> Against misfortune lest it befall her:
> Before Thy altars we beseech Thee
> Our free homeland do Thou return to us, O Lord.
> (Traditional Polish hymn)

> Maybe a communist society is the highest goal
> towards which the history of the world inclines:
> but for it not to become the most terrible irony,
> the most lunatic despotism, it must come at a time
> when the light of Christ turns everyone into a
> saint.
> (Zygmunt Krasiński, 1846(18))

> The state has instituted true freedom of conscience
> and belief together with true equality of citizens
> regardless of their belief or lack of belief.
> Religion has become the private affair of citizens
> as far as the state is concerned.
> (Jerzy Godlewski, official Polish 'expert' on religious mat-
> ters(19))

Apart from the obvious and universal aim of remaining in power, leaders in communist states have the aim of totally controlling the societies they govern. Total control envisages the acquisition of maximum power and its uncontrolled exercise in all spheres of social life.(20) In concrete terms this means the monopoly of all the sanction application mechanisms and the desire for absolute conformity to the demands which the leaders set for the society. It is also important to note the expansionist aims of communist leaders who constantly seek opportunities for extending their sphere of influence beyond the Eastern bloc.(21)

Absolute conformity to the leaders' programme is based on the two principles of 'democratic centralism' and the 'leading role of the party', both of which owe their origin to Lenin and the spirit of which is intended to permeate the whole of Polish political and public life, as indeed it is intended to do in all communist states. As expressed in the 'Statute of the PZPR', democratic centralism embodies the notion of election from below combined with the requirement of binding decisions from above. However, in practice the former has been dispensed with, thus producing a unique feature of communist totalitarianism: 'election' from

above.(22) The 'Statute of the PZPR' describes the functioning
of the binding decisions in this way: 'The resolutions and directives of the higher party organs must be implemented by the
lower ones.' At lower levels there are supervisory bodies
which:(23)

> ensure the implementation of measures deepening the influence
> and authority of the party amongst non-members and which
> strengthen party discipline. They intensify the struggle
> against bureaucratism and activate the society into the rea-
> lization of the tasks set by the party....The bodies function
> under the direction of the party committee of the relevant
> echelon.

The 'influence and authority' of the party are in turn central
to the principle of its 'leading role'. A Polish political handbook
for party members points out:(24)

> The struggle of the PZPR for the strengthening of its lead-
> ing political role in the life of our society and in the function-
> ing of the state has always been an integral part of the
> struggle for the victory of Marxist-Leninist ideas in the
> consciousness of Polish society and for the recognition of the
> ideological leadership of the party.

Marxist-Leninist ideology is undoubtedly the principal source
of legitimacy for any communist leadership. It is far more important than elections which, in any case, do not take place in the
Soviet bloc states.(25) Marxist-Leninist ideology is a total theory
of existence: it covers all metaphysical, moral, social, historal,
political and economic questions in a way that is absolute and
final. There is no room for any truth other than its own. Political
leaders who claim to base themselves on this ideology therefore
invariably claim to possess the absolute and final truth. In this
way they claim the moral right to express and act upon what
they consider to be the objective desires of the population
regardless of what those desires actually are or appear to be.
In such a political context the greatest of all virtues - as far as
the leadership is concerned - becomes the submission of all
activity and thought to the party: this is a virtue not very much
different from the one which the Dukes of Muscovy inherited
from the Tartars. What used to be the will of the Tsar has
become, thanks to Lenin, the will of the party wherever the
party happens to govern. There are no laws, only rules and
decrees - and even these are disregarded at will. Leszek
Kołakowski summarizes communist power as a 'one-party tyranny'.(26)

The 'Theses' submitted by the Central Committee of the PZPR
in 1974 illustrate the leaders' extreme and uncompromising ideological position with respect to their campaign for legitimacy and
popularity:(27)

The socialist character of our life is shaped by an unceasing struggle against all which is alien to socialist ideals, against the remnants of the old order in the social consciousness. We will be consistent in eliminating the mentality and attitudes of petty bourgeois individualism and of social parasitism.

This is clearly a statement of their position with respect to the Church and Catholicism. Article 79(1) of the Constitution is concise on the question of the communist system's fear which is merely the correlate of the oppressive character of the regime: 'Vigilance against the enemies of the nation...is the duty of each citizen of the Polish People's Republic.'(28) It is through the desire for economic betterment and military security on the part of the population that the leaders may strive to mobilize the society for their purposes; the 'Theses' state that: 'the working people...have made Poland a strong country....We are also aware that in the historic advance of Poland only a beginning has been made: in the next twenty years we shall be facing even greater and more complex tasks.'(29)

Marxism-Leninism is therefore very much a philosophy of total power and control; this feature is especially visible when its followers are in positions of political power. Considerations beyond those of the stark realities of power and control all become secondary: Marxist-Leninists, whilst claiming to be in the process of building a morally superior society, do not care much for human rights, civil liberties, freedom of speech, education, trade unionism or conscience;(30) neither is Marx accorded the respect he would have liked.

On the grounds of the leaders' desire for total control alone it is only to be expected that any organization independent of the state will be combated. In Poland the Roman Catholic Church is the only significant organization which has never been state-controlled and which, as a result, remains the greatest single obstacle to the realization of the authorities' aims. Communist leaders in the Soviet Union, long before the communist takeover of Eastern Europe, had already gained experience in combating their own Orthodox Church; the new Polish leaders were therefore aware of the principles according to which they were expected to operate.

The doctrine of total control, however, is not the only element of Marxism-Leninism which is hostile to religion. It is not even the fundamental one. Joseph Bocheński points out that the metaphysical questions concerning religion and its nature lie at the very core of Marxism-Leninism. He is right in observing that this intimate relationship at the heart of the matter has largely gone unnoticed in the vast majority of studies. Bocheński's approach requires us to distinguish between the metaphysical doctrines of Marxism-Leninism and its more familiar social doctrines.(31) The metaphysical doctrines are hostile towards religion in a direct and uncompromising way and it is on them that the social doctrines are based. The basic postulates of

Marxist-Leninist metaphysics, or dialectical materialism, are
four: firstly, the tangible world is the only reality, uncaused
and the cause of all; secondly, the tangible world is constantly
evolving to ever higher forms; thirdly, man reaches consciousness only at the end of a long period of evolution - his consciousness or spirit, therefore, is acquired and not inborn;
man is thus the way in which Nature reaches a state of consciousness. Lastly, consciousness is a product or reflection of
matter and, as such, is ultimately dependent on it. Bocheński
stresses the moral implications of this doctrine, namely, that
man's only duty is to serve progress which depends on him
alone: 'In the face of brute natural and social forces he is called
to transform the world himself in an unending heroic effort.(32)
Religion, according to theory based on such postulates, must
logically succumb to three criticisms: firstly, it is a false and
obsolete science which is conclusively refuted by modern empirical science; secondly, it is a false metaphysics; finally, it
preaches false moral values in the sense that it turns man's
attention away from his tasks here on earth and away from
other men: it teaches him to turn to the chimera God. This final
criticism suggests that religion is egoistic and anti-humanistic
since it preaches individual salvation and admits the existence
of a being above man. These metaphysical doctrines are given
contemporary expression in the writings of Tadeusz Jaroszewski,
a Polish party theoretician. Jaroszewski writes: 'The function
of a religious Weltanschauung (I have Catholicism in mind particularly) consists of weakening the social activity of people in
the struggle for real earthly emancipation.'(33)
    The social doctrines of Marxism-Leninism regarding religion
are better known. They consist of a theoretical elaboration of the
criticism which suggests that religion turns man away from his
duty. In summary they suggest that religion hinders the socialist
revolution, tranquillizes the masses into political passivity and
apathy, aids feudal and capitalist forms of exploitation but will,
nevertheless, finally disappear under the joyous conditions of
socialism. References to the social doctrines are common in the
works of the founding fathers of Marxism-Leninism. In 1844
Marx wrote: 'The abolition of religion as the illusory happiness
of the people is required for their real happiness.'(34) After
him, Lenin wrote: 'All modern religions and Churches, all religious organizations Marxism always regards as organs of bourgeois reaction serving to defend exploitation and stupefy the
working class.'(35) Today the same ideas find their expression
in the writings and statements of party theoreticians and ideologues:(36)

> The Marxist critique of religion stresses primarily, not the
> theoretical 'demolition' of religious dogma... but the neces-
> sity of practical (and revolutionary) measures which will
> destroy the sources of religion. Thus the main task is not a
> theoretical struggle against religion but a struggle for a

society in which religion will have no *raison d'être*.

These sources of religion are, as anyone acquainted with Lenin knows well: 'the socially downtrodden condition of the working masses and their apparently complete helplessness in the face of the blind forces of capitalism...."Fear made the Gods".'(37) Although these are the words of a rabble-rouser and it is doubtful whether even Lenin himself credited them with much cognitive power, they did, nevertheless, become embodied in the principles of communist rule. Particularly striking here is the way in which the early Polish sociology of religion based its view of secularization on this type of metaphysics. In the case of Ludwik Krzywicki there is even a similarity of tone and language.

Since the social doctrine implicitly embodies a claim of openness to empirical investigation it may be thought that a critique may clear up one or two difficulties. Such a critique may run along the lines of suggesting that the doctrine is refuted by factual evidence, that it is nonsensical as a whole on account of the impossibility of accommodating it in any consistent theory of knowledge, that it is in reality closed to empirical investigation, or by confronting it with an alternative and consistent metaphysics. The critique would be of no consequence to Marxism-Leninism for two reasons: firstly, the social doctrine cannot depend on facts and logical consistency if it is to remain the practical expression of dialectical materialism on which the social doctrine is based or, put in another way, because dialectical materialism attacks religion in principle and not for a particular reason; secondly, the abandonment of the social doctrines would weaken the totalitarian justifications of the power structure in a purely practical way: there would be no philosophical justifications for attacking religion and the Church and naked coercion alone would have to be applied - a rather impractical and dangerous solution.

Marxist-Leninist metaphysics is important in defining the relationship which members of a communist society must have to the party: if man's sole duty is to progress and the party is the embodiment of progress then man's duty is to the party and to the party alone. The total abandonment of reason which this demand requires is illustrated by the reminiscences of Leszek Kolakowski who recalls that 'Time and again I have heard old communists say: it is better to make mistakes *with* the party than to be right *against* the party.'(38) On the other hand, life insurance need not represent a total abandonment of reason.

The step from the doctrines of Marxism-Leninism to concrete state policy is a predictable one. Typically, the arguments advanced here are phrased in an order which allows the basing of anti-religious policy on any point which may be convenient at the time. For example, if it becomes important to try to impose limits on the activity of the Church, to keep it out of public life and to counter demands for access to the mass media it is likely that this sort of statement will be issued: 'The state should remain vigilent lest religious activity, and especially religious propaganda, limit individual freedom, come into contradiction with public morality, disturb law and order or stir up anti-state feeling.'(39) These directives have been written into the Polish penal code.(40)

The hostile Marxist-Leninist theory of religion is also taken as the starting point for what could be termed the 'official sociology of religion' which does not attempt serious study of religion but which strives to develop more convincing means of popularizing dialectical materialism, the social doctrine of Marxism-Leninism and general enmity towards the Church.

The doctrinal hostility of Marxism-Leninism towards religion and the Church would have been of comparatively much less significance were it not for the communist leaders' complementary aim of total control.(41) It is through the mechanism of total control that the rulers can implement the materialist metaphysics in terms of concrete policy.

Because of the principle of the outstretched hand and other tactical considerations, all due to Lenin,(42) it is difficult to know with certainty the exact position of the leaders with respect to religion at any one moment. Lenin advocated that Christians should be recruited into the party if they are willing to accept the principles and conditions, a sort of an invitation to suicide. He also insisted that care should be taken in combating religion since 'hurting the religious sentiments of believers...only serves to increase religious fanaticism'.(43) Observation of East European leaders and of their policies, especially in Poland, suggests that there is a continual change of the emphases on the arguments which form the basis of anti-religious policy. It is never entirely clear how they react to changing conditions and how they are affected by pressure from the Kremlin. Even the taking of no obvious anti-religious measures can be justified by the leaders by invoking the argument that religion will die out under socialism or that the taking of such measures will only serve to increase religious fanaticism. On the other hand, the taking of drastic anti-religious measures (persecution, show trials, etc.) may indeed have undesirable results, from the leaders' point of view, other than simply increasing the intensity of belief: firstly, the hostility of the population may be aroused to unmanageable proportions; secondly, the existence of religion is given prominence and publicity by the very taking of the measures; thirdly, in the case of violent anti-religious propaganda, mass suspicions may be aroused regarding the stability of the power structure. All these considerations mean that any prediction regarding specific state policy is impossible. Nevertheless, one point needs to be made in as clear a way as possible. The aim of a Marxist-Leninist state will always be the removal of all forms of religious thought and expression. On this point there is no doubt. What may appear as 'liberalization', therefore, must be understood in terms of changing strategy and tactics on the part of the authorities. What may appear as intransigence on the part of Church

leaders when faced with various offers from the state is no more
than a realistic acceptance of this point. Why accept Lenin's
offer of suicide?
  Having said that the strategy and tactics of the state are
difficult to define, it is nevertheless possible to identify some
patterns. One such pattern was seen to be applied to the Russian Orthodox Church after the communist coup: it was characterized by violence, bloodshed and a determined and outright
effort to destroy the Russian religious culture and establishment.
At least this was the case in the early stages. The authorities
managed to achieve their goal especially as far as the Orthodox
establishment was concerned. These brutal Soviet measures could
not be applied wholesale to Eastern Europe.(44) The Russian
Orthodox Church was a specific case: it was, by and large,
restricted to Russian soil and its spiritual centre was in Moscow;
also, Russian Orthodoxy as a political force had its power base
in Tsarism which, once destroyed, left the institution vulnerable.
Orthodoxy could thus be dealt with internally and with a mini-
mum of fuss. Eastern Europe was different. After the end of the
Second World War the Soviet empire inherited millions of Catholics
who not only shared their faith with millions of other Catholics
outside the empire but who also had the Vatican as their spiritual
centre. This new state of affairs was seen in its most extreme
form in Poland where the percentage of Catholics and the intensity of their belief (measured according to most conventional criteria) were both exceptionally high. In fact, Poland's new leaders
found themselves ruling a society which was more Catholic than
it had ever been: more than 90 per cent of the population as
opposed to 75 per cent on the eve of the war (the changes were
due to Nazi extermination of the majority of the Jews, boundary
changes and population resettlement). In absolute figures, there
were some 22 million practising Catholics in 1944 - a figure which
was to rise to some 29 million by 1970.(45)
  Although what has so far been described are the rationale and
the principles behind the pressure exerted on the Church by
the authorities it is important to bear in mind that the centre
from which the Church in Poland (and in the Eastern bloc as a
whole) is attacked must be finally traced to the Kremlin. In
practice, this means that all Churches and religions in Eastern
Europe and in the Soviet Union are faced with the might of the
Soviet repressive apparatus with which any form of philosophical
discussion of concepts or metaphysics is hardly a viable proposition. It is a mistake to think that the problem of the Church
and religion under communist power can be resolved on the basis
of enlightened discussion: the most that can be hoped for is the
arrival at a temporary accommodation based on a tactical or
strategic rationale.
  How is it possible for the Roman Catholic Church to exist
under such conditions and how can it defend itself against
annihilation? An answer to this question is important for the
understanding of the secularizing and desecularizing pressures

to which the Church as an institution is subject. Before looking at the evidence it is useful to take a closer look at the system of total control.

Poland, in common with most communist states, is still far from being a totally controlled society, despite the strong doctrinal pressure of Marxism-Leninism in that direction. Indeed, since the 1950s it has been becoming less totalitarian although, as we shall see, not as a result of the leaders' altruism or desire for liberalization. Leszek Kołakowski views the system of total control in the following way:(46)

> The system is all torn and tattered - there exists neither the ability nor the will to repatch it and the poverty of ideas shines through in all places. It functions only by forbidding, by terrifying others and by its own fear. However, it constantly strives to destroy everything in the life of the nation and in the life of individuals which is not yet under its command.

But this is a recent view. Earlier appraisals were more cautious:(47)

> It may be argued...that the indigenous Polish communists lacked the resources to establish their control; or that anti-Soviet sentiments alienated the people; or that western traditions and ways were so strongly implanted that Soviet communism, either as a political system of control or as an economic system..., was unsuitable for Poland.

It is likely that all three factors operated to some extent and still operate today. One point does emerge quite clearly: the leaders' level of success is low in terms of the criteria they themselves acknowledge. The intensity of Marxist-Leninist propaganda and the ubiquitous presence of Marxist-Leninist slogans in official statements are further evidence of the communist party's constant struggle for control and legitimacy.

A surer indicator of the failure of the communists totally to control their society has been the frequency and intensity of violent and bloody risings, demonstrations and other disturbances together with the spectacular development in 1980 of Solidarity (Solidarność) - a totally independent workers' trade union movement, claiming a membership of several million, which managed to get itself accepted within the framework of the legal system of the state. Up to this time there had been only 'official trade unions', which were not trade unions but communist party outposts whose function was to keep members in line. What is of particular note in the case of Solidarity is that the initial financial and social demands made by the movement very rapidly gave way to overtly political ones which began to challenge the party.

The 1970 Christmas food riots already appeared to have established a precedent for having social, political and economic issues settled through the exercise of pressure from below; the pressure had then resulted, but not without violence and death, in the removal of party secretary Władysław Gomułka and in the lowering of food prices by Edward Gierek, the new secretary.(48) In 1980 the skilful use of pressure through peaceful strikes, sit-ins and threats led to the acceptance by the party of demands which further weakened the totalitarian structure. An incidental result was the replacement of Edward Gierek by Stanisław Kania and a general purge of party positions was to occur later. The decision as to whether such a process of weakening is to continue or whether overt coercion is to be employed lies primarily with the Soviet Union, but is also partly dependent on external factors such as Western foreign policy and even perhaps Vatican policy.

Another important indicator is the widespread development of an underground political opposition, especially since the end of the 1960s, which today includes intellectuals, Catholic circles, intelligentsia and students. All these groups have assured themselves of a voice through the recently established clandestine press. As we have seen above, these developments have been accompanied by an increasing politicization of the manual workers who must now also be included amongst the ranks of what has become an 'open' underground opposition. The most recent events in Poland indicate that there are now strong opposition currents amongst the peasantry.

The most important indicator of the low level of success of totalitarianism in Poland is the powerful position of the Catholic Church. Although its position has always been strong, the election of the Archbishop of Kraków to the papal throne has given the Polish Church greater prestige than ever before in history.

One of the consequences of the Polish leaders' failure to control totally their society has been noted by Michael Gamarnikow. He suggests that the Church in Poland has been able to contribute a degree of pluralism to what is, in essence, a one-party state. He observes that the political base of the Church has never been as broad as it is under communist rule. After the removal of Mikołajczyk and the liquidation of the rest of the west-oriented opposition in 1947-8 'the Church, although itself under strong pressure, remained as the only major institution which was not identified in the public mind with an alien régime'.(49) Furthermore, others note that 'active participation in the ostensibly purely religious activities became the only legal form of expressing political defiance. Thus even confirmed agnostics began attending Mass regularly to demonstrate their opposition to the régime.'(50)

Perhaps the most important factor militating against an all-out onslaught against the Church is the massive support which it enjoys amongst the population. Paradoxically, this is the very reason which makes it so imperative for the authorities to combat it as quickly and as effectively as possible. It is possible to distinguish two types of support for the Church in Poland:

firstly, there is the support normally given by believers to their Church and, secondly, there is the support given by those who believe that Christianity is the carrier of a cultural tradition without which the very existence of the nation is unimaginable.(51) Individuals quite often show a combination of both types of support although the second type alone is typical of the attitude of many intellectuals. Given this complex situation, the authorities have additional reason for ensuring that, if they are to attack the Church, they must attack carefully and selectively so as not to risk alienating the population as a whole at any one time.(52)

The history of the Catholic Church in communist Poland is yet to be written. The difficulties of writing such a history are enormous: the closeness of the events, the composite picture of Catholicism and the unceasing appearance of re-interpretations, the constantly changing situation and the continual emergence of new facts, the development of new forms of debate and discussion in the uncensored Catholic press(53) are all well-known parts of the contemporary Polish historian's nightmare. Nevertheless, there is evidence enough for a satisfactory sketch of the Church's fortunes to be outlined.

By the nature of things, a passive and acquiescent response on the part of the Church marks weakness or the weakening of the institution and as such can only be accommodated within the structure of the multi-chambered concept of secularization. On the other hand, evidence of vigorous, successful defence and adaptation must be understood in terms of strength, vitality, revival and desecularization.

It is worth recalling that the issue over which there is conflict between Church and state in Poland has been defined by the state. The state demands no less than total allegiance to Caesar. The strategy of the Church is therefore quite clear: it must outlast the totalitarian state without giving in to any demands that might compromise its teaching. At the same time, great tactical advantage is to be gained by both increasing its popular support and undermining that of the state: the former is, after all, part of its defined role. It cannot be overstressed that it is against the background of gains and losses in this particular area that the Church-state conflict must be assessed and not, as has often been popularly done, against a background of gentlemanly 'Church-state relations', simple policy differences or even a left-right dispute between the forces of progress representing the state (or some tendencies in it) and a conservative, obscurantist and anti-reformist Church.

In order to take a closer look at the Church-state conflict it is useful to divide post-war Poland into five periods. The divisions we shall use correspond roughly to ones which have already been found useful by some observers of Church and state in Poland.(54) The periods are as follows: (1) 1944-7; (2) 1947-56; (3) 1956-70; (4) 1970-8; (5) from 1978. We will not attempt any historical explanations. Our aim is more modest: an assessment of the gains and losses over these periods.

Some generalizations can already be made from the changing tactics of the state. Alexander Tomsky has observed that during the 1950s the state had tried to destroy the Church, during the 1960s it had tried to restrict its activities to within the four walls of the Church, and finally, during the 1970s, it has tried to prevent it from growing:(55) hardly an impressive record for the state where each successive period marks a reversal of the intended trend. Not surprisingly, the trend has been paralleled by a weakening of the structures of the total control. Let us now turn to consider the abovementioned periods.

Immediately after the end of the war the communists shared power with non-communists within the provisional government. Although they already dominated in all the key positions they still had some work to do in order to eliminate all political opposition from within the government. These were problems enough for the communists without engaging in an open struggle with the Church. But while maintaining cordiality of relations with the Church they carefully observed and prepared for the future.

One important measure to be taken during this period was the severing of relations with the Vatican; the previous government had maintained relations with the Vatican according to the Concordat of 1925. The Concordat was repudiated in 1945 on the grounds that the Vatican had violated the terms during the war: this was an accusation without foundation but not without tactical rationale.(56) In this way the communists hoped to achieve two ends: firstly, they hoped to discredit the Vatican and the Polish Church; secondly, they saw this measure as a first step in the direction of drawing the Polish Church away from the Vatican in the hope of creating a national church perhaps on the lines of the Orthodox Church in Russia.(57) This latter policy would give them the option of either using the Church as a vehicle through which they could exercise control over the population or of easily destroying a Church which no longer has support outside of Poland. Both of these strategies could, of course, be used in turn. The authorities have not met with any significant successes on either of these two fronts and the latter, since the election of a Polish Pope, must surely be abandoned even as a remote possibility.

One lesson was quickly learned by both the Church and by the communists. Each time the communists failed in an assault on the Church they were penalized: their already low credibility fell by a notch and that of the Church rose by a notch. The communists thus found themselves in a singularly painful dilemma – a dilemma which, to this day, the state authorities have not managed to solve successfully. The Church, on the other hand, was able to make capital merely by defending itself. We have to use the word 'merely' very cautiously since the defence of the Church was to summon its resources to the full. Nevertheless, successful defence became, to the Church, just as important and positive an action as successful attack. During the later periods the skilful use of the Church's uncensored word - the sermon - and the ability to get key issues brought to public attention in the party-controlled press were important factors in maintaining and developing the trust of the population.

At the same time as the Vatican link was cut the idea of using the Catholic Church as a vehicle of communist power caught the imagination of both Polish and Soviet communist leaders although, quite predictably, the interest of the Soviet Union in this idea was far greater and more direct. The Church could be thus used in two complementary ways: for the purposes of internal policy and, much later in time, for the purposes of foreign policy. As far as internal policy is concerned, the Soviet NKVD in conjunction with the Polish communists established the Pax movement and placed at its head the prominent fascist from pre-war days, Bolesław Piasecki.(58) Piasecki, on the Kremlin's instructions, was provided with both the political and the financial resources to build Pax into an exceedingly strong economic giant on condition that he publicized as widely as possible a new 'patriotic line'. This patriotic line consisted of suggestions that the political status quo in Poland was irreversible and that true Polish patriotism requires an attitude of support for the Soviet Union (sic). The line also attempted to establish that there was no contradiction whatsoever between dialectical materialism and Catholicism. Lucjan Blit wrote as follows about Piasecki's philosophy:(59)

> he pleads for those who, like himself, consider themselves non-materialists in the philosophical sense of the word because they are Roman Catholics, to have not only the right to hold to their religious beliefs but also to be accepted as equal participants in the building of the communist system.

This sort of philosophy makes Pax a quite unique phenomenon in the Soviet bloc. Pax is involved in the publishing of books, newspapers and periodicals and also has the monopoly of the sale of holy pictures and other objects used in devotion. Pax was able to play a more sinister role, however. It acted as an important tool in many concrete instances of Church harassment and persecution: the arrest of the Primate, the torture of members of the clergy, the dissemination of disinformation regarding the Catholic Church both at home and abroad, the state takeover of the Catholic Caritas organization, the deportation of nuns, etc.(60) Its aim, at least up to a short time ago, did not stop here. Blit suggests that 'Their ultimate goal can be described in one short sentence. It is power in the state. They hope one day to become the only rulers of the Poles.'(61) But these things were not to be: such might have been the desire of the members of Pax but they lacked the necessary means with the result that the influence of Pax is waning. On 1 January 1979 Piasecki died and his place has been taken by Ryszard Reiff. As well as losing its leader, Pax today appears to have lost both much of its

support from above and much of its sting: instructions are no
longer forthcoming as party leaders struggle to retain their
positions.
How successful has Pax been in mobilizing Catholic support
for the communist rulers? Soon after its establishment a number
of Pax's more talented members left; in 1955 the Vatican placed
its organ, 'Dziś i jutro', on the Index and still more left and,
finally, its political role was superseded by a less amenable
Catholic organization, Znak (The Sign), which managed something that Pax had not: in the 1957 elections the party gave it
five seats in the Sejm (parliament). The rôle of Pax, therefore,
had been most significant in the realm of subversion rather than
in mobilizing the sort of support originally envisaged by
Piasecki.
Associated with Pax were, and still are, the so-called 'patriotic
priests' - consisting of the naïve, disgruntled and easily cor-
ruptible elements of the clergy as well as those game for a morsel
of glory. These priests were to act as a Trojan Horse within the
Catholic community by whipping up support for the party and
spreading the philosophy of Pax. The movement failed in its
objectives for three main reasons: firstly, there were too few
of them; secondly, they were easily identifiable; thirdly, the
Church conducted its own campaign against them. But rewards
were to be had for simply indulging in disagreement, dogmatic
or otherwise, with the Church establishment and there were
always some willing takers. The burden which the 'patriotic
priest' temptation has been to the Catholic Church must be seen
to represent at least a minor victory for the communist regime.
Although the opportunity to use the Catholic Church for the
purposes of foreign policy was a much later development it can
nevertheless be appropriately discussed here. It was the advent
of Pope John XXIII in 1958 that provided the Kremlin leaders
with hitherto unexploited possibilities, namely, the establishment
of formal relations with the Vatican.(62) Dunn suggests that:(63)

First and foremost among Soviet motives in Moscow's apparent
belief that the Church can help in maintaining order in the
Soviet Union and the Soviet empire in Eastern Europe....From
the Catholic Church in Eastern Europe, the Soviets hope to
gain what they tried to achieve at the end of the second world
war. Simply stated, Moscow wants the support of the Catholic
Church to facilitate its supremacy in Eastern Europe....The
Church might even be used for preparing Europe for eventual
assimilation into the Soviet orbit.

The election of Pope John Paul II is particularly significant in
this light since, on the one hand, it would act to intensify the
Soviet desires while, on the other, presenting the Kremlin with
an adversary who is wise to the ways of communist strategy and
tactics and in no way gullible. One of the unknown quantities
here is the effect of the election on all Christians (not only

Catholics) within the Eastern bloc and the Soviet Union: the
idea of a rapprochement with Orthodoxy must surely present
Pope John Paul II with a daunting and even terrifying prospect
– a prospect which undoubtedly terrifies Soviet leaders even
more. The fact is that Orthodoxy is much closer to Catholicism
from a doctrinal point of view than are the reformed churches
of the west. During one of his sermons while in Poland, the Pope
was careful to express his recognition of the importance of
Eastern Christianity to the future of Christian Europe.(64)
Towards the end of the 1944-7 period the communists were so
preoccupied with the rigging of the forthcoming elections of
1947 that they reacted only mildly to a pastoral letter read out
in all churches in Poland urging Catholics not to vote for a
government whose philosophy was incompatible with Catholic
teaching. The year 1947, however, marked the end of all delu-
sions. The Stalinist period had begun. The vicious drive against
the Church was to last until 1956. This period built up to a
frenzied climax when Cardinal Stefan Wyszyński, the new Primate,
was placed under house arrest. The beginning was mild enough:
after the 1947 elections Premier Józef Cyrankiewicz warned
the Catholic clergy not to use religion for political purposes.(65)
In 1952 this warning was written into the Constitution: Article
70 (3) states 'The misuse of freedom of conscience and belief
prejudicial to the interests of the Polish People's Republic is
punishable.'(66) After 1947 there followed massive confiscations
of Church land and property, crippling taxation, the abolition
of Catholic schools, the closure of theological departments at
universities as well as general curtailment of the Church's pastoral activities and privileges. Poland was declared a secular
society. The state takeover in 1950 of the Church-run Caritas,
a charity and welfare organization, the outlawing of Catholic
Action and the establishment of the Office for Religious Affairs
(Urząd do Spraw Wyznań) were among the more far-reaching
of the measures taken by the state. By the end of 1953, in addition to the Primate, there were eight bishops and hundreds of
priests in prison.
These repressive measures were complemented by a campaign
of vilification in the mass media. It was suggested that the
Church had always been anti-Polish, that members of the clergy
and episcopate had collaborated with the Germans during the
war, that the Church was corrupt and had been aiding and
abetting 'fascists' and 'imperialists' after the end of the war.
In 1953 the authorities claimed the right to appoint bishops and
arrested the Primate when he raised his voice in protest.
A balance sheet of these years is not difficult to draw up. The
prime task for the Church was survival and to this end it had to
make itself impregnable in matters of faith and allegiance. There
is no doubt that it succeeded in this respect. One of the main
concerns of the Primate was to set clear limits for the state's
ingressions into Church affairs: indeed, his definition of these
limits was so clear that he was arrested for it. Another concern

was the careful definition of the Church's role in Polish history and society; in other words, the Church took upon itself the function of guardian of both sacred and secular values: truth, freedom, tradition, history and national unity. These were the values that the state was attempting to undermine. The uncensored and spontaneous word from the pulpit was used to good effect. A measure of the success of the Church in these latter two areas is the way in which it soon became recognized as the only organized form of opposition to the communist party – a fact which the party itself had to face up to during years to come. The state takeover of Caritas is a good example of how state policy can misfire. Even thirty years later the Church is still referring to the matter as a totally unnecessary and destructive act.

Another example of the way state policy misfired was the declaration of the separation between Church and state. This measure was intended to weaken the Church by cutting state support and by forcing it to sort out its own material problems. In fact, it would appear that this measure strengthened the Church by giving it the means to resist state interference in its internal affairs.

This period was important in one other respect. Many of the intellectuals who had supported the party for whatever reason during the early stages were confronted with a brutal reality: the perfect embodiment of the socialism that they had supported turned out to be a cruelly oppressive police state.(67)

The death of Stalin in 1953 was to bring changes to the whole of Eastern Europe. But it was not until Krushchev's denouncement of Stalin in 1956 that the full impact was felt. Polish party secretary, Bolesław Bierut, mysteriously died during a trip to Moscow; Władysław Gomułka resurfaced (after his expulsion from the KC in 1948 for 'nationalist deviations') as the new General Secretary of the PZPR; there was visible discontent in the ranks of the intellectuals; there were workers' demonstrations, riots and shooting; a possibility of Soviet military intervention was averted by Gomułka; Marshall Rokossovsky was recalled to the Soviet Union. It is worth recalling that exactly 300 years previously King John Casimir had made his vow to the Virgin Mary. A massive pilgrimage to Częstochowa took place in 1956 and pilgrims prayed for the imprisoned Cardinal Wyszyński. Stefan Wyszyński emerged from house arrest more confident than ever.

The Primate was now set on making Catholicism and the Church an integral and obvious part of Polish national life. However, he was careful to design his strategy in a way that would not permit the state authorities to accuse him of 'interfering with politics': pastoral matters were to come first. The celebration of Poland's 1000 years of Christianity typifies the activity of the Church during the 1956–70 period. The preparations for the 1966 Millennium formed an integral part of the plan: firstly, the Church was to renew King John Casimir's oath to the Virgin Mary and convert it into a national event – the Vows of Jasnogóra;

secondly, there was to be a nine-year period of preparation, the Great Novena, for the Millennium. Work began at once and practically the whole nation was mobilized. Meanwhile the Church worked hard at grass-roots level: it held on to its right to catechize despite state pressure to the contrary, attention was given to family stability and to the problems of alcoholism (a serious problem in Poland). Despite the enormous problems which the campaign involved the Church managed to get permission from the authorities to build the now famous Church of the Queen of Poland in Nowa Huta.(68)

The authorities were dismayed at this massive and concerted show of strength and unity on the part of the whole Catholic community although they must have at least half-known in advance what to expect. Their tactics, less coercive than during the period of Stalinism, were no less determined. The party tried to weaken the Church on many fronts: it tried to lessen the significance of the Millennium by organizing its own state celebrations marking the beginning of the Polish state as opposed to Polish Christianity; it refused Pope Paul VI a visa to visit Poland for the occasion. There was harassment of all forms of lay religious organizations except those which the party itself was encouraging with the hope of seducing, dividing and fragmenting the episcopate and the Catholic community. The regime had already suffered some setbacks with Pax. It was hoped that where it failed the Znak group would succeed.(69) At the same time they allowed the formation of another Catholic group, Więź (The Link), with very similar hopes in mind. The authorities also became interested, for reasons already seen, in the establishment of relations with the Vatican: an integral part of the courtship with the Vatican were the attempts to discredit the Primate vis à vis the population and vis à vis the Vatican by portraying him as an obscurantist and fanatical conservative who was even against conciliar reform. They hoped that they would be able to get him safely out of the way by exploiting reformist and modernist tendencies within the Church. During this period a great boost was given to the Marxist-Leninist study of religion with the aim of eventually developing an intellectually sound anti-religious philosophy and, as a corollary, an effective 'atheizing' policy.

One of the crucial setbacks for the regime during this period is connected with the party's loss of the support of the left-wing intellectuals. At the end of the 1950s the intellectuals' disillusionment with Stalinism gave way to hopes that the totalitarian system would in some way be able to reform or democratize itself 'from within' - that it would acquire a 'human face'. These hopes were marked by a departure by the intellectuals from blind party dogma and, as a result, from the previous blind loyalty to the system. This revisionist tendency led the freethinking left-wing intellectuals gradually to abandon the party and leave behind them an empty carcass incapable of any form of original thought. These intellectuals were to play an important part in the dissident movement which crystallized in the course of the following decade. The 1970 Christmas riots and the authorities' violent reaction to them confirmed the intellectuals' view that they had been both naive and mistaken in their expectations of Marxism-Leninism.

It has since become abundantly clear that the disillusionment of the intellectuals was merely the most prominent aspect of a much more important phenomenon - the development of an almost universal belief in the bankruptcy of both the theory and practice of Marxism-Leninism. In other words, the materialist metaphysics and the promise of fruits by communism in power both began to lose credibility amongst the whole population. At the same time Christianity - associated, moreover, with an institution of high prestige - became even more clearly identified with a realization of those very values which had been sought by the intellectuals in communism. All hope in Marxism-Leninism thus became abandoned and without this hope the philosophy was to become exclusively identified with the self-justifications of an externally controlled and depraved regime. The following decade was to see even the material promises of the regime dissolve into nothingness.

There is one other event of the 1960s which deserves special mention. In 1965 the Polish episcopate had, as a gesture of forgiveness to the German nation, sent a letter of pardon for wartime atrocities to the German bishops. The authorities immediately seized this opportunity in order to revive the German bogey. Although some degree of success on the part of the authorities is not generally doubted, the matter is too complex to be dismissed simply as a miscalculation by the episcopate. Firstly, the episcopate had been anxious to prevent the authorities' use of the German bogey as one of their few holds on the population. The episcopate had carefully chosen a time of high prestige and confidence in order to 'purge' the nation of the spectre. The letter's success or failure, from the purely pragmatic point of view, is not to be judged by the immediate reaction to it but by its long-term effects on the party's use of the German threat. Secondly, and more importantly, the letter was a clear sign of the Church's willingness to take initiative in matters which belong partly at least to the sphere of the political. The letter aroused the fury of the party which itself already had intentions of making an approach to the Federal Republic of Germany.

Post-war Polish history is a succession of convulsions, each one marking the end of an era and the beginning of a new one. Immediately after the 1970 riots Edward Gierek, the new party secretary, hoped to appease the Church by suggesting that relations between Church and state would now be normalized. Instead of the expected nod of approval from the bishops, the party received from the Church a set of conditions. The Church's declaration referred to the sad experience of the riots and called for national self-determination, the freedom of conscience, justice, respect for the Polish Christian tradition and for a relaxation of censorship: unless these conditions were satisfied there could be no talk of normalization. This was an entirely new move since it marked the first sign, since 1946, of a manifest politiciz- ation of the Church's pronouncements. Up to this time analogous pronouncements had been veiled and indirect. The Church was now aware of its strength and of the state's now all too obvious weakness.

The state was too weak to respond to what was, in effect, a challenge. Instead, it continued trying to exploit Vatican Ostpolitik; it attempted to weaken the Church and put pressure on Catholics through constitutional changes; it worked towards the creation of conditions under which religion would eventually die out; it continued to apply the by now customary chicanery. The 1970s in no sense marked a relaxation of the regime's anti- religious policy, but simply a change of tactics. In addition, the state's growing weakness and ever decreasing credibility during this decade must not be confused with relaxation.

Through Ostpolitik it was hoped the Vatican would draw closer to the Warsaw regime over the heads of the episcopate or, at least, over the head of Wyszyński. It was this possibility that worried the experienced Primate who was painfully aware of the naïveté of some of the Vatican assessments of both the Polish Church and of communist aims. Wyszyński also knew that he could not be party to any understanding or compromise with a communist state. As one observer put it: 'In Gierek's scheme "understanding" meant the submission of the Church to the demands of the communist party, and "compromise" meant col- laboration in controlling the people.'(70) Although the party came close to some major successes, events finally overtook Ostpolitik when Pope Paul VI died in 1978.

In 1972 the party decided to tighten its control of Polish society by introducing modifications into the Constitution. In September 1975 the matter was made public and at the beginning of 1976 the party announced the full details of the 'minor' amendments to the Constitution. The most important of these changes for our purposes is the supplement to Article 57. This was to read as follows: 'The rights of citizens are inseparably linked with the thorough and conscientious fulfilling of the duties to the fatherland.'(71) This supplement was clearly aimed at putting pressure on the Church and on the Catholic community. However, Wyszyński's strong criticism - which preceded the famous protest from dissidents(72) - weakened the phraseology to the point of being acceptable.(73)

The communist authorities came over to the view that religion will lose relevance amongst the population as Polish society becomes more affluent and modern.(74) This is a thesis which they based on evidence from western societies. The affluence which Gierek had promised on coming to power appeared to be forthcoming during his early days in power. This may have pro- duced a certain amount of confidence or even complacency which was visible in the almost mocking attitude of the director of the

Office for Church Affairs, Kazimierz Kąkol. However, the
authorities did not refrain from attempts to 'help the process
along'. For example, in 1973 they tried to introduce afternoon
school for children in order to prevent them attending catechism
classes. Secular ritual,(75) was to act as another lubricant in
this process. These rather unsophisticated measures were no
doubt the result of the heavy investment of effort in the theoretical Marxist-Leninist studies of religion initiated during the
previous decade.

The year 1970 marked the beginning of the 'Stanislavian
period' for the Catholic Church in Poland. The 900th anniversary
of the death of St Stanisław in 1079 was drawing closer. The
Church gradually began to take on the role of a guardian of
human rights in the tradition of the Saint. Human rights in
Poland, it argued, are simply non-existent. The Church soon
found itself in the centre of what was rapidly becoming a very
complex mosaic of dissident movements. The Helsinki Agreement
was later to become probably the most important single external
factor which provided the Church and the dissidents with the
additional strength and inspiration in order to pursue the theme
of human rights. Another was the support of the Polish émigré
community which helped in providing moral support and in
publicizing Polish issues in the foreign media. Initially, the
Church had acted as a protector for the dissident groups, but
soon there developed a relationship of symbiosis. Despite harassment by the authorities, the dissident movement continued to
flourish and suddenly a clandestine press appeared. The links
between the Church and the dissident groups remained purposely
vague: they consisted of strong mutual support while avoiding
any formality which might have been seized upon by the authorities. The dissident group closest to the Church is the group
of young intellectuals centred on Spotkania, a clandestine publication. One characteristic feature of this period is the revival of
the old tradition from the days of the partitions, the clandestine
'flying university'.

The Church was becoming more forthright in its demands on
the state. In 1977, at the Vows of Jasnogóra, the Primate declared
that: 'The nation has a duty to watch over its greatest treasure
which is Man - the citizen. The state exists to ensure for its
citizens the necessary conditions for subsistence and for life in
freedom to within the limits of the fundamental human rights
which he fulfils.'(76) This was a clear call for the state to respect principles higher than its own laws. The following year,
Cardinal Wojtyła attacked the atheist views expressed in the mass
media and on the day of St Stanisław the Primate was even more
outspoken. He stated: 'The Polish people are being lied to. In
spite of all the distortions and falsehoods fabricated by the
propaganda, despite the lies they are fed with, the Poles remain
aware of the importance of knowing the truth.'(77) But stronger
language was to come when a pastoral letter condemning totalitarianism was read out in churches on 17 September 1978.

The bishops wrote:(78)

> We all know that the spirit of freedom is the proper climate for
> the full development of a person. Without freedom a person
> is stunted, and all progress dies. Not to allow people with a
> different social and political ideology to speak, as is the prac-
> tice of the state, is unjust. State censorship has always been
> and remains a weapon of totalitarian systems. With the aid of
> censorship, the aim is not only to guide the mental life of
> society, public opinion, but even to paralyse the cultural and
> religious life of the whole people.

The 1970s are now famous for the building of churches. The
final completion of the church in Nowa Huta marked the end of
twenty years of battle with the state over this issue. Since the
communist authorities had generally always refused to grant
permission for the building of churches the consecration of this
church by Cardinal Wojtyła in 1978 marked a major victory. One
way of getting around the problem of obtaining permission to
build churches was to build them without permission, quite
literally overnight. Although this phenomenon occurred in all
parts of Poland the region of Przemyśl has become renowned for
its 'overnight' churches.(79) Often the authorities would demo-
lish them, often peasants would defend them successfully, often
the authorities would fail to find willing hands for such demoli-
tion work. But one thing is certain - the number of churches
is now increasing in Poland. So is the number of stories and
yarns about them which further diminish communist credibility.

In 1978 Cardinal Karol Wojtyła, the Archbishop of Kraków,
became Pope John Paul II. It is more appropriate, however, to
leave the discussion of the significance of this event until the
final chapter of this study.

Although we have to be careful in the sorts of conclusions we
can draw from the limited evidence which we have selected, one
point is quite clear: the evidence does not confirm a thesis of
secularization regarding the institutional Church and its relationship with the Catholic community. Further evidence which we will
note in the final chapter further substantiates this conclusion.
We also observe that the Church is able to build on and develop
a 'tradition of battle' through such events as the pilgrimage of
1956, the Millennium, the tradition of St Stanisław, its outspoken criticism of totalitarianism, etc. Are we therefore entitled
to conclude that there is a process of desecularization taking
place in this area? It has been argued by some observers that
a degree of erosion has occurred as far as the Church's official
(i.e. state-recognized) lay activity is concerned and that during
the period of Ostpolitik the regime may have permanently
encroached on some ground belonging to the Vatican, to the
episcopate and to the Primate. But it is perhaps better to argue
that Vatican Ostpolitik simply presented the greatest danger to
the Church during the post-war period in that the Vatican looked

as though it was going to walk into the trap of by-passing the
Primate and negotiating directly with the Warsaw authorities:
any Vatican naïveté would have been fully exploited by the
communists. It is important, however, not to confuse temporary
crises with erosion or secularization even if such crises may
have produced situations of high risk.

Some erosion has undoubtedly occurred as far as the Church's
pastoral activities are concerned. Administrative measures have
made the practical problems involved with pastoral work quite
enormous in certain areas. As a result the influence of Church
teaching in some areas is not as great as it might have been
under different circumstances. However, such erosion must be
juxtaposed against the complementary increase in the Church's
'clandestine' lay activity.

The evidence also clearly indicates the politicization of the
Church's role. This tendency has been masked to some extent
because during the early post-war years the Church had been
the only form of opposition to the party monolith and, regardless
of its stand, was always seen as a political force. Conversely,
in the 1970s its political stand often became overlooked by
observers who tended to focus attention on the dissident movements. The overall impression often obtained, therefore, does
not reflect the actual trend.

Worth noting here is the rather stark choice which members of
Polish society have to make. The regime, having made religion
a central issue, requires a statement of allegiance either way
and at the same time makes an agnostic position almost impossible
to hold. Meanwhile the Church and Christianity have acquired
new roles associated with freedom from official mendacity, with
relief from the often intolerable pressures of everyday life, with
a return to national pride and tradition and with a commitment
to justice. It is in this way that the desecularizing influence of
the communist regime has to be understood.

Another feature is also evident. This is the decreasing credibility of the regime. This in turn reflects a compromise of the
state's demand for total allegiance. Obedience may be obtained
by the use of threats and coercion, but normal allegiance is out
of the question except amongst an increasingly alienated and
isolated group of party faithful propped up by Soviet guns.

3 TIPS FOR ATHEISTS: THE 'OFFICIAL SOCIOLOGY OF RELIGION' AND SECULARIST PLANNING

> The Polish United Workers' Party considers secularization, understood in the positive terms of Marxist-Leninist teaching, to be a task of prime importance. In pursuing this task, the party stresses a scientific *Weltanschauung*, socialist morality as well as a knowledge of social, philosophical and religious matters. The party thus considers the directing...of the secularizing processes within society...to be one of its fundamental aims.
>
> (Jerzy Godlewski(1))

The steps taken by the authorities in the direction of combating the Church and imposing a Marxist-Leninist Weltanschauung on the population are generally referred to in Poland as 'planned (directed or programmed) secularization'. In this chapter I shall examine some of the theoretical and practical issues concerning the way in which planned secularization operates in Polish society.

The Polish authorities are very serious in their approach to the planned secularization of their society. Evidence of their seriousness is the fact that they have spared very little effort in organizing and conscripting a whole network of bodies and institutions which, in one way or another, are concerned with the formulation and spreading of a 'secular outlook on life'. Colloquially, this network is given the graphic and dramatic description of the 'secular front' (front laicki). Military terminology is quite common in the official ideology of communist states and, in this particular case, it is designed to impart an air of unity of purpose and imperative urgency as well as fundamental importance to the anti-religious policies while at the same time giving them the flavour of a military campaign against an armed enemy.

One of the pivotal bodies in this secularizing machine is the TKKŚ.(2) The object of the TKKŚ is to act both as a processing plant for popular propaganda and discussion concerning the party line on religion and as a symbol of the party's secularist mission. Jerzy Godlewski, one of its members, writes: 'Thus the fundamental aims of the TKKŚ are the dissemination of positive values,(3) wide influence over society, the propagation of secular culture, of socialist human relations, of the struggle against petty bourgeois egoism, nihilism and mammonism.'(4) In 1977 the TKKŚ was granted the status of a 'public body', a

privilege which the Church is denied. The aims of the TKKŚ
will always, of course, reflect the current party attitude towards
religion.

In its desire for the widest possible influence, the TKKŚ both
undertakes its own work and also lectures to and liaises with a
wide variety of bodies the most important of which are the following: the Union of Socialist Youth (Związek Młodzieży Socjalistycznej), the Socialist Union of Rural Youth (Socjalistyczny
Związek Młodzieży Wiejskiej), the Polish Scouts (Związek
Harcerstwa Polskiego), the Socialist Union of Polish Students
(Socjalistyczny Związek Studentów Polskich), the Socialist Military Youth Corps (Koła Socjalistycznej Młodzieży Wojskowej),(5)
parent education bodies, the Centre for the Advanced Training
of Secular Cadres (Centralny Ośrodek Doskonalenia Kadr
Laickich), the Union of Polish Teachers (Związek Nauczycielstwa
Polskiego) and even the Family Planning Society (Towarzystwo
Planowania Rodziny).(6) In maintaining close contact with schools
(e.g. at school level the TKKŚ organizes the Young Rationalists'
Clubs), youth organizations proper or with bodies in some way
connected with the socialization of young citizens (e.g. courses
for engaged couples), the TKKŚ hopes to gain more influence
than through organizations catering for the middle-aged or the
old, who are both less receptive and not such good risks for
ideological investment. Certainly the interest of the TKKŚ in the
Family Planning Society suggests that they mean to waste no
time.

The TKKŚ is also involved in the publication of 'educational'
and 'enlightening' material aimed at all levels of society. Apart
from its official weekly organ, 'Argumenty' ('The Arguments'),
there are the following: 'Rodzina i Szkoła' ('Family and School')
aimed at the lower end of the mass market, 'Wychowanie' ('Education') aimed at the middle level and, finally, the theoretical discussions and academic contributions of 'Człowiek i Światopogląd'
('Man and Weltanschauung').

Another important aspect of the activity of the TKKŚ is concerned with the development and propagation of 'secular ritual'.
The TKKŚ began to work on the introduction of secular ritual at
the beginning of the 1970s in conjunction with a state policy of
indirect anti-religious measures. An innate individual and social
need for ritual and ceremony is assumed by the underlying
theory.(7) It is further assumed that religion is little more than
just one of the ways of satisfying this need. Here we find
attempts to introduce a 'secular wedding ceremony' (in 'Wedding
Palaces'), a name-giving ceremony (a 'secular baptism'?) with
'guardians of honour' (secular 'godparents'?), secular wedding
anniversaries, secular funerals with a master of ceremonies (a
secular 'priest'?) and other socialist life-event ceremonies (secular 'confirmations'?). All these ceremonies are designed to take
place in the absence of clergy and in totally secular surroundings. The TKKŚ's ideas on the subject of secular ritual can
frequently be observed in 'Rodzina i Szkoła'.(8)

It is reasonable to suppose that the authorities introduced secular ritual in the hope that it would be significant in at least four ways: firstly, that it would compete with the already established religious rituals on the 'ritual market' thus drawing people away from religious ritual and commitment; secondly, that it would fill with secular ritual the 'ritual vacuum' of those who had already drifted away from religion so minimizing the chances of their return to religion; thirdly, secular ritual may form the ideal vehicle for the introduction of official ideology into the hitherto impregnable zone of human existence. This final hope indicates that there ought to be no privacy for a citizen under socialism, not even in his innermost thoughts. Such a view was first expressed by Lenin.(9)

The authorities' fourth desire in introducing secular ritual was far more sinister. The original discussions on this subject coincided with discussions of proposals for amendments to the Constitution (already discussed in the previous chapter). The proposed supplement to Article 57, let us recall, was worded as follows: 'The rights of citizens are inseparably linked with the thorough and conscientious fulfilling of the duties to the fatherland.'(10) Might the participation in secular ritual be conceivably construed as a 'duty to the fatherland'? If it were, then the acceptance of this formula would have enabled non-conformity with secular ritual to be punishable by a withdrawal of rights.(11)

So far the authorities have had to depend largely on pressure in order to promote secular ritual: administrative pressure on state functionaries, the use of incentives such as the giving of homes (there is a chronic housing shortage in Poland with many families five or six to a room and with waiting lists up to ten or fifteen years), the ceremonious enrolment of unsuspecting secondary schoolchildren into the PZPR.(12) However, the official emphasis on the practice of secular ritual is not as pronounced as it is in the Soviet Union, for example, although no figures are available as confirmation. It would appear that in Polish society the impact of secular ritual remains a marginal aspect of planned secularization.(13) Rather than producing secularization, it is likely that secular ritual simply picks up those members of society who have already become secularized in other ways although it may have some effect on the gullible and unsuspecting.

The party and the TKKŚ both attach a lot of weight to the backing up and the justification of planned secularization with philosophical and theoretical argumentation. They have invested much effort in the attempt to gather a following of 'secular intellectuals'. The party has two 'intellectual arms' directly responsible to it: the WSNS (a sort of party university) and the IPPML; questions of religion constitute an important, though by no means the only, part of the sphere of interest of these two institutions: a variety of questions relating to Marxism-Leninism, official ideological orthodoxy and party rule are processed by the WSNS and the IPPML. At this level we find that there is an

active contact with similar institutions in the USSR.(14) The
PTR can be regarded as the intellectual arm of the TKKŚ; from
the beginning of 1960 the journal 'Euhemer' became the official
organ of the PTR.

One of the principle aims of this quest for 'intellectualization'
is to endow the anti-religious doctrine of Marxism-Leninism and
the authorities' secularization policy with the prestige, authority
and respectability of an applied academic discipline. The WSNS,
for example, has the status of a university: it confers doctorates
and habilitations, it publishes academic papers and theses. A
constant effort is made in the direction of encouraging all historians, sociologists, philosophers and ex-priests with anti-
religious or anti-Catholic inclinations or grudges to contribute
to 'Argumenty', 'Wychowanie', 'Człowiek i Światopogląd' and
'Euhemer'.

This intellectualization occurred during a period (after 1956)
when the party had abandoned Stalinist coercion and set itself
the task of penetrating the Church. In place of the primitive
abuse of earlier times, the party decided that the Church might
be tempted with ideas of 'dialogue', debate and discussion in
order for it to expose itself to the 'debunking argument'. But all
this required intellectual resources and theoretical backing: a
solution was therefore sought in this vast development of a
'secularist academia'.

It is through the intellectual arms of the party and of the
TKKŚ that the official ideologues broadcast their anti-religious
programme under the respectable-sounding name of 'religious
policy' (polityka wyznaniowa), requiring no further explanation,
and religioznawstwo which, translated literally, means 'knowledge about religion' or Religionswissenschaft. A good translation
of the latter term is effected by the neologism 'religiology'.
Although at one time religiology was quite respectable in Poland
the term has, in recent years, become grossly devalued as a
result of its near-monopoly by the secularizing circles.

Despite their name, party religiologists proper do not engage
in any serious sociological or other research work themselves.
Whenever serious work is to be done the religiologists are careful to engage those sociologists and others willing to embrace
the party cause; they never allow the sociologists a free hand in
research and the results of any work done tend to remain a
closely guarded secret especially if the conclusions do not confirm current party thought. The work which is made public is
mostly of low calibre and oriented towards either the 'showing
up' of religion or illustrating its decline. Religiologists are more
interested in vindications of party policy and in good elabora-
tions of current ideological orthodoxy than in contributing any
new knowledge in the field of religion. They do, of course, welcome all new contributions in the field by academics of repute
since religious policy, in order to be effective, must be founded
on a solid base. Nevertheless, the emphasis is not so much on
facts themselves as on their 'correct interpretation' and on ideas

for suitable policy. Religiology is therefore very much a tool of
the anti-religious policy of the party.

Much of the work of party religiologists consists simply of
sifting all the work done by sociologists (and, of course, by
historians of religion, theologians, philosophers, etc.) through
the ideological sieve. Religiologists are therefore never original
nor can they make any genuine contribution to learning except
by chance. As noted by Martin, a sine qua non of the sorts of
interpretations provided by religiologists is that religion must
be seen as marginal in society, being associated with social
groups which have been artificially 'marginalized'.(15) The very
old, the very young, the least educated and the rural fit classical Marxist-Leninist definitions of marginality perfectly; however, it can be said with no exaggeration that marginality is
being attributed, by implication, to all those elements of society
which are not of current Marxist-Leninist orthodoxy. This means
that at least 93 per cent of the Polish population must count as
marginal in this sense.(16)

Religiological sociology of religion has been characterized at
various times by abuse, by attempts to discredit religion by
associating it with obscurantism and alienation and also by the
emphasis of the role of secular, anti-Catholic and atheist ideas
in Polish history - prominent features of the 1960s;(17) finally,
by the stress of the inevitability of the process of secularization.
Other features of religiology include bad scholarship, abomin-
able literary style and excessive pleonasm, all of which contribute to making the work almost impossible to read.(18) If this
secularizing sociology is what it claims to be, an academic discipline 'requiring especially deep scientific erudition,(19) then
it surely must mark the lowest depth to which scientific erudition
could possibly descend.(20) Party religiology is a discipline
shunned and disowned by men of integrity and can only be
regarded as the illegitimate progeny of scientific and philosophical erudition.

Since the area of religiology is very large, we will limit ourselves to a look at characteristic examples relating to the different
types of state policy (coercion, persuasion, indirect assault).
One important field of religiology particularly characteristic of
the 1960s will be discussed separately in the next chapter.

The party has been largely successful, in numerical terms at
least, in its recruitment of religiologists with the result that
there is a fair number of them in Poland today. A key figure in
their ranks is Tadeusz Jaroszewski. He is perhaps the chief
official theoretician on the subject of secularization: a member of
the KC of the party, his views and articles are generally reckoned to reflect accurately the current party tendencies.
Jaroszewski also holds a post in the IPPML, is the director of
the IFIS PAN and the editor-in-chief of the 'Człowiek i
Światopogląd' as well as exercising other functions in the religiological area.

Jaroszewski's role in an ostensibly non-party academic

institution as is the PAN is an example of the way in which party-controlled thought is able to permeate the society and its academic establishments. The IFIS PAN and other relevant departments at universities (e.g. religiology, sociology) are all encouraged to work according to the principles of party religiology. However, it is impossible even to hazard a guess as to the proportion of the work of these establishments which is thus influenced.

Religiology strives for recognition on a level with genuine and respectable academic analogues. This has the specific advantage of giving the impression that the party has entered into genuine debate and polemics with respectable 'equals' and that, as a result of its superior argumentation, has unquestionably defeated its opponents. The arguments used can, of course, be presented to the public in a way as favourable to the party as required by the skilful use of the mechanism of central censorship. In this way the party hopes to score political victory over 'remnants of bourgeois scholarship' and other similarly undesirable currents of thought which still present it with insoluble problems. Alternatively, the party will always have the option of replacing the genuine product with the religiological one at any convenient moment and pretend that nothing has happened.

Despite the attempts to monopolize the sociology of religion by the party there remains, in addition to the numerous uncommitted individuals, a number of academic institutions unaffected by religiological methodology. The most famous and influential of these institutions, all of which owe their independence to the shield of the Catholic Church, is KUL, which as a university not sponsored and not controlled by the state is a unique phenomenon in the whole of the communist world.(21) The other institutions are the ATK in Warsaw - originally set up by the authorities in order to compete with the Catholic seminaries - and a variety of Church-aided centres and seminaries which the authorities only just tolerate.

In contrast to the general commitment of the religiologists to Marxism-Leninism, the orientations of KUL and the ATK reflect the approaches of Joachim Wach (in the case of Józef Majka, for example, who is now in Wrocław), of Gabriel le Bras and the French school of sociologie religieuse (in the case of Władysław Piwowarski) and of Max Weber and Gerhard Lenski (as illustrated by Andrzej Święcicki of the ATK). None of the work here is related to any identifiable political line either in the Church or anywhere else: it is genuinely independent. By 'political line' we mean more than just a lack of anti-religious or anti-Church bias which is by no means enough to qualify as political; rather, we mean the constant and consistent production of results and conclusions - regardless of their relationship to facts - aimed at vindicating the changing policies of parties, institutions or other bodies.

Areas of study by the independent sociologists include secularization, parish organization and function, the sociology of vocations, religiosity and, recently, historical studies. Relations between these sociologists and the religiologists (and with those sociologists having some sort of religiological commitment) are those of mutual hostility although, not unexpectedly, there is a keen interest in one another's work.

In the past Leszek Kołakowski and Adam Schaff were leading figures in the ranks of the religiologists. Both are now in official disfavour and are living outside Poland. Their past views have contributed to what still remains today as the main substance of the general theoretical approach to religion. Kołakowski's original pronouncements were made during the period of Stalinist repression and therefore contain very strong elements of abuse. His view was that Catholicism must be nonsensical on the grounds that it is based on a philosophical mistake. Writing about claims that religion and science (or even religion and Marxism-Leninism) are congruent, he wrote:(22)

> It is not difficult to demonstrate that not only are they [the claims] baseless fabrications and exist only in the heaven of Catholic fantasy but also that the so-called Thomist Realism is the offspring of the darkest philosophical reaction. Thomist Realism has exactly as much in common with Marxist teaching about objectivity and cognizance of the world as exorcism has in common with medicine.

But the real danger, according to Kołakowski, is that Catholicism exists in association with the evils of imperialism and exploitation; the Catholic Church strives to resurrect Thomism because 'it has become apparent that his teaching is most suitable for the purposes of imperialism and ideally performs the function of sanctifying the capitalist order'.(23) Thomism provides the Church with 'the theoretical bases for the struggle with Marxism and with the workers' movement'.(24) Kołakowski, despite apparent crudeness, is a very astute observer and a very careful writer. A close examination of the above comments reveals three important points: firstly, the argument stands or falls quite independently of Marxist-Leninist assumptions. This means that it cannot be accused of being couched in biased Marxist-Leninist categories and thus can be presented for inspection to those who will have no truck with Marxism-Leninism. The argument is simply about the relationship between Catholicism and Marxism-Leninism; secondly, its venom is designed to arouse the passion of instant and violent disapproval of those committed to the Church and to Thomism as well as arousing the instant approval of Marxist-Leninists and secularists; finally, as an argument, there is a sense in which it cannot be faulted:(25) Thomism is indeed irreconcilable with materialist metaphysics as it is also incompatible with any form of historicism or determinism since it assumes the shaping of the future by the free acts of individuals. What has Thomism got in common with imperialism? Nothing, except that this allusion is required from the point of view of Marxist-Leninist orthodoxy and by the state policy of the period.

The final point can be duly exploited by the propaganda machine if the reaction to the argument in Catholic circles is negative enough. The three points in combination form probably the globally most effective type of verbal attack on the Church and Catholicism; the main thrust of such an attack depends very much on an attempt at an exploitation of the emotions and on the subsequent erosion of confidence in Church circles. The general reaction of the Church to such attacks was to ignore them completely in order not to lay itself open to more damaging action.

Schaff's approach, on the other hand, although it fully accepts the 'mistake' thesis of religion nevertheless stresses the notion of religion as alienation. Schaff writes as follows:(26)

> From a religious standpoint the question of the aim of life is answered very simply. Man is subject to an external purpose, that of God, which he should obey. The only problem is to find out what this purpose is – which is done by study of the scriptures or other records of revelation. The argument against this standpoint must seek to demonstrate scientific-ally the human origins of revelations, to show that God does not create man but man creates God in his own image. But of course, there can be no argument against a believer who will not accept the canons of scientific demonstration.

Schaff's less refined presentation of the attack shows that he is not such a master of the craft as is Kołakowski. However, the formulation does indicate the appearance of an appeal to reason – an attitude typical of the 1960s.

Since Schaff's and Kołakowski's time a synthesis of the 'mistake' and 'alienation' theses of religion has been made by Jaroszewski. Jaroszewski combines this composite view with the 'integrating' or 'social cement' function of religion and, in particular, of Roman Catholicism. He writes that the Church is able to satisfy certain social needs:(27)

> We could call this the 'service' function of religion. Not direct-ly religious, the service function is a response to the real needs of the masses: needs like, for example, the integration of community life in backward areas (especially in the village), the organization of welfare and mutual aid, the satisfaction of man's emotional and aesthetic needs. Religion also imparts ceremony to such events in man's life as name-giving, mar-riage, etc.

But, continues Jaroszewski, already today in countries of the liberated proletariat, this situation is changing: 'the conditions which required the presence of religion to cement the social have disappeared. Similarly, the social sources of religion, rooted in the various forms of alienated social relations, are now disappearing.'(28) Jaroszewski, of course, welcomes secularization, both spontaneous and planned; if religion is alienation then secularization must therefore logically be hailed as a process of de-alienation: secularization is: 'humanism, the reinstatement of the humanistic aims of the revolution, the reinstatement of man'.(29) Under these new conditions, therefore: 'The taking over of the service functions by non-religious institutions and organizations and the increasing satisfaction of the above needs by these institutions and organizations can be put to use as an important instrument of the policy of secularization.'(30) It is thus possible for the Polish authorities to explain 'scientifically' the policy of reducing the totality of religious life to activity within Church walls alone. The most revealing feature of Jaroszewski's elaboration is that it is a very good indicator of the state policies of the 1970s although it was made public as early as 1966. This would suggest that the state's anti-religious policies are not just a response to changing circumstances but the product of a very long-term strategy. Nevertheless, it is likely that the practical implementation of policies may be affected by various changes in the political weather.

At this point it is worth taking a brief look at the curious theory of secularization which arises out of the views so far described. This theory consists of two quite contradictory elements. The first element is the claim that dialectical materialism is absolutely true and, therefore, that any religious belief must be false. In terms of secularization this means that all religious beliefs are doomed if and when the believers finally realize that they are simply not true. This realization will occur as a result of increasing education but only education of a particular - secularist - type. The complete demise of religion becomes as inevitable as the complete triumph of dialectical materialism - the two are complementary. In other words, this element of dialectical materialism is a new form of the old intellectualist critique of magic and religion. The significance here to studies of secularization is twofold: firstly, religiologists tend to assume that religious consciousness becomes secularized not to religious indifference, but to an atheism of the Marxist-Leninist variety. There is no empirical evidence whatsoever for such a claim and, moreover, no studies of 'Marxistosity' have seen the light of day. All the evidence there is tends to support the opposite thesis: that the secularization of religious consciousness is in the direction of religious indifferentism and not in the direction of militant, or any other, atheism. It also needs to be mentioned that 'Marxistosity', while always exceedingly weak in Poland, has undergone a series of spectacular declines since the end of the war. The second element of significance is that religiologists are fond of backing up their claims by reference to studies illustrating the inverse relationship between levels of religiosity and levels of educational achievement. At this point, it is useful to note that the religiologists begin to draw even closer to the pre-war traditions of the sociology of religion.

The other element in this theory of secularization consists of
the claim that religion is the product of specific social conditions.
It is sufficient to change these conditions to those of a higher
order, argue religiologists, for religion, now deprived of substance from which to draw nourishment, to die out automatically.
These two claims cannot both be true at the same time. If they
are taken singly we observe that the provision of the education
required by the first claim would be of no avail if the social
conditions were 'incorrect' and, conversely, all efforts at changing the social conditions may be in vain if the believers do not
realize their mistakes. Taking the two elements and combining
them into a composite theory which states that 'only when social
conditions are changed and people are educated will religion
disappear' has dire consequences for the status of dialectical
materialism as absolute truth: it becomes relegated to a truth
dependent on social conditions. In other words, the inevitable
conclusion is that dialectical materialism cannot be grasped by
those living under the 'wrong' conditions. As well as being at
odds with the facts, such a conclusion is, more importantly,
unacceptable by Marxist-Leninists of any type. The problem is
not removed by invoking the party or the communist movement,
a procedure which is often energetically attempted: as a group
which in a manner similar to some sort of supermen 'stands
apart' and is thus not subject to the above dependence on social
conditions. The argument is that this group can educate itself
autonomously and so act as a carrier of the final truth and as a
catalyst for its acceptance. This sort of explanation has to be
able to deal with the problem of the extent to which thought is
independent of social conditions and hence autonomous - a point
vigorously refuted in other places. It has to be refuted somewhere, since the idea of autonomy of thought and ideas makes
the whole theory of secularization unacceptable. Indeed, the more
closely this view of secularization is examined the more unwieldy
and confusing it becomes.

Ideally, the problems and contradictions can be resolved, not
in a theoretical but in a practical way through the use of force.
The religiologists recommend, therefore, the removal of the
source of the problem - religion. In this way, they formulate
the beginnings of a 'scientific theory of religious persecution'
whereby many conditions are satisfied: religion is removed which,
after all, is the object of the exercise, the claim that religious
belief is 'false' and that it is the product of specific social conditions appears to be vindicated and, finally, theory is shown to
be linked with practice - a characteristic and often generally
repeated claim of Marxist-Leninism.

Jaroszewski does not, of course, see any of the problems connected with his view of religion and secularization.(31) Indeed,
he contributes to the confusion even further. Let us look at his
elaboration of the way in which secularization has been occurring
in the course of history. To Jaroszewski, the Middle Ages are
the high point of Christianity and the very near future marks

its final demise. Secularization, therefore, is not a recent process - it has been going on for hundreds of years. It began in close association with the development of the trade economy and with the removal of the medieval theocratic and corporational forms of political and social life; later, as a result of the increasing influence of secular humanism and democratism, the Church's influence became diminished through both persuasion and administrative pressure. The final stage in the process of secularization, he notes, is the present day where industrialization, urbanization, migration, the development of technology, science, culture and education are all contributing to the demise of Catholicism.(32) This process is accompanied by a 'secularization from within' which takes the form of a rebuilding of Catholic ethics, a rationalization of faith and philosophical systems, the correction of the Church's social doctrine, etc., etc.(33)

This sort of view of secularization has already been criticized by Martin; his most important points are: firstly, that the disassociation of the Church from temporal power and influence can be seen just as legitimately in terms of desecularization;(34) secondly, that unilateralist views of history, of which this is a striking example, tend to employ heuristic devices which are highly selective on facts and events and which, as a result, oversimplify: distortion is the inevitable result;(35) thirdly, that it is medieval Christianity and its associated features which are taken as a point of reference: any change from the medieval pattern is therefore automatically interpreted in terms of secularization;(36) fourthly, the present weakness attributed to Catholicism and the Church under a communist regime is strongly at odds with the facts:(37) this is especially true of Poland. These problems alone demand a radical revision of Jaroszewski's view of secularization.

Jaroszewski's view is further weakened by other shortcomings: he in no way attempts to elucidate the mechanism by which, for example, the trade economy is supposed to encourage the process of secularization or, more generally, the way in which all the main features of today seem to be plotting against God. Also, perhaps more significantly, wherever evidence can be brought to bear, it contradicts rather than confirms his view. We can point here to such examples as the continual development and growth of Catholic doctrine since the Middle Ages right up to today: there has been an increase both in the depth and breadth of appeal (this is especially noticeable in Poland over the last fifty or so years); the constant building up of the heritage of religious or related philosophy, literature, poetry, music, art, architecture, etc. (again, particularly noticeable in Poland) and the already visible, and in any case inevitable, halting of the processes of urbanization, industrialization and migration etc. as we know them. There is, of course, some truth in the claim that the ethos of technocratic society and scientific 'messianism' is conducive to religious apathy, but a claim of direct hostility or contradiction is impossible to uphold. In any case, it is

probable that the relationship between the two is much more
complicated than simply that of a straight correlation. Jaroszewski is right only to the extent that education and culture may
become atheistic and threaten religion directly.

One particularly significant feature of Jaroszewski's view is
the confusion of concepts. Whilst ostensibly dealing with a
unitary process, Jaroszowski first describes the Church's disassociation from temporal power and influence and its retreat
from dominance in the field of culture; secondly, the intellectual
currents of the Enlightenment and their effect on the Catholic
intellectual elite and, finally, the last stage is marked by the
entry of the 'masses' into the arena of religion and secularization.
But these are separate processes in every sense of the word:
Jaroszowski confuses temporal power with the Church's internal
change and with mass religiosity. Each of these should be looked
at separately across the whole period and not just inserted where
convenient from the point of view of the conclusion.

This confusion may not be as serious as Jaroszewski's failure
to distinguish satisfactorily between the causes of secularization
and the causes of religious belief. Common sense tells us that
the same factor cannot cause opposite reactions. Jaroszewski
observes the process of desecularization in Western societies
which, he admits, are the most industrialized, urbanized, tech-
nologically advanced, etc., of all societies so far; but, he suggests, expectations of societal perfection have been betrayed
and instead these societies are riddled with crises, unemployment,
wars, increasing alienation to work and of workers, rule by
financial oligarchies, limitations of democracy and atomization of
the masses.(38) Like Krzywicki's peasant, described in chapter
1, Jaroszewski's Western man lives unstably: 'he is fearful of
atomic extermination, of the social consequences of automation,
of recessions and of new technological achievements turning
against him'.(39) Western man fears the 'Brave New World' where
the 'perfect ones' will have total control of man's existence.(40)
Jaroszewski is fully aware that most of the components of his
description are more applicable to communist societies than they
are to Western societies. The main problem, however, is that
Jaroszewski deliberately fails to distinguish between industrializing and urbanizing societies and those societies which are
already industrialized and urbanized - the post-industrial
societies. It would be difficult for him to do otherwise without
jeopardizing his ideological orthodoxy.

In general terms, Jaroszewski sees the process of secularization as occurring on two distinct levels: firstly, at the level of
the Church as an organization (or the Church 'aparat' as he
calls it, using socialist-realist terminology); here the influence
of the Church and clergy on the life of society is seen to be
diminishing; secondly, at the level of the rank and file believers;
here he outlines three main trends: (1) the loosening of the bond
between believers and their formal organization; (2) the loosening of the bond between the believers themselves, in other words,

a dissolution of the community of believers; and (3) what
Jaroszewski calls 'a process of gradual demise (often very slow
and unnoticed by believers themselves) of religious interests
and the dying away of thinking in terms of religious categories
in the explanation of natural phenomena and social life'.(41)
Jaroszewski's work must not be taken as a serious contribution
to the sociology of religion: it has virtually no sociological value.
It is of value only to the authorities as a piece of propaganda
aimed at secularizing the beliefs of the less discriminating elements of Polish society.

It can be generally observed that all party religiologists take
care to create confusions and misleading arguments like the ones
noted above. Another valuable confusion is the one concerning
the notion that religion must have certain basic conditions in
order for it to be able to survive at all. It is not too difficult
to ensure, for example, that a recommendation of all-out persecution appears merely as a reasonable recommendation for the
removal of the social source of religion: in fact, it is very important that it should appear reasonable otherwise the religiologists
open the door to the accusation, albeit private, restricted or
internal, of religious persecution and as a consequence lose the
little academic respectability and credibility they have. At least,
such are the background rationalizations. In other words, the
pronouncements of the religiologists are always deliberately
milder than the analogous state policy.

One way of dealing with the question of persecution is to suggest, with the help of Lenin,(42) that religion will survive under
any conditions, the worse the conditions are the better religion
survives. Persecution or harassment would, according to this
theory, result in the opposite of the intended effect; the conclusion, therefore, is that there can be no such thing as 'conditions
necessary for the existence of religion', only 'religiogenic'
ones(43) and surely nobody, not even a believer, could possibly
object to the removal of these. In this way religiologists supply
a package which consists of both a theory of secularization and
a blueprint for its acceleration. They can even monitor the application and results by the use of conventional statistical measurement: after the closure of a village catechism centre, for example,
they will observe a substantial drop in the number of children
receiving religious instruction - an indisputable sign of secularization. This sort of approach is often referred to vulgarly and
ironically as a 'dialectical approach' - a rather gross Marxist-
Leninist umbrella term for practice which is at odds with the
expressed intentions: the war for peace is perhaps the most striking example of the dialectical approach.

Party religiologists also strive to blur the differences between
the religions (and also between religion and magic, if possible):
'comparative religions' becomes a key religiological phrase.(44)
This approach is calculated to have at least three effects: firstly,
it can be used to demonstrate the social origins of all religions
(and so leave no room for doubt) by attempting to explain the

differences between them in terms of the differences between
the societies in which they are found; secondly, it enables
priests and popes to be conveniently compared with witch
doctors and magicians of which, it might be suggested, they are
the modern functional equivalents. The step from functional
equivalence to identity is not a very large one. Finally, the
incompatibility of all the claims of all the religions taken as a
whole may be taken as illustrating the fact that 'religion' is
ridiculously self-contradictory; very confusing, but all ideologically sound.

The attempts by religiologists to show up religion in general
and Roman Catholicism in particular are many. The low level of
religious and other knowledge amongst Catholic peasants is often
regarded as incontestable evidence of the absurdity of Catholicism or of the claim that these peasants cannot be truly Catholic;
the fact that Catholics admit to not observing consistently the
required moral ethic is also used as evidence for similar
claims.(45) Some religiologists, like Zygmunt Poniatowski for
example, give reasons for a basic incompatibility between Christian belief and the sciences.(46) Poniatowski makes the point that
the suggestion that many good men of science are believers
could be a low trick designed to increase the prestige of religion.(47) He also argues that all Christians, in order to be consistent in their belief, ought to despise the sciences on the
grounds that they do not lead man to salvation.(48) These almost
unbelievable discourses are what lies behind the great attention
which is paid to the correlations often observed between low
levels of religiosity and high levels of educational achievement;
in practice, this means that those with tertiary education, for
example, admit to lower levels of religiosity than those without.
A closer examination of the figures, however, reveals that the
lowest levels of religiosity tend to be associated with the humani-
ties and not with technical studies and the exact sciences as
Marxist-Leninist religiology requires.(49)

An example taken from Jaroszewski illustrates the way in which
evidence is selected in order to suit the purposes of the writer.
Referring to studies carried out by the Polish Radio, Jaroszewski
points out that 15 per cent of those who declare themselves to
be Catholic believers do not believe that God created the
world.(50) Such a correlation must not be left, as Jaroszewski
leaves it, without reference to possible control situations.
Jaroszewski cares not to mention that the same study shows that
14 per cent of those who declare themselves as atheists believe
that God created the world.(51) The only interim hypothesis
that emerges at this stage is that about one person in seven is
very fundamentally inconsistent assuming, naturally, that they
are not just stupid or simply dishonest; possibly a restructuring
of the questionnaire may be required.

A completely different line of approach is taken by Andrzej
Nowicki, the editor of 'Euhemer'. Nowicki argues that Christian
doctrine has traditionally stifled artistic creativity; he is careful

to add that he is referring to real artistic creativity and not to
the creativity which has occurred within the confines of Church
patronage, in other words, not to the creativity which the Church
did not stifle: the latter is, of course, 'unreal'. Nowicki
writes:(52)

> Artistic creativity was...fettered by religion. 'Thou shalt not
> make to thyself any graven thing, nor the likeness of any
> thing that is in heaven above, or in the earth beneath, nor
> of those things that are in the waters under the earth' said
> God in one of the well-known 'holy writings'.

The opposite view, however, that the strength of artistic expression within the confines of Church patronage may count as evidence for the view that the Church actually encouraged such
expression or might have been the inspiration behind it is not
even given a mention by Nowicki.

Despite the multitude of examples of attempts at the official
sociology of religion by the secular front we will not pursue this
line of thought any further. Some of the sociological issues
which arise will be dealt with in later chapters.

As an afterthought, it might be worth mentioning that Poland
is, nevertheless, still relatively lucky with respect to its sociology of religion. Poland is certainly fortunate in comparison to
other eastern bloc states like Bulgaria, for example, which is
avidly praised by Polish party religiologists. They praise it for
its high degree of secularization and the partial corollary - a
highly developed sense of 'Patriotism' (in Pax's meaning of the
word) amongst its Orthodox clergy.(53) It seems, however, that
they should praise it for yet something else: its entire sociology
of religion has become infested by party religiologists.(54)

This chapter would be incomplete without a mention of the
other instruments of planned secularization. Of particular significance is the apparatus of central censorship, the GUKPPiW.
All material destined for publication(55) must be approved by
the local censorship offices which receive secret directives from
the central office. These directives indicate both the broad outlines and principles which must be adhered to and also give
precise details on the treatment of particular issues.(56) Some
of this classified material managed to find its way to the west but
it is fragmentary and no full picture of the censorship policy
towards religion is available. The impact of central censorship
on religious and related issues can be summarized in terms of the
following consequences: firstly, the encouragement of party
religiology in publication and other media with the prevention of
any open public discussion, debate or polemics on the subject;(57)
secondly, the prevention of public access to vast areas of the
subject which might be, or even sometimes have been, researched,
studied, discussed or simply brought within the general scope
of interest in cultural and other matters;(58) thirdly, the imposition of severe limits on Catholic life in general: news both in

the government media and in the Catholic press which is of
relevance to Catholics is restricted and Catholic intellectual,
cultural and religious life does not have the freedom of expression it requires.(59) A policy applied during the 1970s eliminated
virtually all news relating to Catholicism and to the Church from
all the media except the Catholic periodicals which, as a result
of other restrictions, have a very limited circulation. The object
was to try and quarantine the Church as part of an overall policy
of pushing it towards the margin of its own four walls. Fourthly,
by the monopolization of the media the authorities are able to
instruct the population in dialectical materialism(60) and recommend those patterns of life and general behaviour which are most
adequately suited to socialism and communism.(61) Finally, central censorship enables the deliberate falsification of information
across the whole society. This aspect, often referred to as the
'spreading of lies' is one of the most important instruments in the
system of total control.

Central censorship in Poland presents a particular problem to
the student of the sociology of religion: it is not possible (as is
the case in western liberal democracies) to rely on the published
or publicly expressed word as the exclusive or even main source
of thought on subjects such as religion: such a word is likely to
be ideologically tainted, misleading, restrained or even simply
incorrect; it can certainly be counted on as not reflecting accurately the author's own thoughts on the matter. However, while
due allowance can often be made for remarks obviously aimed at
'pleasing' the censor and for the more eye-catching elements of
incompleteness, it is nevertheless necessary to pay specific
attention to the privately spoken word and to the uncensored
typescript.

It is a well-known fact that many authors manage to evade at
least some of the censor's ingressions. Three methods are commonly employed either singly or in combination when publishing
officially in Poland: firstly, the presentation of the subject can
be made so complicated that only with great effort can the work
be deciphered: the censor may have neither the will nor the
ability to summon such an effort; secondly, the use of historical
or cross-national analogies often gives the impression that a
different subject is being discussed; finally, the presentation
of conclusions at odds with the general argument or with the
evidence (perhaps even no conclusions at all): here the reader
is obliged to argue the case himself. But these are more like
gestures of disapproval than wholesale outwitting of the censor.
Publishing outside Poland has the advantage of totally by-passing
the GUKPPiW but it does mean that the published work is not
available on the Polish mass market: it relies solely on clandestine
importation and private circulation.

Three important qualifications must be made at this point in
order to clarify the position of censorship from the latter half
of the 1970s. Firstly, note must be taken of the development in
Poland of a clandestine press - euphemistically termed 'outside

censorship'. A sort of 'samizdat' literature reflecting opposition
views had been part of the Polish scene for many years, but
1977 witnessed the additional appearance of several independent
publishing houses and presses. These publishing houses began
to print writing of merit rejected by the censor. Today, the
published work includes novels, socio-political commentaries and
discussions of religious matters.(62) The appearance of the final
group is a sure sign of the strength and vitality of Catholic
thought and ideas.(63) Secondly, in 1980 pressure from the
newly-formed independent trade union organization, Solidarity,
has been directed towards weakening the effectiveness of
GUKPPiW. One of Solidarity's demands required a total lifting
of censorship and the granting of access to the media by the
Church. These are demands which the Church itself had been
making for many years. The first demand is unlikely to be conceded willingly while even part of the totalitarian structure
remains intact but the implementation of the second began on 21
September 1980 by the first ever transmissions of Sunday Mass
together with the sermon. This radio broadcast, from the Holy
Cross Church in Warsaw, was the first of its kind since the
coming to power of the communist regime and can only be regarded
as victory for the Church and for Catholicism. Barring a massive
and violent coercive response by the Soviet Union - with or without the consent of the Polish authorities - both the clandestine
press and the direct weakening of censorship will undoubtedly
continue.

A third process is also clearly visible. The mechanism of censorship has been disintegrating spontaneously. Uncensored
material has been coming off official presses and there has been
disarray amongst the censors. There have been many instances
of the Church not submitting work to the censor but simply
having it printed. This process began with the confusion produced in official circles by the election of Pope John Paul II and
by the events of 1980.

In addition to the mechanism of censorship proper there are
ways in which language itself is being deliberately 'washed' of all
possible religious content. Language washing has assumed quite
large proportions in Poland. An anonymous observer has distinguished four areas in which this planned secularization of
language is taking place.(64) Firstly, there is the changing
by the mass media of the names of religious feasts. For example,
the name of the feast of All Souls' has been changed to the
'Day of the Dead'. In all except Catholic publications there are
no references by name to Christmas or Easter. Curiously May
Day remains a 'Holy Day'. The second example concerns the
addressing of priests, nuns and monks. Instead of using the
customary 'Father', 'Sister' or 'Brother' officials and shop
assistants have been instructed to use 'Sir' and 'Madam'. Thirdly,
GUKPPiW has decreed that the Church as an institution is now
to be written in the same way as the church as a building - with
a small letter 'c'. Again confusing but sound in terms of planned

secularization. Finally, all commonly used words and expressions which have some religious association are being replaced by others. The year 1981 A.D. is no longer A.D., but O.E. signifying 'Our Era', and similarly B.C. has become B.O.E.. The observer also describes the increasing monopolization of the term 'science' by Marxist-Leninists. In stressing their materialist Weltanschauung, Marxist-Leninists claim to be 'scientific' and thus constantly repeat the equation between Marxism-Leninism and science. They can therefore begin to refer to non-Marxist-Leninist Weltanschauungen as 'unscientific' or obscurantist.

Another no less important instrument of planned secularization is the Office for Religious Affairs which has ministerial status. The Office is formally charged with the routine running of Church-state relations and informally with the application of statutory instruments to exert pressure on the Church in order to weaken and eventually destroy it. A former director of the Office, Kazimierz Kąkol, did not attempt to disguise his views and during a press conference on religious policy he made the following comments:(65)

> While allowing the Church to function we will never go back on our principles. Even if as a government minister I have to smile in order to inspire confidence as a communist I will unceasingly fight against religion and against the Church both in an ideological and in a philosophical way.

The sense in which Kąkol used the word 'function' is clear from his other statements:(66)

> If we cannot get rid of the Church, we should make sure it does not interfere in the process of building communism. Freedom of religious expression applies only in the church building....We shall never allow any sort of evangelization outside churches or religious instruction in our schools.

Kąkol continues by quite bluntly stating that his object is the establishment of a fully secular society. At the same time, however, he admits that there are some problems to be overcome; he complains about PZPR members who 'ought to put their own house in order' as far as religion is concerned.(67) Reflecting the state policy of the 1970s, Kąkol puts his hope not in the old-style religious persecution but in the promised affluence: 'With a consumer society we should arrive at the sort of rapid decline of religion that has been characteristic of the west.(68)

Another device used against the Church is the sowing of confusion amongst the ranks of the clergy and of the faithful. The role of Pax, of the 'patriotic priests' has already been referred to in this context in the previous chapter. Here it is worth taking as an example the suspicions regarding the function of the monthly 'Ancora', which claims to be the organ of

the Centre for Post-Conciliar Renewal. It rarely appears for
sale in public places but is regularly sent by post to some of
the clergy. No publisher's address is provided and enquiries
have failed to reveal such a centre. The general line of this publication consists of accusing the Polish episcopate of fanatical
conservatism and of an unwillingness to implement any of the
reforms. 'Ancora' also attacks celibacy and has a tendency to
indulge in scandal.

Also in this category are various duplicated materials which
are sometimes distributed to Church congregations or to participants at religious gatherings, etc. These materials have a
typed 'samizdat' appearance. Again, their origin is unknown and
the known dissident groups disown them. Here the arguments
are often the contrary of those to be found in 'Ancora': the
Church is accused of breaking with age-old tradition and of taking part in a heretical council.

Some of the clergy take 'Ancora' and the duplicated materials
at their face-value but it is now becoming accepted that they are
all produced at the instigation of the party in order to fragment
the unity of Catholic opinion. As evidence, it can be noted that
the censor has forbidden the printing of a critique of 'Ancora'
in the Catholic weekly.(69)

The final method of implementing secularism which we will
mention here(70) is by the confiscation or 'secularization' of
Church property, land, organizations and associations - especially of those which are not directly concerned with worship.
The secularization of organizations and associations most often
has taken the form of dissolving them; alternatively, a complete
takeover may be enforced as in the case of Caritas. This policy
has been pursued vigorously since the end of the war and is
directed at the limiting of religious activity to within Church
walls.

The practical effects of planned secularization have not themselves been studied by sociologists - indeed, any attempt to link
them with 'social pathology', for example, is prevented at the
level of study and research and also at the level of publication.(71) As far as the success of planned secularization is concerned there has been no work ever published on the subject.(72)
However, judging from the conclusions of independent sociologists
of religion, it would appear that the desired success is not
observable or even that the policy has had the opposite effect.(73) As Kąkol admits (and he is not the only one), the party
has serious problems with religion even amongst its own members.
The extent of this problem was recognized by the WSNS itself
which engaged some sociologists of religion in order to carry out
a confidential survey of the levels of religiosity of the party actif
(those who are supposedly the most dedicated to Marxism-Leninism
and to the current party line). This work is said to show a surprisingly high degree of belief and practice amongst this most
'secularized' of groups within Polish society.(74)

4 APOCALYPSE WHEN? THE SECULAR MILLENNIUM AND A SECULAR HISTORY OF POLAND

Although religiologists are the official theoreticians and academic spokesmen of the communist authorities on the subject of religion, their central interest is secularization and the creation of a secular society and culture. They thus consider themselves to be secularists.(1) In their position as spokesmen, Polish religiologists, in addition to stressing the Marxist-Leninist parentage of their analyses of religion, consider it necessary to seek roots in Polish historical and cultrual traditions. They no doubt feel that without such roots their claim to the respectability usually associated with traditions of long standing would be difficult, if not impossible, to uphold. What is perhaps most important, however, is that the area of history and tradition is, to secularists, a key area which should itself be secularized. The secularization of the society's reference points, it is hoped, will eventually lead to a fully secularized society. In addition, through the demonstration of such traditional roots the religiologists hope to enhance their and the leaders' intellectual standing in matters of religion. Marxist-Leninist regimes in general consider such standing to be an important prerequisite for political action.

The necessity of producing a secular history must be understood against the background of two important factors. Firstly, there are the exceptionally strong religious reference points in Polish history. The nation-forming role of Christianity has already been mentioned in an earlier chapter. A questioning of the Christian reference points, therefore, amounts to a questioning of the nation - indeed, to an attack on the very soul of the nation. Secondly, the writing of a secular history is an integral part of state policy. Characteristically, it was given special encouragement during the 1960s and reflects the party's hope of using 'reason' against the Church.

While religiologists are normally satisfied with staying within the boundaries of Polish tradition they sometimes reach out to the Ancients in order to acquire some of the dignity of classical thought. Ancients especially popular from this point of view are Epicurus, Democritus and Lucretius.(2) This interest in the Ancients is not new to Marxism-Leninism - the doctoral thesis of Marx himself was concerned with Epicurus and Democritus.

David Martin, in tracing the genealogy of the concept of secularization, notes its derivation from Utopian ideology (Marxism-Leninism and Scientism) which is in turn derived from Christian sectarianism.(3) The sectarian tradition, notes Martin, incorporates the concepts of a past religious 'Golden Age', the

key stratum and universalism. (4) Religiology's central concern
with secularism and secularization enables Martin's categories to
be applied to it with advantage; the concepts incorporated into
the sectarian tradition are found to be reflected in the religiological approach to history.

In the Polish religiologists' approach to history four categories
can be distinguished: firstly, the notion of a secular purpose in
history; secondly, the existence of a 'secular movement'; thirdly,
a curious amalgam of the notions of inevitability, reasonableness
and even moderation of secularism. These three categories so
far are exactly analogous to the concepts listed by Martin. However, Martin might have included a fourth concept, namely, the
concept of the 'True God' which has become secularized to the
atheism of Marxist-Leninist secularism. Atheism can therefore be
regarded as a particular case of the sectarian True God. In
terms of the religiological categories the True God also comes
over as a very strong aggressive element. Not surprisingly
perhaps the whole religiological approach to history is marked
by the continual praise and idolatry of sectarian traditions.

In this chapter we will apply Martin's categories to Polish religiology and expand them to include the concept of the True God.
Firstly, we will look at the religiological approach to history in
general and at the way in which it reflects the four categories.
Secondly, we will examine the secular movement in some detail
bearing in mind that, to religiologists, it is the carrier of the
'traditions in the struggle for the secularization of social life in
Poland'. (5) Finally, there will be a few words about the acceptance of the early Polish sociology of religion by religiologists.

THE RELIGIOLOGICAL CONCEPTION OF HISTORY

Religiological historian and secularist philosopher Andrzej
Nowicki considers the development of a 'history of the critique
of religion' to be a particularly important task of religiology. In
1965 he wrote: (6)

> An assessment of the intellectual value of the contribution of
> Polish thought to the history of atheism is the basic aim of
> studies concerning the history of the critique of religion.
> Such a discipline does not yet exist....A full reconstruction
> of the history of the critique of religion...which would stress
> that which is most valuable and original in that history can
> only be the result of a few decades' intensive work by a
> serious team of historians of atheism who have the ability not
> only to discover interesting texts but also to interpret them
> correctly.

The importance of the history of thought to secularists has been
noted by Martin; (7) in the case of Polish religiologists the treatment of the history of thought is excessively crude: not only is

the thought of one individual liberally attributed to that of a
whole 'movement' by means of simple extrapolation but also a
single thought of an individual - however atypical it may be of
his general ideas - is given privileged status, is extrapolated,
and is finally advanced as representative. There are some analogies here with the political practice of totalitarian regimes.
   The general method, therefore, is to find one crucial thought
by one individual (the more well-known the better but even complete strangers are acceptable), subject it to the 'correct interpretation' and find a whole new world unfolding. Nowicki's interpretation of texts enables him, not unexpectedly, to identify a
strong and important tradition of secularism and atheism(8) in
Poland - a tradition which can even be traced back to the
Ancients. This tradition, according to religiological interpretation, totally eclipses Catholic tradition. This approach also
implies the idea that religiology, as the latest and final stage of
this tradition, marks the highest level of secularism and atheism
- its very perfection - and constitutes, of course, the final word
on the subject of Christianity and religion.
   Let us turn to some remarks concerning the relationship
between the religiological approach to history and an approach
such as the one outlined in chapter 2. The religiological approach
consists of an inversion of the traditional Christian view.(9)
An interesting corollary of this feature is that the traditional
approach already contains within itself the religiological or secular one albeit in an inverted form; it also means that the religiological version is not an entirely new, arbitrary, one but one
which is in many important respects continuous with the old.(10)
From the point of view of Christian theology, the religiological
version of history can be considered as a resurfacing of an evil
which was successfully kept at bay through the ages.
   Religiologists, therefore, do not go as far as rejecting established facts but simply provide a vision of them which is dia-
metrically opposed to the traditional one and which serves the
purposes of the communist leaders. For example, religiologists
suggest that Polish history began, not with Mieszko's baptism
but with the establishment of Poland's statehood. Since the two
events occurred at more or less the same time the religiologists'
departure may appear banal and of no interest. But religiologists
most emphatically do not consider it to be banal. They assign
great weight to changing the nature of an event as important to
the national psyche as the beginning of Poland's history: events
which were previously - and mistakenly they claim - seen as
related to God are now seen in terms of their relationship to the
visible world alone and to the categories of Marxist-Leninist
analysis. In this way religiologists attempt to convert the meaning of events from religious to secular while leaving the events
themselves untouched. Perhaps the classic example of this
inversion can be seen in the celebration of Poland's Millennium
which was organized by the Church hierarchy in 1966. This
celebration was met by its secular and secularizing counterpart

organized by the authorities in the form of a celebration commemorating the founding of the Polish state. Events showed that
the secular celebration was eclipsed by the religious one.

The inversion of history by religiologists is not limited to a
questioning of the relationship between historical events and
God. There are other aspects of this inversion which, although
derivable from the above, are distinct enough to merit special
note. There are two important ones: firstly, the way in which
the concept of the 'toiling masses' is given prominence; secondly,
the way in which alternative heroes are created, traditonal
heroes branded as enemies or converted into a different, secular,
kind of hero.

The emphasis on the role of the toiling masses in the historical
process involves above all the identification of this concept with
Poland and with the Polish nation. In contrast, Poland's kings
and leaders, nobility and gentry, Church and clergy are all
considered to be alien non-Polish elements:(11) the kings on
account of the fact that the system of election brought foreigners
in to reign over the kingdom, the nobility on account of the fact
that it can be shown that they sometimes collaborated with
Poland's enemies (members of the secular movement who collaborated with enemies are always spared this criticism(12)), the
Church for very many reasons but primarily because it was
always subject to the authority of the Vatican which, as well as
itself not being Polish, treated Poland as a pawn on the chess-
board of Europe. All of these elements together are considered
as non-Polish on account of the way in which they readily
absorbed the dubious foreign cultural currents of the more
advanced European states. Religiologists also remind us that it
was these alien elements within the heart of the nation which
were Poland's true enemies and not, as is traditionally maintained,
Poland's non-Christian neighbours. Further, these elements led
the country into the Turkish Wars which so weakened Poland
that she fell victim to the partitioning powers. This view of
history reveals quite a lot about the religiologists' approach to
current political issues.

The masses, however, are considered to be the real patriots
but too weak to be able to oppose the alien 'religious oppression'
by their feudal and capitalist rulers. Thus the only Polish crusade which can be talked about in any realistic way is not the
'croisade permanente' but an anti-Christian 'croisade intérieure'
of the toiling masses against their leaders. It is against this
background that the religiological historian identifies the Polish
secular movement and maintains that it was already a fighting
force on the morrow of Mieszko's baptism.

An example of the Church's lack of concern for the Polish
nation is given by Nowicki. He views Latin as both a tool of
domination and a symbol of contempt:(13)

The contempt for the Polish language amongst the high dignitaries of the Church was linked with a contempt for the nation

which speaks this language; the cynical attitude of the bishops that religion was a tool for keeping the masses in ignorance and obedience was linked with a contempt for the toiling masses. The struggle against the Polish language was one way of defending the old order and one of the ways of inhibiting the intellectual development of our nation.

There is no documentary or other evidence for the assertions made by Nowicki; he does not even suggest that there might be any. The picture is nothing more than the result of an extrapolation of the fact that the liturgy of the Church was in Latin and that Latin was the language of the European Christian elite. It is within this sort of context that the traditional Polish identification of 'Polish' and 'Catholic' (polak-katolik)(14) is dismissed as yet another tool for the stupefaction and subjugation of the masses: to religiologists the notion of polak-katolik is a contradiction in terms.

After these introductory remarks let us turn to a look at the way in which the four categories (secular purpose, secular movement, universalism and the True God) are apparent in the secular version of Polish history. We will deal with them in turn.

The notion of a secular purpose in history is, fundamentally, a notion of purpose. The notion of purpose in history is not at all recent: ideas regarding the role of divine purpose on earth can be traced back through the Judaeo-Christian tradition and can be seen in their starkest form in revolutionary anarchic sectarianism. The secular purpose is analogous to the divine purpose except that the end of history is not God but a union between man and nature. Revolutionary sectarianism and Marxist secularism both declare the imminence and immanence of the millennium: in the first case a Christian millennium based on a sectarian exegesis of the Holy Scriptures and in the second case an inverted, secular, millennium established and organized in accordance with the secular laws (Marxism-Leninism). In both cases the millennium is no more than a return to an earlier state of perfection: the Marxist historical stage of primitive communism is incorporated into the theory of the Secular Golden Age. Applying this theory to Polish history, religiologists suggest that prior to the baptism of Mieszko there existed some sort of idyllic communist society which was atheist in essence though pagan in form. It was the first society and in this sense it was also natural and exemplary: it marks that which man is by nature and that to which he must return in order to reach this-worldly perfection. The Secular Golden Age theory also posits the notion of the Secular Fall as a result of the repressive action of the dark forces of Christianity, feudalism and capitalism. In Poland the Secular Fall occurred quite rapidly and soon the nation was effectively subjugated. The eighteenth century saw Poland pushed into the deepest abyss: the partitions. If Poland produced anything of value during the whole period of Christianity it was either despite the dark forces or attributable to the actions of the early kings who were members of either the Polish Piast dynasty or of the Lithuanian Jagellonian dynasty: these are sometimes excused the epithet 'alien'.

The Middle Ages are normally regarded by religiologists as a model of the lowest point of secularism and of the highest point of Christianity. Martin suggests that such a view of the Middle Ages makes it impossible to cope with subsequent religious change in any way other than in terms of secularization.(15) The view of the Middle Ages as the perfect embodiment of Christianity is not peculiar to religiology but typifies a whole set of general approaches to the problem of secularization - approaches which are quite familiar in Western sociology.(16) In the case of religiology, however, this view of the Middle Ages is related to a whole series of other propositions which are in turn tied up intimately with the Marxist-Leninist Weltanschauung.

Included in the notion of secular purpose are the ideas of the historical stage, the signs, the word, the saints and prophets, etc.. A more concise parody of the original Christian view is difficult to imagine. All these ideas can be seen to derive from the sectarian tradition and are to be observed in the theorizing of the militant sectarians especially. In practice, these ideas mean that the secular purpose gradually unfolds through stages the transition between which is marked by a violent upheaval: the fall of Rome is said to mark the end of the slave-owning era and the onset of feudalism; similarly, the Renaissance marks the transition to capitalism. As well as marking the onset of a new stage these upheavals are accompanied by signs like the increasing exploitation of the proletariat and the onset of imperialism; various disturbances and riots can also be fitted into the schema of the signs. These signs in turn herald the oncoming final and permanent miraculous transformation;(17) those who can be shown to have contributed to this transformation become the secular saints and are given immortality in the books of secular history: they are the Heroes of the Revolution.

Throughout the unfolding of the secular purpose the word is identified with the slightest glimmer of criticism of anything religious, conventional or establishment-linked. The author of such an utterance becomes identified with a sort of embryonic Marxism-Leninism and as the forerunner or predecessor of Marxist communism. He becomes the secular prophet.

Religiological historians identify a whole pléiade of such heroes whom they group together under the evocative-sounding term of 'secular movement'. The term is designed to convey ideas of continuity and intense co-ordinated activity over the last thousand (sometimes few thousand) years - a truly superhuman feat. According to religiologists, all the members of the secular movement, who are said to have consisted of all the intellectual and enlightened members of society, were fighters against a religiously oriented outlook on life, against social injustice and for scientific progress. But they were, above all, the representatives of the toiling masses. Even one of these qualities suffices for

posthumous recruitment into the secular movement. In practice,
therefore, it is difficult to see who can be excluded from the
movement. Even if, as quite often happens, the historical figures
are men of the cloth, the religiologists are careful to explain that
religion is not central to the content of the heroes' beliefs but
represents merely the form or appearance of these beliefs. Religious in form but social in content, runs the argument. It follows, therefore, that a secular hero like Gregory of Sanok
(Grzegorz z Sanoka), the Archbishop of Lwów, was not a 'real'
Christian; nor was Hugo Kołłątaj, despite his assertions that
Catholicism was the only true faith. It is suggested that such
individuals had to speak some sort of language in order to be
understood and that the language of religious imagery was the
only one available at the time. This rather crude treatment of
what belongs to form and what belongs to content is very widespread in religiological literature;(18) also, according to this
treatment, religiousness of form does not qualify as religiousness:
appearances are unreal.

This approach raises a more general problem which is worth
mentioning at this point. If we are to concede that there exists
a criterion for distinguishing between real as opposed to apparent
Christianity (or any other belief) then we cannot at the same
time apply the idea that all religious beliefs and behaviour are
reducible to things social. This means that we cannot reject the
idea that there is such a thing as irreducible or 'real' Christianity
without also rejecting, firstly, the reality of medieval Christianity
(which, let us recall, is taken by religiologists to be the high
point of Christianity) and, secondly, the reality of the process
of secularization which, according to religiology, has ensued.
These questions are important to the general intelligibility of the
religiological approach. Religiology, however, seems to find itself
in a state of undecided oscillation between the acceptance of the
reality of medieval Christianity on one hand, and the reducibility
of religion on the other. In this oscillation the use of the 'form
vs content' device becomes essential: its use suggests an attempt
to salvage the secular history of Poland from absolute bankruptcy.

The Polish secular movement is seen as part of a greater
European secular movement. The suggestion that the secular
movement is a wide and general phenomenon allows religiology
to introduce ideas of inevitability, reasonableness, moderation
and universalism. These ideas are the criteria of the truth and
righteousness of religiologists' claims and they constantly appeal
to them; they ask: is secularism not a natural and all-embracing
European phenomenon? Have not all thinkers of significance
really stood firm against Christianity? Here the religiologists often
quote the very liberal recommendations of the secular movement's
conscripts: the freedom of conscience and belief, the separation
of Church and state, equality of rights for all confessions, etc.
Such aims, claim religiologists, are common to all civilized states,
communist and capitalist alike although realizable only in the

former. These recommendations, moreover, are said to exist in
a state of interdependence with other important and universal
phenomena: scientific and technological progress together with
its fruit, industrialism. Religiologists attempt to establish the
relationship between secularism and scientific progress in the
following way. They claim that members of the secular movement
have always been interested in scientific progress either by
actively contributing to it (Copernicus), by laying the foundations for it (the Arians(19)), or by spreading it (Giordano
Bruno) whereas the Church has no important record of scientific
achievement. The obvious aim is to present individuals such as
Copernicus first and foremost as secularists and only in the
second place as men of science: 'the well-known secularist
Copernicus made an important scientific discovery'. The argument
continues that, since science and religion have always been
incompatible with one another, religion must as a matter of
principle be opposed to scientific progress. It further follows
that religion's opposite - secularism - must always have been in
favour of science. The arguments are all couched in such indignant language as to suggest criminal intent on the part of the
Church and arouse deep passion on the part of the reader. Sometimes the result is quite comical.

The European secular movement has, of course, no more
reality as a movement than the local Polish one: it consists of a
hotch-potch assemblage of for the most part quite remarkable,
though in no general sense anti-religious, individuals whose
only common trait is their apparent rejection of the 'establishment'. To the actions of this assemblage of ideological non-
conformists(20) religiologists attribute by extrapolation and
other less defined means motives like concern for the interests
of the toiling masses, concern for the future, dislike of authority
and even, though implicitly, a love for the yet unborn Marx
and Lenin.

The secular movement becomes a movement of prophets and even
messiahs who are finally to deliver society from the depths of
existence through the proletarian revolution of Russia. Later,
the revolution was exported to Poland and elsewhere in the form
of the Liberation. Religiologists are always at pains to stress the
argument that since the outcome of the movement's struggle is
now a known historical fact its victory must have been inevitable
from the very beginning.

It is perhaps unnecessary to say that the religiologists' suggestion regarding the relationship between the secular movement
and scientific progress is what it is for reasons of definition or,
in other words, because its members have been recruited on
account of their contributions to science as well as for other
reasons. Most striking here is the gross inadequacy of the religiological view of the incompatibility of religion with science.(21)
This view, based to a very large extent on the belief that the
Church has always opposed science, supposing it to undermine
faith, relies on popular misconceptions regarding the disputes in

which the Church was involved during the Renaissance and after.(22) At this point we can see the origins of the 'intellectualist critique' of religion and magic which we have already referred to. The critique is based on the idea that the Church had set itself up as an arbiter of scientific truth - and failed. As a not so serious side it can be noted that the Church's scientific record is in some senses much finer than that of any of the contemporary communist parties: it is in no sense worse except in Marxist-Leninist metaphysics perhaps. If we are to take seriously the explanation that the concern of communist parties with political leadership overshadows their interest in science then we must surely agree that the achievements of a Church so preoccupied with political power and exploitation as it is alleged to have been must be truly remarkable. In any case, it is likely that this type of criticism of the Church is designed only for internal secularist use: apart from its function of provoking and maintaining indignation in anti-Church and anti-religious circles its value as a contribution to the understanding of religion is nil.

The idea that scientific and technical progress and industrialism can happily coexist only with secularism is far too facile an explanation of the incompatibility between religion and science. In fact it is no explanation at all because on close inspection it can be seen that the two spheres have different and non-competing points of reference.(23) This is why, as Martin observes, science and industrialism have a very wide compatibility range which can include a whole variety of beliefs.(24)

The incompatibility argument tends to treat industrialism, for example, as a unitary phenomenon without much attempt to break it down into components: type of industry, type of work, division of labour, trade economy, mobility, disorganization and reorganization of family and social life, urbanization, patterns of life, consumer mentality, etc. The argument also assumes that the degree of incompatibility is directly proportional to the degree of industrialism. This in turn suggests the importance of continued industrial and economic development to the future of secularism. However, there is no reason to believe that the forms which industrialism will take in the future will continue to reflect an intensification of all the present characteristics: the faith in unlimited industrial expansion and economic growth is giving way to the scepticism which is expressed through concerns with quality of life, resources, conservation and environment. Neither Poland nor the rest of the Soviet bloc are immune to the causes of this scepticism.(25)

A prominent place in the secular movement is occupied by sectarians of both revolutionary anarchic and pacifist traditions. The aggressiveness of the Marxist-Leninist secularists, in so far as it is ideologically justified, derives largely from revolutionary anarchic sectarian ideology. Let us for the moment recall, in the words of Norman Cohn, the general paradigm of the central fantasy of revolutionary sectarian eschatology:(26)

The world is dominated by an evil, tyrannous power of
boundless destructiveness - a power moreover which is ima-
gined not simply human but demonic. The tyranny of that
power will become more and more outrageous, the sufferings
of its victims more and more intolerable - until suddenly the
hour will strike when the Saints of God are able to rise and
overthrow it. The Saints themselves, the chosen, holy people
who hitherto have groaned under the oppressor's heel, shall
in their turn inherit dominion over the whole earth. This will
be the culmination of history; the Kingdom of the Saints will
not only surpass in glory all previous kingdoms, it will have
no successors.

It is perfectly clear that the sectarian fantasy differs from Marxism-Leninism not in terms of ideas but only in terms of nomen-
clature. The above passage can be rewritten substituting 'exploitation' for 'tyranny', 'proletariat' or 'exploited masses' for
'victims', 'revolutionaries' for 'Saints of God', etc., etc. Central
to the sectarian fantasy is the identification of the established
Catholic Church with evil and tyranny: it is Antichrist. Their
own doctrine, however, is put forward as the 'true' doctrine of
God. In the secularists' beliefs this place is occupied by another
'true' doctrine but this time one which states that there is no
God. Anything called God is false, they claim. Such a doctrine
has, in present times, some advantages over the previous sectarian one: the difference between the secular sectarianism and
its religious predecessor seems sufficiently great to blur the
similarities and so escape the criticism and suspicion associated
with the latter. In addition, strength is given to the claim that
Marxism-Leninism is an entirely new phenomenon. Marxism-
Leninism, having defined itself as not religion, is now able to
combat religion as a whole with the same vigour which the revolutionary anarchic sectarians applied to other religions. In this
connection the words of the sixteenth-century Anabaptist Thomas
Müntzer to his followers sound remarkably familiar to students of
Soviet history:(27)

Drive Christ's enemies out from amongst the Elect, for you are
the instruments for that purpose. Dearly beloved brethren,
don't put up any shallow pretence that God's might will do it
without your laying on with the sword, otherwise your sword
might rust in its scabbard....Christ is your master. So don't
let them live any longer, the evil-doers who turn us away
from God. For a godless man has no right to live if he hinders
the godly.

Müntzer's attitude towards priests and monks was also quite
blunt: 'The sword is necessary to exterminate them.'(28) Lenin
was not original, therefore, when he wrote: 'The more representatives of the reactionary bourgeoisie and the reactionary clergy
that we manage to shoot the better.'(29)

On the other hand, the pacifist sectarian tradition centres on
the idea that a 'real Christian is not one who states his belief
in the Gospel and yet remains untrue to it in actions'.(30) This
criterion of 'real' Christianity is admired by religiologists because
if applied resolutely it can be used to show that the Pope himself
is well on the way to paganism. However, it is as a criterion of
religiosity that 'real' Christianity is applied by numerous secularists in order to illustrate the process of secularization:(31)
fewer and fewer believers, the argument runs, treat Christianity
seriously enough to bother applying it consistently to their lives;
the reason for this is that its application to modern life is impractical and even impossible.(32) Schaff betrays how the criterion
of 'real' Christianity has entered secularist thought: 'The socialist humanist is ready to make the greatest sacrifices, and appeal
to others to do the same. He accepts the precept of "love thy
neighbour", and has only contempt for those who proclaim this
beautiful precept in words and betray it in deeds.'(33)

The Marxist-Leninist secularist vision of the world exhibits
much continuity with the millennial sectarian vision and manages
to fuse within itself both the anarchic revolutionary traditions
and the pacifist traditions. In practice, however, it is the former
that seem to predominate. One of the central issues of this sectarian vision is the Judaic rejection of the Kingdom of God in
Heaven and the strong complementary emphasis on the kingdom
of this world. Marx's vision of communism is undoubtedly a
vision of God's Kingdom but 'of this World': it is beyond doubt
that his Jewish origins are of particular relevance to this vision.
After Marx, Lenin stressed the 'revolutionary struggle for the
creation of a paradise on earth'.(34)

No account of the religiologists' heritage would be complete
without an introduction to the main heroes of the Polish secular
movement. We shall therefore take a brief look at the movement
and, in doing so, catch a glimpse of the secularist historical
methodology in action.

THE POLISH SECULAR MOVEMENT

The first Polish hero of secularism is Gregory of Sanok (Grzegorz
z Sanoka) who was the Archbishop of Lwów from 1451 up to the
time of his death in 1477. Gregory of Sanok is a rather curious
figure in Polish history, but he left virtually no written words
for posterity. He is known entirely through the writings of his
Italian biographer Filippo Buonacorsi, known in Poland as Kallimach (Callimachus). Because very little is known about Gregory
(even Kallimach's biography is very short) he is an excellent
figure on whom to improvise: the secularist imagination can be
given full rein. Secularists have not managed to recruit any members from the preceding half of Polish history: Gregory of Sanok
is therefore the honoured founder of Polish secularism.

Nowicki describes Gregory of Sanok as a plebeian.(35) However,

the strongest evidence, that of Kallimach himself, suggests that
Gregory was 'a gentleman on his father's as well as on his
mother's side'.(36) Nowicki's insistence shows that the question
of Gregory's origins is not one to be treated lightly: the representation of Gregory as the champion of the toiling masses is
made both much easier and more convincing if his social origins
can be shown to be humble. Humble social origins also make
Gregory really Polish: so please let us ignore the evidence...
Nowicki describes the greatness of Gregory in the following
way:(37)

> From his high position the plebeian Gregory outshone the
> dignitaries of the upper nobility through his political astute-
> ness, thrift and patriotism; he dominated by virtue of his
> education and excelled by virtue of his fine diction....Could
> there be a better argument in favour of the bold granting of
> the highest positions to plebeians? Gregory's life provided
> the townspeople with the weapon they need in their struggle
> for their rights: a precedent was created. The younger
> generation of townspeople was now encouraged to strive for
> more ambitious goals.

Who were these dignitaries whom Gregory outshone? Who was it
that argued for the bold granting of the highest positions to
plebeians? What were the more ambitious goals of the towns-
people? None of these questions are even touched upon by
Nowicki for the simple reason that there is no evidence. Curiously,
Gregory's virtues as noted by Nowicki (political astuteness,
thrift and patriotism) all sound very similar to virtues proclaimed by socialist propaganda aimed at citizens of a communist
state: political astuteness will lead to party membership, thrift
will allow one to cope with widespread shortages of goods and
patriotism suggests a love for the Soviet Union. Gregory must
have been remarkably far-sighted to have foreseen all this.
According to Nowicki's account it turns out that Gregory
possessed a whole gamut of characteristics which communist
leaders try to impose on their societies. We thus read that Gregory was against the Middle Ages, against Scholasticism,
against the Vatican, against backwardness, against the old and
out of date, against parasites and against the dictatorship of
the Church. He was in favour of the future, and of things new,
in favour of the ideology of the oncoming epoch and in favour
of being useful. Such are the perversities of the religiological
understanding of history and Nowicki knows no limit to indecency:
Gregory is also depicted as having stood up against the Teutonic
Knights when, we are informed, all the Polish ruling circles were
very much in favour of their attacks on Poland.(38) Most amazing,
however, is Gregory's uncompromising anti-religious position.
Nowicki writes: 'such strong stress of the irrationality of religion
[by Gregory] could only lead and in fact did lead, in the sixteenth century, to atheist conclusions'.(39)

Religiologists like Nowicki are masters at the art of appearing
to mean more than they actually say. The most striking example
is Nowicki's description of Gregory as a materialist;(40) a dialectical materialist in Poland today, let us not forget, is most
often referred to simply as a materialist. That Gregory might
have been an Epicurean materialist is, in the context of Nowicki's
overall purpose, an irrelevant and even confusing detail. In the
case of Nowicki's biography of Gregory of Sanok we find slight
changes in nuance and emphasis in the translations from the
original Latin, dubious assertions regarding Gregory's social
origins together with an attempt at the creation of an anticipation
on the part of the reader that Gregory must be a hero, albeit
premature, of Marxism-Leninism: all these features combine with
imaginative extrapolations to produce something on the lines of
a secular prophet.

There is, however, one feature of Gregory's thought which
does make him relevant to the history of ideas. Gregory was
undoubtedly already a Renaissance figure who encouraged humanist thought and thinkers such as Kallimach himself. The idea of
man as the measure of all things involved a new approach to
knowledge; this approach involved making a distinction between
that knowledge which is taken 'on trust' and the knowledge
which is readily accessible to the senses. This approach, therefore, managed to view knowledge not in terms of one indivisible
whole - as in the medieval tradition - but as consisting of two
parts. Although Gregory never questioned the Church's com-
petence in matters of faith, he did question it in other matters:
for authority in questions not connected with faith he preferred
to turn to Epicurus.

Medieval thought had nothing but contempt for Epicurean
materialism and sensualism. The beginnings of this sort of humanism, therefore, can be seen as an important milestone on the
winding road leading from Scholasticism to modern versions of
atheism. In other words, the splitting of knowledge is a necessary
first step to the discrediting of one part of it. The secularists
thus do have some claim to Gregory.

Gregory's association with the Renaissance is also of importance
to the secularists. The Renaissance is welcomed by religiological
historians as the bourgeois revolution which replaced medieval
theocentrism with humanism. So important is its interpretation
as the bourgeois revolution that a denial of its occurrence in
Russia would be too incongruous for words: Nowicki, therefore,
identifies the Russian Afanazy Nikitin, no more than a peripatetic
trader who had been to India, as a central Renaissance figure.(41)
The Renaissance is thus a fertile and important period for the
recruitment of secular heroes.

Another important Polish Renaissance figure who has become
a hero of secularism is Andrzej Frycz Modrzewski who died in
1572. Frycz Modrzewski is especially noted for his political
writings where he outlines a theory of the state. In his view,
there should be a constitutionally bound and elective monarchy,

the consistent application of the law with no distinction as to
class or status, a strong treasury and a decisive peace policy.
In religious matters Frycz Modrzewski, although a Catholic,
typified the currents of the Reformation but also believed that
unless the Vatican became less intransigent in the face of the
rapidly occurring changes a Polish National Church may represent the only solution to the Reformation dispute.(42)

Frycz Modrzewski's recommendations, taken out of the original
context, would all appear to reflect either the slogans or the
policies of Poland's communist leaders: the importance of a
constitution, democracy and a democratically elected communist
party; the defence of the underdog, the building of a strong
economy, the stress of peace, criticism of the Vatican, the need
for Church reform, suggestions for a national Church. Religiological historians are also masters at quoting out of context in
the quest for the crucial thought: Nowicki has compiled a whole
book of such quotations.(43) It is probably the discovery of one
such quotation which finally decided Frycz's recruitment into the
secular movement. Nowicki's crucial discovery reads as follows:
'Would it be so curious then if the dogma concerning the Trinity,
for example, or the dual nature of Christ were also to be considered in the future as empty-headed dreams full of stupidity
and error?'(44) A careful inspection of the passage reveals that
a knowledge of the context is essential for full intelligibility;
even taken out of context the statement suggests not the militant
atheism which Nowicki would have us believe but more of an
antitrinitarian position.

Nicholas Copernicus (1473-1543) is too valuable an asset on
account of his fame and status in the history of scientific thought
for the secular movement to pass him by. Copernicus's claim to
fame is that he produced the first valid model of the heliocentric
system. Since Copernicus never wrote anything which directly
criticized or manifested any antipathy towards the Church,
Nowicki is obliged to recruit him in ways that can only be described as devious: firstly, Nowicki stresses the 'materialist
significance of heliocentrism'; secondly, he enlists the help of
Giordano Bruno who accepted the validity of the Copernican
system and admired Copernicus; lastly, Nowicki mentions that
Copernicus's uncle, Watzenrode the Bishop of Warmia, was
acquainted with Kallimach - surely irrefutable proof that Copernicus was a secularist...

Giordano Bruno is considered by Polish religiological historians
to be the leading figure of the European secular movement. His
esteem for Copernicus is therefore very important. Nowicki
writes:(45)

In the philosophy of Giordano Bruno we see the highest point
in the development of Renaissance philosophical thought. His
philosophy is militant, anti-Scholastic and, as a consequence,
anti-feudal. At the core of this philosophy lies the unravelling
and demonstration of the revolutionary, materialistic and

atheistic significance of Copernicus's theory....His death as
a result of the verdict of the Inquisition is a symbol of the
basic conflict between science and religion.

Giordano Bruno is thus hailed as the first martyr of European
secularism. Nowicki wishes to imply here that it was only a
question of pure chance whether it was Bruno or Copernicus who
was burnt. Moreover, implies Nowicki, Bruno died not for himself alone but for the Copernican revolution. In his zeal for
Bruno, Nowicki rather rashly concludes that 'Giordano Bruno
had no intention of reforming, improving or bettering religions
but considered each one of them to be nonsense.'(46)
    It is worth pursuing this line further by asking how others
view Bruno. De Santillana writes as follows: 'In after times,
Giordano Bruno has been glorified as a martyr for free thought,
secularism and democracy. This is fairly absurd, for Bruno was
highly diffident of the untutored multitude, and hardly a
secularist.'(47) De Santillana continues by quoting Bruno's own
words:(48)

> True propositions are never offered by us to the vulgar, but
> only to the wise, who can reach an understanding of our
> point of view. This is why truly religious and learned theo-
> logians have never challenged the freedom of philosophers;
> while the true, civilized and well-organized philosophers have
> always favoured religions.

Although the Inquisition might have found a lot to disagree with
in this statement it is not representative of a secularist position.
Furthermore, while his case was being investigated Bruno 'pitted
his resourcefulness and his vast learning against the Inquisi-
tional mind to prove that he had never deviated from the essential
orthodoxy'.(49)
    It is quite clear that Nowicki is aware of the imperfections in
his work. Taking advantage of central censorship and of the
resultant relative inaccessibility of Western scholarship in Poland
to immunize himself against criticism, he claims that those who
disagree with his interpretation of Renaissance thought are no
more than 'falsifiers of the Renaissance.'(50) In criticizing these
falsifiers Nowicki outlines his own approach:(51)

> With the aim of strengthening their false theses bourgeois
> scholars normally pass over and belittle all that was new,
> progressive and revolutionary in the ideas of Renaissance
> thinkers. They stress, on the other hand, all that was in-
> consequential, anachronistic and a relic of the past. Further-
> more, they re-group thinkers in such a way as to place those
> who were bold and typical - the materialists and atheists -
> in the background and bring to the fore second-rate figures
> of the orthodox Catholic *genre*.

Although Nowicki wrote these words in 1956 they are neverthe-less entirely valid as explanations of the orientation of his much later writings. Indeed, it is difficult to see how his con-tributions could be otherwise explained. This fact indicates the extent to which secularist thought is still characterized by the same uncompromising subservience to party orthodoxy as it was during the time of Stalin.

Among the most important recruits to the Polish secular move-ment are the sectarians known as the Arians. They were origin-ally thus (pejoratively) termed by the Calvinists of the sixteenth century who wished to liken their ideas to those of Arius, a heretic of the fourth century. To Western scholars the Arians are also known as Socinians (after Faust Socinus who made important contributions to Arian doctrine) and as Anabaptists (on account of the re-baptism of their converts). Stanisław Kot, basing himself on the content of their beliefs, refers to them as Antitrinitarians.(52) The name which the Arians finally adopted for themselves was Polish Brethren (Bracia Polscy), an ironical choice perhaps since most of the prominent Arians were not Polish. Western scholars are familiar with the Arians as the pre-decessors of modern Unitarianism.(53)

The Arians, whose ideas percolated into Poland mostly from Transylvania, established themselves as a sect when they broke away from Polish Calvinism in 1565. Because of their extremist ideas regarding both Christian doctrine and socio-political matters, they made themselves rather unpopular in all camps: amongst Catholics, Lutherans and Calvinists as well as with the Polish political circles. In 1569 the Arians founded a colony in southern Poland: this was Raków which was to be their 'New Jerusalem'. To it flocked 'a group of men consisting of social utopians as well as mystics, but principally of millenarians'.(54) In later years Raków became an important centre of Arian thought. The Arians' unpopularity, however, finally led to their being given the choice of either re-converting to Roman Catholicism or being expelled from the land. In 1658 large numbers left Poland for Transylvania and for the Netherlands.

Arian beliefs were in a constant state of flux and even at any given moment the doctrine was never homogenous. Self-contra-diction, confusion and incoherence all typified the Brethren's beliefs. But in broad terms it can be said that the early refuta-tions of all forms of systematized and dogmatic belief, in the course of generations, gave way to systematization and rational-ization. This development was paralleled by the change from pacifism, the rejection of temporal authority and the refusal to hold public office to the justification of the defensive war, the acceptance of the role of citizen and even the defence of the duties of citizenship. Even during times of stress, the Arians did not return to their early pacifism nor did they develop any of the anarcho-revolutionary characteristics.

The tone of Polish religiological writings about the Arians can without exaggeration be described as tearful and heart-rending.

Secularists lament with self-righteous indignation the unjust
treatment the Brethren were accorded by the authorities of the
time, they sympathize with the intellectual and moral integrity
of the Brethren, they praise their progressive thought and
nonconformism both of which they see as an anti-feudal protest,
they admire the Arians' unparalleled work and example and,
finally, they detest any criticism of the Brethren. It is impossible
to avoid thinking that the secularists consider the Arians not
only as the ideological antecedents of Marxist-Leninist secularism
but also as comrades, team-mates or even cronies.

The pacifist character of the Arian beliefs worries the religiological historians who try to seek answers to the question why
the Brethren's anti-feudal protests were so weak that they did
not get past the stage of being expressed in writing.(55)
Typical solutions suggest that the reactionary camp was so
strong that it opposed successfully the full and practical expression of the Arians' ideas; or that the Arians were, on account of
their extreme progressivism, too weak to cope even under conditions which were only averagely oppressive; or that it was not
in fact the case that the Arian beliefs were essentially pacifist.
This last explanation attempts to demonstrate the continuity of
outlook between the Arians and the Anabaptists of Münster.(56)
This suggestion is simply ludicrous.

There are two main reasons for the religiologists' interest in
the Arians: firstly, the 'secularizing' nature of their beliefs and,
secondly, their association with the beginnings of currents of
'rationalization'. The early Arian beliefs were undoubtedly secularizing sectarian beliefs in Martin's sense of the word: they
attempted to 'convert the symbols of ecclesiastical religion into
terrestrial realities: for example communism in property'.(57)
In particular, the early Arians believed that society was in practice hypocritical and evil. It is evil because those who comprise
it, while professing to be Christians, do not live according to
Christian teaching.(58) The following demands were made by the
more radical Arians in 1568:(59)

It was...required of ministers that they resign ministries in
which they live by the labour of others, and that they win
their bread by their own hands. They also said to the brethren of the nobility: it is not right for you to eat bread by
the sweat of your poor serfs, but to work yourselves. Also
it is not right for you to live on such estates, which were
given to your ancestors for shedding blood. Sell then such
estates and distribute to the poor.

But this was in no sense a programme of social reconstruction
which was to benefit the victimized strata, as Ogonowski maintains;(60) nor was it a militant attack on the wrongdoers of
society. It was simply an appeal to conscience. It was the same
sort of appeal which led Peter Gonesius (Piotr Giezek z Goniądza)
to carry a wooden sword in protest againt the use of arms –

hardly a battle-cry. Nevertheless, if it is at all possible to
imagine an indignant battle-cry uttered by one too poor to afford
a steel blade it is most certainly the very same cry which the
secularists consider as the embodiment of their heritage.

The current of rationalization of the later Arians involved
the notion that religious beliefs should be subject to the scrutiny
of reason. It is easy to see why such an idea should appeal to
secularists. Not only can those elements of doctrine or revelation
which are shown to fall short of this yardstick be rejected but
also, hope secularists, the consistent application of reason to
Christianity must lead to one conclusion and one conclusion alone;
secularists all but explicitly state that Christian believers must
be either deficient in reasoning power, proficient liars or
unpleasantly affected by false consciousness. In some cases they
might be the victims of deliberate deception. Secularists admit,
with regret, that the Arians did not push the application of
reason to religion to its logical conclusions but recognize that
their contribution was an important step in that direction.(61)

The banishment of the Polish Brethren and the success of the
Counter-Reformation meant that the secular movement was
weakened for a period of about one hundred years. This secular
Dark Age or, as Nowicki imaginatively terms it, the 'Jesuit
Shroud of Gloom'(62) lifts briefly in 1689 for the death of
Kazimierz Łyszczyński, the first (and only) Polish atheist martyr.
It appears that Łyszczyński was sentenced to death for writing
a treatise entitled 'De non existentia Dei'. This treatise has since
been conveniently lost - presumably destroyed during or shortly
after the trial - and all that remains are a few notes which were
made during the trial. Apart from this and also the fact that
his execution caused some controversy at the time on account
of his being a member of the gentry,(63) next to nothing is
known about Łyszczyński.

Łyszczyński's importance as a martyr of the atheist cause has
led to his romanticization by Nowicki and to his rescue from a
murky cell in the obscure by-ways of history. A copious amount
of writing has appeared concerning both what is not known
about him and what the content of his thought might have been.
Nowicki writes boldly: 'Polish intellectual life cannot boast of
any one figure who could compare with Łyszczyński in terms of
breadth of intellectual horizons, the thoroughness of philosophical erudition and the boldness of thought. He was beyond
doubt the most eminent Polish mind of the epoch.'(64) What a
pity that no one knows what the content of his thought was.

According to the notes made at the trial, Łyszczyński was
curiously 'modern', even to the point of incongruity, in his
critique of religion: all of his remarks might have been made by
Marx or Lenin - an important reason for his popularity amongst
secularists.(65) His ideas belong to the sphere of atheism proper: Łyszczyński clearly states his disbelief in God. The incongruity of this idea, however, lies in an inability to understand
fully its genesis in the context of Polish society at that time:

the sort of atheism which Łyszczyński advocates did not emerge fully until some two centuries later. Further, there is no independent or clear evidence of other individuals with similar inclinations during Łyszczyński's time. To say that Łyszczyński was simply ahead of his time means nothing: it is an admission of the unavailability of an explanation. It is perhaps not possible to get nearer the truth than Martin when he wrote with irony: 'spot the right intellectual and you can know the future'.(66)

Nowicki, on the other hand, has his own explanation which is theatrical, enigmatic and contains imaginative implications. He begins by insinuating that Łyszczyński's use of phrases like 'we atheists believe that...' might indicate a sizeable atheist following.(67) Nowicki does not forget to mention that Łyszczyński was not the first Polish atheist, but nowhere does he suggest who the first atheists were.(68) Perhaps he is referring to Łyszczyński's sizeable following. But Nowicki's greatest inconsequence consists of his comments describing how, during his trial, Łyszczyński had scribbled over the work of Calvinist John Henry Alstedius 'Theologia naturalis adversus atheos'.(69) Nowicki declines to mention either what Alstedius's work was concerned with, or the substance of what Łyszczyński has scribbled if substance there was or, the great enigma, what this occurrence is supposed to illustrate. Nowicki, of course, leaves the reader to assume that Łyszczyński was defacing a work directed against atheism thereby providing further evidence of his own beliefs.

The period of Enlightenment in Poland, as a result of its stress on deism, education, reform and Voltaire, appears to have something to offer to the secularist historian. The two principal Enlightenment figures in Poland were Hugo Kołłątaj and Stanisław Staszic who both typified the currents of the time. Czesław Miłosz writes: 'it can be said that the mainstays of the Enlightenment in Poland were elegant, sceptical, often libertine, priests who displayed all the airs of French politeness.'(70) They have, of course, both been recruited into the secular movement: Kołłątaj on account of his reformism - the next best thing to revolution but only in retrospect; secondly, because of his faith in science and progress - both of which, we have seen it argued, are incompatible with religion; and finally because of his deist tendencies - God without religion is one step nearer towards no God at all; Staszic, on the other hand, has been recruited on account of his atheism (the fact that Staszic appeared, at the same time, to have deist convictions is not a point worth considering, argues Nowicki(71)), his belief in 'natural laws', his concern with the Perfect Society and his typology of societies. All these features thus described may even qualify him as a kind of mini-Marx. It is the opening lines of his most famous work which make him such a great secularist antecedent: 'I will tell you how man subjugated his own race and how his subjugated race regained its rights. Of all the species man is the only one endowed with reason.'(72) Perhaps Staszic should even be put in Marx's place?

The recruitment of figures from the Romantic era is of great importance to religiology on account of the popularity which they enjoy. But because Romantic figures tend to be associated with Catholicism rather than with disbelief, the secularist treatment here has to be far cruder than anywhere else. Nowicki courts Chopin in the following way: 'In any case, it is obvious that in the consciousness of Frédéric Chopin, for example, the central part was...occupied not by thoughts of God and Heaven but by music. George Sand wrote this about Chopin: "His soul is filled exclusively with poetry and music."'(73) Nowicki is, presumably, attempting to confuse the literary with the literal. Are Nowicki's conclusions here perhaps an example of the serious and intensive work which he envisaged earlier?

We have been relying extensively on Nowicki's contributions not because they are necessary typical, but because they represent the most consistent presentation of the secularist case. Nowicki's apparent extremeness is no more than consistency of subjugation to the secularist Weltanschauung: his conclusions are in every way as embarrassing as they are nonsensical. It is difficult not to get the impression that although Nowicki is without doubt considered an intellectual embarrassment even by other secularists - there is a limit to which we can be consistent in our secularism, they might say - he is nevertheless privately revered on account of his ideologically sound and uncompromising beliefs as a 'personal foe of God'. It is perhaps indicative that, as well as editing 'Euhemer' (the secularist journal), he is the president of the PTR and has received state awards for both 'scientific achievements' and for teaching: he was awarded the Cross of Cavalier of Poland Reborn in 1974.(74) Nowicki is thus not to be laughed at, at least not in public.

The second half of the nineteenth century would seem an appropriate point at which to leave the history of the secular movement. This period marks the incorporation into the secular movement of the beginnings of Marxist communism and of the SDKPiL, the development of the Polish freethinkers (wolnomyśliciele) and boasts of producing the father of secularist religiology, Andrzej Niemojewski.(75) In other words, this period can be seen as marking the beginnings of secularism.

It is important to bear in mind that this was also the period of positivism and of the beginnings of the Polish sociology of religion. Positivism and secularism drew on the same philosophical roots with the result that we find that the early sociologists can all be considered to be either secularists or to have strong secularist leanings. Krzywicki's contempt for religion has already been mentioned but let us now draw attention to the similarity between his secularism and that of the Polish religiologists of today. Krzywicki wrote:(76)

The Church is without doubt one of the greatest enemies of
any kind of progress. At every time and in every place we
observe that the Church opposes any kind of free critical
thought. Always and everywhere it condemns to death and
to disapproval all the revolutionaries of thought and deed.

The admiration of secularists today for men like Krzywicki is a
good indicator of the importance to them of this sort of idea.
More importantly, it shows the overlapping origins of secularism
and of the sociology of religion in Poland.
    Although the religiological study of history is a bastard discip-
line with political subservience as the central point of reference,
it does nevertheless develop a logic of its own which attempts
at various points to attach itself to the intelligible world. But the
way in which it manages to explain history and give meaning
to events cannot be seriously considered as competitive with the
sort of view of Polish history that was described in chapter 2.
Even at the best of times the religiological scheme of history
gives the impression of the secular movement as an unsavoury
and perhaps even diabolic presence lurking in the subconscious
of the Polish historical process. It is fair to conclude that it would
no doubt have remained there virtually undetected were it not
for the emergence of one of the greatest evils of recent history
- Soviet communism.

SOCIOLOGY AND SECULARISM

The Utopian and sectarian genealogy of the concept of secularization as used by religiologists and secularists has already been
noted. However, the debt of religiology and also of Marxist or
secularist-inspired sociology of religion to Utopianism and sectarianism is much greater. In this concluding section we will
look at this debt further by examining the question whether it
is possible to understand the curious treatment of religion by
the early Polish sociologists in terms of Utopian ideology and
sectarian tradition. In other words, we will attempt to answer
the question whether the secularist position entails a particular
ideological bias which, firstly, focuses on the peasant specifically
and, secondly, treats him in a characteristic way.
    Insight into these questions can be gained by referring again
to Martin's three categories and their analogues noted above
(the Golden Age, the key stratum and universalism). We shall
argue that the sorts of characteristics exhibited by the peasant
undermine the sectarian use of these categories by questioning
the assumptions behind them. This in turn leads to either a
sociological fascination with the peasant and his beliefs or to a
Marxist secularist contempt for them. The sociological fascination
is derived from the pacifist sectarian tradition while the Marxist
secularist contempt derives from the anarcho-revolutionary
tradition. It is also possible to see the two traditions combining

and so producing the contemptuous fascination of Krzywicki's work.(77) Table 4.1 summarizes and illustrates the secularization of the two sectarian components (anarcho-revolutionary and pacifist) into two important components of religiology and secularizing sociology.

TABLE 4.1 The secularization of the sectarian traditions

	From God as truth: sect	To atheism as truth: religiology or secularism
Pacifist tradition	Appeal to conscience for, or retreat into a 'really Christian' life, e.g. Arians	The 'real Christian' as a criterion of religiosity; e.g. as used in sociology. Also the attempts to secularize by suggesting that nothing is 'really' Christian
Aggressivist (anarcho-revolutionary) tradition	Conversion by force, e.g. Anabaptists	The removal of religiogenic conditions; the marginalization of the peasant and his conversion to an industrial worker; the marginalization of religious believers, e.g. policies of Marxism-Leninism in power

The early Polish sociology of religion, let us recall, limited its investigations to the peasant who was treated as archaic in terms of his life and beliefs and also as outside the reach of modernity. The two opposites, modernity and archaism, were both used in the ideological sense: they designated respectively societies which have and have not reached the signpost on the road to the realization of the secular purpose. The sociological approach, involving attempts at explanation, understanding, detachment, intellectualist critique and the belief that at last the true answer has been found, is reminiscent of the sectarian treatment of the True God according to conscience. This approach contrasts with the Marxist secularist approach which involves a militant dislike of the False God and of the Antichrist and which consequently insists on forcible conversion: this approach does not involve any serious attempt at explanation, etc. Let us now turn to re-examine the peasant.

The important role played by religion in the Polish peasant's life suggests that the truly religious Golden Age is not necessarily

shrouded behind the mists of centuries, but can be found today.
The corollary of this is that the final return of the secular
Golden Age is much further than anticipated. The 'discovery'
of the peasant is therefore accompanied by his marginalization:
he is relegated to the backwaters of the modernizing world by
the insistence that either he must surely be anachronistic or
that he is being slowly but inexorably modernized (or, at least,
should be). This view has important implications for the concept of the religious Golden Age: its remoteness in time is replaced by its remoteness from modernity. In other words, it is
replaced by the notion of the Golden Age of religion at this point
in time but, nevertheless, equally distant in terms of its access
to modernity. The secularist, therefore, must treat the peasant
as an anachronism in order to preserve the remoteness of the
Golden Age of religion and to ensure the closeness of the secular
Golden Age.

To the sociologist interested in the archaic this appears as a
distinct advantage: the past is here and can be studied now.
But the militant secularist tends to dislike such temporal anoma-
lies and prefers to remove them physically in order to facilitate
the coming of the secular age, or perhaps simply in order to
delude himself.

The anachronistic character of the peasant renders difficult
his establishment of a meaningful relationship with the secular
key stratum: indeed, it is difficult to imagine anything further
removed from the secular movement than the peasant. Also, the
importance which secularist universalism attaches to industrialism can only be reconciled with a corresponding neglect or
rejection of things rural or agricultural. The peasant, however,
can be 'industrialized' by converting him into an industrial
worker through the decree that 'agriculture is now industry':
such a declaration also instantly modernizes him; here we can
see the theoretical significance of the communist concept of
'state farms' where the farmers are classified as industrial
workers.

One way out of the difficulty is to suggest that the peasant is
not as religious and, therefore, not as anachronistic as he
appears. In other words, by postulating that the peasant's religion is all rather superficial and that he is not 'really' religious:
what appears to be religion is really something else like ecstasy
or an expression of social cohesion and structure, for example.
This approach, as well as making the peasant ready for modernization, provides sociologists like Krzywicki or Czarnowski with
fertile ground for speculation.

Marxist secularist universalism, being based largely on industrialism and, in Poland and other Eastern bloc states, on the
concept of socialist morality(78) envisages the prompt demise of
the peasant's way of life and of his antiquated beliefs. However,
the extent to which there exists an opposition to the programme
of industrialization and socialist education and also difficulties
in its implementation must be at least a partial indicator of the

non-universality of the secular version of modernism. Since one of the obstacles here is the influence of religion it is not surprising to find that the Church is therefore regarded as an enemy of progress.

One characteristic trend is based on the peasant's conservatism when faced with social change or with new ideas; on the other side of this coin we find his inability to come to terms with new conditions and surroundings. Sociologically, this state of affairs gives rise to the study of the disorganization of peasant communities under conditions of rapid social change (including migration) as exemplified by the work of Thomas and Znaniecki or to the study of patterns of continuity under similarly changing conditions as exemplified by Chałasiński. Today, sociological work in this area is connected with studies of urbanization and industrialization and, in particular, of studies of the secularization of attitudes, beliefs and practices.

The secularist position has traditionally more affinity for the study of the peasant than for the study of any other social group. The reason is that no other group can be marginalized as simply and as effectively as the peasant. Today, the marginal status of the peasant is emphasized comparatively less as greater sections of society are now suffering the onslaught of militant secularist marginalization. The accusation, frequently noted by Polish opposition leaders, that Catholic believers are being treated by the authorities as 'second class citizens' is a further reflection of the policy of marginalization which tends to be applied across the board.

5 ARCHAISM TODAY: SECULAR VIEWS OF CONTEMPORARY CATHOLICISM AND ITS PROSPECTS

Religiology and religious policy are the concern of the ruling circles and their immediate vicinity. Closely allied yet quite distinct is what we shall be referring to as the political realist approach which, although fundamentally Marxist (in the sense of commitment to the regime), is less oriented towards the legitimation of political power; this approach, however, never finds itself at odds with either official orthodoxy or the fundamental tenets of secularism. This approach can be observed in terms of two distinct trends: firstly, a descendant of the Durkheimian-cum-Marxist position of Czarnowski but now flavoured very strongly with political realism and, secondly, the fully fledged Marxist-Leninist political realist position. The former position is illustrated by the work of Edward Ciupak: in examining Ciupak we shall also be taking another look at some of Czarnowski's ideas. The latter position is illustrated by Hieronim Kubiak of the UJ, who stresses the urban environment as a cause of declines in religiosity, and also by Jan Jerschina, also of UJ, who attempts the statistical measurement of the de-alienation of consciousness.

The approach here is one which tends to conserve much of the flavour of the pre-war sociologists. Popular and peasant religiosity are pushed into the foreground as characteristics of Polish Catholicism and condemned for their archaism, nonintellectualism, inconsistency and, most importantly, for their 'lack of future'. Against this is juxtaposed a model of perfect secular society and perfect secular man. We will examine parts of the work of each of the abovementioned sociologists with the aim of illustrating the way in which the official communist orthodoxy reaches even ostensibly academic studies.

Edward Ciupak is one of the best-known of the Polish sociologists of religion today. As well as holding a position in the sociology department of UW, he has been involved in research and teaching at the department of religiology of the WSNS: an indication, perhaps, of his own loyalty to, or at least congruence with, the party line on religion. Ciupak has also participated in le Bras's seminar in Paris.

The beginning of Ciupak's career as a sociologist of religion coincided with the reappearance after the end of Stalinism of the sociology of religion as a recognized academic discipline; previously the sociology of religion had been banned. It is likely that the ban was necessitated by the communist authorities' lack of an adequate formula for the transformation of secularist theory into clear and precise recommendations for empirical sociological investigations; at the same time, it is unlikely that a regime applying repressive measures to religion would be likely to look kindly on studies of the phenomenon it is out to destroy. In 1959 and 1960 a series of articles by Ciupak appeared in 'Euhemer': they were on the subject of the rural parish. Ciupak continues to publish articles and papers in both the learned and the more popular periodicals of the secular front. In terms of sheer volume(1) his published work exceeds that of any other contemporary Polish sociologist of religion. However, the large volume of work is in no sense paralleled by a high sociological value of the contributions: Ciupak suffers from an affliction common amongst writers under communist regimes - longwindedness and repetition (of himself and of others) - the results of being paid according to volume written.

Ciupak's work consists mainly of sociological studies. About the theory underlying his approach Ciupak writes:(2)

> I accept the general methodological assumptions of Stefan Czarnowski which state that religion is a component of social culture; on this basis and using empirical material I attempt to verify some of the early hypotheses of the Polish sociologists of religion. In some cases I apply my own approach.

Ciupak's final product, however, is rather difficult to define on account of multiple imprecisions, inconsistencies (even contradictions) and a liberal eclecticism. For example, quite conspicuous is Ciupak's indiscriminate use of the notions of Catholicism, mass religiosity, political influence and temporal power of the clergy, and the Church authorities as though they were all synonymous or in some way equivalent. This appears to be a widespread failing and has already been noted in Jaroszewski's writings in chapter 3. The overall impression of Ciupak's work is that of a very muddled approach where the only constant and consistent feature is his dislike of religion. The overarching argument, if such there is, suggests the functionality of religion in the primitive rural-agricultural community and its dysfunctionality in the modern socialist urban-industrial community-society.(3) In this sense Ciupak might have been writing between the two wars: he falls squarely into the early tradition of the sociology of religion. Piwowarski, commenting about Ciupak's general approach, politely concludes that his work does not live up to its declared intentions.(4) Finally, it is significant that Ciupak draws attention to the 'early hypotheses of the Polish sociologists of religion': as we have shown, these early hypotheses are far more compatible with Marxist-Leninist secularism than some of the more recent developments in the sociology of religion.

Ciupak's reliance on secondary sources seems somewhat excessive, especially since it is not always made adequately clear whether the interpretations are Ciupak's own or those of the

founding fathers - Krzywicki, Bystroń and Czarnowski.(5)
Features characteristic of Ciupak's approach include his particular interest in the religiosity of rural areas (although he has
also conducted limited investigations of the religiosity of the
urban milieu), his extensive use of the method of participant
observation in the gathering of data and, lastly, his intention
of arriving at a complete explanation of all religious phenomena
in terms of non-religious causes. For our present purposes we
shall take Ciupak's work on popular Catholicism(6) as the most
comprehensive statement of his views although, where necessary,
reference will be made to his other contributions.

It will not be our intention to deal exhaustively with Ciupak's
work: within the available space such an undertaking would be
neither possible nor desirable. Rather, we will concern ourselves with only those principles which bear directly on the question of secularization. We shall therefore limit ourselves to the
non-empirical side of Ciupak's work, namely, the questions
surrounding his notion of 'popular religiosity' which forms the
theoretical starting point for most of his investigations.

The great unfulfilled promise of Ciupak's work is to be found
in the way in which he, following Czarnowski's example, expresses his intention to distinguish between the institutionally defined
model of religiosity and its observable pattern. This observable
pattern is what Czarnowski referred to, in the rural context,
as the religious culture. Restating the case, Ciupak refers to the
pattern as popular religiosity (religijność ludowa). It seems for
one moment that Ciupak is to use Czarnowski as a guide to an
investigation of the rural community: 'The Catholicism of this
community appears more as a "peasant" religion than as the
"Roman" one.'(7) This starting point might have proved most
fertile in so far as, on the one hand, it points to the investigation of a possible relationship between type of milieu and type of
religiosity: such a starting point would stand in direct contrast
to one which is concerned with the relationship between type of
milieu and intensity of religiosity. Work of the latter type is
widespread in both Poland and in Western sociology of religion
and is particularly associated with the sociologie religieuse type
of approach which often centres on the 'instant secularization
thesis'. On the other hand, it might have been possible to form
the basis for the development of quite an original view of Polish
religiology as consisting of a combination of types of religiosity
which together contribute to the specificity of national Polish
religious culture and perhaps even of theological culture. Polish
religiosity might therefore have been presented as a heterogen-
ous composite religiosity where the sub-units exist in a state of
greater or lesser symbiosis with one another.(8)

A key problem of the approach in terms of popular religiosity
is concerned with the nature of the institutionally defined model
- the point of reference and comparison for religious culture.
Is it, for example, an entity which exists as a tangible reality
in its pure form or is it merely the sum total of all the various

regional and national popular religiosities as well as of all the
theological cultures? Or does it consist of the fundamental elements of doctrine and dogma and can it thus be identified with
the idea of Universal Catholicism? A glance at any version of
popular Catholicism is sufficient in order to see that a key position within it is occupied by the institutionally defined model;
also, it is impossible to identify the institutionally defined model
anywhere without finding it in some way, often quite powerfully,
'popularized' or under pressure from some sort of specific
conditions. Most importantly, the definition of the reference
point itself affects the account of popular religiosity which finally
emerges. Because Ciupak does not make his position absolutely
clear on these points, his treatment of the issue is questionable:
firstly, it is clear that he assumes the existence of institutionally
defined religion as a separate and independent entity in the form
of the Universal Church. This Universal Church, it would appear,
consists of priests, bishops, buildings, bibles and a pope - a
clear confusion with the idea of the Church as an institution. It
does not occur to Ciupak to consider whether aspects of the so-
defined Universal Church are not themselves manifestations of
religious culture or, in other words, whether it does not contain
certain elements shaped by pressure of circumstances and
environment. Secondly, Ciupak assumes that the popular Catholicism is more 'real' than the institutionally defined model.
Thirdly, he considers popular Catholicism to be in a very real
way somehow 'independent' of the point of reference. Finally,
Ciupak is quick to grasp the opportunity of defining a Universal
Church where faith and mission are absent. Not sociological,
he would say.

Ciupak's assumptions are, of course, an aspect of the creep-
ing political realism which is found throughout his work: even at
the level of sociological theory the institutional Church must be
separated from its congregation which, in so far as it is a
'mass', is more 'real' than the formal and empty structure of
clergy, episcopate, churches and bibles; the now socially isolated
institution can then be seen to be on the decline.

The next important stage is to establish the relationship between
popular Catholicism and milieu. Before we do this, however, let
us take a brief look at what are possibly Ciupak's major weaknesses. Firstly, there is his attempt at the fusion of a Durkheimian perspective with a Marxist one: the result is an uneasy
coexistence of the two. Czarnowski, let us recall, was happy to
use both Marx and Durkheim but, unlike Ciupak, his clarity of
intention and method is visible throughout. To Czarnowski,
religious culture was the visible manifestation of the collective
conscience as well as being evidence of the way in which society
shapes religion. The lack of a careful synthesis of the two by
Ciupak gives rise to a 'bittiness' of method and to the inconsistencies and even irrelevancies of conclusions. This weakness
is further compounded by the type of Marxism which Ciupak
uses: the political realist version which is based on the alienation

thesis of religion, on the assumption that religious knowledge
is meaningless knowledge and, lastly, on a unilaterist version
of history which incorporates the 'secular movement'. In contrast, Czarnowski's synthesis is rather neat. It consists of
treating a concept of 'class interest' (Czarnowski goes no further) and the notion of religious culture or religiosity as two
variables which could be correlated within a Durkheimian framework. As a particularly vivid example of such a correlation,
Czarnowski took the case of the Polish gentry and showed how
their class position expressed itself through their religiosity.(9)
Such a correlation is, of course, a particular case of the more
general idea derived from Durkheim that society (or aspects of
it) shapes religion to form religious culture. Durkheim thus
formed the more basic framework of analysis in the case of
Czarnowski.

Ciupak's second weakness is concerned with his sociologism.(10)
While the Durkheimian petitio principii can in principle work in
either direction – either reducing religious phenomena to society
or explaining society in terms of a religious 'core' – Ciupak
unambiguously assumes that Catholicism has a 'cause' which can
be traced back to its functions in social life, to man's psychological needs and to physical conditions. Ciupak spares very
little effort in his attempt at a complete reduction of religion and,
in doing so, discards any suggestion that religious knowledge
is knowledge worthy of comment. Ciupak's sociologism arises,
firstly, out of his identification of Catholicism as a belief system
with its popular manifestations as religious culture and, secondly,
out of his application of the legitimate explanation of popular
Catholicism to Catholicism as a belief system. This procedure
is made easier by Ciupak's caveat that it is popular Catholicism
which is 'real'. Józef Majka states that Ciupak's sociologism is
tantamount to an attempt at explaining the activity of fishermen
without taking into account the existence of fish.(11) Perhaps
Ciupak would regard fish as an unnecessary complication?

The third weakness arises out of the above two combined: it
lies in the lack of a systematic operationalization by Ciupak of
his basic categories. This weakness is responsible for the work's
appearance as a haphazard collection of data with little or no
obvious connection between them except their reference to something which vaguely falls under the general heading of Catholic
or traditional.

Let us now turn to a more detailed examination of Ciupak's
work. Although Ciupak does not claim a particular interest in the
question of secularization, it is nevertheless clear that the concept must be treated as central to his work. Writing about the
methodology of sociologists such as himself, Ciupak states:(12)

> They utilize the technique of comparative models in the
> analysis of empirical material; the pattern of traditional
> Catholicism is juxtaposed against the objectively developing
> pattern of secular culture which, in the future, will become

an integral component of the social culture of the nation.

This is indeed what characterizes Ciupak's method. In choosing such methodology Ciupak abandons the incorporation into his approach of what is perhaps Czarnowski's most basic insight: that there is a level at which society is capable of transforming and fashioning religion for its own purposes and according to its own image and likeness.(13) Despite the development of this insight from the thesis that man creates religion, the similarity with Marx is quite superficial: the Marxist thesis, on the one hand, is designed to cover the whole of the religious phenomenon while, on the other hand, Czarnowski was only concerned with the establishment of a relationship between Catholicism and the society in which it is found (this relationship is the key to religious culture); in Czarnowski's case, there is no attempt at a total reduction of Catholicism, but only of certain forms of Catholic expression. Ciupak has retained the idea of religious culture, calling it popular religiosity, and suddenly forgotten about the institutionally defined model of religion. At this point, a sort of substitution of concepts occurs whereby popular Catholicism gradually takes on, in Ciupak's analysis, the role of the religion of the masses. This religion of the masses is then totally reduced to things social. For the sake of clarity, the essentials of Czarnowski's original analysis are presented in diagrammatic form in Table 5.1.

TABLE 5.1 Religious change according to Czarnowski

Patterns	Original state	New state
'Official religion'	Institutionally defined model	Institutionally defined model
Observable pattern of religiosity	Religious culture	Private religiosity
	——————Religious change ——→	
Milieu	Rural-agricultural community; old way of life	New modernized way of life; impact of change; urban-industrial culture?
	———— Social change ————→	

Ciupak's modifications have the effect of obscuring any differences which may occur in the observable pattern of religiosity between different milieux: Ciupak treats both religious culture and private religiosity as the same observable pattern. Next, Ciupak throws in the concept of 'secular culture', as defined by the party, as the end-product of the transformation of popular religiosity. 'Knowing' the future end product means that Ciupak can use it as a comparative measure of the progress (or, perhaps,

regress in this case) of popular Catholicism into the future.
The institutionally defined model is not completely banished,
however, for it remains as another point of comparison for popular Catholicism. A characteristic of Ciupak's methodology at
this point is his oscillation between Church-oriented and 'secular culture-oriented' sociology of religion.(14) The analogous
diagrammatic presentation of Ciupak's modification of Czarnowski
is found in Table 5.2.

TABLE 5.2 Religious change according to Ciupak

Patterns	Original state	New state
'Official religion'	Institutionally defined model	Non-existent (outside the schema?)
	———Disappearance? ——→	
Observable pattern of religiosity (components of social culture)	Popular religiosity; Catholicism of the 'masses'	Secular culture
	——— Gives way to ——→	
Milieu	Rural-agricultural community; urban-industrial capitalism	Rural-agricultural and urban-industrial communism or socialism
	———Revolutionary social change ——→	

Using this scheme, Ciupak attempts to suggest a mechanism
for the rapid decline of popular Catholicism. In this scheme choice
plays an important, if not central, part. The peasant, argues
Ciupak, is able to see the benefits of socialism for himself. He
therefore accepts it as a matter of course for two main reasons:
firstly, because it eliminates class differences, themselves sup-
portive of the Church and, secondly, because the peasant rea-
lizes that 'socialism provides him with a more rational system of
values which he can then use to structure his *Weltanschauung*,
ethical system and morals as well as providing him with a more
attractive life-style'.(15) This sort of view is a typical religious
policy line which can be expressed without any knowledge of the
peasant or of his religiosity. Some comment is therefore appropriate. Firstly, the peasants in Poland have very good reasons
for not supporting socialism: (1) the constant threat of collecti-
vization which was once tried and is abhorred; (2) socialism
attacks the Catholic faith. Secondly, the comments regarding
the more rational system are, without putting too fine a point
to it, mumbo-jumbo. As will be shown in chapter 7, the nearest
the Polish secularists have come to a rational morality is when
Jaroszewski embraced the Decalogue. It is characteristic that
such statements as the one by Ciupak above are never developed
further unless in a context of violent and uncompromising reli-

gious abuse - clearly something Ciupak wishes to avoid. Finally, the more attractive life-style of socialism must surely be taken to mean that the state favours the non-believer and atheist and most certainly makes life difficult for believers. Although Ciupak's orientation suggests that the changes in religiosity lead to secular culture he does, at one point, mention the development of religious indifferentism amongst young people as a result of increasing levels of education. The observation may be correct to some extent although the explanation is probably inadequate. However, it is interesting that because it falls outside his scheme, Ciupak does not develop the question of indifferentism despite its prominence as an element of the secularization of religious belief in Poland.

In developing the idea that secular culture displaces popular Catholicism, Ciupak identifies planned secularization and religious policy, in addition to urbanization and rising levels of education, as important factors in the formation of the secular culture.(16) An interesting analogy to the institutionally defined religion would be a secularism defined in terms of party ideology which could be used as yet another point of comparison in tracing the development of the secular culture. However, no such studies have been attempted, either by Ciupak or anybody else, because of the suppression of all evidence which might suggest that institutionally defined secularism is not percolating down to the populace or that the percolated product does not resemble the original one.

One of the practical difficulties that Ciupak inevitably finds himself in is the inability to produce an adequate definition or specification of the subject-matter. Instead of taking popular Catholicism or even simply Catholicism as his starting point, Ciupak explicitly expresses his desire to deal with the sociology of the 'local community' which, he implies, is the embodiment of Polish popular Catholicism.(17) The local community, he suggests, may be either a village or 'a small town or diffuse community held together by a bond of solidarity and by the pattern of popular Catholicism'; a key characteristic of the local community is the traditionally established authority of the Church within it.(18) Ciupak as good as identifies popular Catholicism with the notion of local community. Treating the subject in this way, Ciupak makes clear that he does not even want to discuss the concept of popular Catholicism itself. Ciupak's approach has got the enormous advantage, from the secularist viewpoint, of producing instant secularization once the local community dissolves or is destroyed.

The prominence of the local community in Ciupak's definition of popular Catholicism is also a reflection of his rejection, albeit implicit, of Czarnowski's methodology. In fact, Ciupak sets out on a train of thought quite different from that which a careful examination of Czarnowski's categories would suggest. Czarnowski was himself quite clear as to the meaning of religious culture: it arises out of the way in which society shapes religion.(19) It

is not, as Ciupak attempts to show, to be observed in the functions or dysfunctions of Catholicism at the local (or at any other)
level or, for that matter, in its use or adaptation to the social
environment in order to survive. We do not wish to deny that
Catholicism has its functions or that it can be misused: but these
are not aspects of the religious culture in the above sense (or
even perhaps in any other sense) - they have nothing to do
with the way in which society impinges upon Catholicism; functions reflect, if anything at all, the way in which religion impinges on society. Furthermore, Catholicism does not 'adapt' to
society, least of all in Ciupak's sense of the word (in terms of a
Darwinian metaphor of a fight for survival); Catholicism may
have undergone various changes in the course of history but
these changes are no more adaptations by religion than is the
changing architectural design of buildings over the ages an
adaptation by buildings. All changes which have occurred must
be seen as the result of decisions taken by members of the
Catholic community and the Church authorities. Ironically, the
truth of this statement should be particularly clear to one who
holds that it is man who is the creator of all religion.

In order to understand why Polish Marxist-Leninist orthodoxy
accepts the idea that religion 'adapts' it is important to realize
the identity of the notion of religion as alienation with the
anthropomorphization of religion. The political rationale is simply
this: an anthropomorphized Catholicism is bound to be a more
effective propaganda weapon than the concept of alienation. In
this way the myth of the sentient dragon was created and presented to the public. This myth runs as follows. Long, long ago,
when society became evil, evil men created religion and used it
for their own purposes and against their fellow men. Once
created, it came alive and has come to be called Dragon Alienation. Dragon Alienation soon learned how to become indispensable
both to the evil men who created him and to those against whom
he was used. Dragon Alienation is a cunning and evil dragon
capable of enslaving the righteous and the hopeless often with
the help of the diabolic powers of the 'lands beyond'. However,
the Hero-party will lead the way to driving this horror back to
its lair, inside the walls of the Church, where it will surely
perish. Before this happens, Chosen Ones, remain awake and
watch, for Dragon Alienation never sleeps.

The dragon, if he is to be feared, cannot be presented as passive and unthinking. Nor can he be allowed to approach too close
for fear of his true nature becoming apparent. Even in sociology,
therefore, he must be kept on the margin of investigations,
pushed to the edge of the page. It is only his evil deeds which
must be stressed and the imagination of the audience exploited.

Ciupak's strong stress of the dysfunctions and misuses of
Catholicism is in keeping with the myth. Ciupak also notes the
deviousness with which Catholicism attempts the futile task of
adapting itself to changing conditions. At the same time the idea
that alien elements are ingested into it so as to produce the very

'stuff' of religious culture is ignored completely.

The ingestion of alien elements into 'official Catholicism' is, of course, also an entry into and fusion with the established meanings of Catholicism. It can also be the creation of new meanings and concepts. Since Ciupak rejects the view that Catholicism can be a system of meaning and knowledge (he limits himself to considering Catholicism as a system of 'patterns and values'(20)), he finds himself obliged to place the meaning of these elements back in the sphere of the social and then to impose a functional interpretation on them. Religious meaning is explained in terms of social function – meaning becomes 'form' and function becomes 'content'.

One or two examples may be in order at this point. Perhaps the best-known case of the ingestion of an external element into the national level of Catholicism in Poland is that of Polish national feeling or Polishness (polskość). This phenomenon has already been referred to. The result of this process is that Polishness has become popularly identified with Catholicism.

Introducing this subject, Ciupak refers to the necessity of studying the 'social product of religion'(21) and points to the 'penetration of matters of nationality by the Church'.(22) Ciupak argues that because there is no 'objective' identity between Catholicism and Polishness – Catholicism is, after all, universal – any identity must exist in the mind alone. This enables him to argue further that the identity exists only because it was successfully propagated by the Church at specific times and under specific circumstances when the need for it coincided with the interests of prominent social groups (e.g. the gentry). It is thus that the Church penetrated matters of nationality.

At the same time, Ciupak deplores the dysfunctionality of the Polish-Catholic equation, arguing that it was in fact a non-integrating and cleaving force within the society.(23) He also deplores the fact that the identity still exists today – a brave admission by Ciupak – and that it is so strong in places that 'it hinders the development of both secular culture and the formation of the socialist personality'.(24) Worse still, it 'infiltrates the educational system, the family, the neighbourhood and the local community'.(25) At least Ciupak lets us know where he stands.

In terms of the survival of a nation subjected to secularist pressure and Sovietization it would appear that the reverse is true: the Polish-Catholic identity has a powerful defence function. It enables the successful protection of Polish traditions and cultural values. But these points do not concern us here. In paying too much attention to functionalism and dysfunctionalism as an aid to understanding, Ciupak seems to have forgotten that while the Church was penetrating Poland with its Christianity it was itself being penetrated by the converts: the primitive Slavs of the region entered the Church with all the cultural goods of their paganism – some of the original marks of Polishness. The same process is still going on today albeit in a changed form.

It is according to such a principle that Catholicism can be understood to have become Polish (at the same time as Poland became Catholic); this point was noted by Czarnowski. Even more important, and less related to any particular historical event, is the notion of the Polish nation as a community of believers: Ciupak does not stop to consider this point. Broadly speaking, the idea is that Christianity also 'converted' the Slavic tribes into a community of believers which later became the nation: it is as though the idea of the Polish nation grew up within the Church and was fed (and still is fed) by the full complement of events and circumstances - geographical, historical, cultural, political, etc. The protection of the community of believers in Poland today is the prime concern of the Church: this would mean that the Catholic Church is both the creator and the guardian of Polish nationhood. The identification of 'Polish' with 'Catholic' acquires significance only through an understanding of the creation of concepts and not through a sort of a Catholic 'imperialism'. Otherwise it becomes impossible to understand why Catholicism is the soul of the Polish nation and the Church is the mother of the nation.

Ciupak has his own explanations of the national consciousness. He attributes it to the development of universal democracy and culture under socialism and suggests that there had been no democracy or culture in Poland before 1945.(26) Culture and democracy in Poland have never been as repressed and stifled as they are under communist totalitarianism and, Ciupak seems reluctant to mention, some of the earliest developments in European democracy took place on Polish soil. Surprising though it may seem, the sum total of Ciupak's arguments would imply that nationality consists of no more than living within designated frontiers.

Another form of ingestion of outside elements into Catholicism occurs at local or village level. Here the cults of patron saints and local madonnas appear in religious 'subcultures'. These figures, we know from Czarnowski, tend to be intimately associated with the problems, sorrows and joys of the locality. It is the members of these local communities who bring their lives and experiences into Catholicism through the agency of the saints and madonnas: in this way the local religious subculture develops and acquires form. This promising area too has been avoided by Ciupak.

Our aim in this chapter is to describe only the way in which official Marxist-Leninist orthodoxy has become expressed through the medium of sociological work. As a result it has not been possible to even begin to describe Ciupak's field investigations. Many of his observations are notable for their grasp of detail and nuance but, as we have shown, the conclusions must suffer on account of the methodology. We thus find Ciupak's conclusions burdened with a litany of polite abuse of popular Catholicism, which is seen as uncivilized(27) and as a barrier to civilization.(28) It is obscure, fanatical and intolerant, he suggests,

but under the influence of urbanism it will become tolerant and
enlightened.(29) Presumably, it will be most tolerant and enlightened when no longer there. It must not be forgotten that Ciupak's criteria of enlightenment, civilization, obscurity, fanaticism
and intolerance are those of the party creed: in this light the
abuse must reflect his perception of the immense strength of
Catholicism in rural areas. Ciupak is also ready to provide
historical reasons for the strength of Catholicism in Poland generally: the retardation of processes of secularization by the
'clericalization of pre-war public opinion', the previous low
academic status of atheism (the absence of formal organizations
combined with the low intellectual level of atheists en masse) and,
lastly, Stalinism. According to Ciupak, Stalin's 'excesses' have
been responsible for the Church's continuing position of dominance in rural areas(30) - not only a startling admission that
even almost forty years after the proletarian revolution the opium
theory may still apply but also an attempt to link the strength
of Polish Catholicism with the only officially admitted public
misery.

Ciupak's contribution to the understanding of secularization
may be summarized by placing him in the tradition of the definition of archaic man on the one hand and, on the other, within
the bounds of the official religiological orthodoxy which hails
the approach of the age of secularism. Particularly characteristic
of Ciupak is that, in seeking a functional explanation of religious culture, he has to present a secular version of the concept
of the nation: it is not difficult to see why this can be an introduction to the idea that Catholicism and the Church are both
enemies of the nation.

Hieronim Kubiak's study of religiosity(31) shares some common
ground with Ciupak's work, but also differs from it in some
fundamental respects. This study is Kubiak's only major contribution to the subject of secularization: he has since turned his
attention to the sociology of Poles abroad (in particular, in the
United States).

Kubiak differs from Ciupak in so far as he is particularly
concerned with the 'instant secularization thesis' which tends to
identify mass religiosity as the key to the sociological understanding of religion in society. The instant secularization thesis
is usually concerned with a correlation of a decrease in the intensity of religiosity with either a rapid rural to urban (or agricultural to industrial) transformation or a rural to urban migration. The decline of religion is then commonly identified with this
decrease in religiosity. In this respect, Kubiak falls squarely
into the category of sociologie religieuse, of the atheistic variety.
His similarity with Ciupak lies in his political realism although
he is far more stark than Ciupak. He writes:(32)

Growing religious indifference is one of the basic signs of
man's liberation from all forms of alienation, including economic and political. It is a result of the gradual development of

man's self-knowledge and of his feeling of control over his
own life and over that of the community; it also results from
his awareness of both individual goals and of the social conditions necessary for their achievement.

This, however, is a statement of belief rather than a conclusion
to an empirical investigation which it purports to be. In the case
of the instant secularization thesis, such political realist interpretations or assumptions do not greatly affect the methodology
of research. This simply means that work of this type should
be assessed in terms of its design and 'mechanics'. From our
point of view, however, a few additional words about the concept of religiosity are necessary at this stage.

Religiosity is one of the many faces of Catholicism and, it is
fair to suppose, of Christianity in general as well as of the
other religions. It has two characteristics which seem to be of
particular appeal to the sociologists: firstly, it can be quantified
and subjected to ever increasing precision of measurement - precision which often goes beyond the limits of meaningfulness;
secondly, it deals with religion in terms of a mass phenomenon
and hence that extraordinarily significant unit, 'the ordinary
man';(33) the latter characteristic may be either an advantage
or a disadvantage depending on one's point of view. The problem
of both of these characteristics is that the all too easy inferences
regarding the decline of religion as a whole which are commonly
drawn often prove illegitimate on close inspection. The basic
principles of data gathering are straightforward: they consist
of either direct questions or observations on the variations of
two basic themes; these themes can be summarized by the questions: 'Are you Catholic?' and 'Do you do Catholic things?'. The
conclusions arrived at in the domain of religiosity cannot be
directly applied to Catholicism in general without a prior understanding of the interrelationship between religiosity and the rest
of Catholicism. It may be, for example, that the perception of
low levels of religiosity amongst the rank and file will release
missionary forces from the centre of the Catholic establishment
or from elsewhere. (Of course, under certain circumstances it
may be legitimate to ask whether such forces are being inter-
cepted by the political authorities.) Alternatively, demoralization
may set in and so dampen missionary ardour. Another completely
different possibility is that religious exhibitionism may be getting
less popular.

Despite the obvious need for caution, investigations of religiosity have gained world-wide popularity over recent years.
An important reason for this is that such investigations appear
to present an easy and precise answer to the question of secularization: that religion has lost its mass appeal, at least this is
how all the investigations would seem to average out. It must
be noted, however, that not all research on religiosity substantiates this thesis: later we will be looking at some work which
stands in contradiction to it.(34)

Kubiak's investigation is concerned with a comparison of the
religiosity of the workers (almost all manual) of the Lenin Steel
Works of Nowa Huta with that of their peasant families living in
the surrounding Nowy Targ district with whom the workers
spent their childhood and youth. The choice of Nowa Huta is not
without significance. Nowa Huta (New Foundry) is a completely
new town whose construction began in the 1950s. Today it is a
huge urban-industrial complex covering 76 km.² with a population of over 200,000 inhabitant-workers.(35) Nowa Huta was
planned to become the first 'true socialist workers' town': its
name and that of its steel works were chosen carefully. What was
perhaps most significant is that it was planned as an atheist
town and, as such, was to have no church. It was hoped that
its atheism and socialism would soon infect nearby Kraków - that
splendid city and extraordinary stronghold of the cultural intelligentsia where Catholicism, traditionalism and good manners
are the order of the day.(36) Nowa Huta is thus not a typical
example of industrialization, urbanization and secularism: it is
probably the most extreme example in almost every way including
the religiosity of the district from which the workers were
drawn: the Nowy Targ district is known for the devoutness of
its population. We might, therefore, expect Kubiak's study to
show a rather extreme and vivid picture of instant secularization.
    Such details concerning the history and intended function of
Nowa Huta are very important considerations in the understanding of religious change in the area and it was a very serious
omission by Kubiak not to even mention them. It was doubtless
Kubiak's intention to convey the idea that Nowa Huta was just a
typical example of industrialization and secularization: this was
made possible by not stepping outside the area of measuring
levels of religiosity.
    Since Kubiak's time, Nowa Huta managed to acquire the famous
Church of Our Lady of Poland (even the army participated by
using a helicopter to aid the positioning of the steeple)(37) and
Kraków has produced a Pope. More still. It was Pope John Paul
II who, as Cardinal Wojtyła, played a leading part in the battles
for the building of the church.
    In examining Kubiak's study, we shall argue that owing to
weaknesses of data and design his conclusions regarding the
instant secularization thesis for Nowa Huta are for the most part
invalid. If the sociological evidence for the instant secularization
thesis is suspect for Nowa Huta, where the trend should be
clearest, it is unlikely that the thesis will be easily confirmed
elsewhere.
    It is Kubiak's intention to examine the following hypothesis:(38)

    That, under the influence of civilizing processes (industrial-
    ization, urbanization, the transport revolution, mass con-
    sumption, the disappearance of the old social and cultural bar-
    riers, horizontal and social mobility, the spread of new ideo-
    logies and value systems, etc.) the gradual changes in reli-

gious consciousness - in the form and frequency of religious practice - lead to an individualization of religious experience and to the diminishing significance of religious communities and of the integrating functions of religion.

Curiously, it could be argued that at least some of the features which Kubiak mentions as leading to secularization of beliefs and practices may well have the very opposite effects. In particular, the spreading of official ideology in Poland has undoubtedly contributed to a desecularization of beliefs as a result of the ideology's aggressive demand for total commitment: Catholic belief has proved to be a very successful form of defence against the encroachment into the innermost recesses of being.

With problems such as this and others connected with the operationalization of the full gamut of the abovementioned features it is perhaps not surprising that Kubiak does not concern himself with the hypothesis as it stands. He simply produces a range of indices with which to measure levels of religiosity in the Nowy Targ region and in Nowa Huta.

In his attempt at the measurement of religiosity, Kubiak draws attention to subjective and objective elements. The subjective element can be observed and measured by the indicators of religious self-identification, an assessment and evaluation of changes in religiosity, convictions concerning the importance of religious norms in individual and collective life and, finally, convictions concerning the role of religious institutions and of the clergy.(39) The objective element can be measured by religious practices: the rites of passage, obligatory practices and, finally, non-obligatory practices.(40) Kubiak is primarily interested in correlating the above with social milieu (urban-industrial and rural-agricultural) although he believes demographic (age, sex) and socio-cultural (education, etc.) factors play a secondary role.(41) The data were gathered using in-depth interviewing technique in 1970.(42)

Again, as in Ciupak's case, it is impossible to give a comprehensive picture of even this one investigation. We shall therefore simply make one or two comments on some of the problems.

The ratio of men to women in Kubiak's sample is about 80:20 as compared to about 50:50 in the rural sample.(43) This difference, in its most extreme interpretation (all women believers, no men believers) would be sufficient to account for the rural believers exceeding the urban believers by a factor of 2.5 (50 per cent of the rural population believers, 20 per cent of the urban); although Kubiak admits that differences between the sexes may 'distort' the data,(44) nowhere does he give any details of religiosity differentials between the sexes. It is likely that sex together with age may account for a significant part of the difference in religiosity between the two samples: 43.5 per cent of those from the rural district are over 60 (a large part of whom are the urban workers' parents) whereas in Nowa Huta there are none over 60.(45) However, Kubiak makes no attempt

to allow for such distortions although it seems that he had all
the data necessary to make such allowances.
What differences does Kubiak find between the two milieux?
Not surprisingly, each of the indicators shows a lower value for
the level of religiosity in the urban milieu: Kubiak sees his
hypothesis as verified and suggests that the final product of
the religious change (which he identifies with the difference in
the values) will be religious indifference which, he stresses,
is not the same as atheism. Before the final stage is reached,
religiosity goes through an intermediate stage of decreasing
significance and relevance to life, both socially and individually:
this is the present stage of Nowa Huta.
Kubiak's view of the civilizing processes mentioned above is
based on characteristic features of urban existence which he
notes as follows: high educational levels, large numbers of radio
and television receivers, high frequencies of cinema and theatre
visits, high levels of readership of books and the popular press,
comparatively high membership of communist party bodies. All
these features are pipelines of ideological orthodoxy – a fact
which would suggest that, even if they had little effect on the
formation of opinion, they certainly make known those opinions
which the party presents as desirable. Indeed, some of the
answers received by Kubiak are remarkably consistent with the
party line both in content and in formulation:(46) 'The Church
should not meddle in the affairs of the state', all Church services
should be 'free of charge', children should not be taught religion
in school but in places suitable for that purpose, 'the Church
should permit the use of contraceptives', 'the Church should
allow abortion'.(47) Of course, such answers may be a true
reflection of the interviewees' opinions but it is just as likely
that they are not, perhaps even more likely.
In connection with this point, it is worth drawing attention to
one particularly important point not always fully appreciated,
namely, that the rational and intellectually honest answer often
attributed to the educated town-dweller of Western Europe (even
here there is some doubt) when responding to questionnaires
need not apply to rural or recently urbanized peasants in Poland
who, moreover, are aware of the party's all-pervading secularist intentions. It is also a well-known fact that the Polish
peasant is very suspicious of communist authority and therefore
responds 'politely' to any probes which may have a conceivable
connection with that authority: clearly, Kubiak gave the game
away by asking such politically charged questions. Although it
is easy to read too much into such reservations, they nevertheless certainly require more consideration in some circumstances
than in others. Some of Kubiak's data have been summarized
in Table 5.3.(48)
A very important shortcoming of Kubiak's investigation is his
failure to take into account the inevitable disorganization and
disintegration which occurs on a massive scale during the process
of establishing an urban-industrial giant such as Nowa Huta and

TABLE 5.3 Extract from Kubiak's data

Elements	Rural district (per cent)	Nowa Huta (per cent)
Deeply believing and practising (self-identification)	39.0	7.0
Believing and practising (self-identification)	55.0	31.7
Systematic prayer	71.0	23.0
Mass attendance: some weekdays, all Sundays	25.0	2.0
Mass attendance: Sundays and Holy Days of Obligation only	57.0	31.5
View that Christmas is traditional (as opposed to religious) in meaning	1.5	28.0
View that a believing man is a morally sound (decent) man	36.0	17.0
View that children should be given religious instruction	97.5	75.5
View that spouse or children should believe	91.0	40.5
View that neighbours should be believers	57.0	12.5
View that pre-marital sexual relations should be subject to religious norms	76.0	44.0
View that marital sexual relations should be subject to religious norms	67.0	24.0
View that the Church should not permit abortion	58.0	12.5
View that sermon should be limited to religious matters alone	75.0	66.5
View that private property in industry should be abolished	77.5	91.5
View that the above is in accordance with Church principles	37.0	49.5
View that the Church's attitude to the state should change	5.0	17.5

also during the migrations themselves.(49) The sorts of factors which would need to be considered and correlated here are as follows: the disruption of previous life routines and the establishment of new ones, the period of residence in Nowa Huta, the availability of pastoral 'services' and places of worship. These factors alone are suffient to explain changes and differences of outlook and behaviour, even the most extreme ones. In the case of Nowa Huta, the change from rural to urban was especially violent. Kubiak, however, argues the reverse implying that the transformation from deep religiosity to the lowest point on the

continuum is gradual. (50) He argues as though he had taken
two points on a graph and extrapolated as shown in Figure 5.1.

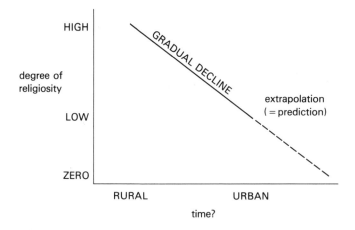

FIGURE 5.1 Kubiak's view of the decline in religiosity

While this graph appears both neat and conclusive, it is, in
fact, neither. The horizontal axis is a composite axis consisting
of at least two variables: firstly, a gradual rural to urban
transformation suggesting degrees of urbanization; this representation is far removed from the rural-urban comparison which
Kubiak presents. A problem is thus encountered in deciding
on the nature of a point mid-way along this axis - a seat in a
train, perhaps. Secondly, a time-scale is superimposed on the
rural-urban migration and then extrapolated; this superimposition is entirely illegitimate although it makes some sort of sense
in terms of orthodox Marxism-Leninism: Kubiak is, in reality,
dealing with two distinct graphs - one of rural religiosity and
one of urban religiosity - with only one point on each. The
migration must be understood as a movement from one of the
graphs to the other: in practice, however, it is probably much
more - the new urban arrivals cannot avoid affecting the already
established urban religiosity as the departure of less devout
Catholics from rural areas cannot avoid raising the levels of
rural religiosity especially if the migrations are massive enough.
We refer here to Figure 5.2.

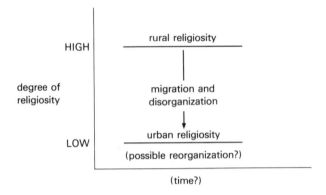

FIGURE 5.2 Schematic representation of the rural to urban migration

It is clear from this modified graph that there must be more information regarding the level of urban religiosity especially if the disorganization-reorganization thesis is to be examined or verified.(51) A closely related question is whether the above-mentioned further influx of peasants into Nowa Huta will eventually raise the level of urban religiosity now that the town is established even assuming that there is no return to higher levels of religiosity by the previously 'secularized' section of the society. In addition, it would be interesting to know whether there occurs any process of selection amongst prospective migrants whereby those of lower levels of religiosity tend to be attracted by the city lights. Even a very slight selection would produce a very large difference in the values of Kubiak's indices.

In contrast to Kubiak's stress of the correlation between secularization and urbanization, Jan Jerschina's study attempts to measure de-alienation in the attitudes of youth. His study consists of an analysis of the selected results of five investigations concerned with the religious attitudes of schoolchildren, students and young workers;(52) it is strongly oriented towards party Marxism-Leninism and has the approval of Jaroszewski and Kubiak as well as owing a large debt to the sociology of Ciupak and Kubiak and to the religiology of Grudzień, Nowicki, Poniatowski and Jaroszewski.(53)

Jerschina's study is in its design and mechanics somewhat similar to Kubiak's: Jerschina even regards it as a further development.(54) Also, the part played by the data is of secondary importance. We shall therefore consider it from the point of view of the theoretical position on which it is based and according to which the data are interpreted. However, we will refer to one, particularly interesting, set of data. Throughout the study, Jerschina's expression of his zealous commitment to the categories of party religiosity is so strong that it is difficult to imagine that he is being serious and not satirical.

For our purposes, Jerschina's data can be simplified and summarized as follows: out of the four groups of young people - schoolchildren, students, young workers and, finally, young workers in the heavy industry of Nowa Huta - the final group scores least in terms of levels of religiosity.

According to Jerschina, the significance of the low level of religiosity of the young Nowa Huta workers can be understood in terms of the concept of 'leading social force'.(55) He writes:(56)

> The notion of the leading social force appears in the works of the Marxist classics whenever they ask the question who or which group in the *context of society or of a class* was the first to develop and perfect a consciousness reflecting most accurately the objective laws and tendencies of social development, the question which social group takes upon itself the aim of accelerating the social embodiment of the potential of its historical epoch, the question which social group occupies a position in the social structure which enables it to influence the consciousness of others and to give a lead.

This group is none other than the secular movement which, after the proletarian revolution, seems to have split into the people's party on the one hand and the rest of the leading force on the other. So the young workers of Nowa Huta, far from being ordinary men, are in terms of consciousness men of the future: we only have to look at their consciousness to see the future consciousness of the whole of proletarian society. What is the significance of the young Nowa Huta workers in particular? What have they in common with, say, Gregory of Sanok that others have not? Jerschina explains: 'their developmental dynamics are amongst the highest both quantitatively and qualitatively'.(57) Helpfully, we are not enlightened as to the meaning of developmental dynamics nor are we given an example of another group of comparable developmental dynamics. However, the choice does make sense in terms of the superimposition of the secular movement on contemporary developments; Nowa Huta is, after all, supposed to be a model socialist town.

Equally, if not more, interesting is Jerschina's redefinition of secularization. It is perhaps not so much a redefinition as the pointing out of yet another process which, in the context of communist proletarian society, is of far greater significance. Assuming the alienation thesis of religion, Jerschina begins by suggesting that alienation can become absorbed into the consciousness as a feeling of powerlessness. Why not, he asks, forget about measuring religiosity as such and come to grips directly with the question of powerlessness. Operationalization

appears as no problem: it is enough to ask (in a questionnaire,
for example) whether respondents feel powerless (or some such
question). In this way, claims Jerschina, 'real' secularization
can be measured.

These suggestions, however, lead Jerschina into some very
strange waters. He begins by criticizing western sociology and
western society; he argues that one of the key failings of both
bourgeois and Catholic sociology is that they deal only with the
change from religious belief to religious indifference and hence
are simply not able to cope with the question of powerlessness.(58) This failure, he continues, is related to the completely
different character of the process of secularization in capitalist
society where the liberation of the bourgeoisie from religion has
made exploitation only more brutal, where ideas of individual
success and competition cause egoism and amorality.(59) Perhaps
the most despicable aspect of the capitalist pattern of secularization is the 'particularly intense effort of production which leaves
little time and strength even for the participation in worship
and prayer for a heavenly recompensation for the buffeting of
this world'.(60) Jerschina attempts to convey a deep sense of
indignation as if to suggest that the wretched, miserable workers
under capitalism are now even denied their opium. Nevertheless,
he notes further, true religion - in the sense of alienation and
powerlessness - still exists under capitalism although it remains
relatively invisible; capitalist conditions are still fundamentally
religiogenic - a point, he stresses, which is confirmed by
Western sociologists such as David Martin.(61) Jerschina concludes that the capitalist pattern of secularization is not necessarily a bad one: on the grounds that it leads to discontent and
misery it can only be regarded as positive. Social discontent,
he notes, gives rise to 'the birth of rebellion of man against
inhuman conditions of life, against force and against the wolfish
laws of social life'.(62) How aptly his comments apply to recent
demonstrations within Poland itself.

Jerschina thus begins to define secularization of consciousness
in terms of the de-alienation of the attitude of powerlessness to
the 'consciousness of the historiogenic role'.(63) He summarizes
the latter phrase as the 'objective attitude'.(64) Jerschina even
goes as far as to suggest that all indicators of religiosity must
be put in question because the objective attitude is far more
widespread than religious indifference or disbelief: the Polish
worker's consciousness is far more secularized than that of a
worker under capitalism 'even though we could multiply by infinity the statistics showing that the Polish worker goes to church
more frequently than the French or American worker'.(65)
Jerschina's approach offers a neat way of avoiding all the
bother and inconvenience of gathering evidence and has the
virtue of yielding politically orthodox conclusions every time.
Jerschina's methodology may yet be the best so far...

Jerschina does, however, provide some data as evidence for
a related claim. For Jerschina this has proved a risky business.

Two tables are provided by Jerschina who suggests that they
measure the degree of alienation and show differences between
the four groups of young people. Table 21 is reproduced here
in its entirety as Table 5.4.(66)

TABLE 5.4 The attitudes of young people to factors determining
their fate. Opinions of youth from five milieux

'What does your future depend on?'	School-children 7-14	School-children above 14	Young workers generally	Young workers of large-scale industry	Students from Krakow
1 On my own efforts	89.3	93.9	68.6	92.4	72.4
2 On my parents' efforts	20.4	9.9	6.3	2.1	9.0
3 On favourable circumstances	26.1	50.3	24.2	12.2	36.1
4 On God's favour	44.0	22.1	25.6	18.2	24.8
5 On keeping God's Commandments	33.0	12.2	16.1	8.4	18.2

Note: percentages do not add up to 100 because respondents were able to choose
several answers. Originally more answers were obtained but these were discarded
as not relevant aspects of the consciousness of youth

The first problem is theoretical. Jerschina, let us recall, has
tried to operationalize the concept of alienation as a feeling of
powerlessness. In fact, he has simply attempted to measure
'pathological' psychological traits associated with a belief in God –
the criteria of pathology are drawn from Marxism-Leninism in
such a way that alienation is presented, not as a view of God,
but as a disease. The intensity of this disease, it is assumed,
is directly proportional to a belief in God. This is yet another
parody of the theologians' view that the belief in God integrates
the personality of man.
    Another problem of the table concerns the ambiguity of the
categories. It is only as a result of this ambiguity that Jerschina
is able to draw attention to the strength of the first category of
answer which, he claims, reflects the objective attitude. The
very high value for young workers in large-scale industry is,
according to Jerschina, the strongest evidence that these workers
are the leading social force. This is most unconvincing since
children over the age of fourteen score even higher and the value
is similar to that for schoolchildren between the ages of seven
and fourteen. The simplest explanation of these figures is that
the school or work environment stresses individual effort but

further evidence would have to be sought here. An interesting
observation here is that earlier Jerschina uncompromisingly
criticized Western society for its individualism.

Another problem concerning this category of answer are the
responses of young workers and students. It is likely that their
lower scores reflect both less stress on individual effort and a
disillusionment with future prospects. In the case of students,
especially, it may be due to a very realistic appraisal of the
facts of life although here again further investigations would be
required for confirmation.

In the question originally asked in the table, 'What does your
future depend on?', 'future' may refer either to 'this life' or to
the 'next life' as far as the respondent is concerned; it is clear
that Jerschina's intention was for it to refer to 'this life'. It is
very likely that different Weltanschauungen would lead to these
two different interpretations of the question. If, for example,
we take 'future' as referring to 'this life', we find that strict
Catholic and strict secularist interpretations of the question
are impossible to separate. By this we mean that an orthodox
Catholic can be affirmative in the answers 1 and 2 (seeing them
in terms of some sort of voluntarism) and also answers 3 and 4
(seeing them as circumstances outside their direct control). The
attitude to answer 5 may be unclear although a negative response
is perfectly in keeping with Catholic belief. However, a convinced secularist or atheist would find it difficult to justify the
denial of any more than answers 4 and 5; his attitude to 2 and 3
may remain unclear but, and this is characteristic of the secularist 'mind', he would claim a positive response to answer 1 as
exclusively his and so resent the Catholic's ingression.

The difficulties of separating Catholic from secularist are
further compounded by the simultaneous alternative interpretation where 'future' is taken to mean 'the next life'. In this case
the orthodox secularist need not concern us. The Catholic will
probably be affirmative about answers 1, 4 and 5 and remain
unclear about 2. He may deny answer 3 although it is by no
means clear what is meant by 'favourable circumstances' - such
circumstances may be spiritual.

The interpretation of these data, therefore, is far more complex than Jerschina would have us believe. What sort of a conclusion are we expected to draw, for example, from a pope who is
affirmative about answer 1 and denies answer 5? Is he of secularized consciousness or is he simply assuming that the question
refers to 'this life'?

In contrast to Jerschina's claim that answer 1 is a crucial
category it would appear that answer 4 is the most informative:
an atheist is unlikely to answer in the affirmative and a Catholic
is unlikely to deny it. This illustrates the futility of the whole
exercise - surely it would have been more useful to ask the
direct question 'Do you believe in God?'? From Jerschina's point
of view such a question would have marked capitulation: he does,
after all, want to keep up appearances of having operationalized

the concept of alienation.

At this stage it is worth asking about the notorious concept of 'false consciousness' which is an integral part of Marxism-Leninism and often used by secularists as a device by which to suggest that individuals can be deluded into utterly false images of themselves. As a Marxist-Leninist, Jerschina would be expected to take into account the possibility of this 'false consciousness' affecting the answers - especially the first answer.

Perhaps the simplest way of operationalizing the concept of powerlessness would be to ask the following question: Do you feel powerless (vis à vis your surroundings)? Alas, under a communist regime such a question can never be asked and the answer made public.

Not very much can be said about the overall impression gained from Jerschina's study except that he seems to have gone to a great deal of trouble to prove virtually nothing of value.

With Jerschina we conclude the survey of the officially based and the officially oriented sociology of religion. We have noted its roots in the view that religion is a feature of archaic man and in a view of the wicked past. The corollaries of this view centre on the discovery of the future, the praise of the modern, the derision of religion, the loyalty to secularist communist power as the imminent future and on the moral absolute of secularism throughout the whole of history. Any discipline based on such assumptions is bound to be sterile and no valid development can be expected from this camp. Work here will undoubtedly continue although the field of interest will be dictated by party policy.

One characteristic feature of this work as a whole has become apparent gradually: it makes some sort of sense in terms of concepts and arguments used except that all of the concepts and arguments exist in a hermetically sealed universe totally out of contact with reality. The work exists as an answer in search of a non-existent question, a system of 'Newspeak' or a Cloud-cuckoo-land of concepts and ideas.

6 CATHOLIC MAN AND RELIGION: SOCIOLOGIE RELIGIEUSE, CATHOLICS AND SECULARIZATION

The public expression of all ideas in Poland is subject to the strictest control by the authorities through the apparatus of central censorship. This control has not always been effective in practice for reasons which we have already mentioned, but it still poses formidable problems for researchers, writers and publishers. Especially affected have been investigations and writings not inspired by Marxism-Leninism or orthodox ideology and the field of religiosity and secularization is particularly hit. In addition to censorship, there are limitations imposed on the numbers of copies which are allowed to be printed and also limitations on the access to information on religiosity (where already existent but in the hands of state bodies). All this has the result that the work of independent investigators (who are in any case discouraged) inevitably suffers. These problems are undoubtedly the major factors affecting both the quality and the quantity of this type of work in Poland today.(1)

The contributions which we shall examine in this chapter are, similarly to those of the previous chapter, centred on the categories of mass religiosity on the one hand and the processes of change connected with industrialization on the other. They differ in so far as they are free from what is often colloquially described as 'primitive atheism'. We will not attempt to distinguish between a 'Catholic' and a 'non-Catholic' approach - indeed, it would be difficult to make a clear-cut case for the division of the Polish sociology of religion into a Catholic and a non-Catholic aproach except, perhaps, in institutional terms.(2) Although there is a deep commitment to Catholic belief by most of the observers dealt with in this chapter their principle unifying characteristic is their refusal to take part in any Marxist-Leninist methodology or apologetics. As a result much of this work can be considered as a genuine attempt at the understanding of religion in Polish society.

The field here is quite large and little more can be done than to outline some of the characteristic tendencies, controversies and conclusions. The sociologist best known for his studies of the changes in mass religiosity in connection with urbanization and industrialization and also for his inspiration of many studies on the subject is without any doubt Władysław Piwowarski. Fr Piwowarski succeeded Fr Józef Majka as head of the Department of the Sociology of Religion at KUL. Of Piwowarski's published works on secularization the most important are his two complementary studies: the first is concerned with the relationship between religiosity and urbanization(3) and the second with religiosity in an urban-industrial milieu.(4) These two studies relate to only some of the localities which Piwowarski has investigated: he is also known for his work on Warmia, Mazuria and various areas in the Pulawy district.

Despite Fr Mirek's pioneer work of 1928 the interest of Catholics, and of priests in particular, in the sociology of religion and in secularization has traditionally not been encouraged by the Polish Church authorities. This is perhaps not surprising in view of the positivistic, scientistic and Marxist orientations of the early sociologists in Poland. The early sociologists of religion were, as a whole, regarded as a threat to the Church as they prodded here and there in their search for possible weaknesses. For a long time the Church's view was motivated by the argument that it is always more politic not to admit to any area of weakness: the process of secularization, it was thought, was surely one such area. This argument was not without a sound strategic basis especially under the later conditions of a planned secularist assault. It was, of course, assumed by the Church that the process of secularization was an indisputable fact of Polish society and was nibbling away at the edges of the Catholic community. It was also maintained that the 'planned secularization of attitudes' was the main, if not exclusive, reason for declines in religiosity. Today, however, the picture is seen quite differently although it still remains indisputable that mass religiosity is changing and that planned secularization does affect attitudes. Piwowarski is symptomatic of this new trend of thought and he is principally concerned with the attempt to place declines in religiosity in a more general context of urbanizing and industrializing society. Piwowarski's emphasis is not exclusively on declining levels of religiosity but on a view which stresses the process of change. It is not surprising, therefore, to find Piwowarski drawing much of his methodology from contemporary Western, and especially French, sociology of religion. The Western methodology has some obvious drawbacks, the most noteworthy of which is the totally different socio-political context in which secularization is investigated.

Piwowarski's study of religiosity and urbanization - the first large published work on the subject by a Catholic in Poland - concludes that mass religiosity is declining.(5) This study was welcomed by secularists, for reasons that are obvious, and also by some Catholic intellectuals not so much on account of the methodology and arguments it used or on account of the conclusions it reached but because it put the sociology of religion 'on the map' and because of its usefulness to pastoral work.(6) Nevertheless, its appearance on the scene was marked by some very violent criticism from Catholics, the polemic with Andrzej Święcicki (head of sociology of religion at ATK) being perhaps the most characteristic.

In ths study, Piwowarski relied extensively on the inspiration of le Bras, L. Dingemans and Rémy, Laloux and Pin. He invest-

igated (using the questionnaire method) four parishes in the area
of the town of Puławy (near Lublin) during the years 1967-70.
This area is of particular significance on account of the recent
construction outside the town of a nitrochemical plant ('Azoty')
which has caused some important changes in the way of life and
attitudes of the local population. However, the choice of these
four parishes may not have been the most appropriate on account
of the many unquantifiable elements of temporary flux which the
building of Azoty indisputably induced in the surrounding count-
ryside. Piwowarski found that the degree of religiosity in each of
the parishes was associated with the degree of urbanization of
the parish.

The mechanics of Piwowarski's method are a good example of an
attempt at excessive precision which results in a failure to bear
the promised fruit. The main problem associated with an attempt
at high degrees of precision in stating, for example, levels of
urbanization or religiosity is that it is not at all clear what constitutes precision: what factors are to be taken into account?
What are the weights to be assigned to them? Faced with such
questions it is likely that even a crude overall impressionistic
type of approach may reflect the situation just as accurately,
especially for comparative purposes as is the case here; this is
due to the clustering effect of the frequencies of the characteristic features.(7) It is quite possible that as soon as the juggling
with the component elements of urbanization and religiosity and
their relative weights begins there will appear no end of 'precise'
statements of levels of urbanization and religiosity some of which
may lie at the opposite end of the scale to others. We do not wish
to suggest that this is indeed the case in Piwowarski's study,
although Święcicki ironically concludes that the very opposite conclusions can be drawn from Piwowarski's data if the correct juggling procedure is followed,(8) but a method which is in principle
open to such reservations is not likely to be a frutiful one.

It would be a mistake to take Piwowarski's statements regarding
levels of religiosity and urbanization as no better than arbitrary;
rather, the indications are that similar conclusions might have
been arrived at, and with considerably less effort, using far
cruder techniques. However, it is likely that such 'precision technique' may have the last word when it comes to persuading those
who are easily impressed by detailed mathematical exposition and
calculation - the so-called 'scientific approach'. The 'precision
technique' is probably a response to such fashion.

Let us now take a look at some concrete examples of Piwowarski's work with the aim of illustrating the way in which his
excessive precision has adversely affected his conclusions; at the
same time we will note the outline of his investigation. Piwowarski
begins by producing values for the levels of urbanization of each
of the parishes; this is done by ranking the percentage values of
'features of urbanization'. The following features were taken into
account: numbers commuting, numbers employed in industry and
services, numbers of young people being educated, numbers of

mortared dwellings, numbers of dwellings with running water
(bathrooms, washing machines), number of electrified villages,
mileage of hard-surface roads, numbers of cars (motorcycles,
mopeds), the attainment of basic levels in education, magazine
readership, numbers of radio receiver and television set own-
ers.(9) The sum total of the ranks for each parish was taken and
the arithmetic mean calculated. The result is reproduced here as
Table 6.1

A few perhaps rather obvious points should be made at this
stage. The first is that urbanization is defined by Piwowarski in
a very specific and limited way which fails to take into account
such features as the size of the built-up area, the population of
the urban area, population density, the types of trade and exchange relations existing in the area, the bureaucratization of
life - to mention only some of the distinguishing features of the
rural-urban difference. The practical consequence of this limit-
ation is that the application of Piwowarski's criteria becomes restricted to the Polish rural-urban difference: rural Britain, for
example, would appear 100 per cent urban according to these criteria. This problem is rather more important than may appear at
first sight, however. Its relevance is not so much to the definition of urbanization or urbanism, but to factors which are able
to affect religiosity: Piwowarski uses the term urbanization merely
as a convenient receptacle for factors which he believes exert
pressure on religious belief and practice. It might have been more
suitable to employ the term modernization. Another point of some
importance is that Piwowarski is looking at rural change which is
one restricted aspect of urbanization or modernization although
the two are closely related in terms of being both a result of industrialization. Here it is both possible and likely that the impact
of urbanization or modernization in the wider sense will not be the
same as the impact of rural change proper. Let us now return to
the question of precision.

TABLE 6.1 The composite indices of urbanization for the four
parishes investigated by Piwowarski

Parish	Index of urbanization	Level of urbanization
A	3.53	Low
B	2.43	-
C	2.10	-
D	1.93	High

The precision of the above values expressing the levels of
urbanization is more apparent than real for two main reasons.
Firstly, on account of the choice of features. Had Piwowarski
omitted bathrooms and running water in his calculations, the values would have been those illustrated in Table 6.2. It is a matter
of speculation what the order would have been had Piwowarski

included such features as, for example, the proportion of the
population working office hours, the number of water taps per
1000 inhabitants, the proportion of dwellings with central heating,
the use of nonstick frying pans, pressure cookers, electric irons,
the readership of newspapers and the number of books in the
house; there is no a priori reason why such features should be
less relevant to religiosity than running water and bathrooms or
even running water in bathrooms. (10)

The second reason which militates against precision is the very
nature of the ranking system which, as Święcicki points out,
'attributes the same weight to differences of 1-2 per cent as it
does to differences of 20-40 per cent'. (11) Again, it is important
to stress, the final figures obtained by Piwowarski are not necessarily meaningless: it is their apparent precision which is confusing. Very similar, even almost identical, levels of urbanization
can still be ranked in the same way and produce a similar distribution in the values of the index to that produced by very different levels.

TABLE 6.2   The change in the values of the indices of urbanization

Parish	New index of urbanization (previous index in brackets)	
A	3.77 (3.53)	Note the rise in the value
B	2.19 (2.43)	for parish A, the inversion
C	2.27 (2.10)	of the order for B and C and
D	1.77 (1.93)	a lowering of the value for D.

One of the implicit claims made by Piwowarski in the early pages
of the study is that the four parishes are reasonably well-suited
for comparison at least partly because the average distance of
their component villages from the parish church are almost identical. They are indeed. Piwowarski does note, however, that in
parish A the distances of the peripheral villages from the church
are rather large but makes no further comment. From Piwowarski's
own data a rough picture of the dispersion of the population in
each of the parishes can be drawn (cf. Table 6.3).

If distance alone were a major factor affecting such aspects of
religiosity as attendance at Mass on Sundays(12) then it would be
expected that parish D should have the highest Mass attendance
rate. Not surprisingly, parish D is indeed shown to have the highest Sunday Mass attendance rate with Piwowarski apparently not
noticing that one half of the parishioners live within easy strolling
distance of their church. (13) It is worth remembering that parish
D is also the most urbanized (according to Piwowarski's criteria)
of the parishes. Piwowarski does note, however, the good communications network of this parish.

The question of accessibility of the parish church is further
complicated by the following: overlaps in the catchment areas of

TABLE 6.3 The dispersion of the population in each of the four parishes

Parish	Average distance of villages from parish church (km.)	Population living less than 2 km from church (per cent)	Population living more than 5 km from church (per cent)
A	5.1	5	53
B	5.1	35	38
C	5.4	24	41
D	4.9	50	25

the parishes studied and of these parishes with other catchment areas; the virtual unquantifiability of accessibility under Polish rural conditions; the fact that some of the elements of accessibility (e.g. the state of roads, the availability of motor transport) have already been incorporated into the indices of urbanization. The latter point is especially problematic since the greater the dependence of the indices of urbanization on elements of church accessibility then the greater is the bias towards a positive correlation between levels of Sunday Mass attendance and levels of urbanization. In other words, urbanization conceived solely in terms of good roads and the possession of a motor vehicle is likely to be associated with an increase in attendance at Sunday Mass.

Let us now turn to a look at what Piwowarski takes to constitute religiosity. Piwowarski accepts the idea that 'popular Catholic religiosity has a different content from the official model of Church religiosity and from the models of Catholicism in other countries'.(14) He notes that already in the nineteenth century the rural communities in Poland began to disintegrate in a way which has been increasing in intensity ever since. As key factors affecting this decline of community, Piwowarski identifies industrialization, urbanization and the rationalization of agriculture.(15) He is aware that the changes, although partly quantitative, have been more significantly qualitative with the result that they are not available for statistical investigation.(16) The changes in rural religiosity occur as an integral part of the broader changes in the overall picture of the rural community(17) or, in other words, a particular state of the rural community can be found to correspond to a particular state of religiosity. This is Piwowarski's fundamental hypothesis around which he builds his statistical investigation. As we will show below, this assumption by Piwowarski is not borne out by facts.

While Piwowarski is aware of the difficulties of observing anything apart from an almost already assumed 'decline' in religiosity, he states:(18)

Much less attention...is paid to the other aspect of this process, namely, the prospects for the deepening of religiosity and for the formation of a religious élite. It is possible to explain this by suggesting that, at least during the initial phases of changes in religious life, there occurs a Dechristianization of rural communities. This phenomenon is easily observed and measured in terms of at least one important indicator - religious practice. However, the formation of conscious and deepened religiosity occurs slowly and is certainly less easily observable and measurable by the sociologist of religion.

Piwowarski is, on the one hand, aware of the difficulties involved in the assessment of religious change and yet, on the other hand, is unable to overcome them: he finally limits himself to simply verifying the existence of an association between the degree of urbanization and the degree of deviation from a model strongly biased towards rural religiosity. While the idea that there is an initial period of dechristianization of the rural community is in principle an acceptable hypothesis under conditions of a rural to urban migration it should, nevertheless, be treated with great caution under conditions of change within the rural milieu.(19)

Piwowarski suggests that religiosity is to be observed in terms of five parameters: the overall attitude to belief (globalny stosunek do wiary), religious ideology, religious practice, religious morality and, lastly, the bond between believers and the parish or Church (i.e. the religious community).(20) Percentage values are calculated from the sample data using the 'official Church requirement' as the point of reference. The percentages are ranked, the ranks are summed, the average is taken and the resulting values of religiosity are juxtaposed against the values obtained for the levels of urbanization. The picture obtained is reproduced in Table 6.4. A graphical representation (not given by Piwowarski) of Table 6.4 is particularly useful in showing clearly the relationship involved; we have shown it as Figure 6.1.

TABLE 6.4 The association between levels of urbanization and levels of religiosity according to Piwowarski's data

Parish	Level of urbanization (average of ranks)	Level of religiosity (average of ranks)
A	3.53	2.33
B	2.43	2.17
C	2.10	2.67
D	1.93	2.83

A glance at the graph is sufficient to see that a relationship may exist but that further confirmation would be required especially in the areas of ranks 1 and 4. This is especially important since Piwowarski was comparing the religiosities of localities which, in absolute terms, were of quite similar degrees of both urbanization and religiosity. Indeed, it might be argued that the variations in levels of religiosity for any one level of urbanization (taken across the whole of the society) are much greater than the insignificant variations between the localities as shown here. This point is argued by Święcicki.

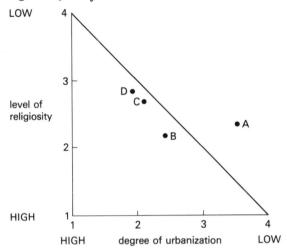

Note: The positions of the four parishes are represented by the four points A, B, C and D. The diagonal represents the 'ideal' inverse correlation between urbanization and religiosity.

FIGURE 6.1 The association between levels of religiosity and levels of urbanization according to Piwowarski's data

According to Piwowarski, a key part in the decline of religiosity in the urbanizing village is played by peasant-workers (chłopi-robotnicy). Peasant-workers are peasant farmers who, in addition to working on the land, have taken up manual or other employment in local industry or elsewhere. In the Pulawy region the nitrochemical plant would be expected to provide most of the employment for the peasant-workers. Piwowarski points to the role of the peasant-workers as the 'importers of urban patterns' into the village. The percentages of peasant-workers in the samples from the four parishes would appear to confirm Piwowarski's hypothesis: A= 12.5, B = 17.4, C = 30.2, D = 31.3.(21)

In a reply to Piwowarski, Święcicki maintains that the conclusions, which point to an association between the processes of urbanization and dechristianization, are unwarranted.(22) Święcicki's tone is harsh and uncompromising; he writes:(23)

As a defender of his own hypothesis, Fr Piwowarski would wish to topple the odds in its favour but as an experienced field-worker he is unable to overlook those facts and figures which are in conflict with the hypothesis. Therefore, as an experienced statistician he is able to play a trick or two in order to make the hypothesis appear confirmed: but the end-product lacks credibility. Finally, as a clergyman Piwowarski sees it his duty to warn the public of the danger of secularization and does not spare criticism, wherever possible, of the rather slow reforms in pastoral methods.

The first and final criticisms, rather than being based on the merits of the case, sound more like personal jibes - no doubt indicative of some very fundamental differences of opinion between Święcicki and Piwowarski or even of strained relations between the sociology of religion at ATK and the sociology of religion at KUL. The second criticism is too important to allow it to pass; however, if Piwowarski consciously relies on tricks one would expect him to make a far better job of it and, for example, make the perfectly legitimate allowance for the population distribution of parishes A and D in order to give weight to his conclusions. But Święcicki is, of course, referring to the problems arising out of Piwowarski's system of weighting the indicators.

One of Święcicki's main objections is that Piwowarski investigated only four parishes; such a small number of units is of very limited statistical significance, notes Święcicki. The ranking system - he continues - in addition to being unable to cope adequately with relative differences becomes top-heavy when totals and averages are taken several times in succession: Piwowarski finally arrives at what can be called a 'third degree rank' - referring to the way in which Piwowarski had selectively summed and averaged the ranks three times in succession.(24)

Another reason why Piwowarski's study is doomed, writes Święcicki, is because, in Poland, the differences in religiosity between town and country are very slight. But perhaps the most important criticism brought to bear by Święcicki concerns the choice of parishes which, he stresses, vary tremendously. It is precisely those differences which Piwowarski did not take into account that may be crucial in determining the relative levels of religiosity. As examples we can take the two extreme parishes of A and D. The parish A, which Piwowarski has classified as the most rural, has an almost century-old tradition of vodka distilling and sugar refining, it is situated only 17 km from Lublin on the busy main highway to Warsaw and, finally, since the last war already two of the parish priests have left the priesthood. One of the consequences of the vodka production is that alcoholism is rife;(25) the alcoholism may be in turn responsible for the generally low moral standards observable in the parish.(26)

In the case of parish D, claimed to be the most urbanized, it is significant that it has been in the orbit of the Azoty for the short period of less than ten years. It is also significant that it possesses a long tradition of carpentry which imparts a specific character to the life of the locality. Carpentry in Poland has always been associated with work away from home and even in distant parts of the country. Such a characteristic would tend to be associated with a cosmopolitan and rather more up to date Catholicism. In addition, there is the good pastoral care which the parish enjoys as well as the newly acquired wealth which has resulted from the Azoty; it is this wealth, notes Święcicki, that Piwowarski has confused with urbanization.

Święcicki's criticism thus stands on the following points; firstly, that Piwowarski's choice of localities for comparison was inappropriate; secondly, that the statistical approach used by Piwowarski can only lead to ambiguity of conclusions and, finally, that Piwowarski has ignored factors which can account very well for the level and type of religiosity observed.

However ambiguous the data gathering and processing might be, Piwowarski's study is characterized by a clarity of intention and exposition. It is not burdened with ideological ballast. As a result, problems and shortcomings are easy to pinpoint. One particularly important feature of the study is the very detailed presentation of all the data obtained so that the work becomes a possible source of raw material for further comment. Piwowarski also includes a sketch map of the area investigated and reproduces the questionnaire used.

As a sociologist of religion,(27) Święcicki is himself well-known as a defender of the thesis that the relationship between religiosity and urbanization as established by Western sociologists and supported by Piwowarski does not hold under Polish conditions; he also holds a view which rejects the generalization of limited sets of observations into laws and trends. Indeed, he is suspicious of any such laws and trends: 'the uniqueness of each situation' is his guiding principle.

In keeping with his recommendations, Święcicki draws attention to a particularly striking pattern in national religious behaviour. Between the years 1960 and 1965 the percentage of the total population practising rarely or not at all declined from 19.1 to 13.9;(28) a similar trend was also observed between 1965 and 1968: the religious self-identification of adults (over 18 years of age, believing and practising) increased during this period by 7.5 per cent (from 63.0 to 67.7 per cent) while the number of non-believers and militant atheists declined by 16.2 per cent (from 5.5 to 4.6 per cent).(29) These examples of possible desecularization are especially significant in view of the widespread general pressures not to admit to any sort of religious belief.

The data used by Święcicki were gathered by a state-sponsored body; it is therefore unlikely that there was any conscious bias in favour of a desecularization thesis. Święcicki explains the observed increase in religiosity over the abovementioned period in terms of events of national importance in Polish Catholic life: the general interest of the population in Vatican II, the discussions of the letter of the Polish bishops to the German bishops and, finally, the period of the Great Novena leading up to the Polish Millennial celebrations. Fragmentary data suggest, continues Święcicki, that this trend has not continued since.(30) More important still, as far as the relationship between religiosity and features of urban-

ization and social modernization is concerned, is the example of
the United States where 98 per cent of the population claim to believe in God as compared with 86 per cent for Poland and 77 per
cent for the UK.(31)

At the level of national data, Święcicki draws attention to the
fact that the provinces of Rzeszów and Katowice, whose indicators
of urbanization are 30 per cent and 78 per cent respectively, have
almost identical levels of religiosity - 70.9 and 71.4 per cent respectively.(32) Taking a closer look at the exceptionally urbanized
Katowice province, we find that the area of Upper Silesia (Górny
Śląsk) has a very much higher level of religiosity than the ad-
jacent and socially almost identical area of the Dabrowa Basin (the
Zagłębie Dąbrowskie which includes the towns of Dąbrowa Górn-
icza, Będzin, Sosnowiec and Zawiercie) and also higher than some
of the surrounding rural areas.(33) This difference can only be
explained in terms of the history and traditions of the two neighbouring areas: during the time of the partitions Upper Silesia was
under German occupation whereas the Dąbrowa Basin was occupied
by Russia. The different socio-economic and political structures
imposed on these two areas resulted, on the one hand, in the
formation of a strong 'workers' Church' and a working-class Catholic tradition and, on the other, a weak Church buffeted by anticlericalism in the Dabrowa Basin and in the other Russian-
occupied urban and rural areas. This process may have occurred
in the following way. In Upper Silesia virtually all capital, large-
scale production and administrative power was in German hands;
the strongly anti-German working-class communities produced
their own recruits for the priesthood who, quite naturally, retained similar sentiments and who sided with their parishioners
during moments of conflict and crisis. As a result, the clergy
were held in very high esteem which in turn resulted in a strong
Church and high religiosity. This strength has lasted up to the
present day. In the Dąbrowa Basin, however, capital, production
and local administrative power all remained in Polish hands while
the Russians exercised jurisdiction. Here the siding of the clergy
with the working-class communities against the local centres of
power did not occur to the same extent: these manifest centres of
power were mostly Polish and the priests often identified with
them. This had the result that any of the workers' ill-feeling towards superiors would have also been directed, at least partly,
against the clergy.(34)

It is clear, therefore, that strong working-class traditions of
developed religiosity and rural traditions of anticlericalism can be
identified in Poland.(35) These traditions go a long way towards
upsetting the classic 'instant secularization thesis'. It is perhaps
this sort of evidence, far more than Święcicki's abovementioned
criticism of Piwowarski, which puts Piwowarski's investigation in
the most useful context: Piwowarski deals with very similar degrees of religiosity (differing only by a few per cent, if that) and
tries to explain them again in terms of only slight differences in
the degree of urbanization; Święcicki shows that huge differences

in the degree of urbanization need not in the least affect levels of religiosity.

Is it possible to identify any contemporary examples of the development of strong working-class traditions of Catholicism? Two examples spring to mind immediately: Nowa Huta and Gdańsk. The factors operating in Nowa Huta can be listed as follows: the strongly religious background of the working-class; the alien and antiseptic character of Nowa Huta itself; the role of the clergy as links with tradition on the one hand and as 'representatives' standing up against the authorities on the other; the prolonged battle for the building of the local Queen of Poland Church; the key part played by the locally born Pope John Paul II (as Cardinal Wojtyła) both in the organization of religious life and in the building of the church in the new town; finally, the Pope's visit to the area of Nowy Targ and Kraków in 1979.

Gdańsk has one of the world's leading shipyards, traditionally run according to the principles of People's Poland and in no way a refuge for archaic rustics. At the end of 1970 discontent and riots in the shipyard toppled a party secretary from his throne. In the summer of 1980 history repeated itself except this time with far greater success: Lech Wałęsa emerged as undisputed leader of an independent trade union movement. The events of 1980 were marked by the prominence of very strong religious overtones: Wałęsa is a devout Catholic who made no attempt to hide the fact that he was both inspired by Catholicism and morally supported by the Church in his struggle for rights and for a better deal – he promptly went to Rome to meet the Pope in whom he ostentatiously showed a far greater interest than in the Western trade unionists; Masses were celebrated and Holy Communion was given to the striking workers during the sit-in; holy images adorned the shipyard walls and the walls of Solidarity's offices; a huge cross commemorating the workers shot during the 1970 disturbances appeared in the shipyard together with a giant portrait of Pope John Paul II; the agreement between Solidarity and the authorities was signed by Watesa using an outsize pen adorned with a portrait of the Pope. This was not all. Part of the workers' demands were concerned with specifically religious issues – the access of the Church to the mass media. The 'instant secularization thesis' is unable to cope with facts like these: to call them 'distortions' or 'deviations' is simply another way of admitting difficulties of interpretation. Religiological methodology has even greater problems in coming to terms with such facts.

Święcicki does not believe that parts of the phenomenon of religion can be 'split off' for study as separate entities: the above examples illustrate the problems which can occur when attempts are made at measuring and explaining separate aspects of religion. Religiosity cannot, for example, be investigated in isolation from socio-economic and political conditions nor can it be isolated from history and tradition. Święcicki suggests that a picture can be obtained only if the following three dimensions are taken into account: firstly, the religiosity of the individual in terms of its

context; secondly, the cultural dimension (the community of language, nation and state); finally, the dimension of the community
of the people of God - worshipping within the context defined by
the Church.(36) We shall return to some of these points in chapter 8.

The importance of the religiosity of Nowa Huta has, therefore,
not escaped the attention of the non-secularist sociologists of religion. Another sociologist, Franciszek Adamski, in his enquiries
into the sociology of the family(37) has paid a good deal of attention to the religiosity of the inhabitants of Nowa Huta. In an investigation carried out in 1971, Adamski was concerned with a
close examination of the often officially advanced thesis that Nowa
Huta is a model 'secular socialist town'.(38)

Adamski investigated the urban district of the Queen of Poland
parish (formerly the rural parish of Bieńczyce). The source of
data consisted of postally distributed and returned questionnaires
covering 1,096 individuals. Adamski concludes that Nowa Huta is
one of the most religious urban centres in Poland.(39) Especially
high levels of religiosity are to be found amongst the working
class - the very group which, according to Jerschina,(40) is the
leading social (secularizing) force of Polish society. Jerschina, let
us recall, also indirectly confirmed Adamski's conclusion by stressing that the leading social force, although secularized, can exhibit high levels of religiosity; according to Jerschina, secularization and religiosity must be treated as entirely independent
variables.(41) One of the most important reasons for the high
levels of religiosity of the Nowa Huta workers, notes Adamski,
lies in their peasant origins. The area from which the first generation was drawn - the Nowy Targ district - is one of the strong-
holds of Polish Catholicism. However, continues Adamski, there
occurs a process of 'practical secularization' which is apparent
above all in the lack of congruence between the moral doctrine of
the Church and the popular attitudes towards marriage: the de-
laying of Church weddings, the support for divorce and the
acceptance of those norms regulating married and social life which
are in conflict with Church teaching. Indicators of these features
all exhibit high values. Adamski suggests that the main explanation of this process lies in a system of pastoral care which is out
of phase with the rapidly changing educational structure of the
younger generation.(42)

Although Adamski is substantially correct in his observations
his conclusions might have been given extra weight if he had
given his work a comparative dimension instead of relying largely
on intuition. He might have suitably compared Nowa Huta both
across time and also with other urban centres in Poland. These
problems can be partly resolved by comparing his data with that
of other sociologists like Piwowarski, for example. It is also a pity
that one of Adamski's key explanatory variables, pastoral care,
has been left untouched beyond a bare mention.

A point concerning the reliability of questionnaire data in general is worth making here. Adamski, in one place, juxtaposes

questionnaire data and statistics obtained from parish records.(43)
Notwithstanding questions of accuracy of the parish records and
the fact that the units of comparison differed slightly,(44) there
appears a rather significant difference between the two sets of
data. For example, parish records show that out of those with a
'basic' education,(45) in 25 per cent of the cases the Church
wedding took place within 1-2 days of the civil marriage ceremony
and in 78.6 per cent of the cases within one year; according to
the questionnaire, the respective figures were 16.6 and 98.6 per
cent. It is not clear what sort of interpretation can be put on
this difference without the availability of additional information
except that factors such as moving house, self-image, misunder-
standing and even perhaps memory played a substantial part.
There is some similarity between Adamski's comparison and Piwowarski's comparison of Mass attendance claims in questionnaires
with Mass attendance counts. In this case also, neither may have
been accurate. Piwowarski has taken the count as presenting a
more accurate picture of the situation. For example, in parish B
33.3 per cent of the sample claimed attendance at each Sunday
Mass and for parish D the figure was 38.9 per cent. According
to the count, the figures were 37.1 per cent and 28.3 per cent
respectively.(46) It is again not clear how to explain these differences in order to eliminate future sources of error.

At this stage we should return to Piwowarski and take a look at
his study of religiosity in an urban-industrial milieu.(47) This
study, while concentrating in depth on the urban centre of Puławy,
includes a general presentation of the values of the indicators of
religiosity for the following urban localities: Puławy (two samples,
N = 941 and N = 113), Kazimierz Dolny (N = 174), Płock (N = 557)
and Nowa Huta (N = 515).(48) This time Piwowarski employs not
five but seven parameters of religiosity: he divides the previously
applied (cf. note 20) parameter of religious ideology into religious
ideology and religious knowledge; he also uses the additional parameter of religious experience.(49) The sizes of the second Puławy sample and of the Kazimierz Dolny sample are perhaps on the
low side. In the case of Puławy it makes little difference on account of the other relatively large sample, but in the case of
Kazimierz Dolny the small size is a distinct disadvantage especially
in view of the fact that out of the four localities it is the odd man
out: it is not a large-scale industrial centre.

In contrast to Piwowarski's earlier study, this investigation
does not include the construction of indices of either religiosity or
urbanization. In this sense, the investigation is not concerned
with the establishment of a relationship between levels of religiosity and degrees of industrialization or urbanization. Piwowarski
is now concerned with an appraisal of the state of religiosity in an
urban-industrial milieu. Here Piwowarski is anxious to draw attention to the effects of the process of urbanizing and industrializing
(including the effects of the migrations involved) on religiosity;
he also pays some attention to the thesis that an urban-industrial
steady state results in a stability of social relations which is con-

ducive to a return to higher levels of religiosity.(50) It is worth looking at this latter thesis in some detail.

Piwowarski examines this thesis by seeking correlations between religiosity and the period of residence in Puławy.(51) Three periods of residence are used in the ordering of the data: (1) from birth, (2) from before 1961 (the beginnings of large-scale industrialization in Puławy), (3) since 1961. The data provided by Piwowarski would appear to be of a high degree of ambiguity. For example, 91.2 per cent of the first category claim to believe and 81.6 per cent claim to practice regularly or often. This contrasts with the respective figures of 85.6 per cent and 75.5 per cent for the pre-1961 residents and with 87.6 per cent and 74.6 per cent for the newcomers after 1961. Investigations of secularization based solely on belief and practice would tend to confirm the above thesis. Piwowarski, however, is cautious and refers to the parameter of belief and practice (the overall attitude to belief) as 'introductory' and only treats the remaining parameters as significant.(52) Piwowarski's caution may not be acceptable to everybody and it might even be argued that belief and practice (even in an overall way) are somehow fundamental. Nevertheless, Piwowarski continues to argue that the ambiguity of the data lies principally in the values of the remaining parameters. There is an almost random distribution of the percentages (never differing by more than 9, often by 2-3 and mostly by 6-7) over the categories for the other parameters. It is quite possible that, similarly to his earlier procedure, Piwowarski is trying to measure differences which are far too slight to register: they may become observable under conditions of longer time-spans, greater disorganization, immense samples, etc. Perhaps Piwowarski had this in mind when he wrote: 'The only conclusion which can be drawn is that an increase in religiosity will only occur amongst those resident in the town over several generations rather than amongst the immigrants.(53)

Piwowarski also examined other correlations. He failed to establish a significant correlation between the degree of religiosity and territorial origin.(54) Piwowarski puts this down to the 'cultural homogeneity' of all the areas of origin investigated including Puławy itself (there may be only minor differences). This cultural homogeneity, according to Piwowarski, has the additional significance of being responsible for the continual strength of religiosity in Puławy. The religiosity is maintained through 'the functionality of the traditional credibility structures which legitimize a specific type of religious attitude and behaviour'.(55)

Piwowarski's examination of the relationship between type of family milieu (in terms of religiosity) and the religiosity of children revealed a characteristic feature.(56) This confirms the conclusions of other studies carried out in Poland. Piwowarski writes: 'in the majority of families, even where religious practice is neglected by the older generation, there exist strong tendencies to continue religious traditions and to exert influence over the younger generation in order to make them maintain these traditions.(57)

So far Piwowarski has been pointing to factors which contribute to the maintenance of popular religiosity in the urban-industrial environment. He has not suggested any ways of identifying possible changes in the religiosity of town-dwellers. There is one set of data, however, which does go some way towards indicating that urban religiosity may be different in type from the popular religiosity of the rural milieu. With the caution typical of this study, Piwowarski is reluctant to draw hasty conclusions, but he makes a point of commenting on the data. The different types of religiosity can be seen from the correlations between religiosity and milieu of upbringing.(58) Piwowarski has data concerning three types of milieu of upbringing: village, small town, town. The data are reproduced in Table 6.5.(59)

TABLE 6.5 Religiosity and milieu of origin (Piwowarski's data)

	Village	Small town	Town
Believers (per cent)	87.1	90.6	83.2
Practising (per cent)	77.0	78.3	70.1

Such data are not entirely unexpected; further information reveals what may prove to be not only a difference between village and town religiosity, but also a possible direction of further changes in urban religiosity. The data are reproduced in Table 6.6.(60) It is to the figures in category (d) that attention needs to be drawn. According to Piwowarski, the religious ritualism of the peasant is being replaced by a consequential type of religiosity which is observable in the town dweller.(61)

Another set of data which may point in the direction of similar changes was presented by Piwowarski in his earlier study of urbanization.(62) An extract of these data is shown in Table 6.7.

What sorts of general changes does Piwowarski identify as occurring in the religiosity of the urban-industrial environment? Using the model of traditional rural Catholicism for comparative purposes, he distinguishes three simultaneous directions of change: firstly, in the direction of what he terms 'selectivism' (wybiór-czość); secondly, in the direction of religious indifference; finally, in the direction of deepening religiosity. Some evidence of these directions can be found in data which have been reproduced in this chapter. The data, even as a whole, are far from complete or conclusive. However, Piwowarski is able to fill and make up the lacunae by informal observation and an intuitive understanding of popular religiosity. The general method, if it can so be called, which Piwowarski employed was one based on the identification of meaningful clusters of characteristics.(63) Let us now take a look at each of these directions in turn.

Piwowarski observes that the dominant form of religiosity and also the starting point for the changes in the rapidly growing

TABLE 6.6 Religious ideology and milieu of origin (Piwowarski's data)

Religious ideology	Village	Small town	Town
(a) Complete or partial knowledge of the Trinity	82.7	77.8	78.5
(b) Complete or partial knowledge of life after death	75.6	69.2	77.0
(c) Agree that Christ is God made man	83.4	82.2	77.6
(d) Agree that the religious duties of a Catholic are:			
religious	23.6	25.5	27.9
ritualistic	46.3	47.0	28.6
moral	27.6	24.2	38.1

Note: The figures are percentages

TABLE 6.7 Reasons for belief (Piwowarski's data)

Why do I believe?	Parish A	Parish B	Parish C	Parish D
Tradition and upbringing	70.7	77.2	68.0	68.7
Own convictions	11.1	20.2	24.6	20.6

Note: The figures are percentages

urban-industrial centres investigated is the traditional rural type. This rural religiosity is characterized by high levels of belief and practice on the one hand, and by little knowledge of fundamental doctrine, a stress of the 'faith of our fathers', ritualism and a generally low score on many of the indicators on the other hand. About 40-45 per cent of the towns' populations fall into this category.(64)

The first direction of change in this traditional religiosity is towards the establishment of selective attitudes, notes Piwowarski. This is primarily a result of the characteristics of urban-industrial culture which gives rise to, firstly, the rationalization of attitudes and, secondly and as a consequence, the appearance of individualism and utilitarianism.(65) Selectivism is characterized by a questioning of some of the fundamental elements of Catholic doctrine, leaving only the belief in God intact: a belief in God as a 'Higher Force', but a belief which owes no allegiance to any religious institution and has little time for tradition; in other words, selectivism is a belief in a dechristianized God. One of the problems involved with the observation of the phenomenon of selectivism is concerned with the difficulty of finding a suitable model to compare it with. Piwowarski writes:(66)

It would be difficult to speak of the spread of the process of
secularization on the grounds that the population uses a completely different model of religious life as a point of reference
for its present religious attitudes. A more specific presentation
of this model is not possible. The abovementioned phenomenon
of selectivism is still in its nascent stage.

While Piwowarski points to the drop in practice and to the breaking with religious institutions - the characteristic feature of
selectivism - he nevertheless does not stop to consider that selectivism might be seen as a stage in the secularization of popular
attitudes. In addition, a knowledge of the dominant 'selected'
beliefs and of the way in which they are 'selected' may be able to
provide a clue as to further changes: this is certainly a direction
which Piwowarski should have developed a bit further. It is likely
that Piwowarski's direction of selectivism is the equivalent of
Adamski's practical secularization and is concerned with the very
same attitudes. According to Piwowarski, selective attitudes are
held by about 25-30 per cent of the populations.
In about 30 per cent of each of the urban populations there
occurs a polarization of religious attitudes with respect to the
model of traditional religiosity. Here Piwowarski identifies the simultaneous changes towards indifferentism and deepening.(67) In
the case of changes towards religious indifference, Piwowarski
fails to identify any significant trend towards atheism (Marxist-
Leninist beliefs or secularism);(68) he also stresses that this
indifferentism is characterized by both the observance of the rites
of passage and by the attendance at church during the important
feasts. It can therefore more usefully be seen in terms of a low
commitment. Piwowarski estimates that the religiously indifferent
make up some 15-20 per cent of the towns' populations.
The remaining 10-15 per cent are characterized by a strengthening of religious attitudes and by increasing religious commitment.
In this category Piwowarski identifies the consequential attitudes
which are manifest in regular practice and in a bond with religious
institutions. In this case too, it is not easy to specify the type of
religiosity which is appearing: does it represent an intensification
of the traditional model or is it an entirely new, say, post-Conciliar
model? Piwowarski suggests that the latter possibility is quite
likely on account of the concern with Church reform. One of the
other characteristics of the population in this category is its participation in religiously oriented informal groups.(69)
The identification of an urban religious culture might have been
made easier by the examination of the very religious Polish urban-
industrial centres such as the old and established ones of Upper
Silesia. Such centres might be usefully compared with centres like
Nowa Huta, Puławy, Płock, Gdańsk or Warsaw. The high level of
religiosity of Silesia has been mentioned in the context of Piwowarski's study by Bishop Herbert Bednorz of Katowice.(70) In a
way similar to Święcicki before him, Bishop Bednorz disagrees
with Piwowarski's caution and restraint and draws attention to the

fact that in the highly urbanized Silesia the Church is far from
marginal. He continues to note that while it is possible that Silesian religiosity may be far more intense than that of the areas
investigated by Piwowarski it is without doubt a striking contrast
with Western Europe. According to Bednorz, it appears that there
are very strong elements of traditionalism in Silesian urban-
industrial religiosity: the 'faith of our fathers' is a particularly
prominent characteristic. This differs somewhat from Piwowarski's
prognosis for Nowa Huta, Pulawy and Plock where traditionalism
is expected to give way to selectivism, religious indifference and
deepened personal commitment. Bednorz also stresses the importance of pastoral care and of church building in the maintenance
of religiosity in all areas.

High dependence on statistical method as a means of identifying
religious cultures (or different forms of religiosity) or as a means
of grasping detail and small differences in correlations is not likely
to produce fully satisfactory results and is very effort-consuming.
In Czarnowski's case, no statistics were referred to and yet a
consistent and illuminating picture was obtained; of the Polish
classics, it is probably Czarnowski who is referred to the most in
contemporary descriptions of Polish religiosity and religious culture.

The comparative model of popular Catholicism as used by Piwowarski is itself a secondary model; the primary model, on which
it is based, is the 'official' Church model. Piwowarski's work is
marked by a distinct bias towards the use of the secondary rather
than the primary model. Such a bias may cause difficulties in the
case of features which are common to, say, both rural and urban
religious culture. An example might be seen in Piwowarski's suggestion that the category of traditional religiosity of urban centres
is, in reality, rural religiosity 'imported' into the town by the
migrants or, alternatively, as a remnant of a disappearing pattern.
The question is particularly important in view of Bednorz's suggestion that the 'faith of our fathers' is a characteristic of Silesian
urban religiosity. The difference in the two views is not merely
one of definition or classification: it reflects a different assessment of the potential for possible future changes in urban religiosity. Piwowarski tends to regard the traditional 'faith of our
fathers' both as a temporary phenomenon under urban conditions
(or, at least, as a phenomenon which is in a state of flux and instability) and, perhaps only partly, as an undesirable form of
religiosity. Bednorz, on the other hand, would tend to see it as
stable and no more or less desirable than any other form of worship or attachment to God. Piwowarski's view, therefore, is also
marked by a strong personal bias in favour of an 'intellectual' version of Catholicism.

The difference between the two views results from the application of different models. The whole question of models, although
very important, is impossible to go into at this stage; however, it
needs to be stressed that a model used cannot be an arbitrary
construct established for comparative use only - it must be seen

to have some sort of 'reality', applicability or sense-giving potential in the eyes of the believers involved although not necessarily
reflecting directly the theology of the beliefs. It is not altogether
clear to what extent Piwowarski's approach to post-Czarnowskian
models of religiosity contains such provisos.

Perhaps ironically, in view of Piwowarski's extensive use of
statistical material, some of the most important observations are of
a statistically unquantifiable nature. These observations are concerned with the reasons for the observed high levels of religiosity
in urban areas; Piwowarski identifies the following factors: the
role of the family milieu, the significance of Catholicism to the
definition of the Polish nation, the role of pastoral care and, finally, the characteristics of the socialist political system.(71)

A chapter devoted to religiosity would be incomplete without a
mention of the work of Anna Pawełczyńska. Pawełczyńska is particularly noted for her statistical work on the correlation of religiosity with other social data at national level. Pawełczyńska worked
mainly with materials obtained by the various projects of the
OBOP of which she was the director. The OBOP was set up during
the initial years of the post-Stalin thaw in order to monitor social
and demographic changes at national level. It began surveys in
1959, but after 1968 no information was made public partly on
account of the re-tightening of the political screw after the 1968
events and also possibly because of the fear that the figures
might continue to contradict the official claims of the party. That
any genuine figures should vindicate the party's ideological claims
is asking rather a lot. Adam Podgórecki, arguing from statistical
data on Polish society, concludes that an examination of contemporary Polish social structure shows it to have nothing in common
with Marxism-Leninism of any description, official or otherwise.(72)
Various surveys have continued since 1968, but their details remain unknown and access to them remains limited to the few.
Pawelczyńska was not the only investigator of religiosity who
worked with OBOP data.(73)

Pawelczyńska was interested in religious self-identification and
claims of religious practice. Material from 1960 illustrates the national differential in religiosity between rural and urban milieux:
in the rural milieu 83.8 per cent believe, 80.00 per cent practise,
in the urban milieu 75.6 per cent believe, 69.6 per cent practise.(74)
An analysis of changing cultural (and religious) patterns by Paw-
leczyńska has been described in English by Jan Siek;(75) on the
basis of national data Pawelczyńska investigated further the relationship between indicators of urbanization and indicators of
religiosity.

It is characteristic of Polish studies of secularization that, despite the very obvious importance of pastoral care as a causal factor
in the process of changing religiosity, very little attention is paid
to it apart from sporadic and ritual references.(76) The term
'pastoral care' must be understood here in its broadest sense
which includes the Primate's and the hierarchy's 'public relations'
work, through the type of education received by seminarists right

down to the parish priest's catechetal work with children and to
the building of local churches. It would be difficult to imagine
the original Christianization of Europe and Poland without the missionary, evangelical and pastoral work of the clergy and of the
religious orders: this process is still taking place in a multitude
of forms and there is no immediately obvious reason why this crucial activity should find itself at the margin of sociological investigations of Christianization and secularization. It would not be
surprising to find, for example, that differences in the type of
parish pastoral care and evangelical zest can account for both
differences in levels of religiosity and for trends in the direction
of Christianization or dechristianization.

It is, of course, possible to speculate on the reasons for this
state of affairs in the sociology of religion. It is very likely that
these reasons, rather than being the result of simple intellectual
oversights and mistakes which they may appear to be at first
sight, are rooted in the pervading secularizing bias which has
also found its way, albeit in a diluted form, into the work of non-
secularist sociologists of religion.

It seems that one of the reasons for the shying away by sociologists from the question of pastoral care may be the fear of the
accusation of 'extreme Church-oriented' sociology of religion.
While it is likely that extreme Church orientation is likely to
dampen the spirit of objective enquiry if due care is not exercised
it is nevertheless true that if work is to be of practical value it
must be 'something-oriented' - a 'nothing-oriented' account is
even difficult to imagine. It is above all the criteria of philosophical and methodological soundness with respect to facts that must
be satisfied by any orientation.

Another reason may be connected with a general malaise affecting institutions,(77) a malaise which may even have affected the
sociology which deals with these institutions.(78) Certainly, judging from studies of secularization in Poland and elsewhere, there
is a distinct tendency amongst sociologists to deal with the 'mass'
aspect of religion and a decided reluctance to consider the aims
and significance of religious institutions.

Yet another reason may be found in an implicit and even subconscious assumption that pastoral care is either an uninteresting
constant or is declining in effectiveness. This assumption may be
found in association with the secularizing belief that the clergy
themselves have seen through the façade of religion and are now
just 'doing a job'. Another possibility here is the similarly secularizing belief that the process of secularization is in some way 'natural' (meaning inevitable) and that the clergy are doing no more
than 'slowing down secularization artificially'. It is easy to see
how signs of desecularization could be easily dismissed here on
the grounds that it is 'artificial'.(79) These final reasons are unlikely to afflict the non-secularist sociology of religion, however.

Each of these reasons taken alone would probably be insufficient
to account for the effective marginalization of pastoral care in
studies of secularization, but a combination of two or more may

begin to constitute a significant degree of pressure. Despite the
almost general reticence amongst sociologists to discuss the question, Bohdan Cywiński – an historian – has argued that the state
of religiosity in Poland today would have been quite different had
it not been for the way in which pastoral care was exercised since
the end of the war.(80) Arguing that levels of mass religiosity
are very sensitive to pastoral care, Cywiński concludes that the
way in which its techniques are adapted to changing conditions is
crucial to the future of Catholicism in Poland.

For the Church itself, pastoral strategy has formed a major
part of its activity throughout history and today the Church has
material, aimed at internal use, on the subject of evangelization
technique.(81) However, even Jan Sadok, who has produced a
typology of strategies of evangelization which have been observable since the end of the First World War, does not disclose much
detail regarding the strategy itself.(82) He observed four types
of strategy: monopolistic, apostolic, defensive and existential
dialogue.

The monopolistic strategy was a feature of the inter-war years
up to 1930. It was characterized by the extensive use of the state
machinery and political pressure by the Church. The apostolic
strategy (1930-9) was based on the ideas of Pope Pius XI and the
principal method employed was the special encouragement of Catholic lay organizations through the agency of the already mentioned
Catholic Action. Most notable here were Marian Sodality and the
Prayer Apostolate.

The most important strategy, however, has been that of defence. This strategy began already in 1939 with the outbreak of
the Second World War and has been continuing ever since. At the
same time the Church, in order not to isolate itself and withdraw
from its role began to take part in widespread discussions with its
opponents on the subject of the meaning of existence. Sadok's
characterization of this final strategy must be treated with caution
since the opponents to whom Sadok refers are not the representatives of totalitarianism but the left-wing intelligentsia whose
antipathy towards the Church and Catholicism dates from before
the Second World War. Sadok writes: 'The Church succeeded in
bridging the abyss separating it from the non-Catholic radical left.
Many of these people are now probably quite sincere in their quest
for institutional guarantees of the defence of human rights.'(83)

An important area is the development of new pastoral techniques.
It is clear from the development of concepts like the 'apostolate of
the lay' (which will be returned to in chapter 8) that this area is
one where changes are occurring – changes which may have far-
reaching consequences.

This is an appropriate point at which to mention the way in
which the question of secularization is seen by the Church. The
area of greatest concern is that of morality where the Church has
identified some alarming trends. These trends are seen to be a
result of the socio-political climate which, in an apparently para-
doxical way, while totalitarian is encouraging forms of liberalism

conducive to the breakdown of traditional values and to an atomization of individuals. The liberalism thus curiously becomes a
means to a totalitarian end. The effect of this sort of social structure has been summed up by Artur Bierutowicz, who wrote:(84)

> The greatest evil in Poland is...that the society is unaware of
> its rights, that the system is bringing up generations of mind-
> less and ignorant barbarians, that the greatest tragedy con-
> sists of the moral havoc and depravity wreaked by over thirty
> years of communist rule.

Although these trends obviously cannot be extrapolated to infinity
they are, nevertheless, of present concern to the Church. The
principal areas where an abandonment of Christian criteria has
clearly taken place are as follows: (1) Alcoholism.(85) This is increasing at an alarming rate and spreading to segments of society
where it had been previously unknown, for instance amongst
women and children; (2) the incidence of divorce is increasing;
(3) the incidence of abortion is one of the highest in Europe; (4)
there is widespread corruption (the greasing of palms is especially
common and accepted), work is not treated seriously (the honest
day's work is hard to find), hypocrisy is rampant. A small incidence of these social problems, although still undesirable, is
tolerable and it may even be difficult to put a limit on what is
tolerable and to define the circumstances under which it is tolerable. But this is a case of epidemic proportions which, Church
leaders point out, is incompatible with the notion of a Christian
society and degrading of the human person.

This depravity is probably indicative of an erosion of some of
the edges of the Catholic community. It would be imprudent to
suggest any more than this since other evidence (some of which
still remains to be noted by us) points both to consolidation at
other edges and to a considerable strengthening of parts of the
core.

7 FROM MARXISM
TO CHRISTIANITY

The approaches to an understanding of the process of secularization examined so far belong to two broad tendencies. The first
of these tendencies centres on two different types of approaches
to the phenomenon of religiosity: firstly, placing it in the context
of a Marxist-Leninist secular Utopia; secondly, observing changes
in religiosity under the impact of the modernizing social processes
associated with science, technology, industrialization and urbanization. These approaches are, of course, properly sociological
according to the Polish definiton of sociology. The first of these
approaches, however, is marked by the inevitable poverty of ideas
associated with Marxist approaches. Another possible approach
within this tendency consists of viewing Catholicism in the context
of secularist assault or religious persecution; as yet this area is
poorly developed.

The second tendency, which we have described in some detail,
attempts to place the process of secularization in a central position
in an alternative vision of the historical process. In Poland, this
tendency is not generally considered to be properly sociological.
The approaches belonging to this tendency suggest, firstly, that
all religion is losing significance as the central pivot of the historical process and will soon become a mere part of history and,
secondly, that there is a complementary and simultaneous process
by which secularism (i.e. the social system based on a philosophy
of a denial of God and on opposition to all religious belief) rises
in significance and eventually becomes the only reference point
and pivot in the whole of the historical process - even in retrospect; the present day is seen here as a 'great turning point' or
apocalypse where the secular triumphs over the religious.

While, on the one hand, the concepts involved in the 'rise of
secularism' thesis are without doubt sociological ones (they pur-
port to explore the relationship between religion and society) and,
on the other hand, the 'great turning point' or the 'final stages'
of the process of secularization are, at least in some sense, capable of being subject to empirical (and even statistical) sociological scrutiny, the overall process remains a terra incognita to the
conventional Polish sociologist of religion of both apologetic and
independent orientation. It is almost as though a conscious decision had been taken by the conventional sociologists to go no
further than, at best, the merest mention of historical and philosophical theorizing: any incursions into territory outside the
preoccupation with empiricism, contemporary data and processes
is regarded with a degree of suspicion. The main reason for this

is probably the legacy of the positivistic and empiricist pattern of thought which easily leads to a preoccupation with the fear of the accusation of 'unscientific'. It is likely that this positivist and empiricist legacy was also partly responsible for the spread of Marxist theory and method in the social sciences in Poland in the early days: Marxists had always claimed that their method was 'scientific' quite regardless of its other drawbacks or inadequacies.

In practice, the problem is solved by a compartmentalization of disciplines: in the case of the official orthodox Marxist-Leninist sociology of religion, work on secularization in a historical perspective, for example, belongs to the sphere of interest of the officially committed historian of religion or historian of atheism.(1) Similarly, within the non-secularist orientations the contemporary statistical data of the Catholic and independent sociologists of religion are complemented by the separate work of historians and philosophers.(2)

In this chapter we shall examine the sociologically relevant contributions of those philosophers and historians whose prime concerns fall somewhat outside the limits we have described. Some of these ideas were designed to prop up official totalitarian wisdom, others were genuinely independent. The only common characteristic of these ideas is the way in which they explore the relationship between Christianity and society: there is no one consistent line of thought nor are there any general categories into which the contributions can be neatly placed. In an indirect way, these contributions strongly demonstrate the failings of discussions centring on 'instant secularization' and 'secular purpose' while remaining cautious about any secularization or desecularization thesis.

We shall be principally concerned with the contributions of Leszek Kołakowski who, as a philosopher and historian, has distinguished himself by his striking reflections on Christianity, history and society. Kołakowski is important for two main reasons: firstly, because of his observations and, secondly, because his own intellectual development can be seen to mirror tendencies which can best be described as desecularizing.

After his uncompromising attacks on Christianity during the Stalinist period Kołakowski's revisionism led him to produce a thesis of a 'contemporary Counter-Reformation'. This thesis was one of the first departures from the ritual repetition of secularization theses by what had apparently been the secularist camp. It is interesting to note that Kołakowski's thesis of the Counter-Reformation appeared several years before the appearance of the bulk of the empirical work on secularization and that his ideas were not referred to by any of the sociologists, secularist or independent, who were concerned with the problem of secularization. Since almost all this work has appeared after Kołakowski's fall from official grace and his subsequent departure from Poland - after the decision that Kołakowski was a non-person and after the forbidding of his name in print by the GUKPPiW - the above is perhaps not surprising.

Kołakowski's Counter-Reformation thesis stresses the point that the Church never remains passive in the face of political, economic, social and cultural change.(3) When Kołakowski advanced the thesis he was clearly moving away from his previous total commitment to the party line. The thesis might never have been published were it not for the fortunate coincidence that the official policy line of the 1956-70 period sought to encourage and exploit any progressive and modernist tendencies within the Church. The party hoped to draw out these tendencies, to weaken them and then use them in order to gain entry into the institutional Church. The authorities no doubt thought that the term Counter-Reformation could be used as an attractive form of bait in this process. On the other hand, the thesis could still in principle be used as a solid argument which would justify the continued taking of anti-religious measures. It might even be used to provide the theoretical basis for the myth of the sentient dragon; this myth was later exploited by Ciupak in his sociological work.(4) In other words, although Kołakowski seemed to be breaking with convention (his view contrasts sharply with that of Nowicki, who tends to see the Church as rooted in unchangeability and opposed to all change)(5) it was by no means clear at the time what the consequences of the departure were to be.(6)

Kołakowski rejected the thesis that religion is capable of dying out automatically even under the conditions of a socialist state. Indeed, he argued that left to its own devices under circumstances where it has been gradually deprived of political influence and material assets, the Church 'perfects the tools of ideological influence and encourages the formation of a Catholic culture which is of an incomparably higher level than that which is possible under the conditions of an intellectual and political dictatorship of the Church.(7) This does not mean that the thesis accepts the triumph of Catholicism in Polish society as inevitable either in the form of a new dictatorship or as a re-emergence of a strong Catholic culture;(8) it merely reflects accurately Kołakowski's own observations of the position of Catholicism in Poland.

The thesis also marks Kołakowski's disappointment with the state of anti-religious propaganda which was inherited from the days of Stalinism. This propaganda consisted, above all, of simple vilification. This was considered as a sufficient form of criticism. Kołakowski stresses that this form of primitive atheism is the natural corollary of primitive obscurantist Catholicism. He also stresses the condition - in many ways obvious but perhaps not appreciated enough by the secularists - that the atheist approach should be designed at attracting believers and not, as was manifestly the case in practice, atheists. He writes: 'Effective propaganda must not demand from those who are being addressed that they must, above all else, admit that they are cretins and scoundrels.'(9) Although this was a taunt it might well have been taken as aptly characterizing the new post-Stalinist 'reasonable' approach to the matter of religion and accepted in good faith as a piece of sound advice especially since Kołakowski himself was guilty of having employed the very approach he now criticizes.

Let us now take a look at Kolakowski's presentation of the thesis. Kołakowski writes:(10)

> The Counter-Reformation...is the totality of measures, undertaken within the world of Christianity beginning from the middle of the sixteenth century, which aim to adapt Christianity to life under new political, economic and cultural conditions....
> The Counter-Reformation is not simply an effort aimed at reinstating the pre-Reformation order of things but an attempt at an internal transformation which will enable the Church to assimilate those values which have existed to the outside of it and despite it; it is an attempt to make these values part of its own body and so ensure that they cease to remain opposing forces. The Counter-Reformation, if it is to be effective, must be practical and self-critical.

Kołakowski adds that the Counter-Reformation does not constitute a consistent and harmonious body of ideas but is full of internal contradictions.(11) Those elements of Catholicism which are prepared to take up the process of self-criticism draw on the argument that 'all human values, regardless of their origins, are suitable for acceptance by Christianity, that - in other words - all human goods are worthy of the support of Christianity simply on the grounds that they are good.'(12) Such are the bare essentials of the Counter-Reformation thesis.

Some of the details of the thesis are of lesser importance. Kołakowski identifies the central Counter-Reforming tendencies with Thomist thought which, he states, has been:(13)

> The philosophical legitimation for the assimilation by Catholicism of those civilizing processes (in politics, philosophy and science) which arose in conflict with Church orthodoxy and which proved to be quite resistant to attempts at destruction. It therefore became necessary to master and exploit them.

Kołakowski takes J. Danielou's Thomist interpretation of history to be the finest example of the central tendency of contemporary historiosophical thought regarding the assimilation of new ideas into Catholicism; Kołakowski writes that in it we find:(14)

> An attempt to *take over* the historiosophical problems of Marxism, *instead of their total negation*, and an attempt to include them in the framework of Christian eschatology as a set of real but subordinated questions. It is also an attempt to take over (in a rather general way) the social postulates of the socialist movement and then to crown them with a Christian superstructure.

The central interest of the Counter-Reformation thesis lies not in the specific form in which it is presented by Kołakowski (the

above formulation is subject to so many objections that it is un-
tenable) but, firstly, in its dominant argument and, secondly, in
the way in which it gives an insight into Kołakowski's intellectual
development. Let us now deal with each of these two points in
turn.

Kołakowski's dominant argument can best be assessed by carefully restating or even modifying it in the following way. It is
undeniable that some changes do occur in the Church (both in
terms of arguments employed and doctrinal emphasis) and that
they are in some way connected with the cultural, economic and
political climate of the time. These changes may lead to a strengthening of the Church and of Christianity (or Catholicism) as, indeed, they may also in principle lead to a weakening. It is also
correct that the original Counter-Reformation was designed with
the aim of such a strengthening. In this context, the age-old observation that persecution serves to strengthen Christianity can
be understood more easily. It can thus be seen that the contemporary Counter-Reformation thesis can easily become stronger,
more convincing and less open to objection while at the same time
becoming somewhat vague, less original and, most importantly,
less of a slave to the communist political wisdom. Put this way, it
is in fact both respectable and nothing new. And it without doubt
becomes valid as an explanation of many of the contemporary
changes in Polish Catholicism.

Two important objections to Kołakowski's thesis must now be
voiced. Firstly, Kołakowski does not make clear the distinction
between those elements in society (or, in this case, in Marxism-
Leninism) which can be absorbed into Catholicism and those which
cannot; it is difficult not to get the impression that Kołakowski is
in some way suggesting that Catholicism is 'infinitely expandable'
or 'infinitely adaptable'. However, this is obviously not the case:
atheism, for example, cannot become absorbed into Catholicism
despite the wishes to the contrary by the secularists. Nor can,
according to some of Kołakowski's own remarks, some contemporary versions of humanism. Secondly and arising out of the above,
a concern by the Church with problems over which Marxism or
socialism claims a monopoly does not imply the 'taking over' of the
content of Marxism or socialism. The appearances of taking over
arise from certain similarities in Marxism and Catholicism; these
similarities stem from the sectarian character of Marxism. Historically, they arose as an attempt to create the 'perfect (according to
Christian criteria) society'.(15) A reassertion of the Christian
criteria within Catholicism, albeit in a way which is not Utopia-
oriented, can easily be misinterpreted as a taking over. It might
be more appropriate to state that it is Marxism-Leninism which
wishes to take over areas which are typically Christian.

The Counter-Reformation can perhaps best be seen for our purposes as a reaction under threatening circumstances: it may be
successful or unsuccessful. It is therefore important not to confuse a threatening situation with the decline of the Church and
religion: the final result may be the reverse. This argument is not

limited to a reaction vis à vis a Marxist or socialist threat to the
Church, but also encompasses reactions in the face of the 'technological Utopia', religious indifference and galloping liberalism.
The main point concerned with Kołakowski's intellectual development is that – in contrast to his earlier position during the Stalinist period – he now leans in favour of Thomism. It is likely that
this volte face was brought on by Kołakowski's gradual realization
that his earlier views of Christianity and of the Catholic Church
were naïve and incorrect, by a belief that the Church under communism was becoming in some way better and by a growing disillusionment with Marxist-Leninist philosophy.
Meanwhile, the secularist camp was repeating the well-worn
attacks on Thomism right into the 1970s. Józef Grudzień, for example, writes as follows:(16)

Up to now, the whole history of the Roman Catholic Church
has been a constant process of adaptation by this institution
and its doctrine to a ceaselessly changing world. The truth of
this thesis is confirmed by both the experts and the theologians
of the Church.

These remarks form the introduction to Grudzień's attack on Thomism to be found in the following pages of the work. Grudzień
argues that Thomism is now in a state of crisis and has not – on
account of its inflexibility – the confidence of leading Catholic
thinkers. He states: 'Thomism has never played a progressive
role in history. Thomas himself and the Thomists represented – in
a forthright way – integrism, clericalism and intolerance.'(17)
These are precisely the very opposite to those described by Kołakowski in the Counter-Reformation thesis. They are more akin to
Kołakowski's remarks during the period of Stalinism and should
most certainly be taken as an indicator of the authorities' harden-
ing intentions with respect to the Church. Grudzień concludes:(18)

Thomism is incapable of dealing with – let alone solving – today's
problems. The attitude of Thomists to problems preoccupying
contemporary man is anachronistic: this is the result of the anachronistic nature of the philosophy's metaphysical assumptions.
The possibility of further developing Thomist philosophy is neg-
ligible since its inflexible structures, which are not related in
an authentic and convincing way to the rapid process of change
occurring in the contemporary world, do not permit it. For this
very reason non-Thomist philosophical thought exhibits greater
signs of dynamic development in those groups of Catholics who
are committed to social progress.

The viciousness of this attack is not immediately apparent to those
not fully acquainted with the issues – indeed, the passage appears
almost reasonable. However, when we take into account the fact
that the backbone of Catholic theology in Poland is Thomist, that
Thomism is asserting itself as a cornerstone of Catholic thought on

the world scale and that Pope John Paul II is a leading protagon-
ist of Thomist ideas we begin to see the nature of the secularist
quarrel with Thomism.

The account of Kołakowski's contributions to the sociology of
religion would be incomplete without mention of his writings since
1968 when he was expelled from the Chair of Philosophy at UW
before finally leaving Poland. It is possible to trace a definite line
of evolution in his thought,(19) a line which has led him from his
original Stalinism to the declaration that 'Marxism has been the
greatest fantasy of our century'.(20) It is inevitable that his
views of religion should also have changed substantially: it is
therefore necessary to note that Kołakowski's recent contributions
are best treated as quite separate from his earlier work.

In these later writings, Kołakowski expresses his distrust of a
particular version of the instant secularization thesis. Caricatur-
ing this version, he writes:(21)

> Are we following scientific method when we base a law of history
> on Church attendance figures gathered over a period of a few
> decades?... Predictions about the decline of religion in our
> society, rather than being based on plain statistics, stem more
> from a particular interpretation of these statistics - an interpre-
> tation which is in turn based on an *ad hoc* theory of human
> nature.

Kołakowski argues that it is a simple instrumentalist theory of religion which is responsible for these predictions.(22) But to say
that religion can be understood only in instrumental terms, writes
Kołakowski,(23)

> Is not merely to fail to recognize all that distinguishes human
> culture and immediate endeavour from biological adaptation, it
> is to make that culture incomprehensible; if there has been a
> passage of society from a state where human needs expressed
> themselves directly to a state where they began to appeal to the
> authority of the sacred in order to express themselves to seek
> support in the 'ideological inversion' this process is in no way
> explained by the content of these needs. Consequently, that
> which was to be explained remains shrouded in mystery.

Kołakowski distinguishes between three forms of 'secularization':
firstly, a decline in mass religiosity;(24) secondly, a decline in
the 'need' for religion (not substantiated by any observational
data, he notes);(25) thirdly, an erasing of the boundary between
the sacred and the profane - if this boundary disappears, all necessarily becomes either sacred or profane. Therefore, in this
sense, secularization is as much the disappearance of the profane
as it is the disappearance of the sacred.(26) This third form of
secularization is seen by Kołakowski as being the dominant one of
the Christian world; it derives principally from a tendency aimed
at the sanctification of the profane world. Kołakowski identifies

this tendency as lying within the Christian tradition itself: it consists of the fundamental choice of either being a 'true' Christian in this world or being in harmony with the exigencies of the world. This is essentially the same type of argument as the one put forward by Martin.(27) This form of the concept of secularization is also, in a sense, the theoretical equivalent of the Church-state relationship in history.

At this point, referring implicitly to the Counter-Reformation thesis, Kołakowski suggests that Christianity(28)

> Obsessed by the panic fear of becoming reduced more and more to the state of an isolated sect...., in order not to be devoured by its enemies seems to be making wild efforts at mimicry - a reaction which, although defensive in appearance, is self-destructive in its consequences. Although Christianity appears to be camouflaging itself with the colours of its surroundings in the hope of saving itself it is in fact losing its identity. This identity is based precisely on the distinction between sacred and profane and on a tension between the two - a tension where the eruption of a conflict is always possible and often inevitable.

This is the very opposite of what Kołakowski was saying and implying when he praised the Counter-Reforming tendencies of Catholicism.(29)

But perhaps the most dramatic reappraisal by Kołakowski of his previous ideas is concerned with his view of the question whether secularization has the virtue of 'liberating' man's energy so that all his efforts can be directed towards the improvement of his life.(30) This question is closely related to the idea of secularization which sees religion as alienation although the element of Utopianism is somewhat weaker because of the lack of stress of the perfect society. Kołakowski's argument is based on a philosophy of culture and takes the form of the defence of the sacred;(31) he argues that the meanings of the fundamental human activities are entirely supra-empirical, as is also the distinction between good and evil: the meanings and distinctions derive directly from a conception of the sacred.(32) A brushing aside of these meanings and distinctions by the elimination of the sacred (either by making all sacred or nothing sacred) amounts to the sanctioning of 'man the animal' - a return to primitive man who reacts only in terms of biological needs and immediate desires and who can be controlled only through force and violence.(33) These comments not only challenge the alienation thesis of religion but invert it: secularization is seen as a return to an even more fundamental primitive state than that of the archaic man described in chapter 1 above.

Although Kołakowski does not refer to any concrete examples of societies when he describes 'man the animal', it is nevertheless clear that he is basing himself both on the extreme dependence of secularist regimes on force and violence (the disappearance of the sacred) and on the orgiastic violence of revolutionary anarchic sectarianism (the disappearance of the profane).

The whole of Kołakowski's argument is constructed around a philosophy of history which conceives the present as a period of conflict between structure and development (conservatism and change). The distinction here must be guarded as must the control of the process of change: the latter is normally the job of tradition; a breakdown of this delicate balance may lead either to stagnation (the refusal of any form of change), the result of an extreme conservativism, or to a disintegration of culture (the total break with tradition and all previous points of reference), the result of uncontrolled change. Central to this scheme is the role of tradition in its capacity as the main stronghold of the sacred.(34) Indeed, the principal way in which the sacred can act on society is through tradition.

Kołakowski thus pleads for a society where the sacred and the profane are able to coexist. The desire to break unconditionally with tradition is also a desire, although perhaps a subconscious one, to shake off the sacred and is thus a clear mark of a secularizing trend.

Kołakowski also notes the close relationship between the idea of secular (unrestricted) man and omnipotent (infinitely perfectable) man who takes the place of God.(35) He observes that:(36)

> The vitality of Christianity certainly lessened in conjunction with the spread of Promethean hopes, in other words, with the growing belief that man's ability to perfect himself and his society knows no limits and that it will either build increasingly magnificent monuments to his greatness or finally bring to humanity a life from which all evil, suffering, aggression, conflict, poverty, unrest and sorrow have been for ever purged. We have witnessed a long-lasting growth of this hope and its two... versions - Nietzsche's and Marx's - produced the ideological blanket serving to legitimize two of the most sinister tyrannies which our century has seen.

Kołakowski continues that, because the Promethean hope is now past its zenith, fertile ground on which Christianity thrives will now increase.(37)

In a subsequent piece, Kołakowski further develops the idea of the disappearance of the boundary between the sacred and the profane.(38) He notes that the boundary risks being blotted out by two, seemingly opposite, currents of thought in Catholicism: integrism and progressism. Although these two currents are both based on ostensibly different - even opposite - political philosophies, both sets of propositions contain the seeds of a secularizing process: they both exert pressure on the boundary, but each in an opposite direction. It is important to stress that these two currents gain in strength under conditions of totalitarianism or dictatorship (Eastern Europe and Latin America are considered fertile ground for these two currents) and that the subsequent secularizing developments must be seen in relation to political con-

ditions and to attitudes taken by the Church with respect to those
conditions.

Kołakowski notes that both integrism and progressism can find
themselves in a position of conflict with the ruling elite. The integrist view under conditions of communist totalitarianism stresses
that the key problem lies in the atheism of the regime and not in
its totalitarianism. Under such circumstances we observe that the
main concern of the Church is apt to become not the transmission
of faith itself but the practical mechanics of implementing policies
reflecting the need to protect the Church and its interests – even
interests which may be at odds with its own teaching. In this way
it is possible to identify totalitarian tendencies(39) within the
Church which can itself in turn become a totalitarian power or
be at least willing to accept totalitarianism provided it were based
on a Christian mythus and the interests of the Church as an institution were safeguarded. The political fuses with the religious,
the sacred-profane boundary substantially weakens: the argument
that 'all is really political' can now be accurately applied to the
Church's role and activities. An obvious practical difficulty with
the integrist position concerns the problem which arises in the
case of a totalitarianism or dictatorship which is based on a
Christian mythus but which does not protect the interests of the
Church.(40) Another difficulty is exemplified by the case of the
extreme integrist position of the Russian Orthodox Church: its
attempts to sanctify the world through its political power led to
its virtual demise after the removal of that power – it is but a
shadow of its former self.

Progressism, argues Kołakowski, stresses that the key problem
in society is that of social inequality and lack of democracy – a
characteristic feature of dictatorial regimes. Here we observe the
tendency of the progressist view to argue strongly in favour of
the Church's role in political opposition movements designed to
implement or restore equality in particular. Indeed, the argument
may even suggest that this is the principal or perhaps only role of
the Church. An acceptance of such a position by the Church as
an institution amounts to a negation of its raison d'être. Once
again, all has now become social and the prime role of the Church
may fall by the wayside. But, as in the case of integrism, there
is also a practical danger. The Church can pursue the course of
social involvement only by joining forces with the Marxist-Leninist
egalitarian crusade – there is no other ally. In this context, it is
often argued that Marxist-Leninist thought is in reality Christian
and that Marxist-Leninists err merely in some minor matters of
theology. The whole of the progressist argument can be seen to
be a variant of the sectarian 'true Christianity'. The result of this
sort of alliance can be inferred immediately from a glance at Eastern Europe: the former ally, when in power, has without exception
always become uncompromisingly and violently hostile to all forms
of religion.(41)

The Church does, nevertheless, have a third option which is
non-secularizing, argues Kołakowski. He suggests that it should

remain independent of the state and, something which cannot occur
in a communist regime, pursue its mission within a framework of
pluralist politics or, if the latter possibility does not exist, to
seek the establishment of a pluralist system.

We shall now make a few comments in order to explore and clarify some of the points made by Kołakowski.

Firstly, Kołakowski is perhaps slightly tendentious in the way
he recommends that the Church should be politically committed to
pluralism. His recommendation is qualified by his claim that liberalism no longer presents a secularizing danger to the Church.
This issue is important since the acceptance of a pluralist political
framework by the Church requires it to take up a position regarding liberalism which forms an integral part of a pluralist system. Kołakowski argues that the Church should not try to impose
politically its Christian vision on society - it should merely argue
for it. However, a difficulty does arise in the case of abortion,
for example. Is the Church, therefore, expected to simply tolerate
an act which seems to answer to the criteria of murder simply on
the grounds that some individuals desire it for their convenience
or is it to take any available measures in order to put a stop to
it?(42) This is exactly the sort of question that Kołakowski wishes
to avoid in arguing for the Church's role as a sort of a bearer of
values, culture and meaning or as a giver of order. Kołakowski
did, of course, mention the tensions existing between the sacred
and the profane and the possibility of conflict between the two
spheres and it is here that we arrive at what is probably the un-
solved question. This question is clearly a two-sided one where
we must ask, on the one hand, at which point does the political
imposition of a Christian vision on society become sectarianism and,
on the other hand, at which point does the tolerance degenerate
into an undermining of the theological structure? The answers are
dependent on conditions and, as such, are subject to change with
time; the success of the Church must depend on the way in which
it can keep furthest from both theological compromise and sectarian
isolation. A re-reading of the post-war history of the Church in
Poland with this question in mind shows that Polish Catholicism
has been largely successful in solving the problem in its own
favour.

The second point is concerned with the inverse relationship, observed by Kołakowski, between Promethean hopes and Christianity.
This inverse relationship is the basis for the secularist view that
progress and Christianity are incompatible (the Promethean hope
equated with progress). Promethean hopes must not, however, be
understood as a cause of secularization: they are merely a logical
corollary or a reflection of the fundamental question 'God or man?'.
It is possible, nevertheless, that the Promethean hopes may at
times compete with Christianity and thus appear as causes of secularization; for example, under some conditions or historical junc-
tures evidence may suggest one direction of causality rather than
another. Thus it may be appropriate to ask whether there exists a
connection between the Nietzschean Superman or the Marxian King-

dom and the incorporation of economic, political or military success, or indeed failure, into the national myth. It is unlikely that a satisfactory answer can be given to this question without also taking traditions of thought into account. One possibility is that the failure of either the Superman or the Kingdom in the realization of promises may produce conditions unsuitable for the widespread growth of faith in man's limitless potential; or, put in another way, the faith itself may become condemned on the grounds that it is morally unacceptable rather than on the grounds that it is materially unproductive. This sort of view is stressed by much of the East European underground opposition movement. A different though analogous scenario may occur under conditions of economic failure.

The third point is concerned with the disintegration of culture, which Kołakowski puts forward as the consequence of secularization. In the case of Marxist-Leninist regimes this disintegration does succeed to the extent that it produces a high degree of social chaos. However, at the same time it is clear that there is a strong reaffirmation of features associated with the sacred (order, tradition, absolute values) from those quarters which are still capable of acting. Possible evidence for this view is that the Church and tradition in Poland have become almost synonymous under conditions of secularizing pressure.

Fourthly, there is the patent inability of Marxist-Leninists to produce any coherent and independent body of ethics.(43) Whilst various noises are made on this subject, the most serious attempt at the formulation of a secular ethics has a result which is remarkably similar to the Christian model without, of course, the support of the motivations of Christian belief. This similarity is not at all surprising since the secular formulations were lifted wholesale from the Judaeo-Christian tradition. In general, it could be said that all attempts in the direction of even considering the idea of ethics may be marked by a fear that the sacred cannot be fully dispensed with while retaining a degree of order supported by a non-coercive structure.

In a lecture delivered to Catholic intellectuals in Warsaw, Jaroszewski remarked that 'It is possible to accept the same values and the same norms while accepting different *Weltanschauungen*'.(44) This argument is similar to the line that Pax has been pursuing since the beginning of communist rule in Poland. What is perhaps most striking about Jaroszewski is that he continues by stating that an extraordinarily good basis for secular ethics could be provided by the Decalogue. While claiming that his choice of the Decalogue is motivated by considerations of practicability and utility, Jaroszewski suggests that it permits the elimination of injustice, the ordering of relations (both social and interpersonal) and raises the moral level of society. But, it must surely be asked, what are the criteria of justice, ideal relations and morality which Jarszweski seeks in the Decalogue? The realization that the answers to such questions need to be sought in the domain of the sacred must lead to the growing disillusionment with attempts to derive the moral from the empirical.

It is a mistake to think, however, that Jaroszewski's quest is first and foremost an intellectual one. It is above all else a means of making a point: it is very easy to see that his is yet another way of presenting secularism as deserving of the support of Christians.

The fifth point to be mentioned concerns the definition of secularization with respect to the thought embodied in the secularizing types of political attitudes (integrism, progressism or excessive liberal tolerance). The question is whether these attitudes (or even forms of sectarianism for that matter) can, regardless of future consequences, be considered already as secularization: latent, potential or hidden secularization. In other words, we are confronted with a phase where transcendental motivations do not play the dominant part in the structure of the claimed Christianity: Christianity begins to acquire meaning only in relation to its role as an eliminator of oppression and instigator of revolution or, in the case of Poland, as a guardian of the national consciousness and as an instrument of political opposition. One possible difficulty here is that latent secularization may, under certain circumstances, be a fully stable form which in no way represents merely a stage between the degeneration of a clear and explicit sacred-profane distinction to no distinction at all. Certainly, the guarding of national consciousness is a more stable form than the struggle for equality. It is quite possible, therefore, that this phase represents not so much a tension between the sacred and the profane as a tension between distinction and identity of sacred and profane. It is also possible that the phase of latent secularization is a reversible one, which means that it can be considered as a case of incomplete Christianization.

As a final note we can sum up Kołakowski's view of religion. He sees Christianity as existing in a state of tension between two extremes in its nature: as a protector and guardian of culture on the one hand, and as a possible participant in the evils of society on the other. Kołakowski's ideas stress indirectly the importance of both a historical perspective and historical material in the understanding of the processes of secularization and desecularization. This is an area which, until recently, had little of relevance to the sociologist of religion. Today, the situation is much more promising with an ever-increasing amount of varied material.

At this point it is appropriate to turn to one such historical account. Historian Bohdan Cywiński wrote a book stressing the importance of the cultural elite and its role in the religious life of the nation.(45) Although Cywiński is writing about events during the period of Poland's occupation, his general allusion to the present situation is clear and unquestionable.

Cywiński notes that the spread of positivism and radicalism during the latter half of the nineteenth century was responsible for the siphoning off of many of the more able minds from the Polish Catholic Church. This resulted in an intellectual impoverishment of the Church. Two distinct trends gradually became

visible within the cultural elite of Polish society: one characterized by the combination of a strong Polish Catholic identity with
intellectual primitivism, the other by the radical, enlightened and
secular 'inteligent'.(46) They were at war with each other.

At the same time, the situation of the Catholic Church had
changed from the favourable Constantinism to what Cywiński
terms Julianism,(47) where the policy of Tsarist Russia was directed at either its subordination to the Russian state or at its destruction by means of a mass conversion to Russian Orthodoxy.(48)
Despite having lost political influence, the Church had gained
immense moral authority as a result of its ability to deal successfully with the tremendous difficulties of the time.

Cywiński describes the relationship between what he sees as the
two great forces of Polish society in this way:(49)

> Although the secularist circles of the radical intelligentsia were
> separated from the Church by a wide rift of mutual antipathy
> and distrust; the differences were, nevertheless, not insur-
> mountable. It appears that even during the time of the greatest
> differences there emerged individuals...who were able to bridge
> the gap.

Here Cywiński has in mind the well-known figures who began
their intellectual development within nineteenth-century secular
radicalism (or even within Marxism itself) and who finally found
themselves clearly within the inspiration of the Church's teaching.
One of the best-known examples of this sort of life-history is
Stanisław Brzozowski who is considered to be one of the pillars of
Polish Marxism;(50) Brzozowski died a Catholic.

The abovementioned historical view begins to add up to a theory
of secularization and desecularization on the application of the
idea that there may be a direction which the logical and consequential development of certain ideas may take or, more specifically, that there is a desecularizing potential embedded in the
secular beliefs of the Christian tradition. In fact, this is the inverse of the view which suggests that Christianity carries within
itself the seeds of secularism and secularization. It would certainly
make sense to argue that the two views, rather than being mut-
ually exclusive, are complementary; further, it could also be
argued that there exists some sort of dynamic equilibrium between
the religious and the secular beliefs of Christian civilization: an
aspect, perhaps, of the tension between distinction and identity
of sacred and profane?

The analogy of Cywiński's account with the present day is particularly interesting although he is careful not to commit himself
on any concrete examples. The drawing of historical analogies to
the present day is a notoriously perilous exercise, the success of
which depends on knowing where to start and where to stop. However, it is not possible to avoid mentioning the two examples which
are popularly associated with Cywiński's thesis: that of Leszek
Kołakowski and that of Adam Michnik.

Kołakowski's intellectual development has already been noted. There is still no evidence to suggest that Kołakowski has arrived at Catholicism(51) after his long journey from Stalinism, but it is beyond doubt that he has evolved from a position of extreme and militant atheism - a personal foe of God(52) - to what appears to be (judging from his own claims) a friend and ally of the Catholic Church and even ready to defend the faith. It is even safe to argue that the doubts raised by Fr Jerzy Mirewicz in 1967 regarding Kołakowski's intellectual position no longer have the same force today.(53) In 1977, in answer to the question 'are you a Christian?', Kołakowski replied: 'Not in the sense of belonging to a Church or a sect. But I consider myself to be a participator in a living Christian culture. Man is both good and evil: evil is a vital force. I believe in original sin.'(54) Kołakowski's sympathetic account of Brzozowski's intellectual development is significant in the sense that it may be indicative of broad changes occurring in the Weltanschauung of Polish secular intellectuals; the importance of Kołakowski in this respect is stressed by Michnik, who writes; 'To our generation - excluding, of course, Catholics - Leszek Kołakowski was *the* example of civic courage, high moral standing and intellectual integrity.' Earlier Michnik had mentioned 'the man who was tacitly accepted by the intellectuals of the "secular left" as its ideologue - Leszek Kołakowski'.(55) The 'secular left' to which Michnik refers is a small but very vocal and well-organized group of intellectuals of the freethinking tradition who had faith either in the Polish regime or in a revision of official Marxism-Leninism during the first two decades of communist power in Poland. Their significance today lies mainly in their very active participation in underground opposition.

The second example, Adam Michnik himself, is significant in so far as the arguments advanced in his book(56) would appear to be at least a partial vindication of Cywiński's theses within the context of Poland's most recent history. As well as accepting Cywiński's view as valid, Michnik traces his own intellectual position from his close association with communist party circles to an expression of Catholic sympathies: he produces a picture very similar to Kołakowski's. Michnik also speaks strongly in favour of a rapprochement between the 'secular left' and the Church; such a rapprochement, he stresses, must be based on a realization that freedom for the Church is the ultimate measure of freedom in society. It is important to recall here the immense gulf which used to separate Michnik and the 'secular left' from the Church in order to appreciate the full significance of his view.

The way in which Michnik's book was received by the Church is indicative of its strong desire to remain independent of political movements and directions. Undoubtedly an important factor here is a fear of latent anti-religious tendencies within this movement. Such tendencies, while accepting the positive role of the Church during periods of occupation and foreign domination, may well turn against the Church under conditions of independence. Another possible factor may be the Church's inability to accept

liberal tenets even into its practical theology: an acceptance of
such tenets would appear to be a precondition of the sort of rapprochement suggested by Michnik.(57)

Such disputes are best seen as evidence that there is still some
ground separating individuals such as Kołakowski or Michnik from
the Church. At the same time, it is impossible to view their intellectual development in terms other than desecularization. In the
case of Kołakowski, in particular, it is clear that he has arrived
at a position where he believes that Christian values form an integral and necessary part of Polish (and European) culture and
civilization and that they must be defended at any cost. He
reached this view as a consequence of his total immersion in
forces erosive of Christianity.

8 WHAT NEXT?

In this chapter we will present a series of reflections and interpretations concerning the material which has been examined in
this study. We will also attempt to give some general impressions
regarding the process of secularization and the state of religion
and religiosity in Poland today. It is unlikely that all the areas
outlined sketchily below can be satisfactorily investigated under
the conditions of a totalitarian state. In this sense, the phenomenon of religion will always remain more of an enigma under totalitarianism than under other, more open, socio-political conditions.

On the basis of the currently available material, it is probably
too early to hope for a satisfactory synthesis. This is partly because, despite the enormous volume of material in some areas, not
all the avenues have been adequately explored.(1) This situation
is rapidly changing although parallel developments in Polish
society itself suggest that it will be some time yet before any clear
picture emerges. However, a preliminary attempt can be made.
Such an attempt at a synthesis should take as its central points
firstly, the weaknesses inherent in certain versions of the concept of secularization and secondly, the lack of convincing evidence in favour of many of the theses of secularization which have
been advanced. At the same time, care must be taken not to lose
sight of the quite convincing hypotheses which suggest desecularization or religious change. The picture which emerges is most
certainly not one of secularization, but one where the conventional
and established methodologies have proved to be inadequate.

One of the more important points illustrated by this study is
that the term secularization needs to be understood in several
senses; still further breakdown is possible into almost independent features. Even here we find that closely related features (or
even the same feature) may exhibit opposite trends simultaneously.
This point is illustrated by Piwowarski's conclusions regarding
the multi-directionality of changes in religiosity which were noted
in chapter 6. Another example concerns the area of political orientation: here we observe how different (in fact opposite) trends can
lead in the same direction (the direction of secularization) by
means of either totally accepting or totally rejecting a political
structure - we refer here to Kołakowski's comments regarding
integrism and progressism.

It has also become clear that any attempt to attribute weights to
the various meanings or senses in which the concept of secularization is used would be both a perilous and a futile exercise. It
is in principle impossible to arrive at any balance which represents

either secularization or desecularization; the practice of weighting is already of dubious value when applied to a mass of indicators of religiosity (or urbanization, industrialization, modernization, etc.): it becomes totally unacceptable when dealing with a cross-section of meanings and with changes which are statistically unquantifiable. Rather, the final picture should be seen to emerge out of an integrated pattern drawn from the totality of the evidence.

As an introduction to a synthesis it is necessary briefly to look at the applicability of the concept of secularization. The concept is notorious on account of its vagueness and variety of meanings - Martin has identified four areas of meaning(2) and Shiner has listed six different meanings of the term: Shiner's list, although it gives a coverage of the general terrain,(3) is incomplete without the additional elaboration by Michael Hill.(4) We shall therefore use Hill's account as a suitable point of departure for relating the Polish material to the context of the Western sociology of religion.

The first meaning of the concept of secularization which was noted by Shiner refers to the decline of religion; this idea has been treated extensively by Bryan Wilson.(5) The area covered by this use of the term includes, in particular, a decline in symbols, religious practice, institutions, doctrine and thinking; the myth of the Golden Age plays an important part in the idea of the decline. This meaning of the concept is perhaps the broadest and, not surprisingly, relates to much of the Polish material examined. Especially prominent in this context are the studies of religiosity and decline in practice which are then extrapolated into a decline of religion. Parallel with this are the secularist attempts at a restructuring of Polish history which, in some of the versions, claims to observe the decline of institutions and symbols over the centuries.

The second meaning of the term secularization is concerned with the shift from 'other-worldly' to 'this-worldly' orientations within the religious groups themselves. The suggestion here is that motivations for behaviour are becoming more and more related to the practicalities of life rather than to the 'other world'. Although this meaning is connected with the above, it is far more specific. Most obviously, it relates to the development of new orientations within broadly defined groups of Catholics as illustrated by the conclusions of Piwowarski (regarding selectivism) and Adamski (regarding practical secularization) noted in chapter 6. This meaning can also be most appropriately related to Kołakowski's notion of the disappearance of the sacred where the Church takes up a position vis à vis the current political issues. This meaning can also be related to the concept of alienation as used by the secularists.

The 'disengagement' of society from religion was noted by Shiner as the third use of the concept of secularization. Explaining this definition, Hill writes: 'Instead of religion's function being that of a primary source of legitimation for the whole of

society, it becomes increasingly a matter for private choice, restricted to the sphere of religiously interested participants.'(6)
A classic example of this view might be seen in Czarnowski's
suggestion of private religion and, today, a major part of the
policy of planned secularization is directed at the administrative
elimination of religion from public life; the general argument for
'disengagement', noted by Hill, might have been advanced by
Polish secularists: 'the traditional religious institutions which at
one time were responsible for educational and welfare functions
have been relieved of these activities by state agencies and...
find themselves more and more in a marginal position in industrial societies.'(7)

The next use of the concept of secularization refers to the
transposition of beliefs and activities in the sense that alternative functional equivalents for religion can be identified. The
Polish material can be seen, firstly, as providing details of the
question whether alternative beliefs and practices are taking
over from Catholicism and, secondly, as illustrating the extent
to which the policy of planned secularization involves a practical
application of these ideas.

The fifth use of the concept of secularization which we will
mention refers to the idea that the world is gradually being deprived of its sacral character. This idea was to be found in
Frazer's evolutionism and in Weber's notion of the 'disenchant-
ment of the world'. Typical of this idea is that modern developments of science and technology, for example, begin to eclipse
all notions of the mysterious and supernatural. This is a form of
scientific or technological messianism. This meaning of the concept is illustrated particularly well by the early Polish sociologists of religion. Its contemporary illustration can be seen in
much of the work of the official sociologists of religion.

Shiner's final use of the concept is concerned with the change
from a 'sacred' to a 'secular' society. The definition of sacred is
based on Howard Becker's idea of resistance to change; secular,
on the other hand, refers to the welcoming of change and to the
spread of utilitarian criteria. This meaning of the concept is
clearly another way of putting Kołakowski's point that the removal of a sacred reference point is impossible without a disintegration of culture.

Hill's additions to Shiner's list consist of the contributions of
Luckmann and Berger.(8) Luckmann stresses the decline in
Church-oriented religion - a process which results in a margin-
alization of the more traditional institutional forms of worship to-
gether with the simultaneous appearance of new forms of worship
and religion.(9) This type of approach is visible in the work of
Piwowarski and is also reflected in Święcicki's opposite view that
Church-oriented religion is not obviously declining in Poland.
Berger refers to the role of religion as a protective device
against meaninglessness(10) - there are very strong echoes of
Kołakowski here - and to the secularizing tendencies inherent in
Christianity.

Despite the apparent comprehensiveness of the list, close inspection reveals that it is of limited applicability to the Polish
material. One reason is that although it happily fits the material,
there turns out to be far more material than can be satisfactorily
accommodated. Secondly, the lack of detailed signposts within
the list is an almost open invitation to the deliberate exclusion
of many relevant features.

One or two examples may make this point clear. In Polish society the policy of planned secularization, together with its
attendant institutions and sociological theory, is an important
part of the Polish picture of secularization. However, it is a feature which is difficult to incorporate into or deduce from any already established Western scheme of classifying approaches to
secularization. At the same time, it cannot be dismissed simply
as religious persecution with the associated images of burning
churches. Also, ideas regarding the Counter-Reformation and its
attendant mechanisms - religious elites, evangelization, pastoral
care - do not immediately spring to mind on reading the list.

This might, therefore, be an appropriate point at which to provide an alternative scheme which would identify the approaches
examined and give an indication of the trends.

One of the most prominent threads which is apparent in the
material examined is that the concept of secularization is strongly
related to a notion of progress within society. Luckmann suggested that 'There is some justification for saying that secularization "theories" are the sociological myth (or counter-myth) of
the origin of modernity.'(11) This statement would appear to be
well illustrated by the Polish material. Indeed, one of the characteristics of the early Polish sociologists of religion was their
strong desire to provide a theory of social change: the theory
envisaged the transition of man from the archaic to the modern
and it is clear that a view of progress in terms of secularization
provided a suitable vehicle for this theory of social change. Even
today, all the work in this field is very strongly oriented towards placing secularization in the light of the processes of
social change.

The history of the secular movement provides a striking example in which a counter-myth is created and used as an explanation of the appearance of the secular communist state. One of
the curious paradoxes of secularism emerges here, namely, that
in order for it to be able to explain itself secularism must take
Christianity as its central reference point: in Western thought
there appears to be no other way of coming to terms with history.
Significantly, this reinforces the notion of a Christian culture.

Let us now turn to look at areas which can be taken as representing the overall picture of secularization and desecularization in Poland today.

Firstly, there is religiosity and religious culture. Religiosity
is in some senses a very basic category since in the absence of
the relevant attitudes and behaviour it is difficult to identify
Christianity (or, indeed, any other religion with which we may

be concerned) except in terms of what might then be justifiably termed historical relics (buildings and architecture, vocabulary, music and other art forms, etc.). But, even under such circumstances, it might be possible to argue a case for incomplete secularization – especially in the presence of even isolated religious institutions.

The sociological starting point for the definition of Polish religiosity was the Polish peasant. One of the keys to the high level of religiosity of the peasant has traditionally been reckoned to be the rural context itself – the material is virtually unanimous on this point. This is not so surprising if we consider that at the very core of the sociological approach to secularization lies the idea that the peasant is the starting-point for the definition of archaism and that modernity can only mean a secular society.

A sub-category concerned with the archaism of the peasant is the role of tradition in archaic society – 'the faith of our fathers' can be used here as an illustration of mindlessness. This example, however, serves to illustrate the secularized sociological viewpoint at its best. This viewpoint secularizes 'in retrospect': the peasant is seen as partly secularized before he actually enters the realm of the secular – he is seen as not 'really' religious, but as a slave of irrational and even undesirable tradition. In addition, his religiosity may be seen as a reaction of terror to the unpredictability of his environment, it may be a reaction to the overwork and to the strenuous conditions of rural existence or it may be 'really' a means of social control. It is characteristic that none of these arguments venture to suggest what it is that constitutes 'real' religiosity. Piwowarski tries to solve this problem by applying the criterion of 'personal commitment' to distinguish religion from tradition, for example; in this sense, there would appear to be a deepening of religiosity as a result of the rural-urban passage. But this procedure is no more than pushing the problem one step further back: it is perfectly easy to conceive of a tradition of personal commitment or of a personal commitment to tradition.

It is, of course, a great temptation to overstate the unpredictability of the rural environment, especially when the imagination is fired by visions of wooden homes burning during times of war, of starving millions during times of famine and of whole families dying from pestilence as well as from cold and exposure during severe winters and gale-force winds: this is the stuff of tales and stories repeated over generations and by no means a general description of the Polish peasant's life-style or society. Similarly, the vision of a stooping, sweating peasant attached to the rear end of a primitive plough pulled by a lean and possibly ill horse belongs to an art gallery rather than to a comparative portrayal – which is what sociology demands – of the rural and urban conditions as experienced by the working man of late nineteenth-century Poland. There are some very fundamental ways in which rural existence is far more predictable than urban existence:

there is the continuity of seasons and harvests, there is little change in the neighbours (except birth and death) and in the immediate surroundings, life patterns have an unquestioned structure which has been handed down with little change for many generations. It is also worth noting the peasant's greater freedom from disease and famine than his slum-dwelling urban counterpart. It can only have been a blind and highly emotional faith in the ideal of progress that could have led observers like Krzywicki to portray such an undisturbed existence of the town-dweller: a sort of an Arcadia in reverse. Krzywicki was, in reality, comparing the peasant not with the working-class urban dweller but simply with himself. Similar arguments and explanations of religiosity are advanced today, except that they also compare types of society and stress the differences between the unpredictability of capitalism and the joys and delights of communist society. Ciupak and Jaroszewski can be identified with this tradition.

The concept of religious culture as developed by Czarnowski has had a tremendous influence on the Polish sociology of religion and especially in the field of secularization. It is here that Czarnowski suggested a parallel between the religious beliefs and rituals of the peasant and the organization of life and society in the rural environment. While Czarnowski was not immediately concerned with the 'explaining away' of religion in terms of this parallel, it is nevertheless possible to use his approach for the purposes of reduction if we assume an identity between the totality of the religious phenomenon and the religious culture. This is the sort of approach that Ciupak tries to use.

It is unfortunate that Czarnowski himself never attempted the investigation of an urban religious culture: an indirect suggestion perhaps that such an analogous culture does not exist(12) or, more likely, that its investigation is a relatively difficult undertaking. Indeed, since Czarnowski's time there have been no systematic attempts to present a picture of the religious culture of the urban working class, nor that of any other urban group for that matter. Question and answer studies and even interviews aimed at arriving at a statement of the level of religiosity (belief and practice) or at the establishment of certain correlations (who believes what and under what conditions) almost invariably lack Czarnowski's imaginative portrayal.

If we are to account for the great differences in the proportion of believers in different localities in Poland - at times far greater than any differences which can be realistically attributed to urbanization and industrialization and at other times far smaller - we must make significant allowances in the typical model of religious culture with particular attention paid to traditions inherited from past socio-political conditions and from the orientations of pastoral care. The partitions and the boundary changes of the Second World War must also be recognized as important factors although they are in a sense 'relics of the past'. In addition, it becomes even more imperative to distinguish between and invest-

igate local religious cultures and milieu religiosity. Such an
approach assumes that although a religious culture (e.g. peasant or working-class) may be identifiable in a particular milieu,
it will, nevertheless, vary within itself from area to area.

The above reservations are particularly well-known examples
of recalcitrant facts in the area of the proposed correlation between religiosity and modernization. The view of rural and religious archaic man does not care for recalcitrant facts: the
evidence is either ignored or explained as having been distorted
by outside factors; given time, all will undoubtedly return to
the 'real' trend. Other examples of recalcitrance can be mentioned: the educated and in every sense modern Catholic intellectual or scientist from town presents a difficult problem as
does, in the case of extreme versions of Marxist-Leninist secularism, the manual worker in heavy industry - especially if he
is also young. Nowa Huta, Silesia and Gdańsk are probably just
the tip of an iceberg. It is also very rarely, if ever, mentioned
that centres of Catholic thought and organization in contemporary Poland tend to be associated with the towns and cities.

An important question connected with the whole issue of dechristianization is concerned with the nature of the final product,
indifference. What are the characteristics of indifference? Can it
be, for example, a return to primitive savagery as Kołakowski's
ideas might suggest? Or will it be a vegetative existence geared
only to the exigencies of the civilization in the manner described
by Max Weber: 'Specialists without spirit, sensualists without
heart; this nullity imagines that it has attained a level of civilization never before achieved.'(13) This point has not received
any attention except the implicit and rather banal suggestion
that it is a non-religious orientation or attitude. We will return
to this point later. Here it is worth noting the secularist attempts
to secularize - or perhaps Marxify is a better word - religious
indifference by claiming a conversion to secularist belief (i.e. to
atheism or to Marxism-Leninism, although these may be described
simply as objective truth). Sociologists, even those with secularist leanings, tend to agree that there is very little conversion to
secularism and accept that the final product of dechristianization
is almost exclusively religious indifference or, at least, something which is neither Christian nor Marxist-Leninist.

It is likely that there is some advantage to be gained by the
secularists from accepting the indifference thesis instead of the
conversion thesis: firstly, in so far as the conversion thesis also
contains an implicit recommendation, total indifference is an in-
trinsically more desirable attitude as far as totalitarian aims are
concerned since intellectually honest attempts at the application
of reason to Marxism-Leninism and atheism are capable of getting
out of hand and turning against the party. The officially desirable orthodoxy relies on loyalty and not reason. Secondly, the
claim that religious belief in Poland is being forsaken in any significant way in favour of Marxist-Leninist secularism is utterly
preposterous. It is not believed by anybody, least of all by

sociologists, philosophers, historians and theologians: it always
raises a good laugh in the most varied of circles. Secularists,
let us not forget, have no sense of humour and do not like being
laughed at. Besides, there still remains some degree of respect
for the maintenance of credibility even amongst the most hard-
ened partisans of official orthodoxy. To claim significant conversions to secularism is to run the risk of being thought of as
a madman. Thirdly, there remains the comfort-producing suggestion, for internal use only, that defections from the ranks of
Marxism-Leninism are the result of a general trend towards indifference which has also affected the secularist circles.

A view which is sometimes advanced suggests that the final
stage in the development of atheism is indifference; if a key
feature of atheism is an opposition to religon – it is argued –
then when religion has finally disappeared the only possible
attitude is one of indifference. In this way, at least, some capital can be made from the admission that indifference, rather
than atheism, tends to be observed: 'We have reached the post-
atheist era!' the secularists might triumphantly declare. The implications of such an argument cause some difficulty, however.
The conclusion invariably suggests that religion in Poland must
have already disappeared, except in the most marginal of cases –
a point which can only be argued by suggesting that appearances are deceptive and that despite what is apparent the society
is really a secular one. Jerschina tends towards this sort of view.

A point which can be appropriately made at this juncture concerns the objectivity of the two basic orientations. This is especially important from the point of view of the foreign observer. It
is a mistake to accept suggestions that a true and objective picture of Polish religiosity can be obtained only by balancing or
weighing up the opposite – Catholic and secularist – orientations.
Such an argument assumes equal and opposite distortions in each
of the orientations or it may assume distortions only as a result
of different intellectual positions. As we have shown in this
study, such assumptions are unacceptable. In the case of the
secularist orientation the distortions arise only secondarily out of
its intellectual position. They arise primarily out of its nature as
an instrument of the anti-religious crusade and out of the monopoly of political power which is enjoyed by that position. The secularist arguments and frameworks, therefore, tend to be political
statements oriented towards the authorities' goal of total control
and of a secular society.

Some of the material examined in this study points towards very
strong reservations which need to be made when generalizing on
the subject of the relationship between religiosity and modernization. Let us add a few examples. One example is the widely
noted decline of anticlericalism (except amongst the orthodox
secularists) in Poland since the beginning of the century and
especially since the end of the Second World War. An important
reason for the decline, which is almost complete today, is the
existence of a political regime which, through its constant pres-

sure on the Church, has given the traditional anticlericalist pro-
gressively less raison d'être: all secularist attempts to revive
anticlericalism have met with nothing but failure.

There is also evidence which points to the importance of elite
religiosity and to the role it has played and still plays in the religious life of Polish society; changes at this level, whilst not
directly indicative of the whole of society, cannot occur without
in some way affecting the whole Catholic community. In examining this elite, particular care needs to be paid to the episcopate
and the clergy and to the cultural intelligentsia as contributors
to the totality of Catholic culture: these are the transmission
belts of Catholicism and of Catholic culture to the wider society.
Święcicki stresses the importance of the Catholic cultural intelligentsia to whom he refers as 'the élite apostolate of the lay'
(elitarne apostolstwo świeckich:(14) it may not be too early to
suggest that the significance of this group is growing in a way
which may soon make their evangelizing role significant in the
maintenance of Catholicism in Poland.

On the other side of the coin to elite religiosity there is the
phenomenon of communist believers. Whilst the presence of a
communist believer amongst the ignorant and uneducated need
not come as much of a surprise since it can easily be explained
in terms of a lack of a full appreciation of the issues involved,
the presence of believers (who practise at their peril - often in-
cognito and in localities far from their usual haunts) in the party
actif or at the higher echelons of the power structure is a very
curious phenomenon. The only explanation which makes sense
requires that they be treated as believers who have succumbed
to the exigencies of life under a communist regime. The alternative explanation, often advanced in secularist circles, is that
they are merely participating in traditional practices and folklore.
However, with the risks that such clandestine practices entail, it
is most unlikely that tradition and folklore alone are sufficiently
strong motivations.

The area of religiosity contains too many variables and the evidence is often so contradictory that no clear-cut conclusion regarding the overall direction of the changes observed can be
successfully drawn. Some parts of it will always remain obscure:
for example, it is doubtful whether it will ever be possible to
consider, through wide-reaching studies, the relationship between religiosity and anti-religious policy. It may be tempting to
apply the French methodology of sociologie religieuse in order
to identify a process of dechristianization: this suffers the draw-
back of not being selective enough with respect to key areas
such as elite religiosity and of not being able to cope with the
elements of religious culture and tradition.

It is clear, therefore, that despite the already large volume of
work done, religiosity is one of the most obvious areas which
require further research. So far, work in this area has been
marred by two major shortcomings. Firstly, there is the strong
tradition of scientism, technological Utopianism and Marxist-

Leninist millennialism. All three elements of this tradition are to
be found in the sociological orientation of the party secularists.
It is doubtful whether even the Catholic orientation has lifted
itself clear of technological Utopianism as one of its central
points of reference. This shortcoming is paralleled by a lack of
significant theoretical investment in this area: it is not possible
to consider the Marxism-Leninism of the secularists to constitute
a useful theoretical framework here although it may, at times,
indicate the way in which religious belief can be used as an instrument of rule. In the case of the Catholic tradition, as represented by Piwowarski, the lack of interest in theoretical and
philosophical discussion tends to produce a very formal picture
of Polish religiosity constructed as a function of either the traditional model or of the official Church model.

The second shortcoming is a practical one and there is little
doubt that it will be gradually made up. This shortcoming is concerned with the rather narrow field of empirical investigation so
far. Studies of the type carried out by Piwowarski, but sacri-
ficing precision for scale, could be carried out in widely differing milieux - ample scope (in theory at least) is provided both
among rural and urban centres. As well as the new industrial
centres of Nowa Huta, Puławy and Płock, other urban centres
would also have to be considered in some detail: the traditional
urban centre of Kraków, the capital Warsaw, centres of working-
class tradition like Łódź, the towns of Silesia and the Dąbrowa
Basin and the coastal industrial centres of the north. Territorial differences would have to be explored carefully - particularly
in the directions indicated by Święcicki: as well as differences
due to the different occupations of Poland, it would be worth
exploring possible differences between the Western territories
(which were German before the Second World War, but which contained numerous Polish communities) and the rest of Poland.(15)
One of the most painful consequences of this second shortcoming
was the bewilderment which followed the exceedingly strong
working-class demonstrations of religious fervour during the
strikes and sit-ins of 1980. An even superficial impressionistic
investigation would have provided an indication of such possibilities.

One exceedingly unlikely possibility must be mentioned here
simply because it is a possibility. We refer here to the access to
the results of the various official surveys and investigations so
far withheld from the public. Provided that this material is not
destroyed it will be possible at some time in the future to gain a
wealth of insights from this information. It is unlikely that this
will occur before the collapse of totalitarian communism in Poland.

The concept of religious culture has been less explored. The
identification of both important historical and traditional factors
and of different religious cultures in different milieux is perhaps
the main task of this area. Apart from a now pressing need to
understand the urban working-class religious culture in relation
to the industrial milieu, there are the additional possibilities

afforded by occupational groups, the technical intelligentsia, the cultural elite, the clergy and even the party actif. In this way it might be possible to step outside the stereotype of religious archaic man and modern secular man. The clergy, in particular, are likely to provide an important gauge of the religious climate: vocations, apostasy and general morale and all features which need to be taken into account.

The attempts which have so far been made in the direction of understanding the religiosity of these groups have been almost entirely based on statistical analyses and, as a result, their explanatory power has been generally low. The few explanations which can be found in this area have little to do with the statistical data: this suggests that it is above all an intuitive understanding which counts in such cases. This area appears, therefore, to be at least in principle ideally suitable for the application of the method of participant observation. In practice, however, apart from the rather banal participant observation in pilgrimages or at Masses, a twofold problem arises with this method. Firstly, there is the problem of the above milieux being far more inaccessible to an outsider (at least to a sociological outsider) than the classic rural milieu of the peasant. In the latter case it would have sufficed, as it no doubt did in Czarnowski's study, to spend some time living in a village and simply observing with little or even no participation. In addition, the sort of participation that might be required is a relatively easy matter: it suffices to go on a pilgrimage or to be at the celebration of a religious feast. The urban milieu, however, is quite different: even such a rough and impressionistic picture is not easy to obtain: where is it possible to observe without participating fully? Simply living in an urban environment is of surprisingly little help: compared with the relative homogeneity of the rural milieu of Czarnowski's time there is the multiplicity of intermingling social groups of today's urban milieu, on the one hand, and the isolation of individuals and families from one another in Polish towns on the other. This isolation is encouraged by communist regimes whose rule is facilitated by high levels of social atomization.

The only remaining possibility for the sociologist is to 'become' a worker or a student, for example, and thus become acquainted with the religious attitudes and interests of that particular group. This raises a problem. The administrative and political difficulties which such a temporary metamorphosis would entail are great. So far, this has been the unique preserve of the secret police. Other areas, like the party actif for example, are restricted to sociologists with impeccable records of party commitment. The same is true of clergy circles, although the restrictions are less and the reasons for suspicion are different. But restrictions of access operate more or less effectively over all areas: 'Who knows what unsavoury details a sociologist may dig up about our workers?' officials would argue on the receipt of a request, 'He may even do some wrecking.'

Even if this problem were avoidable, there would still remain
problems connected with the publication of results. Perhaps the
nearest one can get to participant observation under the current
political conditions is through memoir material; for various
reasons this sort of material is not always entirely satisfactory
although at times it may provide some remarkable insights.

The need to investigate pastoral work has already been noted.
Closely related here is the effect which the personality of the
clergy and of Church leaders has on religiosity. This may occur
both at the local level, where one parish priest may increase the
number of dominicants while another, in an otherwise identical
parish, may severely decrease it, and at the national level,
where the personality of a bishop, Primate or Pope may greatly
affect attitudes towards religion. An obvious example is the
personality of Pope John Paul II. As far as the clergy are concerned, some preliminary work in this field has already been
done.(16)

Closely related to the area of religiosity and religious culture
is the question of social disorganization. Sociologists and others
have long been interested to know whether there exists a relationship between degrees of religiosity and degrees of societal
degeneration, the general assumption being that an inverse
relationship exists. However, no studies have been carried out
on the subject of societal degeneration or on the related question
of social pathology and it is doubtful whether any studies of
these phenomena could ever be undertaken.(17)

The second area is that of planned secularization. Planned
secularization and anti-religious policy, key features of atheist
totalitarianism, are themselves a secular version of the millennial fantasy; planned secularization is typically described by its
proponents as a means to the realization of those values which
Christianity itself postulates but is unable or unwilling to implement. Planned secularization, therefore, is totally outside the
scope and experience of the typical Western sociologist of
religion. In this area we find that the central concern of the
authorities is not religious matters in the narrow sense: it is the
desire to find a secular reference point for all the key elements
of meaning within society - history, nationality, metaphysics,
art, etc. It often gives the impression of being a most haphazard
procedure with only one central point - a deep dislike of religion;
however, planned secularization is very much oriented in its
theory towards the realization of the secular fantasy and in its
practice towards the establishment of a system of total control.

Where secularizing tendencies arising from the policy of planned
secularization enter the sociology of religion they manifest themselves in the following ways: firstly, in the rejection of the
assumption that religious knowledge can be meaningful knowledge
- at best it is mistaken and at worst it is nonsense. In consequence, religion is treated as an epiphenomenon to be understood only in terms of its functions. Secondly, sociological
objectivity tends to be identified with atheism, secularism or

non-belief whereas religious belief on the part of the investigator is taken to constitute a bias. Finally, there appears a
persistent, often totally irrelevant, pursuit of the illogicalities,
the inconsistencies, the dysfunctions and of the hypocrisy
surrounding religion and believers while, of course, ignoring
the analogous and far more glaring defects in the secularist
position.

Planned secularization is typically couched in the language and
terminology of democratic liberalism. Anti-religious and anti-
Church measures are often justified in terms of the 'separation
of the Church from the state'. This principle makes sense only
under the conditions of Western liberal democracy: in communist
societies it becomes a legal and administrative instrument for the
exclusion of both Church and religious belief from any form of
participation in national life. This is simply because under
totalitarianism nothing can be regarded as 'separate' or independent of the central power: the only acceptable form of separation is destruction. In practice, therefore, we find that
Catholic believers who make their beliefs public may be denied
positions of responsibility in Polish society; since the state
controls all of these positions directly, the procedure involved
is not a complicated one. Conversely, prominent atheists and
non-believers tend to be chosen for positions of responsibility on
the grounds of an orthodox secularist attitude alone. The often-
heard justification for this arrangement is that it is no less
reasonable than one which bars, say, a left-winger from a right-
wing political party in any liberal democracy. It is a curious fact
of Polish society that this bias in favour of atheism is never
denied by secularists - but it is not prominently displayed either.
The result of this arrangement is a sort of administrative marginalization of religious belief and institutions in a society where the
religion is anything but marginal in every other respect. In this
sense the official platitude 'we are all atheists here' has an un-
comfortable ring of truth when 'here' refers to positions of power
and responsibility. Although it is possible to find exceptions to
this general rule, the overall tendency is undeniable.

The administrative marginalization of belief must not be confused with the success of planned secularization. One possible
way of treating this marginalization is by considering it in terms
of what could be called 'forced secularization' which is best
likened to trying to remove an object by lifting it up out of sight
and holding it there: it still remains, unseen, and ready to
descend immediately the pressure is relaxed. What we have,
therefore, is a thin veneer of secularism - convincing only to
'tourists' and to the gullible - hanging in shreds from an essentially Christian-oriented culture.

Another aspect of planned secularization is the quite liberal
rewriting of history and the re-definition of the national self-
image. The general aim of this procedure is to produce a new
national myth, presented as a theory of social change, in order
to explain the establishment of the new secular state. The

apparatus of central censorship plays a particularly important part here. Because the central divine reference point connected with the traditional vision of history and of the nation cannot be removed or ignored it must be at least played down and vilified: the trend here is to relegate the hitherto accepted versions of history, the cultural reference points and images to the domain of shame and embarrassment or possibly to the absurd; the hitherto accepted version of the past is portrayed as a mistake, as deception or as injustice. The new myth can therefore justifiably be seen as a parody or inversion of the former vision.

The new myth aims at the secularization of national feeling and culture; the new self-image of society is to be moulded, by the application of the Marxian laws of history, in such a way that it will appear that even in the sphere of religion there has always existed a deep-seated yearning for the secularist ideal or even a visible trend towards the secular society. The typifying rhetorical question from the rewriters of history might be as follows: 'Have not all the early believers been objectively secularist? It is regrettable that these good people all had to carry the burden of religious belief!'

The secularized view of history is consistent in its efforts to subjugate both the historical process and the present time to its central scheme. The secular 'objectivity' which is presented as having been the hidden driving force of history has today become a visible reality: it has become liberated from the fetters of past versions of history. Thus even the use of the term 'liberation' has a greater depth of meaning than simply referring to a liberation from a fascist occupation.(18) Once the party has claimed to be the realization of the historical objectivity and has the necessary monopoly of force it is able to treat all failure to voice agreement with this view in terms of criminality, pathology or, in cases where the circumstances are less extreme, in terms of marginality. The party means to ensure that there will be no escape - physical or spiritual - from the new secular reality; to this end it strives to secularize all cultural reference points and isolate or marginalize all the unsecularizable ones. Thus the concept of the nation becomes secularized, the Church becomes isolated and marginalized (even treated as pathological), movement across frontiers becomes restricted, Western societies become ideologically rejected. This, at least, is the theory and the attempted practice; the result, as we have seen, falls short of the expectations.

Of importance in the area of planned secularization are the frequently advanced arguments concerning the dysfunctionality of religion in society. In general, these arguments are qualified by the additional suggestion that under certain circumstances the Church is capable of playing a positive role in society. If, for instance, the Church pursues a policy which is to lead to its demise then it is clearly seen to be making a major contribution to the life of society and to the national culture. For this it must be praised. In terms of the conditions of a communist regime,

however, the Church's role (and that of religion in general) becomes marginalized to primitive backwaters and underdeveloped
areas and communities: even here only because it is argued that
the state is still unable to take this role upon itself. During
moments of crisis the state may even argue that the Church can
complement secular activity, but only in spheres of extreme
social problems. We see, therefore, that the overall view suggests
that even under the most favourable circumstances the role of the
Church will remain but a shadow of what the state can achieve.

One example of what is considered by secularists to be a particularly noxious function of the Church and, perhaps, of religious belief in general, is that it is responsible for the fettering of
Polish life in the shackles of the anachronistic feudal inheritance,
thus effectively preventing the inevitable establishment of
socialist social relations.(19) Strong indignation is expressed at
the Church's audacity in attempting the morally despicable act
of interfering with the inevitable: turning the inevitable into the
evitable is unthinkable to the secularist mind. Such a view of the
dysfunctionality of religion in turn embodies a view of secularization which is not based, as it may at times appear, on the test-
ing or examination of hypotheses or even on a legitimate conceptual device but on a doctrine of absolute power, a doctrine
with a strong dose of emotional appeal to a historicist myth of
inevitability.

Another example worth noting here concerns the secularist
'struggle against clericalism'. This slogan was used liberally
during the early post-war years. It was claimed that it is unjust
of the clergy to exploit the honest beliefs of simple folk or to act
as the conscience of the people by constantly drawing attention
to the atheism of the Polish state. It is far better, secularists
argue, to keep believers ignorant of such matters so that
harmony in society can be maintained and so that honest and
hard-working people can get down to the task of building a
socialist state.(20) It is easy to see, therefore, how religious
sentiments can become forcibly identified with anti-state sentiments.

In so far as sociological assumptions are called to the service
of planned secularization they tend to rely on the treatment of
religion in terms of its functions. The principal concept employed here is that of functional replacement. It is argued that
religious beliefs, activities and institutions will come to be replaced by analogous secular ones. If, as has been suggested in
various quarters, there is a strong possibility of the development of indifferentism of belief then we might expect the secular
state to respond by providing secular 'replacements' in the areas
of activities, services and organizations. This can certainly be
observed together with the introduction of secularist beliefs as
reference points in these activities, services and organizations.
In this context we have noted the introduction of secular ritual -
not to be mocked or laughed at, insist the authorities. However,
there are many more, perhaps less obvious, functional replace-

ments whose ostensible functional role often lies elsewhere. As an exmpale, we can note architecture and various monuments of secular significance and function. These, together with museums of Marxism-Leninism, are the shrines of secularism and regularly receive groups from schools, factories and sometimes even tourists, especially from other communist bloc states. It might even be possible to include here the almost ritual participation in voluntary work in order to build socialism even more rapidly: groups from schools, factories, universities and colleges are mobilized for work - often on Sundays and religious feast days for reasons which are quite obvious; shirkers are not supposed to go unnoticed. Other aspects include such features as 'activating' meetings or lectures (secular prayer or evangelization?) in the place of work and also the annual May Day Parade (a secular pilgrimage?), ironically on the feast day of St Joseph the Worker, which includes a secular gospel delivered in the shadow of that magnificent monument to the New Order and symbol of Soviet domination - the Palace of Culture and Science in Warsaw. Martin also refers to 'the persistent repetition of the basic formulae of sacred Marxist scriptures in commenting on and explaining the various phenomena of ... society. This provides an equivalent of Christian apologetic formulae.'(21)

On the basis of the material it is impossible to judge the success of planned secularization. Any conclusions here are strictly intuitive and provisional. It is probable that the bulk of the secularist claims remains in the realm of political aims or even political fantasy rather than belonging to reality. At the same time, it is unlikely that the measures simply pass by with no effect at all even though this effect may be the opposite of the intended one. It is also reasonable to expect that where functional replacement does appear to have taken place it is, firstly, generally not associated with the substitution of the alternative belief; secondly, mostly the result of concrete pressure exerted from above and, finally, often associated with continued loyalty to the Church and to Catholic belief. The appearances, therefore, suitably merit the term window-dressing.

Despite the likelihood of very poor results it is beyond any doubt that the total cost of the operation is very high if we take into account administrative effort, the inconvenience caused to almost the entire population and especially to clergy and episcopate, the probable effects on social pathology and also the likely harm caused to the national economy by the exclusion of large numbers of able individuals from key posts on account of their religious belief. But such seem to be the inevitable costs of communist power and its legitimation.

Kołakowski's notion of the Counter-Reformation can be used as a guide to the third area. This area encompasses the process of desecularization or Christianization and is best understood in terms of foci of Christianizing activity. It can be said that for practical purposes there is as yet no specifically sociological work available in this area. It is nevertheless a very important

area and one which has much to offer to the observer interested
in the dynamics of religious change.

The concept of elite religiosity has already been mentioned in
relation to religiosity and religious culture but its significance
is much greater. Apart from the clergy, there is a number of
formal, informal and other Catholic oriented groups and movements within Polish society. The sociology of these groups may
give a clue as to the directions of change of Polish Catholicism
as well as pointing to the main issues of the moment.

The sorts of groups which spring to mind range from the
officially recognised Znak, Więź and the associated KIKi, the
students Pastoral Care (Duszpasterstwo Akademickie) - often
under pressure and harassment, the prohibited groups of
Catholic students and young intellectuals centred on Spotkania.
Associated with the Church and Catholicism is ROPCiO - a
democratic and traditionalist underground political opposition
movement which grew up during the 1970s.

One important example of a semi-formal organization is the
Oazy (Oases) movement. The name of this movement is not
without symbolic significance: oases of truth in a desert of
official lies and spiritual desolation. The Oazy are a Life-Light
Renewal movement based on the idea of 'agape' whose activities
centre on meetings, discussions and summer camp retreats; the
initial steps in organizing the Oazy were taken in the mid-1950s,
the movement began to take on shape and become active in the
1960s and became a strong and integral part of Polish Catholic
life during the 1970s. The activities of the Oazy, although not
specifically outlawed by the authorities, are subject to severe
harassment and limitations; also constant difficulties of a petty
nature are encountered. This suggests that the authorities may
fear an increase in the strength and the influence of this movement. To some extent these fears are justified for two main
reasons: firstly, in 1980 the movement issued statements which
indicated a clear politicization of its views; secondly, the late
1970s saw the appearance of Oazy across the frontier in neighbouring Slovakia.

Another movement within Catholicism which shows signs of
vitality is the Charismatic Renewal Movement which became
established in Warsaw during recent years: its centre is at St
Martin's Church in the Old Town.

Also important is the Institute for the Blind in Laski, commonly
referred to simply as Laski.(22) Laski were established in 1922
and today have about 40 per cent of Polish blind children in their
care. However, Laski today are more than an institute for the
blind, they have become a symbol of humanity within a labyrinth
of symbols of inhumanity. They have become an important focus
for the activity and attention of many Catholic activists.

All these groups tend to have a clear intellectual bias in so far
as they are concerned, in one way or another, with the deepening of knowledge and awareness of doctrinal and other matters
connected with Catholicism; they are undoubtedly an indication

of the existence of different forms of religiosity or devotion
which exist in various segments of the population. The sociological relevance of these groups to the question of secularization is yet to be explored.

It is a tribute to the vagaries of historical, or even sociological, categories that had this book been written a few years
previously this fourth area would not have received any attention, not even in the most speculative way. Yet immediately
after the election of Pope John Paul II one additional and enor-
mously significant factor had to be taken into account in assessments of the position of religion in Polish society. Quite literally
overnight the secularist position had been totally discredited
even outside Poland and the authorities were helpless when confronted with such demonstrations of religious fervour as occurred
immediately after the election.

It is beyond all doubt that the election of Pope John Paul II
will consolidate Christianity and the Church in Poland to an
extent which no other single event could possibly have done.
Significantly, one of the new Pope's first decisions was to visit
Poland during the 900th anniversary of the martyrdom of St
Stanisław in May 1979. The authorities recoiled in horror and
refused him entry and called St Stanisław 'a controversial
figure'; Pope John Paul II was eventually allowed to visit Poland
in June.

The immediate reaction to the Pope's election and visit can best
be seen in terms of mood: there has been a clear development of
confidence and optimism amongst the vast majority of the population. A group of sociologists from KUL carried out a survey of
expectations connected with the new pontificate. (23) It is significant that the greatest prominence was given to hopes of developments in ecumenism, human rights and peace. Soon after the
election a nationwide demand for personal views on the subject
was made by another group from KUL with the result that some
450 accounts were received. The intensity of the effects of the
election are exemplified by this fragment written by a member of
the communist party. He describes watching the Pope on television: (24)

> The cardinals kneel before John Paul II. And I, a member of
> the PZPR, also kneel before the television set together with
> my wife as the Pope raises his hands holding the Host. Some-
> thing breaks inside me. Something throws me to my knees.
> Even though we are not in church and nobody can see us we
> still kneel without looking at each other. Our four-year-old
> daughter also kneels down and something breaks inside me.

This is exactly the sort of possibility which haunted former
director of the Office for Relgious Affairs, Kazimierz Kąkol,
during his happier years at the top.

It is without doubt that one of the resultant trends will be that
of increasing Christianization, both in Poland and in Eastern

Europe. During his sermon in Gniezno on 3 July 1979, Pope John Paul II referred to the often forgotten nations of Eastern Europe and stated: 'Is it not Christ's will, is it not what the Holy Spirit disposes, that this Polish Pope, this Slav Pope, should at this precise moment manifest the spiritual unity of Christian Europe?'(25) To this end the Pope, on the 1,500 anniversary of St Benedict the Patron of Europe, elevated Saints Cyril and Methodius to Co-Patrons of Europe together with Benedict.

As far as Poland itself is concerned, two facts are worthy of note. Firstly, the number of first-year Catholic seminary students in the year following the Pope's election increased by almost 50 per cent over 1977-8.(26) Secondly, shortly after the election Kazimierz Kąkol admitted that the Church was scoring major victories with the younger generation in Poland.(27). It is possible that such optimism may have contributed towards his eventual downfall. There are some signs which suggest that this Christianizing trend is not limited to Poland or Eastern Europe alone, but that it may have world-wide implications: here the statistics of conversions to Roman Catholicism will soon provide an answer.

One development which occurred soon after the Pope's election was the establishment of believers' self-defence committees. The first such committee was formed as early as November 1978 - the month following the election - in the area of Podlesie and two others followed in 1979 in the areas of Przemyśl and Ciszów.(28) The main aim of these committees consisting of laymen is to ensure that believers can exercise without restriction their right to believe. This includes the right to build churches wherever there is a need for them.

Pope John Paul II's central concerns are not with politics but with the Catholic faith - politics nevertheless do enter into the picture when they stand in the way of what are the fundamental requirements of freedom of belief and freedom of activity for the Church.(29) Indeed, under conditions of a totalitarian state a greater stress of such requirements will unavoidably lead to greater destabilization.

The entry of patriotic and national sentiments into the picture is bound to occur. Firstly, there is the obvious reason that the Pope is a 'son of Poland'. Secondly, because the realization of the demands for religious freedom would be a fatal blow to the totalitarian structure quite apart from the consequences of the changes in mood resulting from the election. Thirdly, on account of the immediate association which the event evokes with the messianic elements in Polish culture. During his visit to Poland Pope John Paul was fully aware of the significance of his words when he said:(30)

And I cry - I who am a Son of the land of Poland and who am also Pope John Paul II - I cry from all the depths of this Millennium, I cry on the Vigil of Pentecost: Let your spirit descend, Let your spirit descend and renew the face of the earth, the face of this land.

At the tomb of the Unknown Soldier his remarks were even more to the point when he stated that it is impossible to understand the history of Poland without Christ.(31)

This is a convenient point at which to mention the argument suggesting that the religious fervour surrounding the Pope (and also that surrounding the strikes and sit-ins of 1980) is nothing more than patriotism and nationalism in disguise. This type of reductionism is similar to that which argues that 'religious' is really 'social' and, as such, suffers from similar defects. In this case, however, these defects are particularly obvious. If, for the sake of argument, the religious fervour of the 1980 strikes was mere patriotism, then it is necessary to ask why patriotism needs to be thus disguised. Surely it would have been just as effective, if not more effective, in its original form?

Another of the trends observable here is the effect of the election and visit on the development of political movements opposed to communist rule. It is very unlikely, for example, that the development of Solidarity would have taken the course it did in the absence of the new mood.

What is the attitude of the state to the election of John Paul II? During a talk given to party activists in January 1980, the deputy director of the Office for Religious Affairs, Aleksander Merker, said that 'neither the choice of Pope nor his visit to Poland has had any significant effect on Church-state relations'.(32) Should it have had? According to the evidence in the earlier chapters of the book the nature of the conflict between Church and state is such that it is difficult to identify any possible path in the direction of improvement. Merker was talking to people who are the transmission lines of party orthodoxy and who take this orthodoxy to propaganda outlets. He therefore had to speak not as an objective analyst but as a confident and victorious crusader and this is how his remarks must be understood. The tone of Merker's comments reveals a concern which is echoed in other places. In a similar vein he attempts to play down the welcome given to the Pope in Poland by stating that 'the Pope was received in a secular way by clapping, standing erect, waving... smiling'.(33) Merker argues that this is no less than a success for socialism since without a socialist upbringing the population would have been fanatical in its reaction. Might the Poles have knelt without smiling? If this is the best that the party can do it certainly has reason to worry.

Two other important points emerge from Merker's talk. Firstly, there is the echo of Kąkol's earlier worry about believers within the party itself. This worry must now be assuming mightmare dimensions. Merker states: 'We are fully aware of the fact that we have believers in the ranks of the party.'(34) As if this were not enough, he urges these believers to be Marxist-Leninist at least in outward behaviour and not, as must obviously often be the case, to allow religious ceremonies to take place in their homes.(35)

Secondly, there is every indication that pressure on believers and on the Church will continue unabated. At least, this is the intention. Among the possible areas of pressure and erosive tactics is the attempt to mobilize the Catholic Church for anti-NATO propaganda, the causing of divisions between the Church and the political opposition movements, the drawing away of children and young people from the Church by concentrating secularist efforts on the key areas of sex, love and family and, finally, the continued playing down of the significance of the Pope.

Quite soon after the Pope's election it became clear that the communist authorities were going to do their best to soften the impact of the event. One of their first major acts was to censor a letter sent by the Pope to the Catholic weekly, 'Tygodnik powszechny'. They objected to his reference to St Stanisław as a defender of human rights.(36) Their reaction to his proposed visit has already been mentioned.

During 1979 the regime decided to go ahead with a road-construction plan in Częstochowa which was seen by the epis-copate as an attempt to cut off the shrine of the Black Madonna from the city. The public outcry was considerable and eventually resulted in the authorities' decision to re-route the thorough-fare. These sorts of pressures would have no doubt continued were it not for other developments which managed to push the authorities' concern with religion into second place. The middle of 1980 marked the beginning of an era of headaches for the authorities as the confidence of the independent trade unions began to grow. Indeed, as long as these problems last the Church can expect some respite and may even have a chance to gain new ground.

From the sociological point of view it is important that the election of Cardinal Wojtyła to the papal throne has provided a unique opportunity to observe changes in the Polish Church and in religiosity as well as to test and suggest new hypotheses re-garding the processes of religious change and secularization.

It is useful at this point to turn to the subject of Polish mes-sianism. Polish messianism has often been assumed to be on the way out, if not already out. This demessianization thesis can be likened in many ways to the instant secularization thesis and can also be seen to suffer from similar defects: the central core of the demessianization thesis is that messianism arose under the specific conditions of nineteenth-century Romanticism which no longer apply today. Little attention is paid to the earlier origins of messianism and also to evidence (like the immense popularity of the Polish Bards today) which points in the direction of the continuing significance of messianism as part of the Polish Cath-olic Weltanschauung.

It is also commonly supposed that Catholicism in Poland is characterized by a lack of mysticism which is instead associated with the contemplation of the East or even with the religiosity of Russia. This is perhaps true as far as individual mystics are concerned, but certainly not true of the visions associated with Polish messianism.

Polish messianism and mysticism are both closely associated
with a specific vision of the Polish nation. It is a matter of some
difficulty to give a clear explanation of the way in which this
vision can be unambiguously identified. For our present purposes it will suffice to identify it in terms of key points of reference and symbols within the national culture; these points of
reference and symbols must, of course, be placed in the historical and traditional context described in the early chapters. We
will use three apparently disparate examples in order to draw
out the main elements of this vision.

The first example is the Polish tradition of 'opłatek' (the shar-
ing of bread during Christmas). Although opłatek is clearly part
of the Polish Christian tradition, no authority would care to commit itself as to the exact meaning of this practice within Catholicism. Despite this, it is indisputable that opłatek is a very
important event in the life of the Polish nation and that participation in opłatek is also a participation, mostly (although by no
means necessarily) in the company of one's nearest and dearest,
in the 'oneness' of the whole national or Catholic community.
Opłatek wafers are also sent all over the world to émigrés and
those working abroad. It is generally considered rather odd to
criticize this tradition or to refuse participation; sometimes,
among the secularized and the secularist, folklore or tradition
is given as the excuse for participation. The tradition of opłatek
is reputed to go back to pagan times and in this sense can also
be considered to be a mark of continuity.

The second example is related to another Polish tradition - the
Eastertime visits to Christ's grave. The grave (grób) is in some
ways analogous to the Christmas crib except that it may differ
from one church to another and is often highly symbolic, especially in the larger towns and cities where a suitable 'audience'
can be found. The presentation of the grave varies from year to
year and is often accompanied by a written message. In Warsaw,
many tens of thousands of people spend many hours queuing and
visiting numerous churches just to catch a glimpse of the graves
and perhaps to say a prayer or two. The visits to the graves
are very much a part of the Polish Easter. Those who visited
the grave in the Jesuit Church in the Old Town of Warsaw in
1978 found themselves confronted not with the dead Christ whom
they expected, but with a dead Poland symbolized by the Polish
red and white standard pierced by two swords and surrounded
by barbed wire. The military tone was enhanced by a large and
prominent replica of the Virtuti Militari Cross and by the motto
Semper Fidelis. The message on the standard read as follows:
'And we too will rise again' (i my zmartwychwstaniemy). The
sign of the cross was duly made by all those who filed past.

The third example comes from the area of folk art. Polish folk
art is generally noted for its religious content. One artist whose
work has attracted attention is Józef Lurka, a school caretaker
from Silesia.(37) Lurka's work, consisting of small and medium-
sized sculpture in wood, is concerned, to a large extent, with

the person of Christ; it is striking in its simplicity, orthodox in
its doctrinal messages and yet disturbing in some of its symbolism. It is the final characteristic which is of interest to us here.
We find a constant reaffirmation of the image of Christ the Re-
deemer: we observe a Christ who is suffering yet helping others
who suffer, a Christ unable to walk or carry His Cross yet able
to carry the whole of mankind, Christ making a supreme effort in
lifting a massive chalice, Christ bringing hope to others where
His own situation seems devoid of it, etc. Most striking of all is
Lurka's reaction to the election of Pope John Paul II. He celebrated the election by producing a carving consisting of the
following elements: the White Eagle (the Polish national symbol)
with wings outstretched and viewed from the front; superimposed on the Eagle, the Pope with arms outstretched.(38) Almost under protest we are drawn into an almost never-ending
series of associations and successive thoughts and ideas. We
begin by giving one identity to the following: Eagle, Phoenix,
Poland, Pope, Christ. Then we must continue; we seek out
ashes, the Warsaw Uprising, the Crucifixion, the Resurrection.
The disturbing symbolism of Lurka's work is quite clear if we
refer back to the second example noted above. Is Lurka's popularity and the awe he inspires not itself indicative of a religious
experience and of a participation in a messianic and mystical
vision?

These three examples are all drawn from today's modern Catholic relgiiosity and are clearly related to a messianic view which
establizhes a relationship between the individual, the nation and
the whole of mankind. The idea of the Polish nation as a salvational community is very strongly embedded in this messianic and
mystical vision; other evidence for the existence of this idea has
been indirectly mentioned in some of the preceding chapters.
This idea conceives of the nation as a community of those to be
saved, in some respects a sort of a mini-Catholicism; it also presents the nation as a community which has the power to save
others: the nation has a pre-ordained or chosen role of saving
the rest of mankind through its own suffering. The analogy (or
even near identity) between Christ and the Polish nation is, of
course, closely intertwined with the role of the Virgin Mary as
the Queen (perhaps also Mother) of Poland.(39)

Little imagination is required in order to see the connection
between messianism and political opposition to the communist
regime. Catholicism in Poland, therefore, can be seen to enter
the arena of practical politics along two principle axes: messianism and the concern with human rights. To ignore any one of
them is totally to misunderstand the role of Catholicism in Poland
today.

The area concerned with the Uniates (and also other religions)
deserves a mention. No picture of changes in religion and religiosity in Poland would be complete without taking into account
the problems of the Uniates and those of the other religions.
Despite the claims of the regime, there still remain a number of

Uniates, mostly in the south-eastern upland region of Łemkow-szczyzna. The Uniates have managed to survive intense communist persecution both during and after the war: there have been executions, mass deportations and attempts at forced conversion to Orthodoxy. Even today, the Uniates are regarded as Orthodox by the regime. Currently, there are several thousand (perhaps tens of thousands) Uniates in Poland of whom the vast majority are peasants. Sociological work concerning this area is non-existent in Poland.

Other religious groupings in Poland today include the National Catholic Church (Kościół Polskokatolicki), the Orthodox Church, Protestants, Methodists, Jehovah's Witnesses, Baptists, Jews and Moslems. There is some sociological work available on the National Catholics.

Often forgotten or disregarded by contemporary sociologists is the area of paganism, superstition and magic. Apart from the contributions of the early Polish sociologists and ethnographers, almost no work has been done in this area despite the fertility of the terrain. Factors contributing to the widespread distribution of these and related beliefs (almost invariably held in common with Catholic belief) in the urban as well as the rural milieu have to be sought in terms of the following explanations: firstly, the relatively short (by European standards) history of Christianity in Poland. This means that ancient beliefs and rituals have had less time in which to either disappear under pressure from Catholicism or to acquire new, Christian, meanings. Secondly, there is the apparently high degree of tolerance exhibited by Catholicism towards these and other beliefs provided that they do not directly threaten Catholic belief and the Catholic community. This point has been noted in a rather more general context by Wilson.(40)

Paganism is perhaps the most promising field. A typology of pagan relics can be produced by relating them to Catholicism. There are three main categories: (1) those pagan relics which have become totally absorbed into Catholicism and which, historically, might have 'eased' the acceptance of Christianity on account of certain analogies and parallels; (2) those relics which have become absorbed into Catholicism and given new meaning while retaining elements of original form or meaning;. (3) those which stand outside the meanings of Catholicism although not necessarily challenging those meanings and even often associated with religious festivities or practice.

Examples of the latter two categories are easy to find. The tradition of opłatek has already been mentioned as an example of the second category. The final category would be more general and includes various folk customs and traditions, the belief in spirits (as described by Thomas and Znaniecki and Bystroń in chapter 1), etc. Examples are the 'śmigus-dyngus' custom of the drenching of maidens by young men on Easter Monday, the springtime burning or 'drowning' of an effigy of the ancient Slav goddess of winter (marzanna), the courtship rites like 'puszczanie wianków'.

The first category is the most interesting. It may provide the answer to two questions: firstly, how did Christianity take root so readily and become so strong in such a relatively short period of time? Secondly, how did the specific character of Polish Catholicism develop? At the moment, the connection must be regarded as a mere hypothesis requiring further investigation. Nevertheless it is worth pointing out that historians have generally tended to try to answer these questions in terms of what happened after 966 and, as a result, have failed to deliver the expected goods: these questions must be answered at least partly in terms of the raw pagan material that was around before 966. It is possible that there were even considerable similarities of form which enabled such characteristics of Polish Catholicism as the veneration of the Virgin Mary (always referred to familiarly as the 'Mother of God', 'Matka Boska'), the central importance of the family, the proximity of the Holy Family and even the idea of the nation as a living entity to develop readily. This sort of approach would be based on premisses which are the very opposite of those accepted by Ciupak.(41)

A general theory of secularization, rather than one of Christianization and dechristianization, would have to be able to encompass the changes which occur in these types of beliefs and practices.

The final area requiring some comment centres on Kołakowski's idea of the disappearance of the sacred. Kołakowski, let us recall, suggested that the sacred exists only in so far as it arises from a boundary which separates the sacred from the profane. In this sense it is necessary to consider the disappearance of the profane also in terms of secularization.

One quarrel which is likely to arise here concerns the relationship between God and 'the sacred'. Clearly it is not one of identity since the view of the existence of God which such an identity entails is totally unacceptable. The sacred, therefore, refers to the way in which God is worshipped.

The secular society, according to Kołakowski, is one with no boundary between the sacred and the profane. It has to be considered as one where order is not based on distinctions between right and wrong (Good and Evil) but on violence and fear. It appears from Kołakowski that the fundamental choice is between morality and repression where repression is synonymous with secularism. These sorts of ideas appear to make the case for an invisible religion (based on some sort of Good-Evil dichotomy) stronger than ever although, as Święcicki argues, a society of invisible religion is certainly a dechristianized one. In terms of religiosity, this point is corroborated by Piwowarski's conclusions that the phenomenon of selectivism can be identified as a part of the process of religious change in Polish society.

The most striking example of the disappearance of the boundary might be seen in the Anabaptist community at Münster. Here the distinction between Caesar and God vanished with dramatic results: force, violence, terror and repression became the order of the day and led to the rapid disintegration of the community.

In the context of this discussion of Kołakowski it is as well to mention a certain symmetry between his sacred-profane distinction and the sort of definition of religion mentioned by Hill. Hill states that:(42)

> Religion is characterized by the fact that it draws a distinction between a real, tangible world, which can be ascertained through the senses, and a postulated invisible world, which is equally real but not to be ascertained in the same way; and, moreover, this invisible world is of immense importance in the understanding and maintenance of the tangible world.

Both Kołakowski and Hill speak of a distinction between empirical and supra-empirical. It is clear that neither Kołakowski nor Hill provides a complete definition of religion although, perhaps just as significantly, they do both provide a conceptual terrain on which particular definitions can be constructed. By this is meant that each religion can be treated sociologically as a 'theory' providing an explanation of the sacred or of the supra-empirical world. The definition of religion thus appears as a two-stage process.

The question of the secularization of the Church as an institution can be very fruitfully seen in terms of the disappearance of the sacred. Kołakowski mentioned the importance of avoiding both integrism and progressism. It is not open to any serious doubt that the Polish Church is anxious to avoid the dangers outlined by Kołakowski. However, it would appear that the immediate practical danger posed by integrism is minimal compared with the progressist position.

An examination of the concept of secularization in Polish material has revealed three main points: the concept is used by the political authorities as an instrument of anti-religious policy and repression; the available evidence does not unambiguously confirm a thesis of secularization for Polish society; there is very strong evidence for a thesis of desecularization in Poland. The final point is connected with certain features of Marxism-Leninism in power which appear to have strong desecularizing influences – in particular the failure to solve the problems it sets out to solve like the elimination of injustice and the provision of plenty.

NOTES

INTRODUCTION

1 R. Aron, Ideology and totalitarianism, 'Survey', 1977-8, vol. 23, no. 3, p. 83.
2 Cf. L. Kołakowski and G. Urban, The devil in history, 'Encounter', 1981, vol. LVI, no. 1, pp. 11-15.
3 M. Cranston, Should we cease to speak of totalitarianism? 'Survey', 1977-8, vol. 23, no. 3, p. 67.
4 Ibid., p. 69.
5 An inadequate appreciation of totalitarianism often leads to an inability to grasp the nature of the situation in which religion and the Churches find themselves under communist regimes. For example, cf. V.C. Chrypiński, Polish Catholicism and social change, in B.R. Bociurkiw and J.W. Strong (eds), 'Religion and Atheism in the USSR and Eastern Europe', London, 1975, pp. 241-55. Chrypiński believes that a communist regime can be 'sensitive to the needs of the Church', p. 253.
6 S. Małkowski, Kościoł a totalitaryzm (The Church and totalitarianism), 'Spotkania', (London edition) 1978, no. 3, p. 57.
7 Cf. C.O. Lane, The impact of communist ideology and the Soviet order on Christian religion in the contemporary USSR (1959-1974), unpublished thesis, 1976, University of London.
8 This is not a hard and fast rule and there are exceptions. For example, cf. B. Leś, 'Religijność społeczeństw przemysłowych' (The Religiosity of Industrialized Societies'), Warsaw, 1977. Leś uses the term 'sekularyzacja' when talking about secularization.
9 In particular I have in mind the ideas outlined in D.A. Martin, 'The Religious and the Secular', London, 1969.
10 Cf. G. Simon The Catholic Church and the communist state in the Soviet Union and Eastern Europe, in Bociurkiw and Strong, op. cit., p. 191; also M.T. Staszewski, Polityka wyzaniowa europejskich państw socjalistycznych (The religious policy of the European socialist states), and W. Mysłek, Polityka wyznaniowa Polski Ludowej (The religious policy of People's Poland), both in W. Mysłek and M.T. Staszewski (eds), 'Polityka wyznaniowa' ('Religious Policy'), Warsaw, 1975, pp. 80-120 and pp. 237-87.

1 'ARCHAIC MAN' AND RELIGION

1 J.St. Bystroń, 'Kultura ludowa' ('Folk Culture'), Warsaw, 1936, p. 395. Bystroń used the word 'chłopomania' which does not translate elegantly into English. 'Peasant obsession' might be a better rendering.
2 The play 'Wesele' ('The Wedding') by the playwright Stanisław Wyspiański is set in the context of such a wedding. Wyspiański had been present at the marriage of his friend to a peasant girl and had written the play immediately afterwards.
3 F. Mirek, Socjologia w Polsce (Sociology in Poland), 'Przegląd powszechny', 1930, vol. 47, no. 137, pp. 156-61; cited in W. Piwowarski, Rozwój kierunków, problematyki i metod badań w polskiej socjologii religii (The development of trends, problems and research methods in the Polish sociology of religion), 'Studia warmińskie', 1971, vol. VIII, p. 347.
4 Ibid., pp. 345-87 (including a summary in English).
5 L. Krzywicki, Do Jasnej Góry (To Jasna Góra. Jasna Góra - The Bright Mountain - is where the Abbey of Our Lady of Częstochowa is situated), in L. Krzywicki, 'Studia socjologiczne' ('Sociological Studies'), Warsaw, 1923. It appears from the date at the end of the piece that it was written,

or perhaps first published, in 1895. Krzywicki wrote this piece in answer to Władysław Reymont's account of his participation in a pilgrimage to Częstochowa.
6 In this way Krzywicki attempts to invalidate Reymont's sympathetic account.
7 Krzywicki, op. cit., p. 152.
8 Ibid., p. 159.
9 Ibid., p. 160.
10 Ibid., p. 161
11 Ibid., p. 162
12 Ibid., p. 163.
13 Marxism is a good example. Its theoretical blunders, as illustrated by Karl Popper, have hardly detracted from the sway which it holds over the minds of men.
14 Ibid., p. 163. It is perhaps ironical that the Polish composer Krzysztof Penderecki has produced what may be the most mournful version yet of 'Dies irae, Dies illa' and that this version has proved to be popular amongst the educated urban strata.
15 Ibid., p. 164.
16 Ibid., p. 159.
17 Ibid., p. 163.
18 A similar point has been noted by D.A. Martin, 'The Religious and the Secular', London, 1969, p. 5.
19 W.I. Thomas and F. Znaniecki, 'The Polish Peasant in Europe and America', 2 vols, New York, 1927.
20 Cf. ibid., p. 1523 et seq..
21 F. Mirek, 'Elementy społeczne parafii rzymsko-katolickiej' ('The Social Elements of the Roman Catholic Parish'), Poznań, 1928.
22 Thomas and Znaniecki, op. cit., p. 1280.
23 Ibid., p. 206.
24 Cf. S. Andreski, 'Social Sciences as Sorcery', London, 1974.
25 Thomas and Znaniecki, op. cit., pp. 205-88.
26 Ibid., p. 206.
27 It is from East European folklore that Bram Stoker drew the ideas for his book 'Dracula' in which he 'immortalized' the vampire.
28 Thomas and Znaniecki, op. cit., pp. 237-54.
29 Ibid., p. 254.
30 Krzywicki argued similarly (op. cit., p. 147) when he suggested that the pilgrimage to Częstochowa united the whole of the Polish peasantry. He did not develop this point, however.
31 Thomas and Znaniecki, op. cit., p. 27.
32 Ibid., p. 280.
33 Ibid., p. 287.
34 Ibid., p. 300.
35 Ibid., p. 297.
36 In particular his study of St Patrick, 'Le culte des héros et ses conditions sociales', Paris, 1919, made him famous in Western sociological circles.
37 S. Czarnowski, Kultura religijna wiejskiego ludu polskiego (The religious culture of Polish peasantry), in S. Czarnowski, 'Dzieła' ('Works', 5 vols), Warsaw, 1956, vol. 1, pp. 88-107. This piece is part of Czarnowski's work 'Kultura' ('Culture'), first published in 1938.
38 The 'Tygodnik polski'. This weekly was founded and edited by Czarnowski. It contained articles of principally sociological, political and cultural relevance. The two articles have been reprinted in Czarnowski 'Dzieła', pp. 235-40 under the title Socjologiczne określenie faktu religijnego (The sociological definition of the religious fact).
39 Ibid., p. 235.
40 Ibid., p. 235.
41 Ibid., p. 237.
42 Ibid., p. 237.
43 Ibid., pp. 237-8.
44 'Mana' was also referred to by B. Malinowski, 'Magic, Science and Religion

and Other Essays', London, 1974, passim.
45 Cf. M. Hill, 'A Sociology of Religion', London, 1973, pp. 39-40.
46 It is perhaps safe to assume that Czarnowski was not fully aware of this difficulty.
47 The work of E. Durkheim, 'The Elementary Forms of the Religious Life', London, 1954, was concerned with primitive peoples.
48 S. Czarnowski, Reakcja katolicka w Polsce w końcu XVI i na początku XVII wieku (The Catholic reaction in Poland at the end of the sixteenth and the beginning of the seventeenth centuries), in Czarnowski, 'Dzieła'. This is an historical sketch of the role played by the Polish magnates and gentry in the Polish Counter-Reformation.
49 Ibid., vol. 2, p. 165.
50 Ibid., pp. 165-6.
51 Ibid., pp. 94-5.
52 Ibid., p. 89.
53 Ibid., p. 90.
54 Ibid., p. 104.
55 Ibid., p. 105.
56 Ibid., p. 107.
57 J.St. Bystroń, Rozwój badań historyczno-religijnych (The development of research in the history of religion), 'Przegląd powszechny', 1924, no. 24, p. 357. Cited by Piwowarski, op. cit., p. 357.
58 Bystroń, 'Kultura ludowa'.
59 Ibid., p. 199.
60 J. St. Bystroń, 'Dzieje obyczajów w dawnej Polsce. Wiek XVI-XVIII' ('The History of Customs in Old Poland', 2 vols, Warsaw, 1960 (originally published in 1932), vol. 1, pp. 259-93 passim.
61 Ibid., p. 261.
62 Bystroń, 'Kultura ludowa', p. 421.
63 Bystroń, 'Dzieje obyczajów w dawnej Polsce. Wiek XVI-XVIII', pp. 259-93.
64 Ibid., p. 293.
65 Ibid., pp. 317-18.
66 Bystroń, 'Kultura ludowa', p. 451.
67 Published in Warsaw in 1938 (4 vols).
68 J. Chałasiński, 'Parafia i szkoła parafialna wśród emigracji polskiej w Ameryce. Studium dzielnicy polskiej w południowym Chicago' ('The Parish and the Parish School of the Polish Immigrants in America. A Study of a Polish Area in South Chicago'), *Przegląd Socjologiczny*, 1935, p.11.
69 Thomas and Znaniecki, op. cit., p. 1523.
70 Cf. Mirek, 'Elementy spoleczne parafii rzymsko-katolickiéj' and T. Makarewicz, Emigracja amerykańska a macierzysta grupa parafialna (The immigrants in America and the mother parish), 'Przegląd socjologiczny', 1936, vol. IV, pp. 521-46.
71 Chałasiński, op. cit., pp. 12-13.
72 Ibid., p. 15.
73 Ibid., p. 15.
74 O. Kolberg, 'Lud' ('The People', 20 vols), Warsaw, 1865-90. Piwowarski refers to this mammoth work as a 'mine of information' for the sociologist of religion, op. cit., p. 348. Thomas and Znaniecki used it as a source. Also cf. 'Pamiętniki chłopow' ('The Peasant Diaries'), pub. Instytut Gospodarstwa Społecznego, Warsaw, 1938.
75 Mirek, 'Elementy spałeczne parafii rzymsko-katolickiej'.
76 F. Znaniecki in ibid., pp. xi-xii.
77 Viz. Mirek, Chałasiński and Makarewicz.
78 D.A. Martin, op. cit., pp. 48-57, has pointed to similar ambiguities.

2 FROM PAGANISM TO HEATHENISM VIA CHRISTIANITY: RELIGION IN POLAND PAST AND PRESENT
1 Poland was partitioned between Prussia, Russia and Austria in three stages. The first partition took place in 1772 and the final one in 1795 after which no part of Poland remained independent. Poland regained independence only after the end of the First World War.

2   The Uniates became so called since they were 'reunited' with Catholicism at the Union of Brest ('Unia Brezeska') in 1596.
3   During interregna the Primate would assume power and ensure its constitutional transfer. This function was especially important in Poland on account of the establishment of an elective monarchy.
4   Nobody will be imprisoned unless sentenced by a court of law.
5   Not all Orthodox believers, however, were so reunited.
6   A possible exception is the Polish National Church which was established in the United States of America. It was later re-imported into Poland. Its membership in Poland is only a few thousand.
7   Full text in 'The Polish Daily' (London), 18 November 1978.
8   I do not wish to argue that the criterion of acceptance of these traditions is that they are Polish. The criterion of acceptance must be that of theological soundness. However, theological soundness alone may not be enough to ensure acceptance and some other boost, such as national tradition, may be required.
9   According to the national census of 1931. Figures cited by W. Żyliński, Vue d'ensemble, in J. Modzelewski (ed.), 'Pologne 1919-1939', vol. 1, Neuchâtel, 1946, p. 330.
10 Associated with KUL were the Society for Christian Knowledge (Towarzystwo Wiedzy (Chrześcijańskiej) and the KUL Scientific Society (Towarzystwo Naukowe KUL).
11 This requirement was written into the Constitution (Article 120).
12 There were important exceptions to this rule; cf. A. Święcicki, Les origines institutionelles du mouvement 'Znak'. Analyse de quelques organisations indépendentes issues de l'intellegentsia catholique polonaise, 'Actes de la 12ième conférance de sociologie religieuse' (C.I.S.R.), Lille, 1973.
13 The bodies of some 5,000 of these officers were subsequently discovered by invading German troops. The massacre has since become known as the 'Katyń Affair'.
14 Although these bodies were not in principle necessary for the establishment of Soviet power in Poland, they were, however, important in practice for the future legitimation of communist power which relies on such notions as military tradition, the struggle against fascism and 'popular support'.
15 Mikołajczyk, a member of the pre-war Polish government, had been eventually accepted into the new government. A member of the parliamentary opposition, he was obliged to flee the country after the rigged elections of 1947.
16 Because of the sensitivity of the population on this subject, the term 'communist' has always been avoided as much as possible in all the propaganda. Even the name of the Polish communist party (The Polish United Workers' Party) to this day avoids mention of the word.
17 After the end of the war Stalin engineered a westward shift of Poland's boundaries at the expense of Germany and Poland and to the benefit of the Soviet Union. The land the Soviet Union had occupied in 1939 was never returned. Under such circumstances the population at large has become very susceptible to the German bogey; a dependence of Poland on the Soviet Union for a secure western boundary has also been created - if only from the psychological point of view. If, for example, the pre-war German lands were returned only a tiny Poland would remain.
18 Cited by N. Ustroń, Tak zwana utopia komunistyczna (The so-called communist Utopia), 'Spotkania' (London edition), 1978, nos. 3-4, p. 46.
19 J. Godlewski, Współczesne problemy laicyzacji (Current problems of secularization), in W. Mysłek and M.T. Staszewski (eds), 'Polityka wyznaniowa' ('Religious Policy'), Warsaw, 1975, p. 229.
20 Cf. L. Kołakowski, Hope and hopelessness, 'Survey', 1971, vol. XVII, no. 3, p. 38.
21 This fundamental point of Marxism-Leninism has been stressed by the founding fathers. It is also present in communist 'official ideology' and has been repeated in many official statements. Moreover, it is visible in Soviet foreign policy.

22   M. Fainsod, 'How Russia is Ruled', London, 1963, p. 209. L. Schapiro, 'The Government and Politics of the Soviet Union', London, 1970, pp. 60-2.
23   'Statut Polskiej Zjednoczonej Partii Robotniczej' ('The Statute of the PXPR', revised and amended 1971), 1973, pp. 52 and 116-17.
24   A Kurz and M. Zychowski, 'Partia i ideologia' ('The Party and Ideology'), Warsaw, 1970, p. 29.
25   There does exist a procedure by which the whole nation is encouraged to cast votes for pre-selected candidates and although this procedure is officially termed 'elections', it bears little resemblance to known electoral systems.
26   L. Kołakowski, The Euro-Communist Schism, 'Encounter', 1977, vol. XLIX, no. 2, p. 15.
27   'Tezy Komitetu Centralnego Polskiej Zjednoczonej Partii Robotniczej' ('Theses of the KC of the PZPR'), 1974, p. 70.
28   'Konstytucja PRL', ('The Constitution of the PRL'), final amendment 1973.
29   'Tezy ...', pp. 15 and 81.
30   Kołakowski, 'The Euro-Communist Schism', p. 15.
31   J.M. Bocheński, Marxism-Leninism and Religion, in B.R. Bociurkiw and J.W. Strong (eds), 'Religion and Atheism in the USSR and Eastern Europe', London, 1975, pp. 1-17.
32   Ibid., p. 7.
33   T.M. Jaroszewski, 'Laicyzacja' ('Secularization'), Warsaw, 1966, p. 7. Jaroszewski continues: 'This weakening is brought about through the belief in the primacy of supernatural goals over temporal ones, the belief in man's secondary position with respect to the longing for God, in life after death and in just deserts after death. It is also brought about by belief in the view concerning "man's fallen nature" according to which man is himself unable to do good without the help of God's grace and of the clergy and, finally, through the belief in the view that complete justice and equality of people in this world are impossible on account of "man's fallen nature". In addition, the religious *Weltanschauung* imparts to people a false consciousness which is scientifically unverifiable whereas all effective activity must base itself on experience and must be founded on a rational analysis of real practical conditions and accept as true only that which is scientifically verifiable.'
34   K. Marx and F. Engels, 'On Religion', Moscow, 1957, p. 38.
35   V.I. Lenin, 'On Religion', Moscow, 1965, pp. 18-19.
36   J. Grudzień, Religia jako forma świadomości społecznej (Religion as a form of social consciousness), in J. Grudzień (ed.), 'Wybrane problemy marksistowskiego religioznawstwa' ('Selected Problems of Marxist Religiology'), Warsaw, 1973, pp. 37-8. It is interesting to note that although the general framework of Marxism-Leninism has remained the same, the emphasis has varied according to the anti-religious tactics employed by the state at the time. Thus we can trace three different emphases which correspond to three different types of anti-religious policy: firstly, during the late 1940s and the 1950s there was a strong stress of the association of religion, imperialism, fascism and primitivism. This view complemented a strong policy of repression. Secondly, during the 1960s it was argued that religion was a 'mistake' and represented alienation. This view suited a policy which was less repressive but nevertheless no less determined: it allowed the state to 'talk' with the Church and to try to destroy it from within. The final view, that expressed by Grudzień, suggests that conditions will soon no longer favour the existence of religion and of the Church and they will just die out. This view is the theoretical counterpart of indirect attack on the Church. The different anti-religious policies will be considered below.
37   Lenin, op. cit., p. 21.
38   L. Kołakowski and G. Urban, The devil in history, 'Encounter', 1981, vol. LVI, no. 1, p. 10.
39   E. Grzelak, Stosunek państwa socjalistycznego do religii (The Attitude of a socialist state to religion), in Grudzień, op. cit., pp. 196-7.

40   Articles 192-8 (Crimes against freedom of conscience and belief). Reproduced in Grudzień, op. cit., pp. 322-3.
41   Although this statement is substantially true, it must be stressed that it does not imply that uncompromising doctrinal hostility can exist without the desire for total control: the independence of these two features in practice is difficult, if not impossible, to imagine.
42   Lenin, op. cit., pp. 10 and 49.
43   Ibid., p. 49.
44   These measures were applied selectively to the Polish Uniates who were treated with particular cruelty by the Soviet Union during the last war. Even since the war they have been singled out for repressive measures. To this day the Polish Uniates have not received legal recognition. It is likely that the old Russian fear that the Uniates may form a 'bridge' between Catholicism and Orthodoxy remains very much alive.
45   The figures are difficult to agree upon and such differences as do exist are not important. Some authorities suggest that the percentage of Catholics in Poland is even higher. Lucjan Blit, for example (The insoluble problem: Church and state in Poland, 'Religion in Communist Lands', 1973, vol. 1, no. 3, p. 8), suggests 97 per cent, making the total number of Catholics 32 million. The figures vary, of course, according to the indices used to distinguish Catholics from non-Catholics and also according to the samples used. A particularly low figure of 86 per cent is used by Święcicki (cited in full in chapter 6) who places Poland only in third place (after the United States and Australia) in an international league table of religiosity. For convenience, I have taken a round figure.
46   L. Kołakowski, Słowo wstępne (Introduction), 'Aneks', 1976, no. 12, p. 61.
47   F. Dinka, Sources of conflict between Church and state in Poland, 'The Review of Politics', 1966, vol. 28, no. 3, p. 333.
48   There had been disturbances in Poland before (the events of 1956, for example, are the best known) but it is only recently that they have become associated with a determined and conscious effort of organized opposition covering wide sectors of the society.
49   M. Gamarnikow, Poland: political pluralism in a one-party state, 'Problems of Communism', 1967, vol. VXI, no. 4, p. 12.
50   Ibid., p. 12. D. Lane, Structural and social change in Poland, in D. Lane and G. Kolankiewicz (eds), 'Social Groups in Polish Society', London, 1973, makes similar observations.
51   Cf. Kołakowski, Słowo wstępne, p. 61.
52   E. Valkenier, The Catholic Church in communist Poland 1945-55, 'The Review of Politics', 1956, vol. 18, no. 3, p. 311.
53   Up to this time the centrally censored press dominated (apart from clandestinely imported literature).
54   For example, A. Kamińska, The Polish Pope and the Polish Catholic Church, 'Survey', 1979, vol. 24, no. 4, pp. 204-22 and A. Tomsky, Poland's Church on the road to Gdańsk, 'Religion in Communist Lands', 1981, vol. 9, nos. 1-2, p. 30.
55   Tomsky, op. cit., p. 29.
56   E. Dolan, Post-war Poland and the Church, 'The American Slavic and East European Review', 1955, vol. XIV, February, p. 85.
57   Ibid., p. 84.
58   A study of Piasecki and of Pax has been made by Lucjan Blit, 'The Eastern Pretender', London, 1965.
59   Ibid., pp. 118-19. About Piasecki, Blit writes: 'He agreed to try to win over for communism, and for the Soviet Union as a guardian of post-war Poland, the mass of Catholics in the country, and then to make the Church, its fifteen thousand clergy and its highly esteemed and loyal hierarchy, a collaborator of a communist government in Warsaw. The aim was never kept secret. During his rare public speeches, but more often in writing, published mainly in his daily paper and his authoritative weekly (which had to change its name after being put on the Index by the Vatican), Piasecki has again and again called on the Poles to work for a communist régime in

Poland. And at the same time since he was released from the Soviet prison
he has in every kind of political weather consistently and loyally defended
the rôle of Soviet Russia as "the leader" of the communist world whose
development, successes and eventual world victory are, according to
Piasecki, in the interests of every patriotic Pole' (p. 118).

60 A. Micewski, 'Wspórrządzić czy nie kłamać? Pax i Znak w Polsce 1945-1976'
('Power or Honesty? Pax and Znak in Poland'), Paris, 1978, pp. 138-9.
61 Blit, 'The Eastern Pretender, p. 137.
62 D. Dunn, Papal-communist détente: motivation, 'Survey', 1976, vol. 22,
no. 2, p. 142.
63 Ibid., pp. 148-9 and 151.
64 John Paul II, 'Return to Poland. The Collected Speeches of John Paul II',
Vatican City, 1979, pp. 43-5.
65 During an autumn session of the Sejm. Quoted in the 'Christian Science
Monitor', 16 December 1947.
66 Op. cit. Article 70 (3) was removed from the Constitution in 1976 possibly
to give an impression of relaxation. Its removal has made no practical
difference.
67 P. Raina, 'Political Opposition in Poland 1954-1977', London, 1978, pp.
29-30.
68 The church in Nowa Huta will be returned to in further chapters.
69 Cf. Kamińska, op. cit., p. 208.
70 Ibid., p. 220.
71 Raina, op. cit., p. 215.
72 Micewski, op. cit., p. 244. Ten days later a group of dissidents issued a
document which has become known as 'The Memorandum of the 59'. The
document argued that the Constituion ought to guarantee basic 'freedoms':
religion, work, expression and information, knowledge. These freedoms
are, of course, incompatible with the theory and practice of totalitarianism,
communist or otherwise. The 'Memorandum' marked a very important first
stage in the crystallization of the opposition movements in Poland. It was
also most significant in the way that it reflected the interdependence and
common interests between the Church as an opposition group and other
dissident groups.
73 Cf. Raina, op. cit., pp. 214-19.
74 Cf. Grudzień, op. cit., pp. 37-8 and note 36 above. This point will be
further referred to in the following chapter.
75 Secular ritual will be discussed in the following chapter.
76 A. Ostoja-Ostaszewski et al. (eds), 'Dissent in Poland 1976-77', London,
1977, p. 163.
77 'Kultura' (Paris), 1978, no. 6, p. 88.
78 'Religion in Communist Lands', 1978, vol. 6, no. 4, p. 255.
79 Cf. A. Boniecki, 'Budowa kościołów w diecezji przemyskiej' ('The Building
of Churches in the Przemyśl Diocese'), London, no publication date. The
book is published by 'Spotkania' (London edition) and was printed in 1980.

3 TIPS FOR ATHEISTS

1 J. Godlewski, Współczesne problemy laicyzacji (Current problems of secularization), in W. Mysłek and M.T. Staszewski (eds), 'Polityka wyznaniowa', Warsaw, 1975, p. 235.
2 The TKKŚ was established in 1969 as a result of the fusion of the Society
of the Secular School (Towarzystwo Szkoły Świeckiej) with the Association
of Atheists and Freethinkers (Stowarzyszenie Ateistów i Wolnomyślicieli),
cf. ibid., p. 235. With 13,000 local branches the TKKŚ boasts of a membership of over a quarter of a million (although the majority have been
recruited in 'blocks' with many members not even knowing that they are
members, cf. Z. Słowik, Ruch laicki w Polsce Ludowej (The secular movement in People's Poland), in J. Grudzień (ed.), 'Wybrane problemy marksistowskiego religioznawstwa' ('Selected Problems of Marxist Religiology'),
Warsaw, 1973, p. 333).
3 The use of the adjective 'positive' instead of simply saying 'Marxist-

Leninist' or 'communist' is a favourite habit of Polish ideologues. It is obviously designed to work towards the identification of anything which is not Marxist-Leninist with 'negative'. In addition, it avoids the use of the term 'communist' and is also connected with the authorities' constant fear that Marxism-Leninism might be seen in ways other than 'positive'.

4　This is a direct reference to the statute of the TKKŚ. Cf. Godlewski, op. cit., p. 235. Also cf. Słowik, op. cit., p. 332.

5　Godlewski, op. cit., pp. 235-6.

6　Słowik, op. cit., pp. 335 and 339.

7　Ibid., p. 336.

8　S. Gancarz, Mit państwowego obrzędu (The myth of state ritual), 'Spotkania' (London edition), 1979, nos. 5-6, p. 297.

9　Ibid., p. 293.

10　P. Raina, 'Political Opposition in Poland 1954-1977', London, 1978, p. 215.

11　Gancarz, op. cit., pp. 295-6.

12　Ibid., p. 296.

13　Gancarz gives a figure of 1-2 per cent of the population, ibid., p. 299.

14　Cf. WSNS, 'Materiały i dyskusje nr 19' ('Materials and Discussions no. 19'), Warsaw, 1976, pp. 5-8.

15　D.A. Martin, 'A General Theory of Secularization', Oxford, 1978, p. 216.

16　About 7 per cent of the population are party members. Not many of even these are convinced Marxist-Leninists.

17　They also stress the role of these ideas in world history. This subject will be discussed at length in chapter 4.

18　These features are the result of the way in which writers are paid for their work: it is quantity and not quality that counts. Number of copies sold does not count either: it is the number of copies printed.

19　W. Mysłek, Marksizm-Leninizm o religii i Kościele. Leninowskie założenia polityki wyznaniowej (Marxism-Leninism on religion and the Church. The Leninist principles of religious policy), in Mysłek and Staszewski, op. cit., p. 9.

20　Religiology is not alone, however. The depths to which party-directed studies of economics, politics and philosophy have descended are very similar.

21　As were, of course, the opposition and trade union movements of ments of 1980-1.

22　L. Kołakowski, 'Szkice o filozofii katolickiej' ('Studies of Catholic Philosophy'), Warsaw, 1955, p. 70. The piece cited originally appeared in the weekly 'Nowe Drogi' in 1954.

23　Ibid., p. 8.

24　Ibid., p. 8.

25　The assumptions, however, are unacceptable. For example, the suggestion that there might exist a serious body of Catholic opinion which suggests a congruence between Thomism and Marxism-Leninism is simply not true: quite possibly arguments of the Pax variety may have been the object of attack, although the overall rationale in such a case becomes difficult to comprehend.

26　A. Schaff, 'A Philosophy of Man', London, 1963, pp. 59-60.

27　T.M. Jaroszewski, 'Laicyzacja' ('Secularization'), Warsaw, 1966, p. 10.

28　Ibid., p. 24.

29　Ibid., p. 71; also cf. T.M. Jaroszewski, 'Laicyzacja' ('Secularization'), in Grudzień, op. cit., pp. 269-70.

30　Jaraszewski, 'Laicyzacja', p. 10.

31　Indeed, it would have been surprising if he had. The consequences of stepping out of line are never looked forward to.

32　Ibid., pp. 21-2.

33　Ibid., p. 23.

34　Op. cit., p. 33.

35　Ibid., pp. 65-6.

36　Ibid., p. 66.

37　Ibid., p. 66.

38 Jaroszewski, 'Laicyzacja', p. 26.
39 Ibid., p. 27.
40 Ibid., p. 28.
41 Ibid., pp. 12-16; citation p. 16.
42 V.I. Lenin, 'On Religion', Moscow, 1965, p. 49; here Lenin explains how persecution serves to increase religious fanaticism.
43 Cf. J. Grudzień, Religia jako forma świadomości społecznej (Religion as a form of social consciousness), in Grudzień, op. cit., pp. 19-20. Polish religiologists like to use the unpleasant-sounding term 'religiotwórczy' signifying 'reliogiogenic' to imply some sort of repugnant and pathological social condition.
44 The Zakład Historii i Teorii Religii (Department of the History and Theory of Religion) of the IFIS PAN, under the directorship of Józef Keller (an ex-Catholic priest), has a team which specializes in this sort of approach. Cf. J. Keller (ed.), 'Zarys dziejów religii' ('An Outline of the History of Religion'), Warsaw, 1975; J. Keller (ed.), 'Zwyczaje, obrzędy i symbole religijne' ('Religious Customs, Rites and Symbols'), Warsaw, 1978. The department also publishes a periodical, 'Studia religioznawcze' ('Religiological Studies'), edited by Keller.
45 Jaroszewski, 'Laicyzacja', clearly implies this point, p. 174.
46 Cf. Z. Poniatowski, Religia a nauka (Religion and science), in 'Ateizm a religia' ('Atheism and Religion'), Warsaw, 1960; also Z. Poniatowski, 'Problematyka nauki...' ('The Problem of Science...'), Warsaw, 1961 (summary in English pp. 211-18).
47 Poniatowski, Religia a nauka, p. 256.
48 Ibid., p. 258. Poniatowski also suggests that it would be absurd for Catholics today to accept the findings of science since that would automatically call into question the authority behind the original rejection of heliocentrism by the Church. Since this original rejection is a fact and cannot be altered, Catholics have the choice of either abandoning their faith and accepting Darwinism together with other modern discoveries or remaining Catholic, rejecting all science and staying in the obscure margin of religious superstition. He also maintains that to accept both science and religion as valid is an act of such illogicality and absurdity that it is worthy only of believers: facts, he says, bear this point out. And so they do. During a trip to Poland I wanted to interview Poniatowski. When I eventually did manage to track him down he flatly refused to discuss any of his work with me.
49 Cf. Anna Pawełczyńska, Les attitudes des étudiants varsoviens envers la religion, 'Archives de Sociologie des Religions', 1961, no. 12, p. 112.
50 Jaroszewski, 'Laicyzacja', 1966, p. 174.
51 M. Szaniawska, Światopogląd młodzieży... (The Weltanschauung of young people...), duplicated by OBOP, Warsaw, 1960, p. 27.
52 A. Nowicki (ed.), 'Wypisy z historii krytyki religii' ('Excerpts from the History of the Critique of Religion'), Warsaw, 1962, p. 15.
53 M.T. Staszewski, Polityka wyznaniowa europejskich państw socjalistycznych (The religious policy of the European socialist states), in Mysłek and Staszewski, op. cit., pp. 84-8. The term 'patriotic' is a common socialist realist form of praise applied to those who fully accept the totality of current Marxist-Leninist orthodoxy.
54 At least, this would appear to be the case according to Martin, op. cit., pp. 131-6 and 137-52.
55 M.T. Staszewski, Realizacja zasady wolności sumienia i wyznania w PRL (The realization of freedom of conscience and belief in the PRL), in Mysłek and Staszewski, op. cit., p. 291, admits the role of the GUKPPiW in the religious policy of the Polish state; he writes that the GUKPPiW functions as a check on legality in the sphere of religious policy and prevents the appearence of information which might lead to religious strife. Some publications, e.g. 'Trybuna ludu' ('The People's Tribune', official organ of the PZPR) and Polityka (Policy), do not need the censor's approval for the printing of articles. Their editors are subject to GUKPPiW regulations directly and so act in place of the censor.

56   'Czarna ksiega cenzury PRL' ('The Black Book of Polish Censorship'),
     London, 1977, pp. 7-14. This book is published by 'Aneks'.
57   Cf. ibid., pp. 12, 69, 75 and 110-11. The final paragraph cited reads as
     follows: 'It is forbidden to allow the publication of any materials which
     mock either the secular rituals of name-giving, weddings, funerals, etc.,
     or the propaganda activities connected with their popularization.' This is
     an indication of the seriousness with which secular ritual is treated.
58   Ibid., p. 170. One example is the paragraph which orders the elimination
     of 'formulations which exaggerate the influence of religious inspiration on
     the formation of socially desirable moral attitudes and behaviour'.
59   Ibid., pp. 12 and 75-6. Paragraph 20 reads as follows: 'It is forbidden to
     permit any material concerning the pilgrimage from Poland to Rome which
     is to take place in October 1975. This pilgrimage is part of the so-called
     Jubilee Year celebrations of the Roman Catholic Church. Dated 1.III.1975;
     cancelled 30.X.1975.'
60   Many children's books reflect Marxist-Leninist metaphysics albeit in a
     basic and barely recognizable form. There are even some children's story
     books about Lenin who is portrayed as a father-figure who loves children.
61   Cf. F. Adamski, 'Modele małżeństwa i rodziny a kultura masowa' ('Models
     of Marriage and Family and the Impact of Mass Culture'), Warsaw, 1970.
     Here Adamski examines the impact of the marriage and family patterns
     which were promoted by the popular women's magazine 'Przyjaciółka'
     ('Girl-Friend'). He writes: 'the elements of the pattern of marriage and
     family...are the reflections of a specific ideology which stems from the
     theoretical and political principles of a socialist state... These principles
     are also externally expressed in concretely pursued social policy.'
     pp. 25-6.
62   Cf. L. Ciołkosz, The uncensored press, 'Survey', 1979, vol. 24, no. 4,
     pp. 56-7.
63   Cf. P. Jegliński and A. Tomsky, 'Spotkania' - Journal of the Catholic op-
     position in Poland, 'Religion in Communist Lands', 1979, vol. 7, no. 1,
     pp. 23-8.
64   'Spotkania' (London edition), nos. 5-6, pp. 303-8.
65   'L'Homme Nouveau' (Paris), 1978, 4 June, p. 4.
66   'Religion in Communist Lands', vol. 8, no. 4, p. 351.
67   'L'Homme Nouveau', op. cit..
68   Ibid.
69   A. Boniecki, Etre prêtre en Pologne, in A. Boniecki et al., 'Nous Chrét-
     iens de Pologne', Paris, 1979, p. 138.
70   The general harassment of the clergy and of Catholic intellectuals can also
     be included in this category as can the limitations placed on Catholic pub-
     lications (circulation, supply of paper, etc.). Many more methods of
     implementing secularism can be observed like, for example, compulsory
     catechesis in Marxism-Leninism in both schools and higher education.
71   'Czarna księga...', p. 70. Paragraph 3(a) reads as follows: It is essential
     to eliminate 'all attempts at linking the symptoms of social pathology with
     the limitation or negation of religious values and place the burden of res-
     ponsibility for depraving the nation on the authorities and on social insti-
     tutions (publishing houses, films, theatre, radio and TV).' We will return
     to this accusation in chapter 6.
72   Adamski's study (op. cit.) cannot be regarded as a study of this subject
     in general.
73   Cf. W. Piwowarski, 'Religijność miejska w rejonie uprzemsłowionym' ('Urban
     Religiosity in an Industrialized Area'), Warsaw, 1977, pp. 56-61.
74   I am very grateful to Dr Andrzej Wójtowicz for providing me with this in-
     formation in April 1978.

4 APOCALYPSE WHEN ?
1   Somewhat surprisingly, there is no simple Polish equivalent for the term
     'secularist'. The meaning, however, is conveyed by the use of terms like
     'secular activist' (dzialacz laicki) or 'secular standpoint' (postawa laicka);

most often it is replaced by the word 'atheist'. The phrase 'secularization of public life' (laicyzacja życia publicznego) is often stressed both as a programme and as a system. The word 'laicysta' does not exist, however. Cf. J. Godlewski, Współczesne problemy laicyzacji (Current problems of secularization), in W. Mysłek and M.T. Staszewski (eds), 'Polityka wyznaniowa ('Religious Policy'), Warsaw, 1975, pp. 199 et seq.
2 Cf. A. Nowicki (ed.), 'Wypisy z historii krytyki religii' ('Excerpts from the History of the Critique of Religion'), Warsaw, 1962, pp. 32 et seq. The phrase 'history of the critique of religion', being somewhat unwieldy, has been replaced in the writings of Nowicki by the term 'atheology' (ateoznawstwo); cf. A. Nowicki, Niektóre zagadnienia filozoficznej krytyki religii i teorii ateizmu (The critique of religion and the theory of atheism: some philosophical questions), in D. Kułakowska (ed.), 'Problemy religii i laicyzacji' ('Problems of Religion and Secularization'), Warsaw, 1971, pp. 226 et seq.
3 D.A. Martin, 'The Religious and the Secular', London, 1969, p. 24.
4 Ibid., p. 25.
5 Godlewski, op. cit., p. 221.
6 A. Nowicki, 'Wykłady o krytyce religii w Polsce' ('Lectures on the Critique of Religion in Poland'), Warsaw, 1965, p. 5.
7 Martin, op. cit., p. 29.
8 The terms 'secularism' and 'atheism' are normally used by secularists to convey very similar, if not identical, ideas. Nowicki, Niektóre zagadnienia..., p. 239, writes as though the atheist tradition were the dominant cultural current: 'Studies of the history of atheism in our country demonstrate just how deeply contemporary atheism is rooted in the most progressive traditions of the nation.'
9 Cf. L. Kołakowski and G. Urban, The devil in history, 'Encounter', 1981, vol. LVI, no. 1, p. 11. Kołakowski's remarks about communism in general also apply to the religiological inversion of traditional versions of history: Kołakowski writes that communism 'is not a religion but a caricature of religion which incidentally confirms the theologians' observation that the Devil is an ape of God'.
10 Cf. Martin, op. cit., p. 3.
11 Under some circumstances the king is not considered alien or reactionary. In order to preserve some nominal intelligibility, secularists must in these circumstances stress the monarch's weakness. An example is Nowicki's treatment of Gregory of Sanok's (he will be discussed below) support for the king. He states that Gregory's act was essentially 'progressive' since the king was already struggling against the dominant magnates; cf. A. Nowicki, 'Grezegorz z Sanoka' (Gregory of Sanok), Warsaw, 1958.
12 A reason for the unpopularity of the Arians (to be discussed below) in the seventeenth century was their collaboration with the invading Swedes during the Deluge. Religiologists are quick to point out that this was no stain on the Arians' integrity since Poland was governed by reactionary forces. Apart from this, religiologists add that the Arians 'had no choice' or 'had to! - not explanations which they themselves would be ready to accept as justifications for crimes against 'progressivism'. Perhaps the invastion of Poland by the Soviet Union during the last war is such an example of honourable aggression.
13 Nowicki, 'Wykłady o krytyce religii w Polsce', 1965, p. 41.
14 Cf. chapters 1 and 2.
15 Martin, op. cit., p. 31.
16 In particular I am referring to the sort of approach mentioned by Martin, ibid.
17 Secularists prefer to use the adjective 'heroic' instead of 'miraculous'. The latter is unsuitable on account of its supernatural flavour. The 'heroic act' is, in this context, a sort of secular miracle.
18 Cf. Martin, op. cit., pp. 26, 28 and 66.
19 The Arians will be discussed below. They are considered to have laid the foundations for some key developments in the history of thought.

20   This reflects a good deal of wishful thinking on the part of secularists.
      Most of these nonconformists were in fact more conformist than the sec-
      ularists would care to admit.
21   Cf. Z. Poniatowski, Religia a nauka (Religion and science), in 'Ateizm a
      religia' ('Atheism and Religion'), Warsaw, 1960, pp. 252-8.
22   In particular, it relies on the idea that Copernicus's heliocentric model of
      the solar system was opposed to the basic teaching of Christianity: it is
      claimed that heliocentrism makes nonsense of the metaphysical significance
      and centrality of the Earth and hence of man; cf. A. Nowicki, Mikołaj
      Kopernik (Nicolas Copernicus), in N. Assorodobraj et al. (eds.), 'Z
      dziejów polskiej myśli filozoficznej i społecznej' ('The History of Polish
      Philosophical and Social Thought'), 3 vols, Warsaw, 1956, vol. 1, p. 105-6.
23   This is certainly true of the 'higher religions' and of Christianity in par-
      ticular.
24   Martin, op. cit., pp. 27-8.
25   The problems arising out of pollution, limited resources, energy avail-
      ability, changes in the quality of life - the dysfunctions of industrial-
      ization - are endemic to industrializing societies.
26   N. Cohn, 'The Pursuit of the Millennium', London, 1970, p. 21.
27   Ibid., p. 239.
28   Ibid., p. 239.
29   'Spotkania' (London edition), 1977, no. 1, p. 82.
30   Z. Ogonowski, Antytrynitaryzm w Polsce - wiara i rozum (Antitrinitar-
      ianism in Poland - faith and reason), in B. Baczko (ed.), 'Filozofia polska'
      (Polish Philosophy), Warsaw, 1967, p. 106.
31   Godlewski, op. cit., pp. 232-3.
32   This view can be considered a special case of the 'incompatibility argu-
      ment'.
33   A. Schaff, 'A Philosophy of Man', London, 1963, p. 61.
34   V.I. Lenin, 'On Religion', Moscow, 1965, p. 10.
35   Nowicki, 'Grzegorz z Sanoka', pp. 39 et seq. The whole work is geared to
      presenting Gregory of Sanok as a prototype Marxist-Leninist communist.
36   Kallimach (Filippo Buonacorsi), 'Życie i obyczaje Grzegorza z Sanoka'
      (translated from the Latin: 'De vita et moribus Gregorii Sanocei, Leopol-
      iensis Archiepiscopi'), introduction by T. Sinko, Lwów, 1909, p. 21.
37   Nowicki, 'Grzegorz z Sanoka', pp. 44-5.
38   Ibid., p. 50.
39   Ibid., p. 140. According to Nowicki, examples of atheist conclusions are
      those of Giordano Bruno and Erasmus of Rotterdam; however, as Nowicki
      himself admits elsewhere, it is not yet clear whether Erasmus was in fact
      an atheist. No doubt Nowicki is still working hard on this point.
40   Ibid., pp. 122 et seq.
41   A. Nowicki, 'Wykłady z historii filozofii i myśli społecznej Odrodzenia'
      ('Lectures on the History of Philosophy and Social Thought of the Ren-
      aissance'), Warsaw, 1956, p. 5.
42   Cf. W. Wąsik, 'Historia filozofii polskiej' ('A History of Polish Philosophy'),
      vol. 1, Warsaw, 1958, p. 146; also C. Miłosz, 'The History of Polish Lit-
      erature', New York and London, 1969, p. 39.
43   Nowicki, 'Wypisy z historii krytyki religii'.
44   Ibid., p. 92.
45   Nowicki, 'Wykłady z historii filozofii...', pp. 99-100.
46   Ibid., pp. 108-9.
47   G. de Santillana, 'The Age of Adventure', New York, 1956, p. 247.
48   Ibid., p. 248.
49   Ibid., p. 247.
50   Nowicki, 'Wykłady z historii filozofii...', 1956, p. 7.
51   Ibid., p. 7
52   S. Kot, 'Socinianism in Poland', Boston, 1957.
53   E.M. Wilbur, 'A History of Unitarianism, Socinianism and its Antecedents',
      2 vols, Cambridge, Mass., 1946.
54   Kot, op. cit., p. xix.

55   L. Kołakowski, Problematyka filozofii XV–XVII w. (The problems of 15–
     17th century philosophy), in Assorodobraj et al. op. cit., vol. 1, p. 31.
56   Z. Ogonowski, 'Socynianizm polski' ('Polish Socinianism'), Warsaw, 1960,
     p. 10.
57   Martin, op. cit., p. 23.
58   Cf. Kot, op. cit., pp. 16–30.
59   Ibid., p. 25.
60   Ogonowski, 'Socynianizm polski', pp. 9–10.
61   Godlewski, op. cit., p. 221.
62   Nowicki, 'Wypisy z historii krytyki religii', p. 467.
63   Kołakowski, op. cit., p. 38.
64   Nowicki, 'Wykłady o krytyce religii w Polsce', p. 52. The collective work
     of Assorodobraj et al., op. cit., gives this 'eminent Polish mind' a mention
     in only one sentence out of 1000 pages of sentences. Even here, it is not
     Łyszczyński's ideas that are of interest. It would appear, therefore, that
     Nowicki is suggesting that it is enough to deny the existence of God in
     order to become a formidable intellect: obviously an idea of great appeal
     to the ignorant and unlearned.
65   Cf. Nowicki, 'Wypisy z historii krytyki religii', pp. 143–5. For example:
     'Simple folk are deceived into subjugation by the more clever through the
     false belief in God. These folk, nevertheless, defend their faith with such
     force that even if the wisest of men attempted to liberate them from their
     subjugated state by means of demonstrating the truth to them, these very
     people would throttle him.' Or 'Man is the creator of God who is thus the
     artefact and work of man.'
66   Martin, op. cit., p. 29.
67   Nowicki, 'Wykłady o krytyce religii w Polsce', pp. 59 et seq.. It is per-
     haps unnecessary to mention that Nowicki does not produce any other
     evidence – rather, his treatment of this question suggests that such
     obvious points require no evidence.
68   Ibid., p. 51, unless, of course, Nowicki has in mind Frycz Modrzewski,
     Copernicus or the Arians.
69   Ibid., p. 53.
70   Miłosz, op. cit., p. 160.
71   Nowicki, 'Wykłady o kyrtyce religii w Polsce', p. 72. Staszic is notorious
     for the lack of overall consistency in his ideas and also for his many ob-
     viously contradictory remarks. This means that he can be used as an
     authority in the canvassing of almost any idea.
72   S. Staszic, 'Ród ludzki' ('The Human Race'), 3 vols, vol. 1, Warsaw,
     1959, p. 3.
73   Nowicki, op. cit., 1965, p. 91.
74   Cf. 'Euhemer', 1976, no. 2, p. 138 and 'Euhemer', 1974, no. 4, p. 182.
75   Nowicki, op. cit., 1962, p. 474.
76   Ibdi., pp. 480–2.
77   Cf. chapter 1; in Krzywicki's case, it is unquestionably the contempt
     which predominates.
78   The concept of socialist morality is the contemporary Polish version of the
     well-known concept of the 'New Soviet Man'.

5   ARCHAISM TODAY
 1   Cf. E. Ciupak, 'Parafianie? Wiejska parafia katolicka' ('What About the
     Parishioners? A Rural Catholic Parish'), Warsaw, 1961, 'Kultura religijna
     wsi' ('Rural Religious Culture'), Warsaw, 1961, 'Kult religijny i jego społ-
     eczne podłoże ('The Religious Cult and its Social Foundations'), Warsaw,
     1965, 'Katolicyzm tradycyjny w Polsce' ('Traditional Catholicism in Poland'),
     Warsaw, 1968, 'Katolicyzm ludowy w Polsce' ('Popular Catholicism in Po-
     land'), Warsaw, 1973. The similarity in the titles reflects a similarity of
     content.
 2   Ciupak, 'Kult religijny i jego społeczne podłoże', p. 10. For further dis-
     cussions of Ciupak's methodology cf. W. Piwowarski, Rozwój kierunków,
     problematyki i metod badań w polskiej socjologii religii (The development

of trends, problems and research methods in the Polish sociology of religion), 'Studia warmińskie', 1971, vol. VIII, pp. 345-87 and also K. Judenko and Z. Poniatowski, Socjologia religii (The sociology of religion), 'Euhemer', 1966, vol. 10, no. 6, pp. 38-9.

3 Ciupak's approach can be seen in terms of an operationalization of Jaroszewski's framework of analysis. Cf. chapter 3 and T.M. Jaroszewski, 'Laicyzacja' ('Secularization'), Warsaw, 1966.

4 Piwowarski, op. cit., p. 365.

5 Krzywicki stressed fear as a factor maintaining religion, Bystroń stressed the role of authorities in the locality and Czarnowski the legacy of serfdom.

6 Ciupak, 'Katolicyzm ludowy w Polsce'. Here Ciupak quotes Czarnowski.

7 Ciupak, 'Kultura religijna wsi'.

8 This point will be discussed further in the final chapter of this book.

9 Cf. chapter 1.

10 Cf. J. Majka, Czy taka jest religijność polska? (Is this what Polish religiosity is like?), 'Tygodnik powszechny', 1965, 10 October, and J. Majka (reviewing Ciupak, 'Kult religijny i jego społeczne podłoże', 'Social Compass', 1968, vol. 15, nos. 3-4, pp. 302-5. Also cf. Piwowarski, op. cit., p. 365.

11 Majka, review article 1968, p. 302.

12 Ciupak, 'Katolicyzm ludowy w Polsce', p. 25.

13 S. Czarnowski, 'Dzieła' ('Works, 5 vols), Warsaw, 1956, vol. 1, p. 89.

14 Cf. Thomas Luckmann, 'The Invisible Religion', London, 1967, esp. pp. 17-27.

15 Ciupak, 'Katolicyzm ludowy w Polsce', pp. 288-9.

16 Ibid., p. 291.

17 Ibid., p. 34.

18 Ibid., pp. 34-5.

19 Czarnowski, op. cit., vol. 1, p. 89. This, of course, does not mean that the opposite process does not occur, nor does it mean that Czarnowski did not himself describe any of the functions of Catholicism.

20 Cf. Ciupak, 'Katolicyzm ludowy w Polsce', p. 189.

21 Ibid., p. 189.

22 Ibid., p. 190.

23 Ibid., p. 198.

24 Ibid., p. 195.

25 Ibid., p. 196.

26 Ibid., p. 195.

27 Ibid., p. 292.

28 Ibid., p. 286.

29 Ibid., p. 286.

30 Ibid., pp. 261 and 269.

31 H. Kubiak, 'Religijnożća środowisko społeczne ('Religiosity and Social Milieu'), Kraków, 1972.

32 Ibid., p. 157.

33 Ibid., p. 18; here Kubiak expresses his accordance with the position of J. Maître.

34 I refer here to some of the conclusions of Andrzej Święcicki, whose work will be looked at in the following chapter.

35 F. Adamski, Dynamika przemian światopoglądowych ludności nowego miasta (The Dynamics of Changes in Weltanschauung amongst the Population of a New Town), unpublished typescript in possession of author, 1977. This study contains a fair amount of detail concerning the town of Nowa Huta.

36 Kraków and Nowa Huta today form a large continuous urban agglomeration. There are plans to place both towns under one urban administration whose offices will be situated mid-way between the centres. It is hoped that this will further erode Kraków's cultural and religious significance.

37 The height of the church, however, was not allowed to exceed that of the surrounding blocks of flats, nor was permission granted for the church to be built in a prominent position. The authorities considered it unthinkable

that the church might be visible from a distance.
38 Kubiak, op. cit., p. 18.
39 Ibid., p. 19.
40 Ibid., p. 19.
41 Ibid., pp. 19-20.
42 Ibid., pp. 20-2.
43 Ibid., p. 46.
44 Ibid., p. 47.
45 Ibid., p. 47. If we further assume that men believe only above the age of 60 we find that both age and sex together can account for a staggering figure of 70 per cent believers in the rural sample and for only 20 per cent in Nowa Huta.
46 It is indicative that in the 'civilized' non-communist societies many of these opinions are not to be found.
47 Cf. Ibid., pp. 96, 134-5.
48 Cf. E. Pin, La religion et le passage d'une civilisation pré-industrielle à une civilisation industrielle, in H. Carrier and E. Pin, 'Essais de sociologie religieuse', Paris, 1967. Pin states: 'ce ne serait pas la ville comme telle qui tuerait l'esprit religieux, mais de résider en ville sans y avoir été proprement préparé et sans y être intégré. Aussi bien ce ne sont pas ceux qui résident en ville depuis plusieurs générations qui sont les plus loin de la pratique religieuse, mais ceux qui son nés à la campagne et se voient brusquement, sans préparation, introduits dans la ville et l'industrie', p. 242.
49 Kubiak, op. cit., p. 61.
50 Cf. ibid., pp. 60, 69, 70, 83, 90, 92, 101, 108, 116, 138, 139, 140.
51 This thesis will be referred to again in the following chapter.
52 J. Jerschina, 'Młodzież i procesy laicyzacji świadomości społecznej' ('The Secularization of the Consciousness of Young People'), Warsaw and Kraków, 1978, p. 5.
53 Ibid., pp. 5-6.
54 Ibid., p. 13.
55 Ibid., p. 7 et passim.
56 Ibid., p. 8.
57 Ibid., p. 11.
58 Ibid., pp. 13-14. Ironically, it seems that Kubiak also suffers from this fault.
59 Ibid., p. 111.
60 Ibid., pp. 98-9.
61 Ibid., p. 99 (footnote). B. Wilson and T. Luckmann are also mentioned here in such a way that the reader is almost expected to think that they support Jerschina's thesis.
62 Ibid., p. 111.
63 Ibid., p. 9. It is possible that Jerschina is attempting to define a variant of 'false consciousness' where the consciousness of the historiogenic role is the analogue of class consciousness. In this way he endeavours to incorporate the theory of false consciousness into a theory of secularization.
64 Ibid., pp. 7, 73, 106 et passim.
65 Ibdi., p. 100. Also cf. p. 105.
66 Ibid., pp. 102-3.

6 CATHOLIC MAN AND RELIGION
1 The conditions of work, often most unsatisfactory, and the controls on state finance for research are other important factors; much work is done, however, although the vast mass is unpublished.
2 Majka tends to rely on the institutional divisions. He argues: 'A rather fundamental difference exists between the research conducted by secular centres and that conducted by Catholics. The research differs both in method as well as in the subject matter treated. While secular centres were concerned mainly with research into religious attitudes and used mostly an oral and written interview method (public opinion polls), the

research of Catholic centres, while not neglecting this method, has also included pastoral documents (reports of visitations, etc.), observations, indirect interviews, etc.. The subjects of research are also somewhat different, the range of interest being notably wider.' J. Majka, The character of Polish Catholicism, 'Social Compass', 1968, vol. 15, nos. 3-4, p. 187. Majka was not referring to studies of secularization in particular but to the sociology of religion in general. The remarks concerning the broader methodology and interests of Catholic centres is a clear reference to the seriousness of the research of these centres and to their interest in problems other than secularization which, to secular centres, represents the main area of interest.

3 W. Piwowarski, 'Religijność wiejska w warunkach urbanizacji' ('Rural Religiosity and the Process of Urbanization'), Warsaw, 1971.

4 W. Piwowarski, 'Religijność miejska w rejonie uprzemysłowionym' ('Urban Religiosity in an Industrialized Area'), Warsaw, 1977.

5 Secularists had been, of course, arguing this point for years.

6 J. Eska, Socjologiczne znaki zapytania nad religijnością polską (Sociological question-marks over Polish religiosity), 'Więź', 1973, vol. XVI, no. 11, p. 17.

7 The likelihood of different clustering under different conditions cannot be excluded. In the case of this study by Piwowarski, however, care would have to be taken in the choice of a representative feature on account of a lack of complete homogeneity. Such a procedure is suitable only for overall changes and not for the detection of internal variations.

8 A. Święcicki, 'Religijność wiejska'- hipotezy i fakty ('Rural religiosity' - hypotheses and facts), 'Więź', 1973, vol. XVI, no. 11, p. 34. Święcicki writes: 'By making small changes in the choice of features making up the parameters one can easily almost invert the order of parishes obtained by the author in the conclusion.'

9 Piwowarski, Religijność wieska w warunkach urbanizacji', pp. 85-9. The method is applied as follows. For each of the parishes (A,B,C,D) the percentage of the population exhibiting each of the features of urbanization is noted. For example, in the case of commuters the percentages are as follows: A - 1.64, B - 7.95, C - 7.05, D - 29.5. The rank order is therefore A - 4, B - 2, C - 3, D - 1. The rank order for each of the features of urbanization is noted, the ranks for each parish are summed and the arithmetic mean of the ranks is found.

10 Cases of no running water in bathrooms are quite common in the rural areas of Poland: people often wait for many years for water to be connected to their water taps. Often bathrooms are not used even when water is available and, in some cases, it is doubtful whether the intention to use them was there in the first place: they are sometimes treated exclusively as signs of wealth and as status symbols and can be used as convenient store rooms. This serves as an example of an important characteristic of modernization in countries like Poland: emphasis is often placed by the authorities on the signs or the indices of progress rather than on increased convenience, comfort or even use of facilities. This has the result that figures cease to be a reliable measure of modernization because they tend to overstate the rate of progress.

11 Święcicki, op. cit., p. 34.

12 Distance from the nearest church is undoubtedly an important factor in determining the level of dominicants in the Polish rural milieu especially; rain, snow, mud can make minor roads impassable. Another factor may be the dispersion of the population.

13 Cf. Piwowarski, 'Religijność wiejska w warunkach urbanizacji', pp. 187-8.

14 Ibid., p. 31. Here Piwowarski is accepting Czarnowski's observations of the religious culture of the Polish peasant.

15 Ibid., pp. 31-3.

16 Ibid., pp. 33-5.

17 Ibid., p. 35.

18 Ibid., pp. 35-6.

19   Cf. E. Pin, La religion et le passage d'une civilisation pré-industrielle à
      une civilisation industrielle, in H. Carrier and E. Pin, 'Essais de sociol-
      ogie religieuse', Paris, 1967, p. 242. Although Piwowarski's remarks
      clearly refer to Pin's thesis of a temporary decline in religiosity, the con-
      ditions of modernization in rural areas contrast with Pin's requirement that
      it is the migration to an urban milieu (or even the migration itself) which
      leads to disorganization and to drops in levels of religiosity.
20   The overall attitude to belief is stated in terms of the following sorts of
      indicators: claims of own belief and an assessment of its intensity, rel-
      igious motivation (whether belief is based on tradition or on personal con-
      victions); religious ideology is stated by the following: levels of religious
      knowledge (the Trinity, Christ, life after death, the resurrection of the
      body, the sacraments, the Great Novena), belief in elements of doctrine
      (the Trinity, Christ, etc.), hierarchy of religious duties and interests;
      religious practice is concerned with the rites of passage, regular practice
      and religious duties, devotional practices (mid-week Mass attendance,
      prayer, etc.). Under the parameter of religious morality Piwowarski in-
      cludes both moral opinions (attitudes to divorce, contraception, abortion,
      etc.) and the observance of the Church's moral norms. The religious bond
      is measured in terms of participation in processions, pilgrimages, co-
      operation between parishioners in the upkeep of the local church, the
      attitude regarding the desirability of having a priest as a member of the
      family, etc.. The sample sizes for each of the parishes were as follows:
      A - N = 297, B - N = 252, C - N = 391, D - N = 262.
21   Piwowarski, 'Religijność wiejska w warunkach urbanizacji', p. 326.
22   For the text of the reply cf. Święcicki, op. cit., pp. 33-6; there follows
      further comment by Piwowarski, pp. 36-9.
23   Święcicki, op. cit., p. 34.
24   Ibid., p. 34. Also cf. Piwowarski, 'Religijność wiejska w warunkach urban-
      izacji', p. 340.
25   The high level of alcoholism in parish A was noted by Piwowarski, ibid.,
      p. 238. The figures for the four parishes are as follows: A = 23.2,
      B = 11.1, C = 15.8 and D = 7.6 (all figures are per cent).
26   These were noted by Piwowarski. For example, cf. 'Religijność wiejska w
      warunkach urbanizacji', p. 248.
27   Święcicki is also well known for his previous work on alcoholism.
28   A. Święcicki, Społeczne uwarunkowania polskiej religijności (The social
      determinants of Polish religiosity), paper delivered to the Polish Congress
      of Sociologists of Religion, Ołtarzew, Poland, January 1976. All references
      are to a typescript version in the author's possession; see p. 4 for figures
      quoted. The above paper has been summarized in 'Więź', 1977, vol. XX,
      nos. 5-6, pp. 3-20. During the years referred to (1960-5) the percentage
      of the urban population increased from 48.3 to 49.7 (cf. R. Dyoniziak,
      J. Mikułowski Pomorski and Z. Pucek, 'Społeczeństwo Polskie' ('Polish
      Society'), Kraków, 1972, p. 166).
29   Święcicki, Społeczne uwarunkowania polskiej religijności, pp. 4-5.
30   Ibid., p. 6; the information comes from Mass attendance counts. The trend
      was certainly observable up to 1978.
31   Ibid., p. 6-7. The figure which Święcicki uses for Poland is one of the
      lowest of all estimates.
32   Of those claiming to believe and practice. Cf. ibid., pp. 10-14. Here
      Święcicki compares all seventeen provinces in Poland. Today, the province
      as an administrative unit no longer exists in Poland.
33   A. Święcicki et al., Statystyka praktyk i katechizacji w diecezji częstocho-
      wskiej 1971 r. i 1972 r. (Statistics of practice and catechesis in the
      Czestochowa Diocese during 1971-1972), 'Częstochowskie studia teologiczne',
      1974, no. II, pp. 304-5.
34   Here I express my gratitude to Professor Andrzej Święcicki for a conver-
      sation which I had with him in March 1978. Also in March 1978 Fr Jacek
      Salij in conversation stressed the effect of the partitions on pastoral activ-
      ity. In the Russian occupied zone there was intense persecution of the

clergy with the 'undesirables' rapidly finding their way into Siberian exile. The result was a weak pastoral function and an ineffectual and often scared clergy. In the Prussian zone the activity of the clergy in many lay organizations helped to foster Polish national feeling with which they became associated. The persecution of the clergy was less intense. Lastly, in the Austrian occupied zone the few restrictions imposed resulted in a comparative complacency and a lack of imagination on the part of the clergy. Although the differences in the three pastoral traditions are becoming less significant today on account of the more homogenous conditions and the migrations of both clergy and populations, it is nevertheless important to note that a strong residue remains. In addition, the establishment of a strong religious tradition may be dependent today on who supported the local priest yesterday - whether it was the lord or peasant (or worker); in Nowa Huta today, for example, it is certainly not the lord (in the form of the communist authorities) who supports the local priest. Another example of interest is the case of Poland's western lands (the 'recovered lands' - 'siemie odzyskane'), where the authorities have attempted to both support and mobilize the Church in order to help in consolidating the Polish claim to them.

35   For discussions of rural anticlericalism in Poland cf. E. Ciupak, 'Kult religijny i jego społeczne podłoże' ('The Religious Cult and its Social Foundations'), Warsaw, 1965, pp. 242-51 and E. Ciupak, 'Katolicysm ludowy w Polsce ('Popular Catholicism in Poland'), Warsaw, 1973, pp. 66-7. Ciupak draws heavily on J. Chałasiński, 'Młode pokolenie chłopów' ('The New Peasant Generation'), Warsaw, 1938 and on W. Witos, 'Moje wspomnienia' (́My Memoirs'), Paris, 1964.

36   Swięcicki, Społeczne uwarunkowania polskiej religijności, p. 1.

37   Franciszek Adamski is Professor of the Sociology of the Family at KUL.

38   The material is contained in three articles by Adamski: Przemiany religijności w warunkach urbanizacji (Changes in religiosity under conditions of urbanization), 'Ateneum kapłańskie', 1975, no. 396, pp. 131-50; 1975, no. 397, pp. 294-311; 1975, no. 401, pp. 357-73; also F. Adamski, Dynamika przemian światopoglądowych ludności nowego miasta (The dynamics of changes in Weltanschauung amongst the inhabitants of a new town), typescript in author's possession, dated 1977.

39   No comparative information is given.

40   Cf. J. Jerschina, 'Młodzież i procesy laicyzacji świadomości społecznej' ('The Secularization of the Consciousness of Young People'), Warsaw and Kraków, 1978.

41   It is clear that, although they both use virtually the same sort of data, Adamski and Jerschina come to opposite conclusions.

42   Adamski, Przemiary religijności w warunkach urbanizacji, no. 401, pp. 373-3.

43   Ibid., p. 362.

44   Adamski compares his questionnaire data with parish records over the whole period of the existence of the parish.

45   'Wykształcenie podstawowe' - up to the age of 14 (or 15).

46   Piwowarski, 'Religijność wiejska w warunkach urbanizacji', pp. 182-3. There were two counts: one in spring and one in the autumn; the average was taken. Only two counts may not give a reliable estimate.

47   Piwowarski, 'Religijność miejska w rejonie uprzemysłowionym'.

48   In this study Piwowarski draws on the work of other Catholic sociologists of religion especially on J. Mariański, Więź społeczna parafii miejskiej w rejonie uprzemysłowionym. Studium socjologiczne (The social bond in an urban parish in an industrialized ares), unpublished thesis, 1972, KUL and on N. Karsznia, Przynależność do parafii katolickiej w nowym środowisku wielkomiejskim. Studium psycho-socjologiczne parafii Nowa Huta-Mogiła (Membership of a Catholic parish in a new macro-urban milieu. A psycho-sociological study of the parish Nowa Huta-Mogiła), unpublished thesis, 1973, KUL. Mariański's study is concerned with the town of Płock. Płock is an area of interest on account of the recently established Mazo-

wieckie Zakłady Rafineryjne i Petrochemiczne ('Petrochemia'), a petro-chemical complex. Płock, a town with some very fine architecture and steeped in tradition going back to the tenth century, had up to then been a centre of small-scale industry and trade and a market town.

49   Cf. Piwowarski, 'Religijność meijska w rejonie uprzemysłowionym', pp. 38-41. The list of parameters is now as follows: the overall attitude to belief, religious ideology, religious knowledge, religious experience, religious practice, the religious community (bond) and religious morality.

50   Cf. Pin, op. cit., p. 242.

51   Piwowarski, 'Religijność miejska w rejonie uprzemysłowionym', pp. 331-42.

52   Ibid., p. 360.

53   Ibid., p. 342

54   Ibid., pp. 342-6.

55   Ibid., p. 357.

56   Ibid., pp. 346-51.

57   Ibid., p. 357.

58   Ibid., pp. 346-7.

59   The classification of the milieux is based on the respondents' own assessments of the locality in which they were brought up.

60   Ibid., p. 348; this table is a modification of Piwowarski's original.

61   Ibid., p. 349.

62   Piwowarski, 'Religijność wiejska w warunkach urbanizacji', p. 125 (here Piwowarski's percentages do not add up to 100).

63   Ibid., pp. 30-1.

64   Ibid., pp. 360-2.

65   Ibid., p. 362.

66   Ibid., p. 363.

67   Ibid., pp. 363-4.

68   Trends away from a commitment to Marxism-Leninism (official or otherwise) - a sort of a 'Demarxification' of belief - have already been referred to in chapter 3. It is likely that in many cases Marxist commitment has been abandoned in favour of Catholicism; this would be in keeping with Święcicki's evidence mentioned earlier in this chapter.

69   These informal groups will be referred to again in the final chapter.

70   H. Bednorz, Religijność miejska w rejonie uprzemysłowionym (Urban religiosity in an industrialized area), 'Gość niedzielny' (Katowice), 1978, 23 April.

71   Piwowarski, 'Religijność miejska w rejonie uprzemysłowionym', pp. 56-61.

72   A. Podgórecki, The global analysis of Polish society - a sociological point of view, 'The Polish Sociological Bulletin', 1976, no. 4, pp. 17-30. Podgórecki, for understandable reasons, does not go as far as spelling out this conclusion.

73   For example, J. Górecki and A. Podgórecki, Rozwody w opinii publicznej (General attitudes to divorce), 1964; J. Malanowski, Stosunek społeczeństwa do problemów przyrostu naturalnego (Attitudes to problems of population growth), 1959; Z. Skórzyńska and M. Szaniawska, Światopogląd młodzieży a przynależność do organizacji młodzieżowych (The Weltanschauung of young people and the membership of youth organizations), 1960. For comment cf. W. Piwowarski, Rozwój kierunków, problematyki i metod badań w polskiej socjologii religii (The development of trends, problems and research methods in the Polish sociology of religion), 'Studia Warmińskie', 1971, vol. VIII, pp. 367-9.

74   A. Pawełczyńska, Postawy ludności wiejskiej wobec religii (The attitudes of the rural population to religion), 'Roczniki Socjologii Wsi', 1968, vol. VIII, p. 75.

75   J. Siek, 'Social Compass', 1968, vol. 15, nos. 3-4, pp. 305-14.

76   It has been mentioned at various times by all the non-secularist observers: Piwowarski, Święcicki, Adamski and Bednorz.

77   Cf. D.A. Martin, 'The Religious and the Secular', London, 1969, p. 16.

78   Although this malaise is probably more of a Western phenomenon, the extent to which Polish sociology draws on Western ideas would no doubt reflect the extent to which it also affects Poland.

79 Cf. ibid., pp. 61-9.
80 B. Cywiński, Myśli o polskim duszpasterstwie (Thoughts on the Polish pastorate), 'Znak', 1971, vol. XXIII, no. 204, pp. 689-732. Cywiński remarks that there is very little discussion of the role of pastoral care in the press; it is certain that such discussion is actively discouraged by the censor.
81 Cf., for example, D. Olszewski, Duszpasterstwo młodzieży wobec zagrożeń kultury chrześcijańskiej w Polsce (The pastoral care of youth and the threats to Christian culture in Poland); J. Pałyga, Jak ewangelizować młodzież dzisiaj (How to evangelize youth today). These two pieces are contained in a duplicated publication of the Warsaw Metropolitan Curia, 1978.
82 J. Sadok, Strategia ewangelizacji w Polsce (The strategy of evangelization in Poland), 'Spotkania' (London edition), 1978, nos. 3-4, pp. 150-65.
83 Ibid., p. 161.
84 A. Bierutowicz, O pewnych subtelnościach przepływu informacji (Subtleties and nuances in the flow of information), 'Spotkania' (London edition), 1978-9, nos. 5-6, p. 283.
85 Cf. 'Survey', 1980, vol. 25, no. 1, p. 57.

7 FROM MARXISM TO CHRISTIANITY

1 For example, cf. J. Keller (ed.), 'Zarys dziejów religii' ('An Outline of the History of Religion'), Warsaw, 1975; also cf. A. Nowicki, Niektóre zagadnienia filozoficznej krytyki religii i teorii ateizmu (The critique of religion and the theory of atheism: some philosophical questions), in D. Kułakowska (ed.), 'Problemy religii i laicyzacji' ('Problems of Religion and Secularization'), Warsaw, 1971, pp. 226-53.
2 The matter is less clear-cut in the case of the sociology of religion centring on Catholic institutions, but the compartmentalization is still visible.
3 Kołakowski used the idea of the successful Polish Counter-Reformation as a pattern for this more general concept.
4 Cf. chapter 5 above.
5 Cf. chapter 4 above.
6 Cf. L. Łabędź, Introduction to L. Kołakowski, 'Marxism and Beyond', London, 1971, pp. 7-19. Here Łabędź gives an account of Kołakowski's early development.
7 L. Kołakowski, 'Notatki o współczesnej kontrreformacji' ('Notes on the Contemporary Counter-Reformation'), Warsaw, 1962, p. 51.
8 Ibid., pp. 61-2.
9 Ibid., p. 60.
10 Ibid., p. 5.
11 Ibid., p. 6.
12 Ibid., p. 6-7.
13 Ibid., pp. 27-8.
14 Ibid., p. 41.
15 This point has already been discussed in chapter 4 above.
16 J. Grudzień, 'Kościół w świecie współczesnym ('The Church in the Modern World'), Warsaw (a WSNS internal publication), 1975, p. 5.
17 Ibid., p. 276.
18 Ibid., p. 278. Although Grudzień does not specifically mention it, the 'non-Thomist' philosophical thought is without any doubt an elaboration of Marxism-Leninism or some form of progressism. It is curious to note that Grudzień distinguishes such a division of thought: Thomist and non-Thomist (Marxist-Leninist or related). What has happened to the others?
19 Łabędź, op. cit.
20 L. Kołakowski, 'Main Currents of Marxism', 3 vols, Oxford, 1978, vol. 3, p. 523.
21 L. Kołakowski, La revanche du sacré, 'Contrepoint', 1974, no. 13, pp. 48-9.
22 Ibid., p. 51. Kołakowski has in mind an instrumentalist theory which suggests that religion is nothing more than a tool for achieving certain goals or a medium of expression.

23 Ibid., p. 51.
24 Ibid., pp. 51-2.
25 Ibid., p. 52.
26 Ibid., p. 52.
27 Ibid., p. 54 and D.A. Martin, 'The Religious and the Secular', London, 1969, pp. 23-36; Martin argues that there are two fundamental ways in which secularization has occurred historically: on the one hand, Christian religious passion 'succumbs to bureaucracy and adjusts itself to politics, power and authority' (the lack of conflict with the world) and, on the other, there occurs an attempt at the 'conversion of the symbols of ecclesiastical religion into terrestrial realities' (the attempts to be a 'real Christian' in this world). Ibid., p. 23.
28 Kołakowski, La revanche du sacré, p. 55.
29 Cf. Kołakowski, 'Notatki o współczesnej kontreformacji'. Kołakowski writes (pp. 44-5): 'Thomist historiosophy is thus a proposal of a new Counter-Reformation which would adapt the Church to contemporary changes and ensure that it does not commit itself to a slow death in a world which will stop understanding Christianity and push it into the position of an isolated sect.'
30 Kołakowski La revanche du sacré, p. 55.
31 Ibid., p. 55.
32 Ibid., p. 55.
33 Ibid., p. 60.
34 Ibid., p. 56.
35 Ibdi., p. 59.
36 L. Kołakowski, O tak zwanym kryzysie chrześcijaństwa (On the so-called crisis of Christianity), 'Aneks', 1976, no. 12, p. 166.
37 Ibid., p. 166.
38 L. Kołakowski, Pomyślne proroctwa i pobożne życzenia laika na progu nowego pontyfikatu w wiecznej sprawie praw cesarskich i boskich (Favourable prophesies and pious wishes...), 'Kultura' (Paris), 1978, no. 12, pp. 5-13.
39 During present times these tendencies are so weak that any practical possibility of their realization can be virtually discounted.
40 One way out is to use the argument that the totalitarianism is not basing itself on 'real' Christianity or that it only pretends to be Christian. The integrist position can thus attempt to escape unscathed.
41 In a similar way, Marxism-Leninism in power can always be accused, as indeed it always has been, of a betrayal of its fundamental principles and as a corruption of its true nature. In this way the progressist position would attempt to avoid compromise. It is at least arguable that there is a glaring exception to the general hostility of Marxist-Leninist régimes to religion: Yugoslavia. Yugoslavia would appear to function in a manner more akin to a dictatorship than to a totalitarianism. It has exhibited some of the features of 'change from above' which other communist totalitarianisms have not. It would therefore appear that where the Soviet hold is slacker the greater are the possibilities of inconsistencies in the application of totalitarian and atheist principles.
42 Cf. J. Salij, reviewing book by A. Michnik, 'Kościół, lewica, dialog' ('The Church, the Left and Dialogue'), Paris, 1977, in 'Religion in Communist Lands', 1979, vol. 7, no. 1, pp. 42-6.
43 The attempts of H. Maślińska are typical. Cf., for example, H. Maślińska, Etyka marksistowska a etyka religijna (Marxist ethics and religious ethics), in D. Kułakowska (ed.), op. cit., pp. 276-91 and also H. Maślińska (ed.), 'Podstawowe problemy moralności socjalistyscnej' ('Basic Problems of Socialist Morality'), Warsaw, 1975.
44 T.M. Jaroszewski, Dekalog w oczach marksisty (The Decalogue in the eyes of a Marxist), lecture delivered to KIK, Warsaw. In some respects, it is difficult to take Jaroszewski's argument seriously since it entails his forsaking some very fundamental Marxism-Leninism; Marxism-Leninism's claim to validity is based partly on the assertion of the inadequacy of Christian norms and values.

45 B. Cywiński, 'Rodowody niepokornych' ('The Origins of Polish Defiance'), Warsaw, 1971.
46 This is the clash between the 'polak-katolik' and the 'inteligent-radykał'; the term 'inteligent' can be roughly translated as 'educated man'.
47 The term derives from Julian the Apostate emperor who unleashed a fury of persecution against Christians during the fourth century. His desire was to bring back the ancient beliefs.
48 Ibid., pp. 245-62.
49 Ibid., p. 420.
50 Ibid., pp. 425-62. Cf. H. Skolimowski, 'Polski marksizm' ('Polish Marxism'), London, 1969. According to Skolimowski, the other two pillars are Kołakowski and Schaff. Also cf. L. Kołakowski, 'Main Currents of Marxism', vol. 2, pp. 215-39; according to Kołakowski, Brzozowski is the central figure in the recent history of Polish intellectual development. Kołakowski writes: 'the intellectual history of twentieth-century Poland cannot be understood without reference to the bizarre and disparate effects of his writing and personality', ibid., p. 215.
51 The matter probably still stands as it did when Łabędź wrote: 'It is not true that Kołakowski "has turned into his opposite" in his attitude to religion', op. cit., p. 25.
52 A. Michnik, op. cit., p. 146.
53 J. Mirewicz, 'Emigracyjne sprawy i spory' ('Emigré Affairs and Controversies'), London, 1975, pp. 219-26. In a piece originally written in 1967, Mirewicz argued that Kołakowski was too close to Marxism for any judgment to be made.
54 'Spotkania' (London edition), 1977-8, no. 2, p. 161.
55 Michnik, op. cit., pp. 147 and 89.
56 Ibid..
57 Cf. Salij, op. cit. and S. Małkowski, Kościół a totalitaryzm (The Church and totalitarianism), 'Spotkania', 1978, no. 3, pp. 53-85.

8 WHAT NEXT?
1 The area most widely treated by the Polish sociology of religion is religiosity.
2 Cf. D.A. Martin, 'The Religious and the Secular', London, 1969, pp. 9-22 and 48-57.
3 L. Shiner, The concept of secularization in empirical research, 'Journal for the Scientific Study of Religion', 1967, vol. VI, no. 2, pp. 207-20.
4 M. Hill, 'A Sociology of Religion', London, 1973, pp. 228-51.
5 Cf. B.R. Wilson, 'Religion in Secular Society', London, 1966.
6 Hill, op cit., p. 238.
7 Ibid., p. 238.
8 T. Luckmann, 'The Invisible Religion', New York and London, 1967, and P.L. Berger, 'The Social Reality of Religion', London, 1969.
9 Hill, op. cit., p. 254-5.
10 Ibid., p. 261-2.
11 T. Luckmann, Theories of religion and social change, 'Annual Review of the Social Sciences of Religion', 1977, no. 1, p. 20.
12 I refer here to Czarnowski's implicit bias which militates against a concern with modern religious man.
13 M. Weber, 'The Protestant Ethic and the Spirit of Capitalism', 1930, p. 182.
14 A. Święcicki, Społeczne unwarunkowania polskiej religijności (The social determinants of Polish religiosity), paper delivered to the Polish Congress of Sociologists of Religion, Ołtarzew, Poland, January 1976. Typescript version in author's possession, p. 55.
15 The awareness of this issue goes back to immediately after the end of the Second World War; cf. S. Ossowski, Zagadnienia więzi regionalnej i więzi narodowej na Śląsku opolskim (The question of regional identity and national identity in the Opole region of Silesia), 'Przegląd socjologiczny', 1947, vol. IX, pp. 102-3. This piece must, of course, be understood in the light of Poland's new boundaries which now include this region.

16 For example cf. W. Piwowarski, Księża w opinii parafian wiejskich (The image of the priest in the eyes of rural parishioners), 'Homo Dei', 1963, no. 2; also W. Piwowarski, Księża w opinii parafian miejskich (The image of the priest in the eyes of urban parishioners), 'Więź', no. 5, 1964.
17 As long as the totalitarian structure remains intact and relatively functional. Cf. A. Podgórecki, The global analysis of Polish society - a sociological point of view, 'The Polish Sociological Bulletin', 1976, no. 4, p. 28. Also cf. chapter 3, note 71 above.
18 It would appear from such examples as the Nazi-Soviet Pact and the Warsaw Uprising that the Soviet communist party does not have such a strong line in favour of liberation in this specific political sense.
19 W. Mysłek, Polityka wyznaniowa Polski Ludowej (The religious policy of People's Poland), in W. Mysłek and M.T. Staszewski (eds), 'Polityka wyznaniowa' ('Religious Policy'), Warsaw, 1975, p. 240.
20 Ibid., p. 253.
21 D.A. Martin, 'The Dilemmas of Contemporary Religion', Oxford, 1978, p. 84.
22 Cf. W. Gołąb, Wychowankowie Lasek (The alumni of Laski) and S. Wilkanowicz, Laski po 50 latach (Laski 50 years on), both in 'Więź', 1974, vol. XVII, no. 3, pp. 135-9 and 139-42 respectively.
23 A. Biela, Z. Chlewiński and A. Stanowski, Oczekiwania związane z pontyfikatem Jana Pawła II (Expectations connected with the pontificate of John Paul II), 'Zeszyty Naukowe KUL', 1979, vol. 22, nos. 1-3, pp. 208-16.
24 'Spotkania' (Lublin edition), 1979, no. 8, p. 5.
25 John Paul II, 'Return to Poland. The Collected Speeches of John Paul II', Vatican City, 1979, p. 43.
26 Religion in Communist Lands, 1980, vol. 8, no. 3, p. 239.
27 'The Polish Daily', 18 July 1979.
28 Cf. 'Survey', 1979, vol. 24, no. 4, pp. 227-9.
29 Cf. Papal Encyclical 'Redemptor Hominis' (Polish edition), Vatican City, 1979, p. 63.
30 John Paul II, op. cit., p. 30.
31 Ibid., p. 29.
32 A. Merker, Aktualne stosunki Państwo-Kościoł (Current state-Church relations), 1980, 14 January (Keston College Document), p. 5.
33 Ibid., p. 8.
34 Ibid., p. 8.
35 Ibdi., p. 8.
36 'Religion in Communist Lands', 1979, vol. 7, no. 2, p. 126.
37 I am indebted here to Fr Stanisław Małkowski for first bringing the work of Lurka to my attention; I also express my gratitude to Ludwig Zimmerer of Saska Kępa, Warsaw, for having very kindly invited me to visit his magnificent private collection of Polish folk art which includes some exceptionally fine examples of Lurka's work.
38 For picture cf. 'Wspólny dom', 1980, May, opp. p. 7.
39 An interesting aspect of the salvational community is its internal belief structure where it is arguable that the so called basic truths of Catholicism may not be required by all in order to be saved: those who do not know these truths or even those who deviate from them might conceivably be 'carried' by the strictly orthodox. In this sense it might be possible to speak of a differentiated religiosity within the nation. The often noted importance of the Catholic élite (episcopate, clergy, lay leaders of the Catholic community) acquires an additional dimension here: the élite is often considered and considers itself to be the guardian of the soul of the nation. All these ideas are not part of any consistent and ordered body of concepts nor are they generally accepted in any one characteristic form. Most significant of all, perhaps, is that they are not part of orthodox Catholic teaching (and may even be in conflict with it) yet seem to be tolerated within Catholic universalism.
40 B.R. Wilson, 'Magic and the Millennium', London, 1975, p. 107.

41   E. Ciupak, 'Katolicyzm ludowy w Polsce' ('Popular Catholicism in Poland'),
     Warsaw, 1973, p. 200. Here Ciupak accepts the view of G. Labuda.
42   Hill, op. cit., p. 42.

SELECT BIBLIOGRAPHY

Note: figures in brackets refer to the chapters in which the work is cited in this book

Adamski, F., 'Modele małżeństwa i rodziny a kultura masowa' ('Models of Marriage and Family and the Impact of Mass Culture'), Warsaw, 1970. (3)
Adamski, F., Przemiany religijności w warunkach urbanizacji (Changes in religiosity under conditions of urbanization, 3 articles), 'Ateneum kapłańskie', 1975, nos. 396, 397, 401. (6)
Aron, R., Ideology and totalitarianism, 'Survey', 1977-8, vol. 23, no. 3. (Introduction)
Assorodobraj, N., et al. (eds), 'Z dziejów polskiej myśli filozoficznej i społecznej' ('The History of Polish Philosophical and Social Thought'), 3 vols, Warsaw, 1956. (4)
'Ateizm a religia' ('Atheism and Religion'), Warsaw, 1960. (3, 4)
Baczko, B. (ed.), 'Filozofia polska' ('Polish Philosophy'), Warsaw, 1967. (4)
Beeson, T., 'Discretion and Valour', London, 1974.
Berger, P.L., 'The Social Reality of Religion', London, 1969. (8)
Bethell, N., 'Gomułka: His Poland His Communism', London, 1972. (2)
Biela, A., Chlewiński, Z., and Stanowski, A., Oczekiwania związane z pontyfikatem Jana Pawła II (Expectations connected with the pontificate of John Paul II), 'Zeszyty Naukowe KUL', 1979, vol. 22, nos. 1-3. (8)
Blit, L., 'The Eastern Pretender', London, 1965. (2)
Blit, L., The insoluble problem: Church and state in Poland, 'Religion in Communist Lands', 1973, vol. 1, no. 3. (2)
Bociurkiw, B.R., and Strong, J.W. (eds), 'Religion and Atheism in the USSR and Eastern Europe', London, 1975. (Introduction, 2)
Boniecki, A., et al., 'Nous Chrétiens de Pologne', Paris, 1979. (3)
Bystroń, J.St., Rozwój badań historyczno-religijnych (The development of research in the history of religion), 'Przegląd współczesny', 1924, no. 24. (1)
Bystroń, J.St., 'Kultura ludowa' ('Folk Culture'), Warsaw, 1936. (1)
Bystroń, J.St., 'Dzieje obyczajów w dawnej Polsce. Wiek XVI-XVIII' ('The History of Customs in Old Poland'), 2 vols, Warsaw, 1960. (1)
Chałasiński, J., 'Parafia i szkoła parafialna wśród emigracji polskiej w Ameryce. Studium dzielnicy polskiej w poł. Chicago ('The Parish and the Parish School of the Polish Immigrants in America. A Study of a Polish Area in South Chicago'), Przegląd socjologiczny, 1935. (1)
Ciołkosz, L., The uncensored press, 'Survey', 1979, vol. 24, no. 4. (3)
Ciupak, E., 'Kultura religijna wsi' ('Rural Religious Culture'), Warsaw, 1961. (2, 5)
Ciupak, E., 'Parafianie? Wiejska parafia katolicka' ('What About the Parishioners? A Rural Catholic Parish'), Warsaw, 1961. (5)
Ciupak, E., 'Kult religijny i jego społeczne podłoże' ('The Religious Cult and its Social Foundations'), Warsaw, 1965. (5, 6)
Ciupak, E., 'Katolicyzm tradycyjny w Polsce' ('Traditional Catholicism in Poland'), Warsaw, 1968. (5)
Ciupak, E., 'Katolicyzm ludowy w Polsce' ('Popular Catholicism in Poland'), Warsaw, 1973. (5, 6, 8)
Cohn, N., 'The Pursuit of the Millennium', London, 1970. (4)
Cranston, M., Should we cease to speak of totalitarianism? 'Survey', 1977-8, vol. 23, no. 3. (Introduction)
Cywiński, B., 'Rodowody niepokornych' ('The Origins of Polish Defiance'), Warsaw, 1971. (7)

Cywiński, B., Myśli o polskim duszpasterstwie (Thoughts on the Polish pastorate), 'Znak', 1971, vol. XXIII, no. 204, 1971. (6)
'Czarna księga cenzury PRL' ('The Black Book of Polish Censorship'), London, 1977 (published by 'Aneks'). (3)
Czarnowski, S., 'Dzieła' ('Works'), 5 vols, Warsaw, 1956. (1, 5)
Dinka, F., Sources of conflict between Church and state in Poland, 'Review of Politics', 1966, vol. 28, no. 3. (2)
Dolan, E., Post-war Poland and the Church, 'The American Slavic and East European Review', 1955, vol. XIV, February. (2)
Dunn, D., Papal-communist détente: motivation, 'Survey', 1976, vol. 22, no. 2. (2)
Dziewanowski, M.K., 'The Communist Party of Poland: An Outline of History', Massachusetts, 1959. (2)
Eska, J., Socjologiczne znaki zapytania nad religijnością polską (Sociological question-marks over Polish religiosity), 'Więź', 1973, vol. XVI, no. 11. (6)
Fainsod, M., 'How Russia is Ruled', London, 1963. (2)
Gamarnikow, M., Poland: political pluralism in a one-party state, 'Problems of Communism', 1967, vol. XVI, no. 4. (2)
Gancarz, S., Mit państwowego obrzędu (The myth of state ritual), 'Spotkania' (London edition), 1979, nos. 5-6. (3)
Grudzień, J. (ed.), 'Wybrane problemy marksistowskiego religioznawstwa' ('Selected Problems of Marxist Religiology'), Warsaw, 1973. (2, 3)
Grudzien, J., 'Kościół w świecie współczesnym' ('The Church in the Modern World'), Warsaw (a WSNS internal publication), 1975. (7)
Halecki, O., 'Tysiąclecie Polski Katolickiej' ('The One Thousand Years of Catholic Poland'), London, 1966.
Halecki, O., 'A History of Poland', London, 1978.
Hill, M., 'A Sociology of Religion', London, 1973. (1, 8)
Jaroszewski, T.M., 'Laicyzacja' ('Secularization'), Warsaw, 1966. (2, 3, 5)
Jegliński, P., and Tomsky, A., 'Spotkania' - journal of the Catholic opposition in Poland, 'Religion in Communist Lands', 1979, vol. 7, no. 1. (3)
Jerschina, J., 'Młodzież i procesy laicyzacji świadomości społecznej' ('The Secularization of the Consciousness of Young People'), Warsaw and Kraków, 1978. (5, 6)
John Paul II, 'Return to Poland. The Collected Speeches of John Paul II', Vatican City, 1979. (2, 8)
Judenko, K., and Poniatowski, Z., Socjologia religii (The sociology of religion), 'Euhemer', 1966, vol. 10, no. 6. (5)
Kąkol, K., 'L'Homme Nouveau', 1978, 4 June.
Kałwa, P., et al. (eds), 'Księga Tysiąclecia Katolicyzmu w Polsce' ('A Thousand Years of Catholicism in Poland'), 3 vols and 1 vol. containing translated pieces, Lublin, 1969. (2)
Kamińska, A., The Polish Pope and the Polish Catholic Church, 'Survey', 1979, vol. 24, no. 4. (2)
Keller, J. (ed.) 'Zarys dziejów religii' ('An Outline of the History of Religions'), Warsaw, 1975. (3, 7)
Keller, J. (ed.), 'Zwyczaje, obrzędy i symbole religijne' ('Religious Customs, Rites and Symbols'), Warsaw, 1978. (3)
Kisielewski, S., Stosunki Kościół-państwo w PRL (Relations between Church and State in the Polish People's Republic), 'Zeszyty Historyczne - 49', Paris, vol. 307, 1979, pp. 3-23.
Kłoczowski, J. (ed.), 'Chrześcijaństwo w Polsce' (Christianity in Poland), Lublin, 1980.
Kołakowski, L., 'Szkice of filozofii katolickiej' ('Studies of Catholic Philosophy'), Warsaw, 1955. (3)
Kołakowski, L., 'Notatki o współczesnej kontrreformacji' ('Notes on the Contemporary Counter-Reformation'), Warsaw, 1962, (7)
Kołakowski, L., Hope and hopelessness, 'Survey', 1971, vol. XVII, no. 3. (2)
Kołakowski, L., 'Marxism and Beyond: On Historical Understanding and Individual Responsibility', London, 1971. (7)
Kołakowski, L., O tak zwanym kryzysie chrześcijaństwa (On the so-called crisis

of Christianity), 'Aneks', 1976, no. 12. (7)
Kołakowski, L., Słowo wstępne (Introduction), 'Aneks', 1976, no. 12. (2)
Kołakowski, L., The Euro-Communist schism, 'Encounter', 1977, vol. XLIX,
no. 2. (2)
Kołakowski, L., La revanche du sacré, 'Contrepoint', 1977, no. 13. (7)
Kołakowski, L., 'Main Currents of Marxism', 3 vols, Oxford, 1978. (7)
Kołakowski, L., Pomyślne proroctwa i pobożne życzenia... (Favourable pro-
phesies and pious wishes...), 'Kultura' (Paris), 1978, no. 12. (7)
Kołakowski, L., and Urban, G., The devil in history, 'Encounter', 1981, vol.
LVI, no. 1. (Introduction, 2, 4)
Kolberg, O., 'Lud' ('The People'), 20 vols, Warsaw, 1865-90. (1)
Krzywicki, L., 'Studia socjologiczne' ('Sociological Studies'), Warsaw, 1923. (1)
Kubiak, H., 'Religijność a środowisko społeczne', Kraków, 1972. (5)
Kułakowska, D. (ed.), 'Problemy religii i laicyzacji' ('Problems of Religion and
Secularization'), Warsaw, 1971. (4, 7)
Kurz, A. and Zychowski, M., 'Partia i ideologia' ('The Party and Ideology'),
Warsaw, 1970. (2)
Lenert, P., 'The Church in Poland', London, 1963.
Lenin, V.I., 'On Religion', Moscow, 1965. (2, 3, 4)
Leś, B., 'Religijność społeczeństw przemysłowych' ('The Religiosity of Indus-
trialized Societies'), Warsaw, 1977. (Introduction)
Luckmann, T., 'The Invisible Religion', New York and London, 1967. (5, 8)
Majka, J., Czy taka jest religijność polska? (Is this what Polish religiosity is
like?), 'Tygodnik powszechny', 1965, 10 October. (5)
Majka, J., The character of Polish Catholicism, 'Social Compass', 1968, vol. 15,
nos. 3-4. (6)
Makarewicz, T., Emigracja amerykańska a macierzysta grupa parafialna (The
immigrants in America and the mother parish), 'Przegląd socjologiczny', 1936,
vol. IV. (1)
Malinowski, B., 'Magic, Science and Religion and Other Essays', London, 1974.
(1)
Małkowski, S., Kościół a totalitaryzm (The Church and totalitarianism), 'Spot-
kania' (London edition), 1978, no. 3. (Introduction, 7)
Martin, A., 'La Pologne défend son âme', Paris-Fribourg, 1977.
Martin, D.A., 'The Religious and the Secular', London, 1969. (Introduction,
1, 3, 4, 6, 7, 8)
Martin, D.A., 'A General Theory of Secularization', Oxford, 1978. (3)
Martin, D.A., 'The Dilemmas of Contemporary Religion', Oxford, 1978. (8)
Marx, K. and Engels, F., 'On Religion', Moscow, 1965. (2)
Meysztowicz, V., 'La Pologne dans la Chrétienté 966-1966', Paris, 1966. (2)
Micewski, A., 'Współrządzić czy nie kłamać? Pax i Znak w Polsce 1945-1976'
('Power or Honesty? Pax and Znak in Poland'), Paris, 1978. (2)
Michnik, A., 'Kościół, lewica, dialog' ('The Church, the Left and Dialogue'),
Paris, 1977. (7)
Miłosz, C., 'The History of Polish Literature', New York and London, 1969.
(2, 4)
Mirek, F., 'Elementy społeczne parafii rzymsko-katolickiej' ('The Social Ele-
ments of the Roman Catholic Parish'), Poznań, 1928. (1)
Modzelewski, J. (ed.), 'Pologne 1919-1939' (3 vols), Neuchâtel, 1946.
Mysłek, W., and Staszewski, M.T. (eds), 'Polityka wyznaniowa' ('Religious
Policy'), Warsaw, 1975. (Introduction, 2, 3, 4, 8)
Nowicki, A., 'Grzegorz z Sanoka' ('Gregory of Sanok'), Warsaw, 1958. (4)
Nowicki, A. (ed.), 'Wypisy z historii krytyki religii' ('Excerpts from the Hist-
ory of the Critique of Religion'), Warsaw, 1962. (3, 4)
Nowicki, A., 'Wykłady o krytyce religii' ('Lectures on the Critique of Religion'),
Warsaw, 1963. (4)
Nowicki, A., 'Wykłady o krytyce religii w Polsce' ('Lectures on the Critique of
Religion in Poland'), Warsaw, 1965. (4)
Ostoja-Ostaszewski, A., et al. (eds), 'Dissent in Poland 1976-77', London,
1977.
Pawełczyńska, A., Postawy ludności wiejskiej wobec religii (The attitudes of

the rural population to religion), 'Roczniki socjologii wsi', 1970, vol. VIII.
(6)
Pin, E., La religion et le passage d'une civilisation pré-industrielle à une civilisation industrielle, in H. Carrier and E. Pin, 'Essais de sociologie religieuse',
Paris, 1967. (5, 6)
Piwowarski, W., 'Religijność wiejska w warunkach urbanizacji' ('Rural Religiosity and the Process of Urbanization'), Warsaw, 1971. (6)
Piwowarski, W., Rozwój kierunków, problematyki i metod badań w polskiej socjologii religii (The development of trends, problems and research methods in
the Polish sociology of religion), 'Studia warmińskie', 1971, vol. VIII. (1, 5,
6)
Piwowarski, W., 'Religijność miejska w rejonie uprzemysłowionym' ('Urban Rel-
igiosity in an Industrialized Area'), Warsaw, 1977. (3, 6)
Poniatowski, Z., 'Problematyka nauki...' ('The Problem of Science...'), War-
saw, 1961. (3)
Raina, P., 'Political Opposition in Poland 1954-1977', London, 1978. (2, 3)
Raina, P., 'Kardynał Wyszyński' ('Cardinal Wyszyński'), vol. 1, London,
1979.
Schaff, A., 'A Philosophy of Man', London, 1963. (3, 4)
Schapiro, L., 'The Government and Politics of the Soviet Union', London, 1970.
(2)
Shiner, L. The concept of secularization in empirical research, 'Journal for the
Scientific Study of Religion', 1967, vol. VI, no. 2. (8)
Skolimowski, H., 'Polski marksizm' ('Polish Marxism'), London, 1969. (7)
Święcicki, A., Les origines institutionelles du mouvement 'Znak', 'Actes de la
12ième conférance de sociologie religieuse' (C.I.S.R.), Lille, 1973. (2, 8)
Święcicki, A., 'Religijność wiejska' - hipotezy i fakty ('Rural Religiosity' -
hypotheses and facts), 'Więź', 1973, vol. XVI, no. 11. (6)
Święcicki, A., Społeczne uwarunkowania polskiej religijności (The social deter-
minants of Polish religiosity), paper delivered to the Polish Congress of
Sociologists of Religion, Ołtarzew, Poland, January 1976; typescript version
in author's possession. (6, 8)
Święcicki, A., Społeczne uwarunkowania polskiej religijności (The social deter-
minants of Polish religiosity), 'Więź', 1977, vol. XX, nos. 5-6. (6)
Szaniawska, M., Swiatopogląd młodzieży... (The Weltanschauung of young
people...), duplicated by OBOP, Warsaw, 1960. (3)
Szczepański, J., 'Polish Society', New York, 1970. (2)
Thomas, W.I., and Znaniecki, F., 'The Polish Peasant in Europe and America',
2 vols, New York, 1927. (1)
Tomsky, A., Poland's Church on the road to Gdańsk, 'Religion in Communist
Lands', 1981, vol. 9, nos. 1-2. (2)
Urban, W., 'Ostatni etap dziejów Kosciota w Polsce przed nowym tysiącleciem
(1815-1965)' ('The Final Stage in the History of the Church in Poland before
the New Millennium'), Rome, 1966.
Ustroń, N., Tak zwana utopia komunistyczna (The so-called communist Utopia),
'Spotkania' (London edition), 1978, nos. 3-4. (2)
Valkenier, E., The Catholic Church in communist Poland 1945-55, 'The Review
of Politics', 1956, vol. 18, no. 3. (2)
Wąsik, W., 'Historia filozofii polskiej' ('The History of Polish Philosophy'),
Warsaw, vol. 1, 1958, vol. 2, 1966. (2, 4)
Wilson, B.R., 'Religion in Secular Society', London, 1966. (8)
Wilson, B.R., 'Magic and the Millennium', London, 1975. (8)
WSNS, 'Materiały i dyskusje nr 19' ('Materials and Discussions no. 19'), War-
saw, 1976. (3)
Zatko, J.J. (ed.), 'The Valley of Silence: Catholic thought in contemporary
Poland', Indiana, 1967.

INDEX

Routledge Social Science Series

Routledge & Kegan Paul   London, Henley and Boston

39 Store Street,
London WC1E 7DD
Broadway House,
Newtown Road,
Henley-on-Thames,
Oxon RG9 1EN
9 Park Street,
Boston, Mass. 02108

Contents

*Authors wishing to submit manuscripts for any series
in this catalogue should send them to the Social Science Editor,
Routledge & Kegan Paul Ltd, 39 Store Street,
London WC1E 7DD.*
● *Books so marked are available in paperback.*
○ *Books so marked are available in paperback only.*
*All books are in metric Demy 8vo format (216 × 138mm approx.)
unless otherwise stated.*

International Library of Sociology
General Editor John Rex

GENERAL SOCIOLOGY

Barnsley, J. H. The Social Reality of Ethics. *464 pp.*
Brown, Robert. Explanation in Social Science. *208 pp.*
● Rules and Laws in Sociology. *192 pp.*
Bruford, W. H. Chekhov and His Russia. *A Sociological Study. 244 pp.*
Burton, F. and **Carlen, P.** Official Discourse. *On Discourse Analysis, Government Publications, Ideology. About 140 pp.*
Cain, Maureen E. Society and the Policeman's Role. *326 pp.*
● **Fletcher, Colin.** Beneath the Surface. *An Account of Three Styles of Sociological Research. 221 pp.*
Gibson, Quentin. The Logic of Social Enquiry. *240 pp.*
Glassner, B. Essential Interactionism. *208 pp.*
Glucksmann, M. Structuralist Analysis in Contemporary Social Thought. *212 pp.*
Gurvitch, Georges. Sociology of Law. *Foreword by Roscoe Pound. 264 pp.*
Hinkle, R. Founding Theory of American Sociology 1881–1913. *About 350 pp.*
Homans, George C. Sentiments and Activities. *336 pp.*
Johnson, Harry M. Sociology: *A Systematic Introduction. Foreword by Robert K. Merton. 710 pp.*
● **Keat, Russell** and **Urry, John.** Social Theory as Science. *278 pp.*
Mannheim, Karl. Essays on Sociology and Social Psychology. *Edited by Paul Keckskemeti. With Editorial Note by Adolph Lowe. 344 pp.*
Martindale, Don. The Nature and Types of Sociological Theory. *292 pp.*
● **Maus, Heinz.** A Short History of Sociology. *234 pp.*
Myrdal, Gunnar. Value in Social Theory: *A Collection of Essays on Methodology. Edited by Paul Streeten. 332 pp.*
Ogburn, William F. and **Nimkoff, Meyer F.** A Handbook of Sociology. *Preface by Karl Mannheim. 656 pp. 46 figures. 35 tables.*
Parsons, Talcott and **Smelser, Neil J.** Economy and Society: *A Study in the Integration of Economic and Social Theory. 362 pp.*
Payne, G., Dingwall, R., Payne, J. and **Carter, M.** Sociology and Social Research. *About 250 pp.*
Podgórecki, A. Practical Social Sciences. *About 200 pp.*
Podgórecki, A. and **Łos, M.** Multidimensional Sociology. *268 pp.*
Raffel, S. Matters of Fact. *A Sociological Inquiry. 152 pp.*
● **Rex, John.** Key Problems of Sociological Theory. *220 pp.*
Sociology and the Demystification of the Modern World. *282 pp.*
● **Rex, John.** (Ed.) Approaches to Sociology. *Contributions by Peter Abell, Frank Bechhofer, Basil Bernstein, Ronald Fletcher, David Frisby, Miriam Glucksmann, Peter Lassman, Herminio Martins, John Rex, Roland Robertson, John Westergaard and Jock Young. 302 pp.*
Rigby, A. Alternative Realities. *352 pp.*
Roche, M. Phenomenology, Language and the Social Sciences. *374 pp.*
Sahay, A. Sociological Analysis. *220 pp.*
Strasser, Hermann. The Normative Structure of Sociology. *Conservative and Emancipatory Themes in Social Thought. About 340 pp.*
Strong, P. Ceremonial Order of the Clinic. *267 pp.*
Urry, John. Reference Groups and the Theory of Revolution. *244 pp.*
Weinberg, E. Development of Sociology in the Soviet Union. *173 pp.*

FOREIGN CLASSICS OF SOCIOLOGY

● **Gerth, H. H.** and **Mills, C. Wright.** From Max Weber: *Essays in Sociology. 502 pp.*

● **Tönnies, Ferdinand.** Community and Association *(Gemeinschaft und Gesell-schaft).\Translated and Supplemented by Charles P. Loomis. Foreword by Pitirim A. Sorokin. 334 pp.*

SOCIAL STRUCTURE

Andreski, Stanislav. Military Organization and Society. *Foreword by Professor A. R. Radcliffe-Brown. 226 pp. 1 folder.*

Broom, L., Lancaster Jones, F., McDonnell, P. and **Williams, T.** The Inheritance of Inequality. *About 180 pp.*

Carlton, Eric. Ideology and Social Order. *Foreword by Professor Philip Abrahams. About 320 pp.*

Clegg, S. and **Dunkerley, D.** Organization, Class and Control. *614 pp.*

Coontz, Sydney H. Population Theories and the Economic Interpretation. *202 pp.*

Coser, Lewis. The Functions of Social Conflict. *204 pp.*

Crook, I. and **D.** The First Years of the Yangyi Commune. *304 pp., illustrated.*

Dickie-Clark, H. F. Marginal Situation: *A Sociological Study of a Coloured Group. 240 pp. 11 tables.*

Giner, S. and **Archer, M. S.** (Eds) Contemporary Europe: *Social Structures and Cultural Patterns, 336 pp.*

● **Glaser, Barney** and **Strauss, Anselm L.** Status Passage: *A Formal Theory. 212 pp.*

Glass, D. V. (Ed.) Social Mobility in Britain. *Contributions by J. Berent, T. Bottomore, R. C. Chambers, J. Floud, D. V. Glass, J. R. Hall, H. T. Himmelweit, R. K. Kelsall, F. M. Martin, C. A. Moser, R. Mukherjee and W. Ziegel. 420 pp.*

Kelsall, R. K. Higher Civil Servants in Britain: *From 1870 to the Present Day. 268 pp. 31 tables.*

● **Lawton, Denis.** Social Class, Language and Education. *192 pp.*

McLeish, John. The Theory of Social Change: *Four Views Considered. 128 pp.*

● **Marsh, David C.** The Changing Social Structure of England and Wales, 1871–1961. *Revised edition. 288 pp.*

Menzies, Ken. Talcott Parsons and the Social Image of Man. *About 208 pp.*

● **Mouzelis, Nicos.** Organization and Bureaucracy. *An Analysis of Modern Theories. 240 pp.*

● **Ossowski, Stanislaw.** Class Structure in the Social Consciousness. *210 pp.*

● **Podgórecki, Adam.** Law and Society. *302 pp.*

Renner, Karl. Institutions of Private Law and Their Social Functions. *Edited, with an Introduction and Notes, by O. Kahn-Freud. Translated by Agnes Schwarzschild. 316 pp.*

Rex, J. and **Tomlinson, S.** Colonial Immigrants in a British City. *A Class Analysis. 368 pp.*

Smooha, S. Israel: Pluralism and Conflict. *472 pp.*

Wesolowski, W. Class, Strata and Power. *Trans. and with Introduction by G. Kolankiewicz. 160 pp.*

Zureik, E. Palestinians in Israel. *A Study in Internal Colonialism. 264 pp.*

SOCIOLOGY AND POLITICS

Acton, T. A. Gypsy Politics and Social Change. *316 pp.*

Burton, F. Politics of Legitimacy. *Struggles in a Belfast Community. 250 pp.*

Crook, I. and **D.** Revolution in a Chinese Village. *Ten Mile Inn. 216 pp., illustrated.*

Etzioni-Halevy, E. Political Manipulation and Administrative Power. *A Comparative Study. About 200 pp.*

Fielding, N. The National Front. *About 250 pp.*

● **Hechter, Michael.** Internal Colonialism. *The Celtic Fringe in British National Development, 1536–1966. 380 pp.*

Kornhauser, William. The Politics of Mass Society. *272 pp. 20 tables.*

Korpi, W. The Working Class in Welfare Capitalism. *Work, Unions and Politics in Sweden. 472 pp.*

Kroes, R. Soldiers and Students. *A Study of Right- and Left-wing Students. 174 pp.*

Martin, Roderick. Sociology of Power. *About 272 pp.*

Merquior, J. G. Rousseau and Weber. *A Study in the Theory of Legitimacy. About 288 pp.*

Myrdal, Gunnar. The Political Element in the Development of Economic Theory. *Translated from the German by Paul Streeten. 282 pp.*

Varma, B. N. The Sociology and Politics of Development. *A Theoretical Study. 236 pp.*

Wong, S.-L. Sociology and Socialism in Contemporary China. *160 pp.*

Wootton, Graham. Workers, Unions and the State. *188 pp.*

CRIMINOLOGY

Ancel, Marc. Social Defence: *A Modern Approach to Criminal Problems. Foreword by Leon Radzinowicz. 240 pp.*

Athens, L. Violent Criminal Acts and Actors. *104 pp.*

Cain, Maureen E. Society and the Policeman's Role. *326 pp.*

Cloward, Richard A. and **Ohlin, Lloyd E.** Delinquency and Opportunity: *A Theory of Delinquent Gangs. 248 pp.*

Downes, David M. The Delinquent Solution. *A Study in Subcultural Theory. 296 pp.*

Friedlander, Kate. The Psycho-Analytical Approach to Juvenile Delinquency: *Theory, Case Studies, Treatment. 320 pp.*

Gleuck, Sheldon and **Eleanor.** Family Environment and Delinquency. *With the statistical assistance of Rose W. Kneznek. 340 pp.*

Lopez-Rey, Manuel. Crime. *An Analytical Appraisal. 288 pp.*

Mannheim, Hermann. Comparative Criminology: *A Text Book. Two volumes. 442 pp. and 380 pp.*

Morris, Terence. The Criminal Area: *A Study in Social Ecology. Foreword by Hermann Mannheim. 232 pp. 25 tables. 4 maps.*

Rock, Paul. Making People Pay. *338 pp.*

● **Taylor, Ian, Walton, Paul** and **Young, Jock.** The New Criminology. *For a Social Theory of Deviance. 325 pp.*

● **Taylor, Ian, Walton, Paul** and **Young, Jock.** (Eds) Critical Criminology. *268 pp.*

SOCIAL PSYCHOLOGY

Bagley, Christopher. The Social Psychology of the Epileptic Child. *320 pp.*

Brittan, Arthur. Meanings and Situations. *224 pp.*

Carroll, J. Break-Out from the Crystal Palace. *200 pp.*

● **Fleming, C. M.** Adolescence: Its Social Psychology. *With an Introduction to recent findings from the fields of Anthropology, Physiology, Medicine, Psychometrics and Sociometry. 288 pp.*

● The Social Psychology of Education: *An Introduction and Guide to Its Study. 136 pp.*

Linton, Ralph. The Cultural Background of Personality. *132 pp.*

● **Mayo, Elton.** The Social Problems of an Industrial Civilization. *With an Appendix on the Political Problem. 180 pp.*

Ottaway, A. K. C. Learning Through Group Experience. *176 pp.*

Plummer, Ken. Sexual Stigma. *An Interactionist Account. 254 pp.*

● **Rose, Arnold M.** (Ed.) Human Behaviour and Social Processes: *an Interactionist Approach. Contributions by Arnold M. Rose, Ralph H. Turner, Anselm Strauss, Everett C. Hughes, E. Franklin Frazier, Howard S. Becker et al. 696 pp.*

Smelser, Neil J. Theory of Collective Behaviour. *448 pp.*

Stephenson, Geoffrey M. The Development of Conscience. *128 pp.*

Young, Kimball. Handbook of Social Psychology. *658 pp. 16 figures. 10 tables.*

SOCIOLOGY OF THE FAMILY

Bell, Colin R. Middle Class Families: *Social and Geographical Mobility. 224 pp.*
Burton, Lindy. Vulnerable Children. *272 pp.*
Gavron, Hannah. The Captive Wife: *Conflicts of Household Mothers. 190 pp.*
George, Victor and **Wilding, Paul.** Motherless Families. *248 pp.*
Klein, Josephine. Samples from English Cultures.
    1. Three Preliminary Studies and Aspects of Adult Life in England. *447 pp.*
    2. Child-Rearing Practices and Index. *247 pp.*
Klein, Viola. The Feminine Character. *History of an Ideology. 244 pp.*
McWhinnie, Alexina M. Adopted Children. *How They Grow Up. 304 pp.*
● **Morgan, D. H. J.** Social Theory and the Family. *About 320 pp.*
● **Myrdal, Alva** and **Klein, Viola.** Women's Two Roles: *Home and Work. 238 pp. 27 tables.*
Parsons, Talcott and **Bales, Robert F.** Family: Socialization and Interaction Process. *In collaboration with James Olds, Morris Zelditch and Philip E. Slater. 456 pp. 50 figures and tables.*

SOCIAL SERVICES

Bastide, Roger. The Sociology of Mental Disorder. *Translated from the French by Jean McNeil. 260 pp.*
Carlebach, Julius. Caring For Children in Trouble. *266 pp.*
George, Victor. Foster Care. *Theory and Practice. 234 pp.*
    Social Security: *Beveridge and After. 258 pp.*
George, V. and **Wilding, P.** Motherless Families. *248 pp.*
● **Goetschius, George W.** Working with Community Groups. *256 pp.*
Goetschius, George W. and **Tash, Joan.** Working with Unattached Youth. *416 pp.*
Heywood, Jean S. Children in Care. *The Development of the Service for the Deprived Child. Third revised edition. 284 pp.*
King, Roy D., Ranes, Norma V. and **Tizard, Jack.** Patterns of Residential Care. *356 pp.*
Leigh, John. Young People and Leisure. *256 pp.*
● **Mays, John.** (Ed.) Penelope Hall's Social Services of England and Wales. *368 pp.*
Morris, Mary. Voluntary Work and the Welfare State. *300 pp.*
Nokes, P. L. The Professional Task in Welfare Practice. *152 pp.*
Timms, Noel. Psychiatric Social Work in Great Britain (1939–1962). *280 pp.*
●   Social Casework: *Principles and Practice. 256 pp.*

SOCIOLOGY OF EDUCATION

Banks, Olive. Parity and Prestige in English Secondary Education: a Study in Educational Sociology. *272 pp.*
● **Blyth, W. A. L.** English Primary Education. *A Sociological Description.*
    2. Background. *168 pp.*
Collier, K. G. The Social Purposes of Education: *Personal and Social Values in Education. 268 pp.*
Evans, K. M. Sociometry and Education. *158 pp.*
● **Ford, Julienne.** Social Class and the Comprehensive School. *192 pp.*
Foster, P. J. Education and Social Change in Ghana. *336 pp. 3 maps.*
Fraser, W. R. Education and Society in Modern France. *150 pp.*
Grace, Gerald R. Role Conflict and the Teacher. *150 pp.*
Hans, Nicholas. New Trends in Education in the Eighteenth Century. *278 pp. 19 tables.*
●   Comparative Education: *A Study of Educational Factors and Traditions. 360 pp.*
● **Hargreaves, David.** Interpersonal Relations and Education. *432 pp.*
●   Social Relations in a Secondary School. *240 pp.*
    School Organization and Pupil Involvement. *A Study of Secondary Schools.*

● **Mannheim, Karl** and **Stewart, W. A. C.** An Introduction to the Sociology of Education. *206 pp.*
● **Musgrove, F.** Youth and the Social Order. *176 pp.*
● **Ottaway, A. K. C.** Education and Society: An Introduction to the Sociology of Education. *With an Introduction by W. O. Lester Smith. 212 pp.*
Peers, Robert. Adult Education: *A Comparative Study. Revised edition. 398 pp.*
Stratta, Erica. The Education of Borstal Boys. *A Study of their Educational Experiences prior to, and during, Borstal Training. 256 pp.*
● **Taylor, P. H., Reid, W. A.** and **Holley, B. J.** The English Sixth Form. *A Case Study in Curriculum Research. 198 pp.*

SOCIOLOGY OF CULTURE

Eppel, E. M. and **M.** Adolescents and Morality: *A Study of some Moral Values and Dilemmas of Working Adolescents in the Context of a changing Climate of Opinion. Foreword by W. J. H. Sprott. 268 pp. 39 tables.*
● **Fromm, Erich.** The Fear of Freedom. *286 pp.*
● The Sane Society. *400 pp.*
Johnson, L. The Cultural Critics. *From Matthew Arnold to Raymond Williams. 233 pp.*
Mannheim, Karl. Essays on the Sociology of Culture. *Edited by Ernst Mannheim in co-operation with Paul Kecskemeti. Editorial Note by Adolph Lowe. 280 pp.*
Merquior, J. G. The Veil and the Mask. *Essays on Culture and Ideology. Foreword by Ernest Gellner. 140 pp.*
Zijderfeld, A. C. On Clichés. *The Supersedure of Meaning by Function in Modernity. 150 pp.*

SOCIOLOGY OF RELIGION

Argyle, Michael and **Beit-Hallahmi, Benjamin.** The Social Psychology of Religion. *256 pp.*
Glasner, Peter E. The Sociology of Secularisation. *A Critique of a Concept. 146 pp.*
Hall, J. R. The Ways Out. *Utopian Communal Groups in an Age of Babylon. 280 pp.*
Ranson, S., Hinings, B. and **Bryman, A.** Clergy, Ministers and Priests. *216 pp.*
Stark, Werner. The Sociology of Religion. *A Study of Christendom.*
　Volume II. *Sectarian Religion. 368 pp.*
　Volume III. *The Universal Church. 464 pp.*
　Volume IV. *Types of Religious Man. 352 pp.*
　Volume V. *Types of Religious Culture. 464 pp.*
Turner, B. S. Weber and Islam. *216 pp.*
Watt, W. Montgomery. Islam and the Integration of Society. *320 pp.*

SOCIOLOGY OF ART AND LITERATURE

Jarvie, Ian C. Towards a Sociology of the Cinema. *A Comparative Essay on the Structure and Functioning of a Major Entertainment Industry. 405 pp.*
Rust, Frances S. Dance in Society. *An Analysis of the Relationships between the Social Dance and Society in England from the Middle Ages to the Present Day. 256 pp. 8 pp. of plates.*
Schücking, L. L. The Sociology of Literary Taste. *112 pp.*
Wolff, Janet. Hermeneutic Philosophy and the Sociology of Art. *150 pp.*

SOCIOLOGY OF KNOWLEDGE

Diesing, P. Patterns of Discovery in the Social Sciences. *262 pp.*

● **Douglas, J. D.** (Ed.) Understanding Everyday Life. *370 pp.*
● **Hamilton, P.** Knowledge and Social Structure. *174 pp.*
Jarvie, I. C. Concepts and Society. *232 pp.*
Mannheim, Karl. Essays on the Sociology of Knowledge. *Edited by Paul Kecskemeti. Editorial Note by Adolph Lowe. 353 pp.*
Remmling, Gunter W. The Sociology of Karl Mannheim. *With a Bibliographical Guide to the Sociology of Knowledge, Ideological Analysis, and Social Planning. 255 pp.*
Remmling, Gunter W. (Ed.) Towards the Sociology of Knowledge. *Origin and Development of a Sociological Thought Style. 463 pp.*
Scheler, M. Problems of a Sociology of Knowledge. *Trans. by M. S. Frings. Edited and with an Introduction by K. Stikkers. 232 pp.*

URBAN SOCIOLOGY

Aldridge, M. The British New Towns. *A Programme Without a Policy. 232 pp.*
Ashworth, William. The Genesis of Modern British Town Planning: *A Study in Economic and Social History of the Nineteenth and Twentieth Centuries. 288 pp.*
Brittan, A. The Privatised World. *196 pp.*
Cullingworth, J. B. Housing Needs and Planning Policy: *A Restatement of the Problems of Housing Need and 'Overspill' in England and Wales. 232 pp. 44 tables. 8 maps.*
Dickinson, Robert E. City and Region: *A Geographical Interpretation. 608 pp. 125 figures.*
The West European City: *A Geographical Interpretation. 600 pp. 129 maps. 29 plates.*
Humphreys, Alexander J. New Dubliners: *Urbanization and the Irish Family. Foreword by George C. Homans. 304 pp.*
Jackson, Brian. Working Class Community: *Some General Notions raised by a Series of Studies in Northern England. 192 pp.*
● **Mann, P. H.** An Approach to Urban Sociology. *240 pp.*
Mellor, J. R. Urban Sociology in an Urbanized Society. *326 pp.*
Morris, R. N. and **Mogey, J.** The Sociology of Housing. *Studies at Berinsfield. 232 pp. 4 pp. plates.*
Mullan, R. Stevenage Ltd. *About 250 pp.*
Rex, J. and **Tomlinson, S.** Colonial Immigrants in a British City. *A Class Analysis. 368 pp.*
Rosser, C. and **Harris, C.** The Family and Social Change. *A Study of Family and Kinship in a South Wales Town. 352 pp. 8 maps.*
● **Stacey, Margaret, Batsone, Eric, Bell, Colin** and **Thurcott, Anne.** Power, Persistence and Change. *A Second Study of Banbury. 196 pp.*

RURAL SOCIOLOGY

Mayer, Adrian C. Peasants in the Pacific. *A Study of Fiji Indian Rural Society. 248 pp. 20 plates.*
Williams, W. M. The Sociology of an English Village: *Gosforth. 272 pp. 12 figures. 13 tables.*

SOCIOLOGY OF INDUSTRY AND DISTRIBUTION

Dunkerley, David. The Foreman. *Aspects of Task and Structure. 192 pp.*
Eldridge, J. E. T. Industrial Disputes. *Essays in the Sociology of Industrial Relations. 288 pp.*
Hollowell, Peter G. The Lorry Driver. *272 pp.*
● **Oxaal, I., Barnett, T.** and **Booth, D.** (Eds) Beyond the Sociology of Development.

Economy and Society in Latin America and Africa. 295 pp.

Smelser, Neil J. Social Change in the Industrial Revolution: *An Application of Theory to the Lancashire Cotton Industry, 1770–1840. 468 pp. 12 figures. 14 tables.*

Watson, T. J. The Personnel Managers. *A Study in the Sociology of Work and Employment, 262 pp.*

ANTHROPOLOGY

Brandel-Syrier, Mia. Reeftown Elite. *A Study of Social Mobility in a Modern African Community on the Reef. 376 pp.*

Dickie-Clark, H. F. The Marginal Situation. *A Sociological Study of a Coloured Group. 236 pp.*

Dube, S. C. Indian Village. *Foreword by Morris Edward Opler. 276 pp. 4 plates.*
India's Changing Villages: *Human Factors in Community Development. 260 pp. 8 plates. 1 map.*

Fei, H.-T. Peasant Life in China. *A Field Study of Country Life in the Yangtze Valley. With a foreword by Bronislaw Malinowski. 328 pp. 16 pp. plates.*

Firth, Raymond. Malay Fishermen. *Their Peasant Economy. 420 pp. 17 pp. plates.*

Gulliver, P. H. Social Control in an African Society: a Study of the Arusha, Agricultural Masai of Northern Tanganyika. *320 pp. 8 plates. 10 figures.*
Family Herds. *288 pp.*

Jarvie, Ian C. The Revolution in Anthropology. *268 pp.*

Little, Kenneth L. Mende of Sierra Leone. *308 pp. and folder.*
Negroes in Britain. *With a New Introduction and Contemporary Study by Leonard Bloom. 320 pp.*

Tambs-Lyche, H. London Patidars. *About 180 pp.*

Madan, G. R. Western Sociologists on Indian Society. *Marx, Spencer, Weber, Durkheim, Pareto. 384 pp.*

Mayer, A. C. Peasants in the Pacific. *A Study of Fiji Indian Rural Society. 248 pp.*

Meer, Fatima. Race and Suicide in South Africa. *325 pp.*

Smith, Raymond T. The Negro Family in British Guiana: *Family Structure and Social Status in the Villages. With a Foreword by Meyer Fortes. 314 pp. 8 plates. 1 figure. 4 maps.*

SOCIOLOGY AND PHILOSOPHY

Adriaansens, H. Talcott Parsons and the Conceptual Dilemma. *About 224 pp.*

Barnsley, John H. The Social Reality of Ethics. *A Comparative Analysis of Moral Codes. 448 pp.*

Diesing, Paul. Patterns of Discovery in the Social Sciences. *362 pp.*

● **Douglas, Jack D.** (Ed.) Understanding Everyday Life. *Toward the Reconstruction of Sociological Knowledge. Contributions by Alan F. Blum, Aaron W. Cicourel, Norman K. Denzin, Jack D. Douglas, John Heeren, Peter McHugh, Peter K. Manning, Melvin Power, Matthew Speier, Roy Turner, D. Lawrence Wieder, Thomas P. Wilson and Don H. Zimmerman. 370 pp.*

Gorman, Robert A. The Dual Vision. *Alfred Schutz and the Myth of Phenomenological Social Science. 240 pp.*

Jarvie, Ian C. Concepts and Society. *216 pp.*

Kilminster, R. Praxis and Method. *A Sociological Dialogue with Lukács, Gramsci and the Early Frankfurt School. 334 pp.*

● **Pelz, Werner.** The Scope of Understanding in Sociology. *Towards a More Radical Reorientation in the Social Humanistic Sciences. 283 pp.*

Roche, Maurice. Phenomenology, Language and the Social Sciences. *371 pp.*

Sahay, Arun. Sociological Analysis. *212 pp.*

● **Slater, P.** Origin and Significance of the Frankfurt School. *A Marxist Perspective. 185 pp.*

Spurling, L. Phenomenology and the Social World. *The Philosophy of Merleau-Ponty and its Relation to the Social Sciences. 222 pp.*

Wilson, H. T. The American Ideology. *Science, Technology and Organization as Modes of Rationality. 368 pp.*

International Library of Anthropology
General Editor Adam Kuper

● Ahmed, A. S. Millennium and Charisma Among Pathans. *A Critical Essay in Social Anthropology. 192 pp.*
Pukhtun Economy and Society. *Traditional Structure and Economic Development. About 360 pp.*

Barth, F. Selected Essays. *Volume I. About 250 pp.* Selected Essays. *Volume II. About 250 pp.*

Brown, Paula. The Chimbu. *A Study of Change in the New Guinea Highlands. 151 pp.*

Foner, N. Jamaica Farewell. *200 pp.*

Gudeman, Stephen. Relationships, Residence and the Individual. *A Rural Panamanian Community. 288 pp. 11 plates, 5 figures, 2 maps, 10 tables.*
The Demise of a Rural Economy. *From Subsistence to Capitalism in a Latin American Village. 160 pp.*

Hamnett, Ian. Chieftainship and Legitimacy. *An Anthropological Study of Executive Law in Lesotho. 163 pp.*

Hanson, F. Allan. Meaning in Culture. *127 pp.*

Hazan, H. The Limbo People. *A Study of the Constitution of the Time Universe Among the Aged. About 192 pp.*

Humphreys, S. C. Anthropology and the Greeks. *288 pp.*

Karp, I. Fields of Change Among the Iteso of Kenya. *140 pp.*

Lloyd, P. C. Power and Independence. *Urban Africans' Perception of Social Inequality. 264 pp.*

Parry, J. P. Caste and Kinship in Kangra. *352 pp. Illustrated.*

Pettigrew, Joyce. Robber Noblemen. *A Study of the Political System of the Sikh Jats. 284 pp.*

Street, Brian V. The Savage in Literature. *Representations of 'Primitive' Society in English Fiction, 1858–1920. 207 pp.*

Van Den Berghe, Pierre L. Power and Privilege at an African University. *278 pp.*

International Library of Phenomenology and Moral Sciences
General Editor John O'Neill

Apel, K.-O. Towards a Transformation of Philosophy. *308 pp.*

Bologh, R. W. Dialectical Phenomenology. *Marx's Method. 287 pp.*

Fekete, J. The Critical Twilight. *Explorations in the Ideology of Anglo-American Literary Theory from Eliot to McLuhan. 300 pp.*

Medina, A. Reflection, Time and the Novel. *Towards a Communicative Theory of Literature. 143 pp.*

International Library of Social Policy
General Editor Kathleen Jones

Bayley, M. Mental Handicap and Community Care. *426 pp.*

Bottoms, A. E. and McClean, J. D. Defendants in the Criminal Process. *284 pp.*

Bradshaw, J. The Family Fund. *An Initiative in Social Policy. About 224 pp.*

Butler, J. R. Family Doctors and Public Policy. *208 pp.*
Davies, Martin. Prisoners of Society. *Attitudes and Aftercare. 204 pp.*
Gittus, Elizabeth. Flats, Families and the Under-Fives. *285 pp.*
Holman, Robert. Trading in Children. *A Study of Private Fostering. 355 pp.*
Jeffs, A. Young People and the Youth Service. *160 pp.*
Jones, Howard and Cornes, Paul. Open Prisons. *288 pp.*
Jones, Kathleen. History of the Mental Health Service. *428 pp.*
Jones, Kathleen with **Brown, John, Cunningham, W. J., Roberts, Julian** and
    Williams, Peter. Opening the Door. *A Study of New Policies for the Mentally
    Handicapped. 278 pp.*
Karn, Valerie. Retiring to the Seaside. *400 pp. 2 maps. Numerous tables.*
King, R. D. and **Elliot, K. W.** Albany: Birth of a Prison—End of an Era. *394 pp.*
Thomas, J. E. The English Prison Officer since 1850: *A Study in Conflict. 258 pp.*
Walton, R. G. Women in Social Work. *303 pp.*
● **Woodward, J.** To Do the Sick No Harm. *A Study of the British Voluntary Hospital
    System to 1875. 234 pp.*

International Library of Welfare and Philosophy
General Editors   Noel Timms and David Watson

● **McDermott, F. E.** (Ed.) Self-Determination in Social Work. *A Collection of Essays
    on Self-determination and Related Concepts by Philosophers and Social Work
    Theorists. Contributors: F. P. Biestek, S. Bernstein, A. Keith-Lucas, D. Sayer,
    H. H. Perelman, C. Whittington, R. F. Stalley, F. E. McDermott, I. Berlin, H. J.
    McCloskey, H. L. A. Hart, J. Wilson, A. I. Melden, S. I. Benn. 254 pp.*
● **Plant, Raymond.** Community and Ideology. *104 pp.*
Ragg, Nicholas M. People Not Cases. *A Philosophical Approach to Social Work.
    168 pp.*
● **Timms, Noel** and **Watson, David.** (Eds) Talking About Welfare. *Readings in
    Philosophy and Social Policy. Contributors: T. H. Marshall, R. B. Brandt, G. H.
    von Wright, K. Nielsen, M. Cranston, R. M. Titmuss, R. S. Downie, E. Telfer, D.
    Donnison, J. Benson, P. Leonard, A. Keith-Lucas, D. Walsh, I. T. Ramsey.
    320 pp.*
● Philosophy in Social Work. *250 pp.*
● **Weale, A.** Equality and Social Policy. *164 pp.*

Library of Social Work
General Editor   Noel Timms

● **Baldock, Peter.** Community Work and Social Work. *140 pp.*
○ **Beedell, Christopher.** Residential Life with Children. *210 pp. Crown 8vo.*
● **Berry, Juliet.** Daily Experience in Residential Life. *A Study of Children and their
    Care-givers. 202 pp.*
○ Social Work with Children. *190 pp. Crown 8vo.*
● **Brearley, C. Paul.** Residential Work with the Elderly. *116 pp.*
● Social Work, Ageing and Society. *126 pp.*
● **Cheetham, Juliet.** Social Work with Immigrants. *240 pp. Crown 8vo.*
● **Cross, Crispin P.** (Ed.) Interviewing and Communication in Social Work.
    *Contributions by C. P. Cross, D. Laurenson, B. Strutt, S. Raven. 192 pp. Crown
    8vo.*

- **Curnock, Kathleen** and **Hardiker, Pauline.** Towards Practice Theory. *Skills and Methods in Social Assessments. 208 pp.*
- **Davies, Bernard.** The Use of Groups in Social Work Practice. *158 pp.*
- **Davies, Martin.** Support Systems in Social Work. *144 pp.*
  Ellis, June. (Ed.) West African Families in Britain. *A Meeting of Two Cultures. Contributions by Pat Stapleton, Vivien Biggs. 150 pp. 1 Map.*
- **Hart, John.** Social Work and Sexual Conduct. *230 pp.*
- **Hutten, Joan M.** Short-Term Contracts in Social Work. *Contributions by Stella M. Hall, Elsie Osborne, Mannie Sher, Eva Sternberg, Elizabeth Tuters. 134 pp.*
  Jackson, Michael P. and **Valencia, B. Michael.** Financial Aid Through Social Work. *140 pp.*
- **Jones, Howard.** The Residential Community. *A Setting for Social Work. 150 pp.*
- (Ed.) Towards a New Social Work. *Contributions by Howard Jones, D. A. Fowler, J. R. Cypher, R. G. Walton, Geoffrey Mungham, Philip Priestley, Ian Shaw, M. Bartley, R. Deacon, Irwin Epstein, Geoffrey Pearson. 184 pp.*
  Jones, Ray and **Pritchard, Colin.** (Eds) Social Work With Adolescents. *Contributions by Ray Jones, Colin Pritchard, Jack Dunham, Florence Rossetti, Andrew Kerslake, John Burns, William Gregory, Graham Templeman, Kenneth E. Reid, Audrey Taylor. About 170 pp.*
- ○ **Jordon, William.** The Social Worker in Family Situations. *160 pp. Crown 8vo.*
- **Laycock, A. L.** Adolescents and Social Work. *128 pp. Crown 8vo.*
- **Lees, Ray.** Politics and Social Work. *128 pp. Crown 8vo.*
- Research Strategies for Social Welfare. *112 pp. Tables.*
- ○ **McCullough, M. K.** and **Ely, Peter J.** Social Work with Groups. *127 pp. Crown 8vo.*
- **Moffett, Jonathan.** Concepts in Casework Treatment. *128 pp. Crown 8vo.*
  Parsloe, Phyllida. Juvenile Justice in Britain and the United States. *The Balance of Needs and Rights. 336 pp.*
- **Plant, Raymond.** Social and Moral Theory in Casework. *112 pp. Crown 8vo.*
  Priestley, Philip, Fears, Denise and **Fuller, Roger.** Justice for Juveniles. *The 1969 Children and Young Persons Act: A Case for Reform? 128 pp.*
- **Pritchard, Colin** and **Taylor, Richard.** Social Work: Reform or Revolution? *170 pp.*
- ○ **Pugh, Elisabeth.** Social Work in Child Care. *128 pp. Crown 8vo.*
- **Robinson, Margaret.** Schools and Social Work. *282 pp.*
- ○ **Ruddock, Ralph.** Roles and Relationships. *128 pp. Crown 8vo.*
- **Sainsbury, Eric.** Social Diagnosis in Casework. *118 pp. Crown 8vo.*
- Social Work with Families. *Perceptions of Social Casework among Clients of a Family Service. 188 pp.*
  Seed, Philip. The Expansion of Social Work in Britain. *128 pp. Crown 8vo.*
- **Shaw, John.** The Self in Social Work. *124 pp.*
  Smale, Gerald G. Prophecy, Behaviour and Change. *An Examination of Self-fulfilling Prophecies in Helping Relationships. 116 pp. Crown 8vo.*
  Smith, Gilbert. Social Need. *Policy, Practice and Research. 155 pp.*
- Social Work and the Sociology of Organisations. *124 pp. Revised edition.*
- **Sutton, Carole.** Psychology for Social Workers and Counsellors. *An Introduction. 248 pp.*
- **Timms, Noel.** Language of Social Casework. *122 pp. Crown 8vo.*
- Recording in Social Work. *124 pp. Crown 8vo.*
- **Todd, F. Joan.** Social Work with the Mentally Subnormal. *96 pp. Crown 8vo.*
- **Walrond-Skinner, Sue.** Family Therapy. *The Treatment of Natural Systems. 172 pp.*
- **Warham, Joyce.** An Introduction to Administration for Social Workers. *Revised edition. 112 pp.*
- An Open Case. *The Organisational Context of Social Work. 172 pp.*
- ○ **Wittenberg, Isca Salzberger.** Psycho-Analytic Insight and Relationships. *A Kleinian Approach. 196 pp. Crown 8vo.*

Primary Socialization, Language and Education
General Editor   Basil Bernstein

Adlam, Diana S., *with the assistance of Geoffrey Turner and Lesley Lineker.* Code in Context. *272 pp.*
Bernstein, Basil. Class, Codes and Control. *3 volumes.*
● 1. *Theoretical Studies Towards a Sociology of Language. 254 pp.*
2. *Applied Studies Towards a Sociology of Language. 377 pp.*
● 3. *Towards a Theory of Educational Transmission. 167 pp.*
Brandis, W. and **Bernstein, B.** Selection and Control. *176 pp.*
Brandis, Walter and **Henderson, Dorothy.** Social Class, Language and Communication. *288 pp.*
Cook-Gumperz, Jenny. Social Control and Socialization. *A Study of Class Differences in the Language of Maternal Control. 290 pp.*
● **Gahagan, D. M.** and **G. A.** Talk Reform. *Exploration in Language for Infant School Children. 160 pp.*
Hawkins, P. R. Social Class, the Nominal Group and Verbal Strategies. *About 220 pp.*
Robinson, W. P. and **Rackstraw, Susan D. A.** A Question of Answers. *2 volumes. 192 pp. and 180 pp.*
Turner, Geoffrey J. and **Mohan, Bernard A.** A Linguistic Description and Computer Programme for Children's Speech. *208 pp.*

Reports of the Institute of Community Studies

Baker, J. The Neighbourhood Advice Centre. A Community Project in Camden. *320 pp.*
● **Cartwright, Ann.** Patients and their Doctors. *A Study of General Practice. 304 pp.*
Dench, Geoff. Maltese in London. *A Case-study in the Erosion of Ethnic Consciousness. 302 pp.*
Jackson, Brian and **Marsden, Dennis.** Education and the Working Class: *Some General Themes Raised by a Study of 88 Working-class Children in a Northern Industrial City. 268 pp. 2 folders.*
Marris, Peter. The Experience of Higher Education. *232 pp. 27 tables.*
● Loss and Change. *192 pp.*
Marris, Peter and **Rein, Martin.** Dilemmas of Social Reform. *Poverty and Community Action in the United States. 256 pp.*
Marris, Peter and **Somerset, Anthony.** African Businessmen. *A Study of Entrepreneurship and Development in Kenya. 256 pp.*
Mills, Richard. Young Outsiders: *a Study in Alternative Communities. 216 pp.*
Runciman, W. G. Relative Deprivation and Social Justice. *A Study of Attitudes to Social Inequality in Twentieth-Century England. 352 pp.*
Willmott, Peter. Adolescent Boys in East London. *230 pp.*
Willmott, Peter and **Young, Michael.** Family and Class in a London Suburb. *202 pp. 47 tables.*
Young, Michael and **McGeeney, Patrick.** Learning Begins at Home. *A Study of a Junior School and its Parents. 128 pp.*
Young, Michael and **Willmott, Peter.** Family and Kinship in East London. *Foreword by Richard M. Titmuss. 252 pp. 39 tables.*
The Symmetrical Family. *410 pp.*

Reports of the Institute for Social Studies in Medical Care

Cartwright, Ann, Hockey, Lisbeth and **Anderson, John J.** Life Before Death. *310 pp.*
Dunnell, Karen and **Cartwright, Ann.** Medicine Takers, Prescribers and Hoarders. *190 pp.*
Farrell, C. My Mother Said. . . *A Study of the Way Young People Learned About Sex and Birth Control. 288 pp.*

Medicine, Illness and Society
General Editor W. M. Williams

Hall, David J. Social Relations & Innovation. *Changing the State of Play in Hospitals. 232 pp.*
Hall, David J. and **Stacey, M.** (Eds) Beyond Separation. *234 pp.*
Robinson, David. The Process of Becoming Ill. *142 pp.*
Stacey, Margaret *et al.* Hospitals, Children and Their Families. *The Report of a Pilot Study. 202 pp.*
Stimson, G. V. and **Webb, B.** Going to See the Doctor. *The Consultation Process in General Practice. 155 pp.*

Monographs in Social Theory
General Editor Arthur Brittan

● **Barnes, B.** Scientific Knowledge and Sociological Theory. *192 pp.*
Bauman, Zygmunt. Culture as Praxis. *204 pp.*
● **Dixon, Keith.** Sociological Theory. *Pretence and Possibility. 142 pp.*
   The Sociology of Belief. *Fallacy and Foundation. About 160 pp.*
Goff, T. W. Marx and Mead. *Contributions to a Sociology of Knowledge. 176 pp.*
Meltzer, B. N., Petras, J. W. and **Reynolds, L. T.** Symbolic Interactionism. *Genesis, Varieties and Criticisms. 144 pp.*
● **Smith, Anthony D.** The Concept of Social Change. *A Critique of the Functionalist Theory of Social Change. 208 pp.*

Routledge Social Science Journals

The British Journal of Sociology. *Editor – Angus Stewart; Associate Editor – Leslie Sklair. Vol. 1, No. 1 – March 1950 and Quarterly. Roy. 8vo. All back issues available. An international journal publishing original papers in the field of sociology and related areas.*
Community Work. *Edited by David Jones and Marjorie Mayo. 1973. Published annually.*
Economy and Society. *Vol. 1, No. 1. February 1972 and Quarterly. Metric Roy. 8vo. A journal for all social scientists covering sociology, philosophy, anthropology, economics and history. All back numbers available.*

14

Social and Psychological Aspects of Medical Practice
Editor   Trevor Silverstone

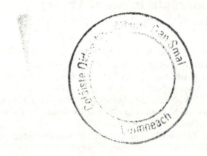

Printed and bound in Great Britain by
Redwood Burn Limited, Trowbridge & Esher